THE SEPTEMBER SIX

AND THE STRUGGLE FOR THE SOUL OF MORMONISM

THE SEPTEMBER SIX

AND THE STRUGGLE FOR THE SOUL OF MORMONISM

SARA M. PATTERSON

SIGNATURE BOOKS | 2023 | SALT LAKE CITY

for my parents

Join our mail list at www.signaturebooks.com for details on events and related titles we think you'll enjoy.

Design by Jason Francis

FIRST EDITION | 2023

LIBRARY OF CONGRESS CONTROL NUMBER: 2023942690

Hardback ISBN: 978-1-56085-466-1
Ebook ISBN: 978-1-56085-483-8

CONTENTS

INTRODUCTION

> *"I am inescapably a Mormon. I am not on the outside looking in. I just have another way of being inside."*
> —David P. Wright

When his Latter-day Saint bishop asked him to meet to discuss his scholarship in February 1994, biblical studies scholar David Wright chose to turn him down. They had met ten months before and it had not gone well. Wright felt that further meetings would cause more stress and anxiety without bringing any resolution. That night he had a dream that, rather than avoiding his bishop, he sought him out. He wanted to share his opinions about what was happening throughout the institutional church. In the dream, the two men met in a church classroom and the bishop, rather than openly listening to and engaging Wright, kept running away. The bishop did everything he could to escape the room and what Wright had to say. When he could not get out, he simply put his hands over his ears, refusing to hear Wright speak.[1]

Wright's dream reflected feelings he had had in his experiences with church leaders, experiences he felt echoed those colloquially known as the "September Six," a group of six intellectuals and activists who were subjected to disciplinary councils by the Church of Jesus Christ of Latter-day Saints (LDS) in September 1993.[2]

---

1. David P. Wright, Journal, February 9, 1994.

2. The stylistic guide for the Church of Jesus Christ of Latter-day Saints asks that people writing about the church refer to it by its full name rather than using the term "Mormon." In this work I have referred to the church using its full name and then refer to it as LDS Church when discussing the institution. I also use the term "Mormon" in this work. First, it applies to all of the traditions that sprang from Joseph Smith Jr.'s revelations, of which the LDS Church is but one. Second, I am writing about a time when the term Mormon was used freely to describe the LDS Church and its members.

The excommunications weighed on Wright. Part of that weight was the mystery surrounding it all. How exactly did those decisions get made? Why was the church meting out its harshest punishment so universally? It felt as though no one he knew could see the full picture. And those who could were not talking.

Even though the process of excommunication took place at the local level, people could not imagine all six disciplinary councils happening in a single month without someone orchestrating them from the church hierarchy. Wright wondered if perhaps he was supposed to have been part of that group. Church members like him did not know how the power centers of the church worked behind the scenes. When scary things happen and there is no clear explanation, fear spreads like wildfire. For Wright, it was an anxiety that was spiritual, emotional, and extremely personal. In the midst of the confusion surrounding the September Six, he recalled, "I didn't know what to do to weather the storm."[3] And what he wanted more than anything was to weather the storm.

The struggles between the institutional church and the September Six had at their foundation different understandings of what it meant to be a restoration church. When Joseph Smith Jr. first founded the church in 1830, he asserted that it was the Restoration of the "true church," one that had been absent from the earth since the time of Jesus and his disciples. While Smith declared that his was the true church, what the Restoration looked like was not a one-and-done deal. Restoration was a process and not everyone agreed about what its end goal should be. This was true during Smith's lifetime and it continues to be true in the various branches of the Mormon tradition that sprang from his movement. What Wright and his contemporaries in the LDS Church struggled over were different visions of the Restoration, struggles that shaped their view of the church's past, present, and future.

Therefore, when my sources use the term, I follow suit. Finally, because I am talking about a group of people who were excommunicated from the LDS Church, I will use the broader term Mormon to describe them when appropriate. To call people who were excommunicated from a church using the nomenclature preferred by the institution—unless the people themselves do—is to continue to place them in relationship to an institution that expelled them.

3. David P. Wright, oral history with author, March 24–25, 2023.

Early on, Wright pondered avoiding altogether the meetings and questions of his bishop and stake president, the person above the bishop in the church hierarchy. The allure of just walking away was powerful. During one of his meetings with his bishop, Wright brought up the September Six and their disciplinary councils. Wright explained that the church hierarchy had recently established the Strengthening Church Members Committee (SCMC) to ensure doctrinal purity by searching church members' speeches and publications for any instances that "did not correlate with doctrine."[4] In fact, the bishop had already received a copy of Wright's 1992 Sunstone article titled "Historical Criticism: A Necessary Element in the Search for Religious Truth" from someone above him in the church hierarchy.

In the article, Wright had argued for a new approach to reading scripture that took into account the historical context of the text and asked questions about the claims scripture made.[5] Wright outlined two different modes of studying scripture, moving from the "traditionalist" to the "historical critical" mode required what he called a "conversion experience," during which the person realized the problems of the traditionalist approach (which assumes that what a particular religious tradition has taught about a text is true) and sees the strengths of the alternative mode. He saw a primary strength of the historical-critical mode was an understanding that what a text claims to be and what it actually is can be two entirely different things. In order to take part in this second approach, a person has to have an open-ended research approach in which conclusions are not driving the study but can be subject to change based on the evidence presented.[6]

The historical-critical approach takes context into account. The method first led Wright to examine biblical texts and make arguments about how to reconcile current LDS beliefs and practices with a historical-critical reading of those same texts. Then he turned his historical-critical eye to the Book of Mormon, arguing that, "Over time I came to see that...the 'ancient' scriptures produced by

4. David P. Wright, Journal, October 28, 1993.

5. David P. Wright, "Historical Criticism: A Necessary Element in the Search for Religious Truth," *Sunstone* 16, no. 3 (September 1992): 28–38.

6. Ibid, 28.

Joseph Smith were not really ancient but his own compositions."[7] One example that Wright explained was the Book of Mormon's use of sections from the biblical Isaiah. The field of historical criticism had long claimed that Isaiah was written not by one person, but by multiple people in different periods. Thus, Wright observed, Lehi (a Book of Mormon figure who went on a journey to the Americas) would not have had the portions of Isaiah that appear in the Book of Mormon with him when he left on his journey. Those portions were written "some sixty years after the family came to the new world."[8]

While Wright provided several examples of how he came to understand the Book of Mormon in a new way, the crux of his argument lay in borrowing a distinction that non-LDS biblical scholars had long been making. That was the difference between "judgments about historical matters and judgments about spiritual worth." This, then, was the focus of Wright's article. While the historical-critical method may challenge the historical claims of the Book of Mormon, he felt that it encouraged new revelations about Joseph Smith and his prophetic worldview. He believed claims to historicity limited what could be learned from the text; whereas a historical-critical approach opened readers up to asking new questions and therefore finding new layers of meaning.[9]

The concerns of members of the church hierarchy who understood the field of historical criticism in which Wright was standing would have been strong. His article declared that the scriptural and historical foundations of the church were not what they claimed to be. The potential outcome for some readers may well be that if the scriptural and historical foundations were not true, the entire edifice could crumble. Wright was introducing questions about scripture that most people simply did not ask. And while he was providing a faithful way to reconcile scriptural inconsistencies, the simple fact of those inconsistencies could become a stumbling block for many people of faith.

At the meeting where they discussed the SCMC, the bishop's copy of Wright's article was covered with notations and marginalia

7. Ibid, 33.
8. Ibid, 34.
9. Ibid, 34–35.

that he knew the bishop had not made. Wright observed: "He did not do the underlining. He wasn't sure if the stake president or Salt Lake [headquarters] made the underlining."[10] Wright noted to the bishop that what was happening with his process was the same as what happened with the September Six disciplinary processes. The bishop agreed. He was not trying to hide it. He said that their goal was to get Wright "to be orthodox or [they would] hold a disciplinary council."[11]

Frustrated, Wright wrote in his journal that he believed the institutional church had played the bully with scholars for too long and that church leaders had "exercised dominion uncharitably and unwisely."[12] In part, he wanted to protest what he had seen the church do to others, and in part, he wanted to protect himself and his family from what seemed inevitable.

But there was a hitch. He could not simply walk away because he wanted to perform ordinances for his family, especially the baptism of his eight-year-old son, a ritual symbolizing entry into church membership, and the priesthood ordination of his older son. The priesthood is bestowed on male church members deemed worthy by the institution as early as age twelve. At that age they can receive the Aaronic priesthood, which allows them to minister to the believing community through various rituals. Ordination into this priesthood functions culturally as a rite of passage into manhood. Both baptism and ordination mark key moments in the life of a church member. In the system's patriarchal structure, they would normally be performed by the person's father if the father was an ordained priesthood holder. Wright wanted to play that role as his sons' father and priesthood holder. So he had to be diplomatic.[13]

These rituals were big moments in his sons' lives and in the life of their family. For Wright, whose family had branches stretching back in church history to the pioneer exodus from Illinois to the Salt Lake Valley, the church "is a cultural home. It's my cultural heritage." He explained that even when he wanted to turn and walk away, "You

10. Wright, Journal, April 28, 1993.
11. Ibid, October 28, 1993.
12. Ibid, June 6, 1993.
13. Ibid, June 6, 1993, and David Wright to Bishop Reeder, letter, February 17, 1994.

don't want to jump out of that. You want to help [the church] and to improve it and make it not only a better place for you and your family, but for those people around you."[14] In addition to making the tradition better, Wright also wanted to participate in its rituals. It was for the kids, but not just for them. It was also for their grandparents "whose total identity is the traditional church."[15]

Before he could do any of this, though, Wright had to be deemed worthy by his local priesthood leaders. He recalled that, "Everybody knows of cases where people win the so-called 'Bishop Roulette' and are able to do things and participate in church activities even though they ... are not completely kosher."[16] Wright's bishop and stake president were primarily concerned with orthodoxy and so Wright had to pass whatever orthodoxy test came his way. In one of their meetings in July 1993, his bishop asked questions that Wright found "inquisitional," ones that were "asked with categorical starkness and that required immediate unreserved yes or no answers." Wright wanted to just walk out, but he stayed because his ability to perform the ordinances for his sons was on the line.

The bishop peppered him with questions like, "Do you believe that Joseph Smith was a prophet? Do you sustain Joseph Smith as a prophet? Do you believe that Joseph Smith was visited by John the Baptist and received the Aaronic Priesthood from him?" As Wright experienced it, the rigid questions suggested that there was only one right answer and he could not be nuanced in his response. Out of exasperation Wright eventually blurted out what he thought, "I said I viewed Joseph Smith as a prophet, that he was inspired of God. I said that the Church was good and beneficial, and that I wanted to be part of it and I wanted my children to be part of it. I said it was part of our family identity." Even as he affirmed the role that the church and religion had played in his life—a central, not peripheral role—Wright also felt he had to explain his views that probably differed from the bishop's. His "questions presupposed ... the view that God communicates clearly and unambiguously and that prophets properly understand and convey to their audience what is so revealed."[17]

---

14. Wright, oral history with author.
15. Ibid.
16. Ibid.
17. Wright, Journal, July 11, 1993.

Instead, Wright believed that while Smith was inspired, his revelations were shaped not just by divine hands but came through the vehicle of human experience and therefore could contain both revelation and human input and error. When the discussion was over, Wright felt they had reached an impasse. The church the bishop imagined was "for perfect beings and not for those who are seeking to improve and to learn and to grow." He understood that the bishop saw membership in the church as following a series of requirements and affirming a set of orthodox beliefs.[18] "His main point was that we must 'hold on to the iron rod,' to the 'stake of truth which has been driven in the ground' by the restoration.... In essence he said that, measured against this truth, my views could be judged apostate."[19] What he recalled hearing from his bishop was that the Restoration was not a process, but a done deal that had created an orthodox measuring stick. That stick could then be used to measure the orthodoxy of any church member.

But Wright saw the Restoration differently. Perhaps his view was most succinctly captured in a letter written by his wife, Dianne, to their bishop on February 17, 1994. She argued that Wright was someone who pursued the truth, wherever it might lead: "This church was founded on the search for truth by Joseph Smith. Joseph used every means available to him to find truth. Indeed, one of the great joys we have on this earth is our quest to find truth."[20] From Dianne Wright's perspective, her husband's scholarship represented the vision of the Restoration that Smith had begun: a collection of individuals pursuing the highest truths and embracing wherever that path led. Whether the Restoration was an iron rod or a continued search for truth shaped the way they understood the church and its future.

The last meeting with his bishop was a pivotal moment for Wright. When he left he knew his time in the church was coming to an end: "I really don't have a home in Mormonism no matter how much I desire it. Only orthodoxy is tolerated."[21] Because he could not affirm the orthodox claims of his local church leaders, be-

18. Ibid.
19. Ibid, April 28, 1993.
20. Dianne Wright to Bishop Reeder, February 17, 1994.
21. Ibid.

cause he had a different vision of the Restoration, Wright saw that there was no hope that he would be allowed to perform his sons' ordinances. Instead, a neighbor friend in their ward performed the rituals. Wright watched from the sidelines, unable to even stand in the ordinance circle for his elder son.

After the ritual, church leaders encouraged Wright's son to hug his mother, but throughout the ritual and after, no one acknowledged David Wright.[22] For him the experience was "like being a disembodied spirit … you know, how people talk about how they are on the operating table and they can see themselves on the table and they are sort of removed from that? It felt like I was there but not there."[23] This hit Wright hard. His church leaders were not allowing him to be the kind of believer and the kind of father he wanted to be. They had stripped him of the ritual aspects of the priesthood role he had carried since he was young. They had pushed him to the sidelines as an observer. All this made him realize that "for the first time personally, I got a sense of how women must feel in the church, of having to sit and watch and never participate in the ritual life of the church."[24]

Reading Scriptures

Every time Wright met with his bishop and stake president they placed great emphasis on orthodoxy and obedience. Here Wright experienced a pattern that appeared in the cases of six other church members in September 1993. What may have begun as concern about scholarship and publications slowly shifted toward the question of obedience to authority. Leaders at the local level often were not prepared to engage ideas or issues of scholarship and so framed any disagreement as disobedience, focusing their attention on it rather than the complex issues at hand. But unquestioning obedience to authority was not in Wright's character. Since young adulthood he had been pushing back against orthodox views of scripture and revelation. His thinking about these topics had become his life's work.

At nineteen Wright had embarked on his two-year LDS mission to Oregon even as he knew that what he most wanted was to study

22. Wright, Journal, July 21, 1993.
23. Wright, oral history with author.
24. Ibid.

the ancient Near East. In fact, he hoped to become the next Hugh Nibley, a popular apologetic biblical scholar teaching at Brigham Young University. Wright had dreamed of being an apologetic defender of his faith, the Book of Mormon, and the other scriptures of the Latter-day Saint tradition. After his mission he attended the University of Utah in order to pursue that dream.

In his undergraduate years at the University of Utah, Wright first began to see inconsistencies in what scripture claimed to be and what the evidence suggested. He recalled finding "certain bits of data [that] made it look as though the Book of Mormon, the Book of Abraham, and other of Joseph Smith's ancient scriptures were not ancient."[25] Wright's initial impulse was to quit his studies, to turn away from his findings. Quitting would allow him to put his questions on a shelf and not have to wrestle with the fact that leaders of the church and scholars of the faith like Hugh Nibley now appeared "flawed," "not rigorous," and "sometimes illogical."[26] Ultimately, though, Wright decided to go to graduate school at University of California–Berkeley, hoping to better understand and therefore defend his faith with accurate information.

But as his studies continued, his questions only multiplied. Wright became confident that the evidence pointed him to a knowledge that the Book of Mormon and other Mormon canon were modern-day scriptures rather than ancient ones. This led him to a new crisis of faith: he either had to get rid of his faith system and community or come to a new understanding of the value of Mormon scriptures.

It was his professors in graduate school who helped him see that his faith need not rest on the historicity of the texts. "For example, many of my professors were Jewish, and religiously devout," he recalled, "but accepted the critical conclusion that Moses did not write the Pentateuch or Torah."[27] Wright remembered that his experiences allowed him to be just such a mentor to his own students. They "were trying to figure out how they could deal with similar struggles as well."[28] Wright's professors' model helped him look to Mormon scriptures for

25. David P. Wright, Statement for Disciplinary Council, April 6, 1994.
26. Ibid.
27. Ibid.
28. Wright, oral history with author.

the truth that they offered even if their claims as ancient texts did not stand up to evidentiary expectations. Of Joseph Smith, he concluded: "that prophets 'translate' revelation into their own words in terms of their cultural situation. Thus a revelation, or rather a product of revelation ... has a certain amount of humanness which can account for error and even misperception on the part of the prophet."[29]

Feeling confident in a newly reconstructed faith, Wright went to teach at Brigham Young University in the Asian and Near Eastern Languages department from 1984 to 1989. He arrived at BYU optimistic. He had heard Jeffrey R. Holland, then president of BYU, call the university the "Harvard of the West" and felt he could be happy there "if that was the direction BYU was going." And so he took the job, hoping to turn "scriptural scholarship in the church in a more academic direction. That doesn't mean an antagonistic direction, but it certainly meant to rethink things and to re-understand our history."[30]

Wright's desire to reframe thinking about scripture at BYU met obstacles at every step. He may have understood this best when a colleague, sitting in Wright's office at Brigham Young University said to him, "I wouldn't call you Mormon." Though Wright's general optimism and rosy outlook on the future won out for a time, things came to a head in his 1987–88 Continuing Faculty Status review. People in his department shared with the review committee some of Wright's emails that discussed his plan to give a talk addressing contradictions in creation stories. Where he wanted to have open dialogue about inconsistencies and how they might be understood, others thought it best not to bring those inconsistencies to people's attention. What people did not know or had not yet encountered could not injure their faith. The review committee sided with his colleagues and terminated Wright, asserting that the cause of his termination was his unorthodox teachings that challenged the historicity of the Book of Mormon, even though he never spoke about these ideas in his classes.[31] He knew that colleagues who were also

29. Wright, Statement for Disciplinary Council.

30. Wright, oral history with author.

31. Wright, oral history with author. See also Gregory A. Prince, *Leonard Arrington and the Writing of Mormon History* (Salt Lake City: The University of Utah Press, 2016), 432.

friends had not supported his continuation at their institution. They simply could not imagine his type of scholarship at BYU.

After his next and final year at BYU, Wright went to Hebrew University in Jerusalem on a one-year Fulbright. But BYU was still with him halfway around the world. Weekly church meetings were held at the BYU Jerusalem Center, meaning that the Wrights attended church in a building tied to the university that had just ousted him. After the Wrights returned to the United States, David taught for a year at Middlebury College in Vermont before receiving a tenure-track position at Brandeis University in Massachusetts.

At Brandeis, Wright finally felt a sense of relief, fully free from the stress of still being tied to BYU and free to publish what he wanted to publish.[32] And so he published his 1992 article, "Historical Criticism: A Necessary Element in the Search for Religious Truth" in *Sunstone*. It was this article that his bishop brought to their meeting, the article that caused concern for the church hierarchy and represented Wright's refusal to stay in line.

Not long after, in 1993 Wright also published an essay, "'In Plain Terms that We May Understand': Joseph Smith's Transformation of Hebrews in Alma 12–13," in Brent Metcalfe's edited collection titled *New Approaches to the Book of Mormon: Explorations in Critical Methodology*.[33] Knowing that church leaders were already alarmed about his writings, Wright provided his local leaders with a copy of the essay, "because I didn't want to blindside any of them."[34] Even though he sought a collegial relationship, a church disciplinary process was already in motion.

This meant that because Wright held the Melchizedek priesthood (the second and higher order of priesthood that allows worthy men to teach and preach to outsiders), a twelve-person council (made up of local men who had the same priesthood status) would be convened by his bishop. At the council, Wright would be given a chance to speak and bring witnesses for his defense. The bishop and stake president would also be able to offer evidence against Wright,

32. Wright, oral history with author.

33. Brent Metcalfe, ed., *New Approaches to the Book of Mormon: Explorations in Critical Methodology* (Salt Lake City: Signature Books, 1993). Metcalfe was excommunicated in 1994 for publishing this scholarship.

34. Wright, oral history with author.

arguing that he had become apostate. After all evidence was presented the council would meet without Wright present to determine if any discipline or punishment was necessary.

Wright was not the only person at this time who faced disciplinary proceedings for similar issues. Brent Metcalfe, the editor of the book that contained Wright's second essay, was also brought before a disciplinary council and ultimately excommunicated. *New Approaches to the Book of Mormon* was written by scholars who employed the historical-critical method in their studies. Many in the collection, including Metcalfe, argued that the Book of Mormon was a nineteenth-century document, using context to make their claims. Some church leaders perceived both Wright and Metcalfe as dangerous. They were publishing works, and therefore making public, arguments that could raise doubts in other believers.

David Wright and Brent Metcalfe could see the writing on the wall not only at the local level, but also because their work was clearly on the radar of the most powerful men in the church, and those leaders were not pleased. One of them was Dallin H. Oaks, who throughout his adult life committed himself to making sure that the boundaries around church doctrine were firm, not porous. He and other church leaders understood themselves to be managing the watchtower of purity in the LDS Church. And David Wright and Brent Metcalfe, along with many others, were on their list.

In some ways, Oaks had been training to be a custodian of the faith his whole life. After graduating University of Chicago law school in 1957, he became a law clerk to Supreme Court Chief Justice Earl Warren. He later taught as a law professor at the University of Chicago while he simultaneously served as a stake leader. In 1971 he became the president of BYU, helping the institution expand and grow. He left after a decade, wanting the institution to create and achieve new goals under a new leadership. In 1980 he accepted an appointment as a Utah Supreme Court Justice, where he served until, in 1984, he was ordained a Latter-day Saint apostle on the same day that Russell M. Nelson was ordained.[35] All these activities—from serving in the judicial system, to presiding over the church's

35. See Richard E. Turley Jr., *In the Hands of the Lord: The Life of Dallin H. Oaks* (Salt Lake City: Deseret Book, 2021).

flagship university, to entering the highest body of church authority—allowed Oaks to hone and offer his law-abiding, rule-enforcing traits. These traits worked well in service of an institution that was organized around purity and believed God to be a holy being concerned about the holiness and worthiness of church members.

In October 1993, just after the September Six disciplinary actions and during David Wright's struggle with his local leaders, Oaks gave a speech titled "The Historicity of the Book of Mormon," in which he explored these questions. Oaks announced that there were some church members who claimed to be faithful Latter-day Saints who "abandon claims that [the Book of Mormon] is a historical record of the ancient peoples of the Americas." Labeling them "practitioners of so-called 'higher criticism,'" Oaks declared that the Book of Mormon was fact, not fable. History not story. While he said he would use reason in his exploration, he also said he would "approach the question of the historicity of the Book of Mormon from the standpoint of faith and revelation."[36] Oaks warned that those who relied only on scholarship and rejected revelatory knowledge fulfilled the Book of Mormon prophet Nephi's prediction that in the final days "men shall teach with their learning, and deny the Holy Ghost, which giveth utterance."

Oaks argued that only the Holy Spirit could serve as a witness to the authenticity of the Book of Mormon, and he spoke of his admiration for scholars who were able to keep faith and revelation at the forefront of their work. Those who did not "can also take what is sublime and make it mundane."[37] The danger for Oaks was obvious. Suggesting that the Book of Mormon was inspired story rather than historical fact rooted in revelation was to suggest that it was just another book, one among many from which humanity could learn. This idea upset the foundation on which the church hierarchy had built its understanding of the Restoration. Without the institution's particular perspective on history, that foundation might begin to crumble as people debated the meaning of the story and the role of human error in its foundational texts.

---

36. Dallin Harris Oaks, "The Historicity of the Book of Mormon" (Provo, UT: Foundation for Ancient Research and Mormon Studies, 1993), 1–2.

37. Ibid, 6–7.

Oaks likened what was happening in Book of Mormon studies to what had happened in the historical Jesus movement. In that movement, scholars of ancient Israel sought to peel back the layers of Christian theology that had accrued around the figure of Jesus, making him the Christ. The scholars went in search of the historical man, attempting to separate out the theological claims made about him after his death from the historical teachings he preached during his life. In so doing, they were making their own claims about what was significant: focusing on Jesus's life rather than the significance of his death, on who he had been to his immediate community, rather than how the community remembered him in later decades. As they sought out the 'real' Jesus, they emphasized the importance of historical criticism to their pursuit. They provided evidence that the gospels included in the Christian bible were written decades after Jesus's life and were not, as they claimed to be, firsthand, eyewitness accounts.

All of these arguments were part of the historical criticism movement in the late twentieth century. Perhaps nowhere can this be seen more than in the work of the Jesus Seminar, which began in 1985. The Seminar gathered together biblical scholars from around the globe to vote about the historical accuracy of sayings and stories attributed to Jesus. While voting may seem an odd approach, the goals of the Seminar were to find out where there was consensus and to offer those aspects of the biblical story that they felt could be traced back to Jesus himself. The Seminar used different colored beads that scholars placed in a box: Red votes represented the strongest claim that Jesus said something; pink votes represented a feeling that the saying was something like what Jesus would have said; gray stood for a sense that it was less likely Jesus made the statement; and black represented the position that Jesus did not make the statement.[38]

Oaks described scholarly explorations like these as an attempt to "dissect a sacred subject with a secular scalpel" and, because of this dissection, "in the confusion of categories of truth the patient dies on the operating table."[39] Using inappropriate tools for the study of sacred matters sullied them, made impure what was pure. The

38. Marcus Borg, *Meeting Jesus Again for the First Time* (New York: HarperCollins, 1995), 20–22.

39. Oaks, "Historicity of the Book of Mormon," 12.

scholarly endeavor had to be curtailed before the foundation cracked and the entire thing fell to pieces.

Before finishing, Oaks made a critique of a seemingly unrelated topic: diversity. "Diversity is one of the favorite buzz words of our time," he argued. When "properly applied," it could encourage human relationships and growth, but it could be damaging and detrimental to faith. To answer how, Oaks turned to a letter to the editor found in the October 20, 1993, *Deseret News*. In her letter, a woman had written, "Certainly 'God cherishes diversity' in almost everything—except his followers' loyalties and beliefs. The LDS Church exists as evidence of his rejection of diversity in beliefs."[40] While the woman was referring to church members attending symposia rather than paying attention to the lessons of general conference, Oaks wanted to suggest an even larger connection to the secular study of scripture: diversity of perspectives was not a boon to the church.

Instead Oaks and many of his fellow members of the church hierarchy saw diverse perspectives as a threat to their vision of the Restoration. There was one way to be faithful, not many. They had a calling to staff the watchtowers, to ensure that the church was not led astray from its mission and goals. These members of the church hierarchy were anxious that the growing diversity of perspectives in the church community would lead to a disintegration, not just of the institution, but of the Restoration itself. Their work, as they understood it, was to be the centripetal force holding the church together against the centrifugal tides that sought to tear it apart.

It was only a few months after Oaks's talk that Wright's disciplinary council happened on April 5, 1994. When it arrived, Wright felt ready—ready to be excommunicated. He was ready to move on from the unproductive relationships with church leaders that caused him spiritual and social harm. The twelve-person council asked him questions that his bishop and stake president had asked him before. He acknowledged that he considered the prophets to be "wise and instructive individuals, but not infallible." When asked if he would follow his bishop's counsel even if the bishop told him to quit publishing about these topics, Wright said he would not, that research and writing were part of his scholarly work and his pursuit of truth.

40. Ibid, 15.

While Wright's ideas were problematic from the council's perspective—they disrupted a sense of orthodoxy, after all—Wright, like others, became subject to disciplinary action because he published and spoke publicly about his unorthodox views.[41] He had aired his doubts and questions, shared his alternative perspective. In his defense, Wright explained that he had "suffered a loss of community" because of "ecclesiastical suspicion and investigation of my honest work." He then concluded, "if I am guilty of anything, it is of trying to find a way to believe and appreciate my religious tradition, of trying to see Joseph as a prophet and to understand his work as spiritually valuable to me, my family, and my Mormon community."[42]

Wright felt as though the church that was holding the disciplinary council was "not the church that I had striven to be part of and to which I had tried to commit my loyalties." Instead, he saw a church that was wrapped up in what he called "prophetic fundamentalism," where prophets were seen as infallible, as always having been in perfect agreement with one another, and as leaders who could not be challenged or questioned. This was not the church that Wright wanted to embrace.[43]

In his defense at his disciplinary council, Wright noted that all of his studies grew "out of a desire to cultivate faith, not disbelief." He did not want to attack the church, he insisted, but to offer members an alternative path of maintaining a faith that was not rooted in claims to historicity. In the articles in which he addressed such topics, he wrote about how believers could interpret evidence in a faithful way while still accepting the rigorous scholarship of scriptural studies. And in his writing he "explicitly supported the prophet's right to interpret prophecy for our time."[44]

The council saw things differently. When his stake president came out of the meeting room to tell Wright that he had been excommunicated, he also told Wright that he should no longer wear his temple garments or pay tithing. But he made clear that he wanted Wright to continue to attend church. Wright had too much pride, he explained,

41. Wright, Letter to Bishop Reeder.
42. Wright, Statement for Disciplinary Council.
43. Wright, Journal, April 5, 1994.
44. Wright, Statement for Disciplinary Council.

and needed to "learn to subordinate scholarship to what the prophet said. The prophet's words (in his prophetic office) are not contravenable or liable to revision on the basis of scholarship." He went on to tell Wright something that those experiencing church discipline often hear—that the disciplinary proceedings and their outcomes were rooted in love. He then shook Wright's hand and gave him a hug.[45] From Wright's perspective, the council was not about love, but the enforcement of orthodoxy and conformity. And he was relieved that it was over. Looking back thirty years later, he would call the claim that the council was motivated by love, "bullshit."[46]

In his official letter written after the council and announcing Wright's excommunication, his stake president wrote: "We represent the Savior and our prophets and recognize that they alone have the right and authority through inspiration to direct the affairs on this earth. When our prophets speak in their office and calling, they will be directed by inspiration and when they speak as such all debate should stop. The prophet is the only person on the earth authorized to interpret the doctrine of the Church."[47] Here the stake president had reinforced an orthodoxy rooted in the idea that prophets and prophetic authority should not be challenged. No one, save the prophet, was able to interpret the teachings of orthodoxy in the church. Thus, hierarchy and orthodoxy were cemented to one another.

Even at the time, Wright's excommunication did not receive as much attention as the councils of the September Six just eight months before. Perhaps because his did not occur in Utah along with several others in the same month, and perhaps because attention to the church's excommunications had started to wane. Yet some in the academic community raised a flag of concern. In an April 30, 1994, letter from Apostle Hugh B. Brown's great-grandson, Edwin Firmage Jr., who also studied the ancient Near East at Berkeley, to scholar Bryan Waterman and counselor Stephanie Smith-Waterman, Firmage declared that Wright was excommunicated "for publicly advocating an historical-critical approach to the Bible and Mormon scriptures." From Firmage's perspective, the

45. Wright, Journal, April 5, 1994.
46. Wright, oral history with author.
47. President Wheeler, Letter to David P. Wright, April 6, 1993.

excommunication was "an attack on freedom of thought and demands a response from all of us for whom the life of the mind is vital." In his letter Firmage enclosed an open letter from LDS scholars to the First Presidency and the Quorum of the Twelve. The letter asserted that the September Six disciplinary actions and Wright's excommunication demonstrated that the leadership of the church "is determined to silence dissent, even when it is offered in a spirit of good will and fellowship." This approach to intellectual inquiry, the signers maintained, made the church lose credibility even as it claimed to seek the truth. "By insisting on unquestioning conformance to their version of history," the letter declared that "church leaders also deny members the opportunity to think and choose for themselves." That letter, signed by eighty-seven past and present church members and seventy-six non-members, appeared in the Salt Lake Tribune on July 3, 1994.

After his excommunication, Wright wrestled with his grief and frustration over the loss of his Latter-day Saint community. D. Michael Quinn, a historian and one of the September Six, had counseled him that he would experience all the stages of grief. Wright turned to the internet and found some solace in an online "hunt-and-peck community" that never met in person but had experienced being excommunicated. His wife and children felt as though they had been excommunicated as well. The community had rejected them. When Wright told a friend that he was not a Mormon anymore, she disagreed. This friend, along with the community at Sunstone conferences who enjoyed exploring issues of faith, and his online community made him realize she was right. In his journal he wrote, "I am inescapably a Mormon. I am not on the outside looking in. I just have another way of being inside."[48]

48. David P. Wright, "Exile to Reconstruction," May 6, 1994. Decades later, Wright explained that his Mormon identity was primary or central to who he was, and yet "I can't escape my past and that is what is in my background. I don't want to deny it or reject it." What happened to him in 1994 is part of who he was. Now Wright describes himself as "humanistic," arguing that "we need to live together. We need to work together." After retiring from Brandeis, Wright returned to playing music, something he loved in his youth and felt he did not have enough time for during his working life. For him, music brings "great joy" because he can "offer [his] talents" to the public. Wright, oral history with author.

Remembering the September Six

Why begin a story about the September Six with David Wright and Dallin Oaks? Wright's journey and his struggles with the institution begin to challenge and revise how narratives of the September Six have been told. While his disciplinary proceedings were still in process during September 1993, his story shows that what happened in September 1993 was not an anomaly. Instead it was part of a much larger pattern stretching long before and long after that month. While alliterations are alluring, they do not provide us with the explanatory power to truly understand what was at work in the church during this time.

The human mind is always looking for patterns, clustering events so as to make them more memorable. We have a strong urge to make sense and order out of things that seem sloppy and chaotic. This is especially true when it comes to historical memory. We want to impose limitations and boundaries, to imbue those limitations with meaning so that we can store them in our minds in neat chunks. "Oh yes," we can then say, "that happened during X period or Y time." While those clusters can be helpful in quickly communicating with one another, they can become so cemented in our minds that we look no further than the meaning that has already been conveyed. This is very true of an episode that is typically remembered as "The September Six," when six feminists and intellectuals were disciplined by the LDS Church in September 1993. People remember confidently that there were six and we know the reasons why.

Explanations have accrued about that month in roughly two patterns. On one side are those who remember the September Six as a time when the conservative and anti-intellectual institutional church clamped down on public expression of free thinking and personal conscience in its membership, sending a clear message that one must stay in line or get out. On the other side are those who defend the church's choices as difficult ones, but necessary to prevent the church from decaying away from the "true church" Joseph Smith restored. Necessary because they could create unity and a strong sense of purpose in the church membership as it was rapidly expanding around the globe.

These explanations have become overly and destructively simplified by the limitations placed around the September Six, leaving us unable to see not just a month, but an era in which church leadership clashed with church members over what the faith and the meaning of the Restoration would be. People on all sides of these debates defined the culture of Mormonism for years to come.

The late twentieth century was a period of growing pains in the LDS Church, when different visions of the Restoration came to a head, with questions surfacing about which one would take hold. Restoration claims are always contextual, but also have an ahistoric component built in. In this case, Joseph Smith and his tradition argued that the "true church" instituted by Jesus had left the earth after the death of his apostles, where it waited to be restored by Smith and his companions in the modern day. Restoration movements like Smith's assert that they are transcending history, moving back in time, skipping over the bad parts and returning to all that is true and good. They are shaped by their context. Yet those involved deny that context as they claim to be resurrecting an authentic, pristine past.

Within the LDS Church, an understanding of the Restoration is central. The notion of the Restoration has been defined over and against the concept of apostasy, a category that is always pushing back, making clear distinctions between self and other.[49] The dualisms in this understanding of the Restoration are striking. The words of the 2004 "Preach My Gospel" missionary handbook help illustrate this point:

> With the death of the Apostles, priesthood keys and the presiding priesthood authority were taken from the earth. The Apostles had kept the doctrines of the gospel pure and maintained the order and standard of worthiness for Church members. Without the Apostles, over time the doctrines were corrupted, and unauthorized changes were made in Church organization and priesthood ordinances, such as baptism and conferring the gift of the Holy Ghost. Without revelation and priesthood authority, people relied on human wisdom to interpret the scriptures.[50]

---

49. Miranda Wilcox and John D. Young, "Introduction," in Miranda Wilcox and John D. Young, eds., *Standing Apart: Mormon Historical Consciousness and the Concept of Apostasy* (Oxford University Press, 2014), 2–3. See also Terryl Givens, "'We Have Only the Old Thing': Rethinking Mormon Restoration," in *Standing Apart*, 336–38.

50. "Preach My Gospel: A Guide to Missionary Service," (Salt Lake City: The Church of Jesus Christ of Latter-day Saints, 2004), 35.

And so the 'true church' disappeared from the earth for a time and God waited for the right circumstances to bring back the revelation and priesthood authority that were its central components.

Evident here is the idea that doctrine must remain pure and that without careful boundary maintenance, apostasy looms, ever attempting to pull the church off its narrow path. The handbook goes on to state: "[A] restoration, not a reformation, was required. Priesthood authority did not continue in an unbroken line of succession from the Apostle Peter. To reform is to change what already exists; to restore is to bring back something in its original form. Thus, restoration of priesthood authority through divine messengers was the only possible way to overcome the Great Apostasy."[51]

This narrative, taught to potential converts, creates its own set of patterns and history-telling. It contains a critique of Catholicism, which claims an unbroken succession from the apostle Peter and a critique of the Protestant Reformation, which sought to reject what had been added to Christianity over time, peeling back to the movement's essence. Finally, it is set over and against the notion of Apostasy, the threat that the church once did fall off the correct path due to worldly ways and thus could do so again.

During the period of the disciplinary councils in the 1990s, historian and church member Dean May noted that "the Restoration arose as a dissent from mainstream Christianity, and most of the Restoration churches arose as a further dissent from that movement." Because there was no officially orthodox position when Joseph Smith died, each movement that grew out of that tradition was its own Restoration, and its own form of dissent. For this reason, dissent was baked into the concept of the Restoration: "A faith that at its outset so boldly rejects the claims of other traditions must insist upon the right of its converts to dissent from those traditions."[52]

Just months after September 1993, May asserted that the institutional concerns about the September Six were primarily about their challenge to the position of the prophet. The Latter-day Saint community had enough room for individual dissent, but "when a

51. "Preach My Gospel," 36.

52. Dean L. May, "Dissent and Authority in Two Latter-day Saint Traditions," *Sunstone* 17, no. 1 (June 1994): 16–17.

member speaks out in a highly public way on matters about which Church authorities have made special pronouncements," they challenge the very heart of the institution. May argued that the concern "is [over] authority more than doctrine." He noted that any public fissure that challenged the authority of the church hierarchy was deemed "a most egregious act."[53] He characterized the upside of the avoidance of airing dissent and dirty laundry as the ability to "avoid precise definitions of orthodoxy in creed, doctrine and even conduct." "The stress … upon prophetic authority," May finally argued, "has choked off avenues of formal dissent."[54]

Any movement toward prophetic or hierarchical infallibility or unquestionability means that democratic impulses that do not conform must be silenced or condemned. The church in the 1990s very clearly defined orthodoxy at the doctrinal and behavioral levels. The actions around the September 1993 disciplinary councils demonstrate that in addition to the concept of prophetic authority, the church was constructing a new understanding of orthodoxy that had been in development for decades. This entailed a commitment to a purity system, an understanding of God that suggested God's ultimate concerns were about holiness and purity, maintaining the purity of those on the inside and protecting them from those on the outside.

On the institutional side, there was an emphasis on the need to draw firm boundaries around the "true church." After all, the claim of the Restoration was that the true church had left the earth as worldly concerns polluted God's vision, making it necessary for a latter-day prophet to come and bring it back. Restorationist claims are always, in part, claims to a type of purity. Things were once right and true and good. In this case, Jesus knew the way that the one true church should look. Restorationists argue that the church got muddied along the way, so much so that it was no longer recognizable as the true church. They claim that they are bringing back what was so corrupted, so impure that it was no longer what God had envisioned.

And so in some sense to see that the LDS Church in the late twentieth century was grasping at purity is to see it as simply part of a restoration movement. At the same time, though, the church

53. Ibid.
54. Ibid.

was fostering within its ranks a purity system that sought to measure everything by its level of purity. The church hierarchy worked to create and maintain firm boundaries around what was acceptable and unacceptable. For the institution, the theological message about God's holiness, and therefore God's emphasis on purity, was key. Church leaders argued that they were simply maintaining the course that Joseph Smith had set. That the institution had not changed in any dramatic ways over time. That the true church would not change because of the ways of the world.

On the other hand, there were scholars, intellectuals, feminists, and others, both in the center and on the margins, who had a different view of the Restoration. They, too, made an argument about original intent. They believed that when Joseph Smith instituted the true church it was a radical move that democratized theological claims and made new experiences and spiritual authority open to everyone. These dissenters wanted to pursue the truth wherever it led. Subsequently, they argued, the ideas and practices that democratized Christianity in order to restore it had been slowly erased by institutional leaders who wanted a clearly defined hierarchy with power shored up at the top. They wanted to unearth a history that they thought was rich with equality, the Spirit, and emphasis on being driven by personal conscience and personal revelation. For them the Restoration was about egalitarianism and the democratization of spiritual authority. It was chock-full of new theological and social innovations that pushed the community toward a more rewarding path.

Sources

A note on sources is necessary here. While the church hierarchy was very much a part of constructing the purity system that led to the September Six disciplinary councils, many of the documents tied to those councils on the institutional side are not open to research. In addition, the personal papers of many church leaders are closed to research. The focus of Part I, in which I explore the church's construction of the purity system concentrates on public talks, sermons, and discourses. This is as it should be. While individual church leaders may or may not have agreed with everything taking place, the institution operates in a unified way. It is the public discourse that created and encouraged a vision of the Restoration that emphasized the purity system in place at the time. For church leaders, the institution and understandings of tradition were significant sources of theological authority, offering great wisdom about what the Restoration should be.

On the other hand, Part II, in which I explore the stories of the September Six alongside a handful of others facing church disciplinary proceedings, focuses on documents and interviews tied to the personal experiences of the Six and others. This, too, is as it should be. While they knew one another, they were not operating in concert. They were not a counter-institution. They were individuals. And they located spiritual authority in personal experience and conscience. These, they argued, were important sites of knowledge. Their words describe their experiences and highlight the complexities of individuals navigating a complex institution. Their individual narratives illustrate their understandings of what the Restoration ought to look like.

Neither side in this struggle was immune to external political forces or contextual movements around them. In the late twentieth century, the institutional church worked hard to align itself with the Religious Right. Its anti-intellectualism, emphasis on the historicity of scriptures, its political activism and theological arguments against anything other than heterosexual monogamy, and its claims about women, the family and the home, worked to cement the church's social and political bonds with conservative evangelical social and political forces.

The September Six—less Avraham Gileadi, who will be discussed in Chapter 2—and other dissenters at the time contested in various ways the very idea that God was most concerned with holiness and purity. They were molded by feminist theologies and political activism. They were formed by new historical methodologies that shaped history-telling in both ancient and modern times. They were framed within an era of civil rights in which the movements for Black, women's, and LGBTQ+ rights enhanced their vision of egalitarianism. They offered a different vision of the Restoration.

All of these visions of the Restoration looked to history to make their claims. All argued that theirs was the vision rooted in the "true church." Each side claimed that its vision was the one that had not wavered from Joseph Smith's—that the other side had been swayed by contextual forces that had knocked it off the path. In this one way, at least, both sides were wrong. All of the people involved in this story were profoundly shaped by the cultural and theological ideas swirling around them. Their arguments had roots both external to the Mormon tradition and indigenous to it. They were all products of their time, arguing for what the meaning of the Restoration might be, struggling for the soul of Mormonism.

PART I
THE PURITY SYSTEM

"There is nothing in your lives that will destroy you if you will follow the Brethren."
—Boyd K. Packer

On May 18, 1993, Boyd K. Packer gave a talk to the All-Church Coordinating Council (ACCC), the body in the church that oversaw teaching and standardization. Packer gave the talk because he was worried. He was worried that the church to which he had dedicated his life was moving in the wrong direction, that it was turning away from what was true and godly. And Packer wanted to provide some redirection: "It is so easy to be turned about without realizing it is happening to us," he warned. Because of this concern, Packer clearly outlined what he saw as the three greatest threats to the church at the end of the twentieth century: "so-called intellectualism," feminism, and the "gay-lesbian movement."[1] He portrayed the three threats as foreign, external threats trying to invade a happy community. There was an urgency to his message. The political and social agitation that the three movements caused were infiltrating the church. He warned that sympathy with the three movements could feel "reasonable and right," but the dangers were immediate and the stakes were high.

To illustrate the problems that manifest from these movements, often at their intersections, Packer offered an extensive discussion of the issue of working mothers. Demonstrating the conservative stance that the church hierarchy had increasingly embraced over the past century, Packer saw the issue of working mothers as a problem.

1. Boyd K. Packer, "Talk to the All-Church Coordinating Council," May 18, 1993.

Not long before, in 1987, church President Ezra Taft Benson had insisted a woman's role was tied to the home and to children. Packer noted that some church members had reacted negatively to Benson's talk in ways that demonstrated the extent to which intellectualism, feminism, and the gay-lesbian rights movement had already become secondhand.[2] It was a sign of the strife external movements could cause. "Some mothers must work out of the home," he acknowledged. They had to do that for their families and "in this they are justified and for this they should not be criticized."[3] Nonetheless, the gender ideals and a complementarian model of gender, one that imagined a gender binary with entirely separate domains coming together to make up one whole, remained in place. It had been "taught by the prophets from the beginning of this dispensation," he argued, suggesting that church teachings about women had not changed over time. And so Packer allowed that a new day might mean women taking on new roles, but the best form of womanhood was still tied to home and family. It was the measure of a woman's creation.

From Packer's perspective, the solution to all of these problems was simple. Believers needed to step into line, to listen to those in the church hierarchy who knew better and who wanted to protect the faith lives of the membership. There was a genuine urgency to his sense that something had to be done. While some believers thought that support for the three groups was reasonable, others were sympathetic to these causes because it felt right on an emotional level. In the end it did not matter; too many good believers were losing their faith. A believer who found sympathy for these movements "needs to understand that the doctrines of the gospel are revealed through the Spirit to prophets, not through the intellect to scholars."[4]

Part of demonstrating faithfulness meant appreciating the work of correlation, the church's name for the process that ensured its teachings and messages were always the same, bracing against any kind of heresy or dangerous speculation. "The principle of correlation

2. In this work I will use the phrase "gay-lesbian rights movement" when referring to the LGBTQ+ political movement for rights in the 1990. At that time, bisexuals and transgender individuals were marginalized and invisibilized in the movement, something I will discuss in chapter 4.

3. Ezra Taft Benson, "To the Mothers of Zion," February 1987.

4. Ibid.

is a sound principle," Packer argued. It allowed the church to be a global institution without losing its doctrinal core.

His position was that globalization created an outward push, members could go in all kinds of directions, while correlation was an inward pull, ensuring that orthodoxy remained even as the church grew increasingly diverse. "If we neglect it," he preached, "we will pay a very, very heavy price one day." That meant those in the hierarchy who worked on correlation had really important jobs. They were hired to be "generalists," Packer explained, so that they could not only see how one speech or activity fit into church doctrine but could also see how all of the puzzle pieces—the speeches, essays, books, and talks that were happening everywhere—fit together. Their job was to ensure that the resulting puzzle was unified doctrinally and fit into the hierarchy's picture of the Restoration.

Even though Packer's May 1993 talk is often used as shorthand for the church's stance in the period surrounding September 1993, the audience to whom Packer was speaking is only ever given passing mention, the All-Church Coordinating Council. As always, and especially in this instance, audience mattered. Packer was speaking directly to the committee responsible for correlation in the church, the committee charged with creating a well-functioning organization with an emphasis on orthodoxy. He was preaching to the choir. And, as he did so, he was letting that choir know exactly who the enemies were: intellectualism, feminism, and the gay-lesbian rights movement. From the perspective of Maxine Hanks, one of the September Six, Packer had "named the shadow" that other general authorities had been unwilling to name.[5] He had placed his finger on their worst fears.

The ACCC was set to coordinate the Sunday curriculum, but also to ensure that how the gospel was taught at every level was in step with the goals and teachings of the church hierarchy. When the prophet David O. McKay had asked Harold B. Lee to head the ACCC in 1960, Lee had a dramatic vision for the group's goals. He thought he could transform the organizational structure of the church while also strengthening the religious lives of believers. In

5. Maxine Hanks, oral history with author, August 18, 2022.

doing this the ACCC would simplify structures and curriculums and centralize the priesthood that Lee felt had been marginalized in the church.[6]

The ACCC and the correlation movement headed by Harold B. Lee comprised only an updated view of correlation, a process that Joseph F. Smith had envisioned as a way to fortify the church in the early twentieth century. At that time, Smith wanted to make some organizational changes, but he also wanted to make theological ones. After the end of the practice of plural marriage, a practice that defined not just the social and communal aspects of life, but the theological as well, Smith felt the need to re-emphasize other aspects of the church's theology. Correlation would help support moving polygamy away from the center of church theology and create a more individualized view of faith. The shift in focus also caused church leaders to look back in history, especially at Joseph Smith Jr, to find new stories for the church's newly reconfigured identity.[7] This historical move made the concept of restorationism all the more central to the church's identity.

There were a lot of church leaders who saw correlation as the solution to multiple problems. It emphasized orthodoxy, conformity, and hierarchy at a time when the church was globalizing rapidly.[8] Having almost tripled in size between 1950 and 1970 under the leadership of David O. McKay, the church just continued to grow.[9] During that same period, the church stabilized its presence in countries throughout the world.[10] The statistics were clear, too, that the growth of the church did not come from internal fertility rates, but from convert baptisms. As an example, in 1991, 75,000 baptisms

6. Matthew Bowman, "Zion: The Progressive Roots of Mormon Correlation," in Patrick Q. Mason, ed., *Directions for Mormon Studies in the Twenty-First Century* (Salt Lake City: University of Utah Press, 2016), 22–27.

7. Ibid, 15–16. See also Kathleen Flake, *The Politics of American Religious Identity: The Seating of Senator Reed Smoot, Mormon Apostle* (Chapel Hill: University of North Carolina Press, 2004).

8. Terryl L. Givens, *Stretching the Heavens: The Life of Eugene England and the Crisis of Modern Mormonism* (University of North Carolina Press, 2021), 152.

9. Matthew Bowman, *The Mormon People: The Making of an American Faith* (New York: Random House, 2012), 188–90.

10. Gregory A. Prince and Wm. Robert Wright, *David O. McKay and the Rise of Modern Mormonism* (Salt Lake City: The University of Utah Press, 2005), 139.

were for children of church members, whereas 297,770 baptisms were converts.[11] Church leaders felt that this growth signified the success of the church at bringing the message of the Restoration to the world. At the same time, the sheer numbers also represented greater cultural and geographic diversity.[12] Some church leaders had the impulse to clench, to create firm boundaries between who was an insider and an outsider. The system of boundaries that correlation helped create was set up on the basis of holiness and purity.

Prior to Lee's correlation process, all of the auxiliaries in the church—the Relief Society (the organization for women), the Young Men's and Young Women's (for teenaged believers), the Primary (for children), and the Sunday School were all operating fairly independently which made them difficult to manage. It was often the case that each auxiliary had its own curriculum, its own budgets, and its own goals.[13] With all of this seeming chaos, correlation sought to reorganize the church's structures and simplify its educational system. The reorganization brought all of the auxiliaries under the supervision of the Quorum of the Twelve and unified the curriculum so that people everywhere in the world would be hearing the same messages on Sunday morning and throughout the week.[14]

The auxiliaries lost their independent budgets, which became part of the general church funds. They also had their independent publications closed so that the ACCC could review all statements coming from the institution and place them in what became just three church magazines: *Friend* (for children), *New Era* (for youth), and *Ensign* (for adults). The standard that Lee used for the new structure was a corporate one, based on a business model that valued simplicity and standardization. Manuals for teaching members of any age told teachers not to go beyond the content the church provided in what they taught. And the curriculum focused on short

11. Claudia L. Bushman, *Contemporary Mormonism: Latter-day Saints in Modern America* (Westport, CT: Praeger, 2006), 2.

12. Prince and Wright, *David O. McKay*, 151–55.

13. Bowman, *Mormon People*, 194.

14. Andrea G. Radke-Moss, "Women and Gender" in Matthew L. Harris, ed., *Thunder from the Right* (University of Illinois Press, 2019), 191, and Bowman, *Mormon People*, 191–97.

soundbites of doctrine that were easily digested and memorized.[15] This move, of course, centralized the position of orthodoxy in the church. Right thinking was important if the church was going to operate in a unified fashion.

In addition to simplifying teachings in order to make them broadly available, correlation dramatically limited the power of women in the church. While this may have been envisioned from the start, it also was a by-product of the centralization of the priesthood. In a church where all worthy males over the age of twelve hold the priesthood, making priesthood central also made patriarchal authority central.[16] Where the Relief Society had once operated as an auxiliary fully in the charge of women, with its own goals and education, after 1971 it was firmly under the watchful eye of the men at the top of the church structures, meaning that women's power to help shape the direction of the church had been severely limited.[17] Correlation also emphasized not only the hierarchical structure of the church, but also of the nuclear family, where it attempted to place more emphasis.

In many ways correlation operated at the institutional level, but it was designed to seep into the lives of families and individuals. The church wanted to participate in every aspect of people's lives, deepening their spirituality, their connection to the community, and their relationship to the institution. The correlation program promoted Family Home Evening, one evening a week where families would pray, share lessons, and engage in activities together. This, church leaders believed, would pull the family together around a shared

15. Bowman, *Mormon People*, 195–97. See also, Robert Gottlieb and Peter Wiley, *America's Saints: The Rise of Mormon Power* (San Diego: Harcourt Brace Jovanovich, Publishers, 1986), 197–99 and Kristine L. Haglund, *Eugene England: A Mormon Liberal* (University of Illinois Press, 2021), 71–73.

16. Matthew Bowman, "Zion," 23–25.

17. Marti Bradley has noted that after 1971, "All LDS women automatically became members of the Relief Society, dues were no longer collected, and they were forbidden to have separate fundraising activities or budgets. Local wards no longer staged bazaars, bake sales, and other traditional activities that helped create and sustain female ward networks. The LDS Church made considerable efforts to draw boundaries between traditional women and feminists. Increasingly the feminist was portrayed as the enemy of home, family, and traditional religious values." Martha Sontag Bradley, "The Struggle to Emerge: Leaving Brigham Young University," in George D. Smith, *Religion, Feminism, and Freedom of Conscience* (Salt Lake City: Signature Books, 2014), 129–30.

faith. As the patriarchs and priesthood holders of their families, men were told they should oversee, guide, protect, and provide. The father was the church representative in the home.[18] In addition, the new programming brought with it an emphasis on living according to a strict moral code that shaped the daily eating habits, clothing choices, and sexual practices of believers.

A focus on bodily purity and integrity accompanied the correlation process that sought to shape and manage the experiences of believers on a daily and weekly basis. Any Sunday, anywhere in the world, church members were learning the same materials produced by the institution and overseen by the hierarchy.[19] The correlation impulse even shaped church architecture with a desire to make new buildings uniform.[20] Thus the feel of things was McDonaldized in many ways: church members could be anywhere and walk into a church building and feel comfortable. They would know what was happening, the order of things, the rituals, the content of lessons, and the spaces that surrounded them. They might even be encouraged to feel the Spirit working in their lives in a standardized way.

Some observers and participants have seen correlation as a necessary and important move for the church as it was globalizing, one that helped the institution financially flourish and come together in a united effort. Others have viewed it as a consolidation of power with a subsequent loss of the spiritual gifts that accompanied early Mormonism. They argue that organizing on a corporate model leaves little room for spiritual experiences other than ones that affirm the truthfulness and importance of the church hierarchy. And perhaps both are true to a degree.

What is most important here is that it was to the ACCC that Boyd K. Packer was talking that day as he outlined the external dangers of intellectualism, feminism, and the gay-lesbian rights movement that he hoped this group would root out. He hailed the ACCC and the hierarchy as the ones responsible for the orthodoxy of the church. If they failed, the church would fall off course and it

18. Radke-Moss, "Women and Gender," 191–92; Bowman, *Mormon People*, 191; Gottlieb and Wiley, *America's Saints*, 195–97.

19. J. B. Haws, *The Mormon Image in the American Mind: Fifty Years of Public Perception* (New York: Oxford University Press, 2013), 75–76.

20. Ibid, 76.

would lose its ability to make the claims that Joseph Smith once had: that the church was the Restoration of the true church of Jesus Christ. While human errors and foibles had caused Christ's church to be lost from this earth for centuries after his death, Packer and his peers believed that Joseph Smith had restored it and that the committee members with whom he spoke would ensure that the past did not repeat itself.

Packer's Calling

When Harold B. Lee saw the need for correlation, he had asked Boyd K. Packer to design a presentation in support of the process. And Packer, then supervisor for seminaries and institutes (both places where the young and faithful would be educated about their faith), was the perfect person to make the presentation. He, too, understood the benefit of correlating.

As he presented his report, Packer created a metaphor for thinking about the need for correlation. He drew a picture of a home that was being torn apart by an axe. The home represented the church and the axe was the fact that the Relief Society, the Sunday School and the Primary were not in line with one another. This meant that each auxiliary was operating as a "church within the Church," doing its own thing with little oversight and at times working at cross-purposes.[21] For Packer, this metaphor was perfect. Not just for correlation, but for how he understood the best mode for church operations. If too many of the different people within the church were doing their own thing, some of them, if not a lot of them, would probably be heading away from God. His job was to create a centripetal force in the face of all of the centrifugal things happening in the church. He wanted to hold things together.

When discussing the events surrounding the September Six, Boyd K. Packer's name comes up more than any other. For some, Packer was a man who was doing his job, looking after the flock whose care he was given in all of his church callings. For others, he was the central villain in this story, the one behind each of the disciplinary councils, the one pulling all of the strings. They claim that "it

21. Qtd in Lucile C. Tate, *Boyd K. Packer: A Watchman on the Tower* (Salt Lake City: Bookcraft, 1995), 136.

was all Boyd K. Packer." And it seems that that is a powerful way of narrating this story. If there is a clear villain, then what happened in September 1993 was an aberration in the church's history, a moment when one villain had too much control and the system of checks and balances to power did not work.

But it's never that simple. Even if Packer bore much of the responsibility for what happened, he did so with the authority and power of the church behind him. No one stopped him. And there were many who saw his actions as heroic. While he may have been a leader with power, institutions and people granted him that power. He operated in a church culture where there was a desire for correlative efforts, a desire to quash heterogeneity of many kinds just as the church was facing new types of diversity in its rapid expansion. Packer represented the impulse to trust hierarchy and enforce orthodoxy against the centrifugal tides that were facing the church at the end of the twentieth century.

When Packer was called to the Quorum of the Twelve in 1970, he became part of the highest governing body in the church alongside the President and his First and Second Counselors. He was only forty-five, young for that position. Before that time he had slowly worked his way up through the ranks. Because of his love of and commitment to education rooted in faith and for the faithful, his early callings in the church were tied to education. He became supervisor of seminaries and institutes in 1955. Later he was appointed to the Administrative council at BYU, part of the Church Board of Education, and a BYU trustee. Part of that commitment to education manifested in the degrees he earned at BYU, culminating in a Doctor of Education on May 25, 1962.[22] Those positions and degrees also allowed him to move up in the church hierarchy as a general authority, helping with the oversight of the church as an international body. In 1961, he first became an Assistant to the Twelve, before becoming a member of the Twelve.[23] In 1994, when Howard Hunter became the president and prophet, Packer also ascended to serve as the acting president of the Twelve.[24]

22. Tate, *Boyd K. Packer*, 128.
23. Ibid, 125–27.
24. Ibid, 289.

Because he held all of these positions, Packer understood the way that the hierarchy of the church worked and he embraced it as the force keeping the church together even if context sought to tear it apart. Packer wanted to study every aspect of every level of the church, and his studies continuously brought him back to his belief that the priesthood was the glue that held things together. He loved to write and teach about the priesthood.[25] He saw the priesthood as the structural foundation of the family. When he performed marriages, he spoke about how the priesthood was the basis of order within the family.

When Packer served as the president of the New England mission in 1965, Loren C. Dunn assisted as his counselor. Dunn recalled that he learned "more from [Packer] about how the priesthood should operate than from any other person." Dunn described Packer's leadership style as powerful and driven by a vision, "a vision of the Church and how it should operate and what it should do."[26] He recalled that Packer was an excellent president of the mission: "As we counseled together, we received direction and inspiration.... There is a power present because it is what the Lord has ordained as part of church government."[27] Dunn's comments reveal that Packer's teachings about priesthood authority were rooted in spiritual experiences, the sense that they were being guided in their leadership by God. Even though he emphasized spiritual knowledge, Packer made sure it was hierarchized, applying only to those over whom one had priesthood authority.

In a fireside talk for the Boston Stake on May 5, 1968, Packer counseled that church members should "get your lives in order." Foretelling a theme that would echo throughout the disciplinary actions of the 1980s and 1990s, Packer asserted, "Some among us would rather criticize the Lord and His church than concentrate on the problems." Rather than asking questions or raising concerns, he taught that church members should "follow the Brethren." "If you don't understand a problem or a position of the Church, restrain your tongue," he advised. "Check the mote in your own eye before

25. Ibid, 239, 258.
26. Ibid, 149–50.
27. Ibid, 150.

you criticize."[28] Turning it back on those who asked questions, suggesting that they should not criticize lest they be criticized, Packer assured them that, "There is nothing in your lives that will destroy you if you will follow the Brethren."[29] From very early on Packer taught that the priesthood authority of church leaders carried with it a type of inerrancy. Inspired by and speaking in the voice of the Spirit, they would not lead people astray, but would maintain the successful functioning of the church.

That authority structure, rooted in the priesthood, was patriarchal at its very core. Men held the priesthood and were to lead their families through their revelations. While women may be given some spiritual power in the temple, Packer firmly held that men were to provide and protect and they were also to guide their families. One of the things he was asked to do as a general authority was to serve as the adviser to the Relief Society for several years. In that capacity he worked with Belle S. Spafford, general president of the Relief Society from 1945 to 1974. Spafford was a woman Packer admired, precisely because she understood where she did and did not have power. Packer explained: "She had a fierceness about sustaining the priesthood. She would say 'The Brethren have said this, and sisters, this is our duty. We will do it.'"[30] And so Spafford represented Packer's ideal woman, one who knew that sustaining general authorities in their oversight of the church was her most important duty.

Part of the process of understanding how and why the church functioned as it did was tied to education. And Packer had a great love of education, so long as it was understood through the lens of faith. While reason was valuable, revelation was the source of truth, and he feared that some scholars had forgotten that. As the disciplinary proceedings began and progressed in the 1990s, and as people often fingered Packer as the villain in the story, he grew frustrated. He felt strongly that he was not the anti-intellectual others claimed, but that he knew how to balance faith and new knowledge. Out of his frustration, Packer once penned a poem titled "Academic Freedom":

28. Ibid, 157.
29. Ibid.
30. Ibid, 135.

They say we're anti-intellect,
Afraid to even think—
Our paranoid, deep fear of truth
Has caused our minds to shrink.

We're bigoted and prejudiced,
Withdrawn, afraid, regressive.
They must speak out and save the Church;
Someone must be progressive.
But them! How could we dare believe?
No! No! They're nowhere near it.
For shame that we should think the thought
That they are anti-spirit.[31]

Signed "A Narrow-Minded Bigot," Packer's poem clearly frames what he saw as the battle between reason and revelation, or intellect and experience.

One of the things that set Packer apart from other members of the church hierarchy was that he was not shy about saying what he thought. He was confident in his faith and in his calling and was not concerned about how others might perceive him. In May 1993, the same month he gave his talk to the ACCC, he wrote an article for *Ensign* that sheds light on his position. Titled "The Temple, the Priesthood," Packer linked the two concepts that he felt were central to Latter-day Saint identity. He began by emphasizing the role of temples in the tradition, noting that even when the church community could not build a temple, believers still set apart spaces for them wherever they went.[32] This act immediately divided sacred space from other spaces.

Packer noted throughout the talk that nineteenth-century believers were often unable to build their temples or had to move away from them because of the anti-Mormon sentiment of their fellow Americans. Here he tapped into the persecution narrative that had been a strong glue in group cohesiveness throughout the Restoration's history, particularly for the Utah branch of the Mormon movement. Packer noted that even in the midst of oppression from

31. Ibid, 265.
32. Boyd K. Packer, "The Temple, the Priesthood," *Ensign*, May 1993.

outsiders, the church was careful as it built its temples. When cracks were discovered in the foundation of the Salt Lake Temple, the base was ripped out and replaced. The Saints were not going to allow for a faulty foundation for the future.[33]

Next, Packer discussed the relationship between the temple and the priesthood. It was in the temple that "the fulness of the priesthood" had been restored. He then turned, with a bit of vagueness unusual for him, to those in the church who "are now teaching that priesthood is some kind of a free-floating authority which can be assumed by anyone who has had the endowment. They claim that this automatically gives one authority to perform priesthood ordinances." Whether women arguing for the priesthood, ultraconservative members, or those outside the orthodox church who had once been members claiming they could still pass on the priesthood, Packer was clear that the priesthood could only come through ordination by "one who has authority." And, in a nod to church-endorsed histories, he stated that "it has been so since the beginning."[34] If the institution did not recognize an individual's "proper authority," that person did not have the authority to ordain.

Finally, Packer reminded his audience that those who did not follow the call of God would not receive any blessing. "Say the word temple," he commanded. "Add the word holy. Holy Temple. Say it as though it were capitalized."[35] Seeing the temple as the heart of purity, Packer reinforced the hierarchy that oversaw the temple as the font of religious authority. The temple and access to the temple marked whether or not individuals were worthy. He concluded with a request: "May God grant that we may be worthy to enter there and receive the fulness of the blessings of His priesthood."[36] And so Packer captured that the temple and the priesthood authority that ran from the prophet of the church down through the household's male priesthood holder, the patriarchal authority of the Restoration, would ensure that the church stayed on track. It was to the priesthood leaders that people should turn for counsel.

33. Ibid.
34. Ibid.
35. Ibid.
36. Ibid.

The Purity System

Packer was one of the primary boosters for a vision of the Restoration that had the process of correlation and priesthood authority at its core. As the church expanded around the world in the late twentieth century, the church hierarchy responded to new diversity and membership numbers by constructing a vision of the Restoration rooted in a purity system, where the categories of pure and impure, clean and unclean, worthy and unworthy, insider and outsider, came to carry great significance. Purity systems are not built into any culture or historical context, rather they are constructed and maintained in particular cultural times and places. Because the church was experiencing new growth and because the institution was increasingly aligning itself with the Religious Right, a movement that understood itself and its values to be under attack by forces in the broader culture, the church hierarchy came to focus on purity as its central concern. Individual bodily purity was certainly a component of that purity culture, but purity is not only individual. A purity system is structured around standards of purity and is political to its core.

In a purity system, activities, geographies, individuals, and social groups are all mapped onto the categories of pure and impure. In the words of Marcus Borg, "[Purity systems] are systems of classifications, lines and boundaries."[37] Borg explains that in the context of first-century Judaism, the purity system was centered around the temple and the priesthood. This observation, too, applies to the LDS Church in the late twentieth century. Priesthood holders were at the center of the purity system and dictated both its boundaries and its terms. And this system also had a vision of God as a being who was primarily concerned with living a "life of requirements," following the rules and rewarding those who bound themselves to the hierarchies of the system.

The church rooted its purity system in its history-telling. And church leaders' history-telling was about the nature of the Restoration.

---

37. Borg's discussion of purity cultures and systems has influenced my own understanding of these systems. While this work will bring in discussions of purity cultures in more recent history, Borg's work helped to shape my understanding of how purity systems work when he discussed the purity system in Jesus's historical context. See Marcus J. Borg, *Meeting Jesus Again for the First Time* (New York: HarperOne, 1995), 49–78.

They understood their work as protecting orthodoxy. They described intellectualism, feminism, and the gay-lesbian rights movement as outside infiltrators, not indigenous to the institution. Portraying these as outsider threats to the Restoration made the discipline of believers who fell into those categories all the more easy and imperative. Their very existence threatened the ability of the institution to stay its course.

All purity systems have histories that endorse their structures and hierarchies. In the instance of a Restoration purity system, this is even more the case. Ancient history, the founding of the Restoration movement, and the present, are all imagined as perfectly aligned and speaking the same truths. This vision of history requires faithful narrators who confidently proclaim the *one* history of the movement. On the foundation of the official historical narratives that the LDS Church narrated stood three pillars of the late twentieth century purity system:

1) Doctrinal purity: The purity system emphasized the importance of orthodoxy or right-thinking to the institutional church. It occurred to the extent that the church created its own intellectual culture, one that stood apart from mainstream academia and rooted its epistemological claims in distinct sources. During the late twentieth century the church maintained very strict boundaries and used the process of discipline and excommunication to indicate to all believers that their beliefs mattered.

2) Familial purity: The church emphasized the value of the family as the basic unit to both its theological and social frameworks. Within the family, relationships and roles were rigid. A heterosexual, monogamous temple marriage between a male priesthood holder and a wife who fulfilled the role of mother was set up as ideal. The hierarchy viewed feminism as a social movement that threatened to undermine the very nature of the family structure that was rooted in a patriarchal understanding of the primacy of the priesthood.

3) Bodily and Sexual purity: The third pillar, a bodily and sexual purity, focused on policing the male priesthood holder's body in particular. While many late-twentieth-century purity cultures focused on female bodies, the LDS Church, while still aligning itself with conservative religious groups concerned with female purity, also

acted out of anxiety about the possible pollution of the priesthood holder's body—and imagined a subsequent pollution of the church body—both in terms of health and sexuality.

It was no accident that Boyd K. Packer talked about intellectualism, feminism, and the gay-lesbian rights movement as the three major threats facing the church. His May 1993 speech encapsulated the concerns of the hierarchy's anxieties about purity. He was calling all the watchdogs to come and defend their church.

The rhetoric of the institutional church highlighted the hierarchy's emphasis on purity. After the September disciplinary councils, they wanted the public to know that "we have the responsibility to preserve the doctrinal purity of the church. We are united in this objective."[38] The institution was after the preservation of purity at the same time that observers, including Elbert Peck, executive director of Sunstone, noted that church officials felt "the church is fragmenting into factions and this crackdown is an attempt to keep us together." Peck recognized that this doctrinal fragmentation caused particular anxiety in restoration movements. The church was concerned that there could be "churchwide apostasy, which Mormons believe destroyed the ancient church established by Jesus Christ and his apostles."[39]

The pressure felt immense: managing the theological teachings of a global church was a herculean task. Excommunications and disciplinary actions surely felt like a necessary warning sign to those who might lead others astray. Added to that immense pressure was the comfort that, in the words of Gordon B. Hinckley, "Our responsibility is not to please the world, but rather to do the will of the Lord, and from the beginning the divine will has been so often contrary to the ways of the world."[40] Thus church leaders assured church members that criticism from the world may well be evidence that the church was on the right path; it had to keep the community pure,

---

38. Peggy Fletcher Stack, "More Stories Point to LDS Leaders as Source of Dissident Crackdown," *Salt Lake Tribune*, October 16, 1993; "LDS Church Leaders State Their Position," *Salt Lake Tribune*, October 17, 1993.

39. "Six Mormon Scholars Say They Are Being Punished as Dissidents," *New York Times* September 19, 1993.

40. Peggy Fletcher Stack and Peter Scarlet, "Church Critics Are Few, Hinckley Tells Faithful," *Salt Lake Tribune*, October 4, 1993.

and the impure world would attempt to call that out, to pull the church away from its restoration project.

Even as the three pillars stood independently on a foundation rooted in history-telling, there was also significant overlap. That overlap demonstrates the extent to which the institutional church sought to enter into the lives and daily experiences of believers in order to uphold its hierarchical and patriarchal structure. One example here will suffice as others arise later. The purity system had as a key component the understanding that the church functioned as a family on a large scale. And, much like the concept of omerta in Italian cultures, talking about the family's problems to outsiders is an act of betrayal. For example, when Kate Kelly, a feminist who argued that women should be ordained to the priesthood was excommunicated in 2014, Kathleen Flake, a religious historian, explained that the LDS Church functions like a family, "and if the family's going to fight, it's very disloyal to have that fight outside the family."[41] This expectation, that to speak of problems outside of the church community is a betrayal of the church, played a profound role in late-twentieth-century policing of the church's boundaries. A purity system stood at the heart of the LDS Church in the last decades of the twentieth century. To break the rules marked a person as impure. To publicize a story about the discord marked a person as a Judas, someone who betrayed the entire community and its values.

41. Jane Little, "Push to Ordain Mormon Women Leads to Excommunication," *BBC News*, August 26, 2014.

1: HISTORY TELLING

"Some things that are true are not very useful."
—Boyd K. Packer

Writing his 1976 yearly report in his personal journal, official Church Historian Leonard J. Arrington looked back on what had been a hard and heart-breaking year. "This is the Lord's work; of that I am sure," he wrote about his position. But that did not mean that history-telling in the church had been easy. That year, *Story of the Latter-day Saints* appeared. It was the first church-sponsored history of the Restoration since the early decades of the twentieth century. Writing it had come at a price. Arrington described the context this way: members of the LDS Church's history department worked to publish "intelligent, competent, honest history," while they were under the same conditions as "a political dictatorship." Always optimistic, though, Arrington hoped that in the future he would have the patience and understanding to continue to do the fraught work.[1]

Members of the Quorum of the Twelve and the First Presidency, who had to approve of any new history of the church, had mixed reviews of *Story of the Latter-day Saints*. But those who viewed it negatively had the loudest voices: "They particularly noted the absence of inspiration—descriptions of occurrences in Church history without attributing their cause to God or to his direction and inspiration."[2] These church leaders believed that the history relied too much on sources that they deemed anti-Mormon and that the book

1. "Yearly Report on My Work as Church Historian," in Leonard J. Arrington, *Confessions of a Mormon Historian: The Diaries of Leonard J. Arrington, 1971–1997*, 3 vols. (Salt Lake City: Signature Books, 2018). Hereafter LJIA.

2. LJIA, August 18, 1976.

was secular through and through.[3] They "felt very strongly that we should not put anything in any of our history that reflects badly on the church."[4] These church leaders knew that history-telling was tied to identity maintenance and public image—and they felt that both had been tarnished by the new book. "I have been hurt by this episode," Arrington wrote in his journal.[5] He felt as though his faithfulness and his professionalism were being called into question.

On September 21, 1976, Arrington had met with the First Presidency and some members of the Twelve. Several admitted to having only read portions of the book, but they still had a lot to say. Apostle Ezra Taft Benson was adamant that "the book would cause young people to lose faith." Over the coming days, Arrington would conclude that those who opposed it "want the glorious stories of the Restoration, unsullied by discussions of practical problems and controversial evidence."[6] They wanted historians in the church's employ to focus on the believing audience, to write hagiographies that would inspire faith, without a care about whether professional historians would deem the work up to their discipline's standards.

In this meeting, too, Arrington learned that he would "be watched like a hawk." Henceforth the work that he and his colleagues produced would have to be read and approved by the highest bodies in the church. While acquiescing to the future plan, he hoped that others would not be told what was happening—that everyone could keep the secret. He was concerned about "diminishing our credibility as historians and raising the cry of censorship of our works."[7] He quickly learned that those hopes would not be met. The censorship of his office became public knowledge almost immediately.

Arrington was shaken by the whole ordeal. He lost sleep. His "mind was in a turmoil." He wondered, "Do I really have a function? If we were to go as far as to write primarily for young people in a faith-promoting manner there are dozens of persons who would be a far better Church Historian than I."[8] Ever optimistic, Arrington de-

3. Ibid, September 6, 1976.
4. Ibid, September 7, 1976.
5. Ibid, September 6, 1976.
6. Ibid, September 21, 1976 and September 22, 1976.
7. Ibid.
8. Ibid, October 22, 1976.

cided to forge ahead, certain that accurate and honest history would enhance people's faith.

But the church authorities who viewed the book as a secular history would not waver. Their goal was to defend the history of the church from what they perceived as unfair attacks from the inside. Their understanding of the Restoration was rooted in a sanitized version of history that lay at the foundation of the purity system that they felt charged to uphold. They were not going to rest until the history of the Restoration was narrated their way. They believed, in the words of Boyd K. Packer, that "some things that are true are not very useful."[9]

During the late twentieth century, the church hierarchy worked hard to police a sanitized version of history: it dictated who could tell history and what that history could and could not include. All of this was in service of enforcing its claims to authority and maintaining boundaries. In so doing, members of the church hierarchy were calling upon not just the notion of history, but also the concept of tradition. The stakes surrounding the institution's narratives of history were all the higher because they had to suggest that there was a tradition, that things have always been as they are. The concept of tradition is central to the persuasive power of religion precisely for this reason.

Religions call to believers, promising that they are entering into what sociologist Danielle Hervieu-Leger calls a "chain of memory" that has stretched back through time.[10] For restoration movements, historical narratives are particularly important and complex. These movements argue that the true church existed on this earth during the lifetime of Jesus (and so stretch back thousands of years), while also arguing that the true church left the earth when believers failed to participate in its upkeep. Thus restoration movements, including the Mormon traditions following Joseph Smith Jr., also understand their more recent history of reinstituting the "true church" as being very significant. In Hervieu-Leger's descriptions, religions have

9. Boyd K. Packer, "The Mantle Is Far, Far Greater Than the Intellect" BYU Address, August 22, 1981.

10. Danielle Hervieu-Leger, *Religion as a Chain of Memory* (New Brunswick: Rutgers University Press, 2000), 76.

three components: 1) "the expression of believing;" 2) "the memory of continuity;" and 3) "the legitimizing reference to an authorized version of such a memory, that is to say tradition."[11] Restoration movements have to narrate their histories in such a way that the memory of continuity extends back thousands of years through the history of the restoration movement itself.

Feminist theologian Sallie McFague offers important cautions about how the concept of tradition operates within Christianity. McFague points out that "tradition" often carries the weight of a seemingly unchanging version of history (a "we've always done it this way" sense), yet McFague reminds us that tradition always falls "within the realm of experience and that all experience is interpreted."[12] Thus it is imperative to ask questions when people call upon the notion of tradition. Who has the power to write the histories? What is at stake in the history-telling? Who benefits from telling the story this way? Only when asking these questions does it become apparent that tradition is the accumulation of experiences that have been declared normative by those who hold power. Critical interpretation of those versions of history must assess who and what is being left out.

Doing so in the context of the LDS Church in the 1990s will help to see the ways that history-telling had extremely high stakes. It formed identity. It narrated the distinctions between insiders and outsiders. And it laid at the foundation of the church's purity system, supporting the doctrinal, familial, and bodily pillars. Because of this, church leaders worked hard to control the narrative and to make authorized and official versions of history the story that believers knew.

Racial Bans and the Restoration

"There once was a time, albeit brief, when a 'Negro problem' did not exist for The Church of Jesus Christ of Latter-day Saints," wrote Lester Bush in his ground-breaking 1973 *Dialogue* article.[13] Bush

11. Ibid, 97.

12. Salle McFague, *Models of God: Theology for an Ecological, Nuclear Age* (Philadelphia: Fortress, 1987), 42–43.

13. Before Bush published his article, Stephen G. Taggart wrote a short book addressing similar issues. In it, he argued that the racial restrictions originated in the Missouri church. Lester E. Bush Jr., "Mormonism's Negro Doctrine: An Historical Overview" *Dialogue: A Journal of Mormon Thought* 8, no. 1 (Spring 1973): 11–68.

showed in one sentence precisely what his argument sought to prove with historical evidence. He was making his own restoration claim. If there once was a time when the racial priesthood ban was not in place, then, as a restoration movement, the church could return to that time. Over the course of the next fifty some pages, Bush showed that through the decades church teachings about race changed as the church sought to respond to the historical context in which slavery was a hotly debated topic. In addition, he argued that, "There is not contemporary evidence that the Prophet [Joseph Smith] limited priesthood eligibility because of race or biblical lineage; on the contrary, the only definite information presently available reveals that he allowed a black to be ordained an elder, and later a seventy, in the Melchizedek priesthood."[14]

It was subsequent prophets and church leaders who slowly rationalized and theologized explanations for a racial ban and argued that it had always been so: their arguments for the ban spanned from an interpretation of the biblical Curse of Cain to Latter-day Saint theories about what had happened in the pre-mortal existence, a time when individual spirits existed with God prior to entering the mortal world. Thus they attempted to root the ban not only in time immemorial, but to construct arguments that it was divine decree.

Over the course of the nineteenth century, the church also added to the priesthood ban a temple ban, meaning that Black church members could not have access to the temple and therefore no access to the central rituals of the faith.[15] By the mid-twentieth century, a historical amnesia about the past had set in and most members of the church assumed that as the First Presidency in 1949 declared, "The attitude of the Church with reference to Negroes remains as it has always stood."[16] So much so that most were surely not surprised nor did they challenge the First Presidency of 1960, when they declared that "Negroes [are] not yet to receive the priesthood, for reasons which we believe are known to God, but which He has not made fully known to man."[17]

14. Ibid, 21–22.

15. Ibid, 32. See also W. Paul Reeve, *Let's Talk about Race and the Priesthood* (Salt Lake City: Deseret Book, 2023).

16. Qtd in Bush, Jr., "Mormonism's Negro Doctrine," 39.

17. Qtd in ibid, 44.

Bush's article hit like a bombshell. The issue quickly sold out and then the article was reprinted as a free-standing pamphlet that stayed in print until *Dialogue* moved all of its back issues to the internet with free access.[18] Members of the church hierarchy had mixed responses to the article. Prior to its publication, Bush met with Boyd K. Packer and discussed the arguments. Toward the end of the conversation, Bush, sensing the church leader's discomfort, asked Packer if he should contact the journal to delay the issue and Packer's response was, "No, no, if those people thought we were interested in delaying, they would just hurry faster to get it published."[19] Here Packer vocalized the concern that he and others in the church hierarchy had about the argument. It would challenge the sanitized version of history that the institution had been telling; it revealed that prophets and other church leaders were swayed by and proponents of the racist culture in which they lived to the extent that they would participate in retelling what became official church narratives to support the systemic racism of the church.

As part of his research, Bush had access to Apostle Adam S. Bennion's papers at Brigham Young University's Special Collections. In Bennion's papers, which contained First Presidency journals and documents, Bush found a lot of information. The papers helped him to see that church leaders at the turn of the century and after, including President Joseph F. Smith, had known Joseph Smith Jr. had ordained a Black man named Elijah Abel to the priesthood and those same leaders had subsequently worked to create a narrative that Smith had voided the ordination or that it had never happened. They therefore helped foster the historical amnesia about their church's prior racial openness.[20] Packer investigated how Bush received access to the Bennion Papers and found that the librarian, Chad Flake, had given Bush greater access than the general public even though certain files had been removed or restricted.[21]

18. Gregory A. Prince, *Leonard Arrington and the Writing of Mormon History* (Salt Lake City: University of Utah Press, 2016), 495n34.

19. Lester E. Bush Jr., "Writing 'Mormonism's Negro Doctrine: An Historical Overview' (1973): Context and Reflections, 1998" *Journal of Mormon History* 25, no. 1 (Spring 1999): 229–71, esp. 253.

20. Bush Jr., "Mormonism's Negro Doctrine," 33–34. See Bush's footnotes for a sense of all that he learned from the Bennion Papers.

21. Prince, *Leonard Arrington*, 311–13.

Bush's article inspired institutional pushback. In addition to Packer's apprehensions about access to documents, Apostle Mark E. Petersen had concerns about intellectuals in the church and what they were writing about the faith. He worked with Roy W. Doxey, who oversaw correlation, to identify authors who were making "problematic" arguments. Petersen would then reach out to the local stake leaders of the authors and ask them to investigate whether the authors were promoting faith and worthy of their membership. At least fourteen scholars were called to meet with their local leaders. Because of this list, on March 28, 1983, Bush met with his stake president, J. Willard Marriott Jr., who, after a long interview, decided there was no reason for concern.[22]

Leaders of the church had understood and been concerned about the ramifications of the racial bans for a church that made universal claims that its truth applied to all of humanity. When President Harold B. Lee died in 1973, he was succeeded by Spencer W. Kimball as president of the church. Both men had experienced some of the ways that the church's goals were being practically inhibited by the racial bans.[23]

Throughout the twentieth century, proponents of expanding the priesthood to all worthy males were up against much more than just practical concerns, though. The church hierarchy and lay folklore had developed an entire theology of race over the course of its existence. That theology suggested that there was something essential about race that began in the pre-mortal realm. There, some of the spirit children of God who had not been valiant in following God's plan, were set aside to live a mortal life different from and not as blessed as that of other spirit beings. They would be the descendants of the biblical Cain, who was "marked" for his offenses against God.[24]

This theology, which justified a racial hierarchy, shared similarities with other Christian theologies of race in the United States while also embedding it in the Latter-day Saint theology of the Plan of Salvation. In the Plan of Salvation, spirit beings move through a

22. Prince, *Leonard Arrington* 416–17. See also Devery Anderson, "A History of *Dialogue* Part III," *Dialogue: A Journal of Mormon Thought* 35, no. (2002): 15–19.

23. Armand L. Mauss, *All Abraham's Children: Changing Mormon Conceptions of Race and Lineage* (Urbana: University of Illinois Press, 2003), 232.

24. Ibid, 255.

process of progressing through the pre-mortal realm into the mortal where they gain physical bodies and finally the post-mortal where their eternal futures will be determined by the choices they have made. Thus the church's theology of race did not just permeate social relationships in the church, but also the theological worldview, creating divine justifications for systemic, cultural, and personal racism throughout the church.

During his leadership of the church from 1973 to 1985, Kimball was increasingly aware of the fact that the racial bans were making it difficult to accomplish some of what the church was attempting to do in the world. The church had struggled in its South African mission in the 1940s because of the bans.[25] Because the country's government refused entry to LDS missionaries after learning about the bans, the church's work to establish itself in Nigeria had not succeeded, even though there was a strong desire on the part of some Nigerians who had begun their own congregations.[26] On top of that, in 1975, the church had announced a new temple in Sao Paulo, Brazil. This move meant that the institution would face similar concerns because of the temple and priesthood bans. Brazil's complicated history of racism and of racial "mixing" made the bans a serious obstacle to the success of the church in that country.

The institutional church struggled with its policy that any amount of Black ancestry would disqualify someone from the priesthood. Just as was true with any similar policies in the larger culture, there was no way to confidently confirm someone's ancestry one way or another.[27] This proved that racial hierarchies were cultural constructions rather than biological fact. As the church encountered pressure from other nations to change its policies, it also encountered push-back in the United States. Protests of the church and its racial doctrines happened with greater frequency and often in the context of Brigham Young University.

At the same time that these issues faced the church in the global and national arena, the institution witnessed minor changes in the United States. Perhaps most significantly, in 1971, three Black church

25. Prince, *Leonard Arrington*, 315–17.

26. Reeve, *Race and Priesthood*, 98–99. Mauss, *All Abraham's Children*, 236–37.

27. Prince, *Leonard*, 315–17.

members proposed to the hierarchy that they create a Black branch of the church. What eventually transpired out of the request was the creation of the Genesis Group, a support group for Black Latter-day Saints.[28] The creation of Genesis marked a turning point for Black members, who understood they shared a collective experience as faithful and also marginalized members of the church. All of the pressures—both internal and external—were building up to move toward broad-scale institutional change.

On June 1, 1978, Kimball, who was seeking consensus in church leadership for changing the racial bans, met with his counselors and ten of the twelve apostles. This strategic move came on the heels of his request for historical research so that he could better understand the roots of the bans. Feeling as though he saw how to move forward, Kimball called a meeting of the top leaders of the church. The leaders prayed together for divine guidance. After that successful meeting, the circle expanded and he met with forty-six other leaders in the church. On June 9, 1978, the church issued an official announcement of a revelation that lifted the priesthood and temple bans for Black church members. With the new revelation, the institution moved quickly to provide priesthood ordinations, temple rituals, and temple marriages for its Black membership.[29]

Within months of the revelation, Apostle Bruce R. McConkie, who had previously defended the racial bans, said at BYU: "It doesn't make a particle of difference what anybody ever said about the Negro matter before the first day of June this year.… Forget everything … that is contrary to the present revelation. We spoke with a limited understanding and without the light and knowledge that now has come into the world."[30] McConkie's comments show a distinct understanding of Latter-day Saint history, one that can be interrupted and changed relatively quickly. Revelation speaks to the historical context in which the church finds itself and has the possibility of upsetting what had been considered tradition.

Writing about his article twenty-five years later, Bush noted of

28. Mauss, *All Abraham's Children*, 235.

29. W. Paul Reeve, *Religion of a Different Color: Race and the Mormon Struggle for Whiteness* (New York: Oxford University Press, 2017), 259.

30. Qtd in Reeve, *Religion of a Different Color*, 271.

the June 1978 revelation that it declared that "all worthy male members of the Church may be ordained to the priesthood without regard for race or color." In the statement he saw careful word choices that avoided any discussion of Blackness and the priesthood. As well, there was no reference to past teachings or doctrine on the topic; it said nothing of the theologies of race permeating the community. One year later, Bush reflected that in the revelation he saw the "subject quietly but firmly declared dead." But even twenty-five years later, he would argue that, in fact, "the subject is not dead."[31]

Bush's 1973 article was important on many counts: it challenged the institution's narratives about Black men and the priesthood by pointing out the ban was neither true to Joseph Smith's time nor rooted in divine revelation. Those institutional narratives then reinforced not only the structural and systemic racism of the patriarchal priesthood, but also the everyday racism of church members. What Bush revealed was that there had been a concerted effort on the part of church leaders after Smith to erase the role of Black members in the church. This was a strategic and intentional form of historical forgetfulness that enabled the church to make a claim to whiteness.[32]

The history of Bush's article and its impact reveal much about history-telling in the LDS Church. First, it shows the lengths to which the institution went to present a particular version of history, closing documents to research, asserting false narratives about the status quo being "as it has always stood." The impact also demonstrates the importance of history-telling for the institution. The stakes were high precisely because history-telling stood at the foundation of the church's construction of its norms and practices. Bush's example demonstrates what later believers and scholars understood well: for change to happen, it would have to be rooted in narratives about the past.

Memory is always in process. We remember what is useful to our understandings of individual and collective identities and we forget what does not easily fit into our narratives about who we are. Even as it is true that Latter-day Saints believe revelation can change the course of their histories, making what was once true false in a moment, this

31. Bush Jr., "Writing 'Mormonism's Negro Doctrine,'" 270–71.

32. Reeve, *Religion of a Different Color*, 247–72.

does not mean that historical narratives and memory can easily be changed. Memory takes work. Sometimes forgetting takes even more work. Sociologist Armand Mauss describes what he calls the "myth of time-filtered history" operating in LDS memory. Mauss notes that even as Latter-day Saints are largely willing to accept new revelation and the changes it may cause, they are reluctant to challenge the old narratives told by and about their ancestors.

The church did not narrate the 1978 revelation as a rupture or reversal, but rather something that was always bound to happen. When history is viewed as time-filtered, there is an expectation that apologies are not necessary, that past offenses should be gotten over, and that everyone should happily work toward a new future.[33] This is an expectation that glosses over the feelings of and reasonable expectations for an acknowledgement of past wrongs by those who have been injured.

In the case of the 1978 revelation, it operated as the starting point of a new history for many white Latter-day Saints. For them, historical racism was erased with the 1978 revelation. There was no need for an apology. There was no need for a narrative of church history that reckoned with all of the work the white hierarchy had done to sanitize its past. There was no need to see how history-telling had been used to support present-day racism. There was no need to address the racism running throughout the LDS community.

This was true precisely because many white church members were willing to accept a new teaching about race, but they were not willing to accept that their ancestors and past prophets had done anything morally wrong. They were not willing to make a moral judgment about what had happened in the past.

History is much more than just a recollection of past events. It is the foundation for narrating identity. And so the refusal to recognize a past injustice or the need for an apology is also an act that defines identity. It is an act of power. It creates one group that has greater access to claim membership in "us" over another group that is marginalized.[34] The refusal to acknowledge past wrongs is a rejection of

33. Mauss, *All Abraham's Children*, 262–63.

34. For discussions of the politics of apologies, see: Brian A. Weiner, *Sins of the Parents: The Politics of National Apologies in the United States* (Philadelphia: Temple

the identity of people who have been wronged. Not everyone can forget past harm with the snap of divine fingers. Marginalized members of the community may remember a complex counter-narrative. If the institution refuses to acknowledge that complex counter-narrative, the refusal perpetuates marginalization.

A history of systemic and cultural racism was not the only element of its history that the institutional church wanted to sanitize or forget. The institution had also become quite practiced at re-narrating and hiding aspects of its polygamous past. It worked to do this because those are difficult historical topics that challenge present-day norms and morality in the church and the broader culture. And so the institution worked to ignore those complicated historical narratives, knowing it could do so as long as it maintained control of history-telling.

Several Mormon studies scholars have made the case that history in the LDS Church often serves as the foundation for theology.[35] In the late twentieth century, history-telling about Joseph Smith's Restoration, and history-telling about the ancient world, undergirded the three pillars—doctrinal, familial, and bodily—of the institution's purity system. For that reason the traditional, historical narrative had to be fought for, policed, and continuously sanitized in the face of newly emerging evidence.

Narratives of Church and Nation

Maintaining sanitized histories is the labor of many institutions. As the United States experienced its bicentennial in 1976, Americans expressed a renewed interest in their history, engaging in it to support identity. For conservative Americans, especially of the religious sort, an emphasis on a particular type of history-telling took hold. Their narrative showed them that American history had recently gone awry. They imagined the United States as a Christian

---

University Press, 2005); Roy L. Brooks, ed., *When Sorry Isn't Enough: The Controversy over Apologies and Reparations for Human Injustice* (New York: New York University Press, 1999); Charles L. Griswold, *Forgiveness: A Philosophical Exploration* (Cambridge: Cambridge University Press, 2007); and Elazar Barkan and Alexander Karn, eds., *Taking Wrongs Seriously: Apologies and Reconciliation* (Stanford: Stanford University Press, 2006).

35. J. B. Haws, *The Mormon Image in the American Mind: Fifty Years of Public Perception* (Oxford University Press, 2013), 133.

"city upon a hill"—a nation unlike any other nation—and they read the culture of the late twentieth century as evidence that Americans were turning away from their divine calling.[36]

In 1976, Apostle Ezra Taft Benson, gave a speech at BYU titled "God's Hand in Our Nation's History" that easily could have been read from evangelical pulpits across the nation. In it he argued that "the destiny of America was divinely decreed." He went on to explain how the land itself was sacralized and set apart by God and how the nation was foretold by prophets.

Benson warned his listeners that secular scholarship was incomplete and inaccurate, precisely because it did not acknowledge God's role in history. "Why is it that this view of our history is almost lost in classrooms in America?" he asked. Here, he aligned himself with conservative evangelicals in their rhetoric that the nation was turning away from its divinely sanctioned origins. Instead, it was embracing secularism, "a view of life with the idea that God isn't in the picture." Nowhere could this change be seen better than in universities around the country that had become agnostic and "ethically neutral."[37] Students were being taught that all events could be explained through rational, humanistic terms.

Benson critiqued "new" historians who challenged the heroism and leadership qualities of the nation's founders. This, he claimed, destroyed American character and was simply bad history. Those who wrote that version of history had biases and agendas. He called what was happening "slander and defamation." What was more, Benson was concerned that the same trends in the telling of American history were also creeping into the telling of church history.

He saw in historians a desire to downplay revelation and the models of life set forth by the prophets. Most of all, he chafed at historians' suggestion that "the Church has not been telling the truth."[38] For these reasons, Benson argued for an understanding of history that was chock-full of divine providence; the success of the nation and the growth of the church were evidence of that divine

36. Andrew Hartman, *A War for the Soul of America: A History of the Culture Wars* (Chicago: University of Chicago Press, 2015), 253–54.

37. Ezra Taft Benson, "God's Hand in Our Nation's History," Fireside at BYU, March 28, 1976.

38. Ibid.

favor. He encouraged his listeners not to believe those who narrated history otherwise. Instead, they should hold firm to the testimony that God worked in and through history.

The practice of history-telling in academia had moved far away from narratives like Benson's. It continued to transform as professional historians were becoming more comfortable with the idea that history was not an objective accounting of the facts, but was always perspectival and partial, as well as contextually located. Long a central component to the academic practice of history-telling, the idea of objectivity contained a lot of practices, expectations, and assumptions. Objectivity for historians assumed that there were facts to be dug up and narrated without consideration for the social location of the narrator or the historical figure. Facts were facts, simply waiting to be revealed by the historian whose work transparently did so.[39]

Objectivity, then, had initially stood at the center of how historians understood their craft. Yet in the final decades of the twentieth century, social historians especially sought to tell history from the perspective of those who did not have power. In this act, they understood that history was not a neutral endeavor, but a political one.[40] Where once professional historians were expected to claim neutrality, to offer a bird's eye view of the facts, now they were expected to acknowledge their perspectives and biases, to name and claim their stance.[41]

Even as the work of professional historians gained a wider audience, the way that professional historians told history was growing increasingly different from the history most Americans had consumed in their schools and other public venues. That history was frequently rooted in American exceptionalism and nationalism.[42] In 1991, the Smithsonian created an exhibit at the National Museum of American Art called "The West as America." The exhibit's narrative critiqued the stories of manifest destiny and American exceptionalism, showing that professional historians were challenging the mythology of American culture, and providing evidence of the

39. Peter Novick, *That Noble Dream: The 'Objectivity Question' and the American Historical Profession* (New York: Cambridge University Press, 1988), 2.

40. Hartman, *War for the Soul of America*, 256–60.

41. Peter Novick, *That Noble Dream*, 458.

42. Hartman, *War for the Soul of America*, 260.

widening gap between folk and professional history-telling.[43] Many Americans, especially white Americans, were not ready for the kind of history that they had not heard in school and they pushed back against institutions that participated in that kind of story-telling.

What has been called the "New Mormon History," an approach to historical inquiry embraced by a number of the September Six, was part of a larger movement in the academic discipline of history that looked to new sources and gathered the perspectives of historical figures whose stories had not yet been told.[44] New Mormon historians acknowledged perspective. They asked the same questions as other social and cultural historians. They embraced new methodologies. Because of this, they faced push back on many fronts.

Boyd K. Packer was one who pushed back as hard as he could. He saw the dangers in losing a proper balance of reason and revelation throughout academia but came to see historians as the primary problem. He believed that the discipline had trained them to critique the church to the point that they felt comfortable questioning the inspiration and heroism of previous church leaders. Perhaps the best-known articulation of his concerns came in a speech that he gave at BYU, an institution that he was determined to protect from what he saw as secularizing trends at several other universities.

Alarmed about the growing number of Latter-day Saint intellectuals who were presenting and publishing on topics that he felt went against the doctrinal purity of the church, Packer gave a speech in 1981 to religious educators at BYU. That speech articulated more extensively the problems that he saw with intellectualism. From his perspective, the academic world offered a different type of knowledge to budding scholars than the church did. That knowledge was powerful and alluring. It could inspire believers to excel in the world, but it was also dangerous in that it could lead them away from their faith. Their new knowledge might cause them to believe they could "judge the Church, its doctrine, organization, and leadership, present and past, by the principles of their own profession."[45]

43. Ibid.

44. Neil J. Young, "A New Mormon History of D. Michael Quinn," in Benjamin E. Park, ed., *DNA Mormon: Perspectives on the Legacy of Historian D. Michael Quinn* (Salt Lake City: Signature Books, 2022), 8–11.

45. Packer, "Mantle Is Far, Far Greater."

Instead, Packer insisted that academic fields and knowledge should not be used to "judge the professions of man against the revealed word of the Lord."[46] For him, intellectualism was a slippery slope. If a scholar did not rank the two properly—things of the Spirit over things of scholarship—then ranking the Spirit as second would creep into every aspect of life.[47] Scholars had to be careful and wise in order to get things right.

As he progressed, Packer revealed that his primary, perhaps only, concern was historians. The generic academic, of whom he spoke, was a historian, particularly a historian of the church. Listeners surely knew his most specific subject was historian D. Michael Quinn, who was a professor at BYU and would later be one of the September Six. Even though he never named Quinn, Packer used a strategy that many in the church hierarchy did. He spoke broadly, knowing some in his audience would understand precisely whom he meant. Packer focused on Quinn because he researched prophets and church leaders of the past and narrated their lives and teachings for others. Quinn, though, wanted to present an accurate picture of those leaders even if the picture was not so rosy.

A history of the church, Packer claimed, could not be written accurately and objectively "without consideration of the spiritual powers that attend this work."[48] So Packer believed church history had to be told while acknowledging all of the ways that the Spirit worked in human history, particularly in the revelations of prophets. That was not the way that historians were trained. They were trained to contextualize and to explain how culture and context shaped human events. When this happened in relation to the history of the church, Packer thought that it led people away from their faith rather than towards it: "If not properly written or properly taught, it may be a faith destroyer."[49]

Historians also had a tendency to want to tell their readers everything. And that made a lot of sense. But, Packer cautioned, "Some

46. Ibid.

47. In the Church of Jesus Christ of Latter-day Saints, the Holy Ghost or Spirit operates on a very personal level, providing believers with embodied surety about their beliefs and actions.

48. Packer, "Mantle Is Far, Far Greater."

49. Ibid.

things that are true are not very useful."[50] Just like the lure of new knowledge that academia offered, so too did it demand from scholars that they say something new. And Packer thought that historians were often tempted to say something about figures in church history that was tied to the "weakness or mistake of a prominent figure."[51] That would cause problems. He offered as an example an unnamed professor at BYU (clearly again Quinn) who gave a talk about one of the past presidents of the church that showed that the prophet "was a man subject to the foibles of men."[52] In this way, Packer concluded, "He has taken something away from the memory of a prophet. He has destroyed faith."[53]

So while the faith of the historian was one issue, it was minor when compared to the faith of the historian's audience. Strong church members would be rooted in their faith, able to see that a secular version of the church's history was lacking. Because they operated by the Spirit, Packer felt confident that they would have the spiritual skills to tell when someone else was not. But others had a more juvenile or beginner's faith, which could easily be upended by a dangerous secular history.

For this reason, Packer introduced what he called the "principle of prerequisites." This principle ruled that just as one would not put a first-year college student into a graduate level course, so, too, must believers be gradually introduced to information about their church's history.[54] Under the guise of objectivity or neutrality, he claimed, historians were giving too much time to "the adversary," or Satan, who would prosper under this new style of telling history. The danger was clear: a "testimony in seedling stage may be crushed."[55] And so Packer gave a warning; historians were dealing with information that could wreak havoc and they were morally responsible for the outcomes. Packer ended by showing historians the stick: If they had "carefully purged their work of any religious faith in the name of academic freedom or so-called honesty [they] ought not expect to be accommodated in

50. Ibid.
51. Ibid.
52. Ibid.
53. Ibid.
54. Ibid.
55. Ibid.

their researches or to be paid by the Church to do it."[56] Their spiritual lives and their ability to provide for themselves hung in the balance. They had to stay on the tightrope or plummet to their peril.

History-Telling at the Center

Within the LDS Church, the stakes surrounding history-telling were high and the accusations against those who told alternative narratives flowed freely. But the debates happening in the church mirrored the larger debates taking place in American culture about higher education and the academic study of history and religion. Often portrayed in evangelical discourse as opposed to religion, church leaders at times villainized intellectuals, depicting them as trying to bring about a secular, godless society, a goal they described as anti-American.[57] The shift within the academy toward post-modernism, relativism, and deconstructionism signaled to evangelicals that truth with a capital T was at stake. On both sides, objectivity became both a justification and a shield. And nowhere could this be seen more clearly than in the LDS Church Historian's Office.

In the early 1970s, two important shifts took place in quick succession in the church's history department that continue to have ripple effects to this day. In 1970, when Joseph Fielding Smith became president of the church, Apostle Howard W. Hunter replaced him as the Church Historian. Hunter began to reorganize the department. He hired based on professional experience, moved away from a historically defensive position, and opened access to the archives, even to First Presidency material.

Quinn, a young historian at the time, remembered the period of Hunter's leadership as one of openness. He recalled "if you could explain what you wanted to see in a way that the reception people could identify what you wanted, they would go back and bring it out to you. It didn't matter what you asked for."[58] This move for more openness in the archives and toward professionalization was part of an openness found in many US denominations at the time,

56. Ibid.

57. Hartman, *War for the Soul of America*, 222–27.

58. D. Michael Quinn, interview with Gregory A. Prince, December 5, 2005. Signature Books Collection.

including the Catholic Church.[59] Hunter believed the church could survive historical investigation and, in fact, he welcomed it.[60] Building on that newfound openness and as part of a reorganization in 1972, church authorities named Leonard J. Arrington, a historian then teaching at Utah State University, as the new Church Historian.

This marked a notable shift for the church hierarchy that was not lost on observers. Arrington was the first person named to the position who was trained as a professional historian and held a PhD in the field.[61] Arrington recorded in his diary that Hunter had told him that the church "was mature enough that our history should be honest." It was ready to move beyond overlooking, hiding, or locking away sources, and ready to face external scrutiny.[62]

Heartened by this perspective, Arrington assembled his own team of promising young scholars—James Allen (from BYU) and Davis Bitton (from the University of Utah)—as his Assistant Church Historians and set out to face church history with a faithful but critical lens. In his position and in addition to creating the office's own historical research agenda, Arrington also nurtured new scholarly journals like *Dialogue*, participated in the success of the Mormon Historical Association, and supported historical inquiry for believers as well as professionals.[63] Hunter and Arrington's move to professionalize the Church History office was also not distinct during this time; it was part of a larger trend in Christian denominations in the United States that sought to institutionalize structures, professionalize labor, and make use of their membership in as many ways possible.[64]

Historians of Arrington's life believe that he was naïve in his dealings with members of the church hierarchy as evidenced in the events surrounding *Story of the Latter-day Saints*. He thought that if he could just show the church hierarchy the facts they would better understand and change their perspectives.[65] But the desire to

59. Young, "New Mormon History of D. Michael Quinn," 9–10.

60. Haws, *Mormon Image*, 134. See also Prince, *Leonard Arrington*, 82–84.

61. Benjamin E. Park, *American Zion: A New History of Mormonism* (New York: Liveright, forthcoming 2024), chapter 8. See also Haws, *Mormon Image*, 134.

62. LJIA, January 26, 1972.

63. Prince, *Leonard Arrington*, 160–62.

64. Young, "New Mormon History of D. Michael Quinn," 9–10.

65. Prince, *Leonard Arrington*, 284–85.

control and keep pure the historical narratives of the church was powerful. Even as some leaders like Hunter suggested that the church could withstand historical critique, no one was ready to test that unproven hypothesis. The church hierarchy soon realized that if people outside of church employ told the church's history, the hierarchy could at least distance itself from their claims. Although outsider historians were not easily controlled, the greatest danger came from within.[66]

Much of the conflict during Arrington's call as Church Historian was tied to the same debates taking place in the broader culture with very different views on how to tell history and the purpose of that history. Arrington was trained as a professional historian, and because learning a different history from the institution's sanitized version had not changed his faith but deepened it, he assumed that that would be true for all believers. He believed that the institutional church needed to be open about what had happened—to share its warts-and-all history and frame it for their audience. He trusted that embracing an objective history was going to be the way the church would enter the future as a strong institution.[67] From his perspective, history was important for its own sake. It was beautiful in its human messiness.

At the same time, Arrington acknowledged that there was a tension for faithful historians. There were certain topics that were taboo: polygamy, the early church's relationship to masonry, Mountain Meadows Massacre, race and the priesthood, and temple practices. These were aspects that had been shorn from institutional narratives.

He also understood that there was an impulse for the church and believers to be driven to find morality and meaning in historical events. Yet he saw that there was a danger in this path. In his December 1, 1973, journal entry he wrote, "If history is going to be an aspect of doctrine and missionary work, then our department should not exist."[68] In this way Arrington sought to disentangle the writing of church history from the utilitarian ends of the institution. Even as he cautioned against precisely what the church was doing in its Sunday curriculum and at its historic sites, Arrington

66. Ibid, 407.
67. Ibid, 177–80 and 350–53.
68. LJIA, December 1, 1973.

straddled a line that he thought was important. Historians could still meet the standards of their trade because honest history could strengthen faith.

In 1977, and in part because of the events surrounding *Story of the Latter-day Saints*, the church changed Arrington's title from Church Historian to Director of the History Division, restraining his power and placing the department more firmly under the oversight of the church hierarchy. His opponents in the church hierarchy felt that little should happen in the church's history department except for the preservation of documents. These documents could serve as a resource to church leaders, but not necessarily to professional historians or the general public.[69]

Beginning in 1980, Apostle Gordon B. Hinckley oversaw the transfer of Arrington's division to the new Joseph Fielding Smith Institution for LDS History at BYU.[70] This was another move to take power away from him. Arrington taught some classes at BYU, but was devastated when he found out that a few students were spying on him and reporting what he taught to Apostles Petersen, Packer, and Benson. Historian Quinn, also a BYU professor, recalled that devastation: "Leonard had a sense that students were innocent ... completely trustworthy because they were innocent.... [He found out] at the end of the semester, that three or more students had been spying on him and reporting back anything he said that they thought was non-faith-promoting."[71]

Devastation followed devastation. Arrington had imagined that his church was entering a new era in which both the hierarchy and church members would be comfortable with their history, a history that he loved. Instead he was met with continual professional roadblocks, one of the last being the hardest. The hierarchy was watching his every move.

In 1982, church authorities canceled the multi-volume church history Arrington and his team had planned. The department was instructed to spend its time preserving documents rather than writing histories of the church. The move also signaled a restriction on

69. Prince, *Leonard Arrington*, 304.

70. Park, *American Zion*, chapter 8. See also Haws, *Mormon Image*, 136–37.

71. Quinn, interview with Prince.

access to archival documents and the commitment of church leaders to stop history-telling that they thought might be damaging to faith.[72] Paralleling the movement of Arrington away from the centers of power was a staged closing of archival access. First Presidency papers were restricted, then the boundary expanded to include other documents. The church was learning that restricting archives and distancing itself from insider professional historians would better suit its purposes of keeping the historical narrative pure.[73]

New Documents, Old Narratives

When a young student named Mark Hofmann arrived at the office of AJ Simmonds, the curator of the Utah State University's Special Collections and Archives department, with a seventeenth-century Cambridge Bible he said he had purchased recently, the two grew increasingly excited.[74] Two of the pages of the Bible were glued together. When Hofmann had brought the book home and showed his wife, Dori, the couple had started to pull a sheet of paper out from between the two glued pages. They did not get far because they were afraid they would tear the old paper. Nonetheless, what they could see had a clear signature: "Joseph Smith, Jr." Hofmann took the book to Simmonds so that a book expert could help him extricate the page. Sure enough, the paper they removed appeared to be an important missing document from early Mormon history. Even though Hofmann refused to say where he purchased the Bible, the church's historical community was abuzz with excitement about the new discovery.

As he was translating the Book of Mormon, Joseph Smith Jr. created a transcription of the characters from what he proclaimed to be ancient gold plates. He did this in order to assuage the doubts of some of his earliest followers. After writing down the characters, Smith sent Martin Harris, one of his trusted scribes, to visit Columbia College's Professor Charles Anthon, a professor of Greek and Latin. He thought Anthon would verify the characters as Reformed

72. Taylor G. Petrey, *Tabernacles of Clay: Sexuality and Gender in Modern Mormonism* (Chapel Hill: University of North Carolina Press, 2020), 190.

73. Prince, *Leonard Arrington*, 339–47.

74. Jerald Tanner, *Tracking the White Salamander: The Story of Mark Hofmann, Murder and Forged Mormon Documents* (Salt Lake City: Utah Lighthouse Ministry, 1987), 74.

Egyptian letters. Harris returned from the trip even more confident that the Book of Mormon was precisely what Smith claimed it was: ancient American scripture that had been buried in a hill only to be brought forth when God was ready to restore the true church.

The Anthon document helped solidify the importance of the restoration project in the minds of the early community. In the late twentieth century, Hofmann's professed discovery of the document promised to bolster the version of history that had become a much-beloved story in the church.

By the end of the summer in 1980, the LDS Church's Historical Department had spent months examining the document—including using infrared and ultraviolet photography and handwriting analysis. Dean Jessee, an expert on Joseph Smith's handwriting, declared that it was indeed Smith's.[75] The Anthon document was a treasure for the church's collections. It also solidified Hofmann's identity as a serious document hunter and trader who seemed to have an endless supply of sources and buyers. And Hofmann's documents changed the politics of history-telling in the church, altering the church's openness to would-be history tellers and archive searchers.

In February 1981, Hofmann showed LDS Church Archivist Don Schmidt a photocopy of a blessing dated January 17, 1844. In the blessing, recorded by Thomas Bullock, Joseph Smith named his son Joseph Smith III as his future successor in the leadership of the church he had founded.[76] The document threatened to disrupt traditional church narratives about priesthood authority and the position of prophet. For detractors, it "undermined the entire concept of an unbroken chain of succession in the presidency of the church."[77] The text of the blessing read: "For he shall be my successor to the Presidency of the High Priesthood: a Seer, and a Revelator, and a Prophet, unto the Church."[78]

75. Richard E. Turley Jr., *Victims: The LDS Church and the Mark Hofmann Case* (Urbana: University of Illinois Press, 1992), 249.

76. Ronald V. Huggins, *Lighthouse: Jerald & Sandra Tanner, Despised and Beloved Critics of Mormonism* (Salt Lake City: Signature Books, 2022), 248.

77. Tanner, *Tracking the White Salamander*, 83, and Linda Sillitoe and Allen D. Roberts, *Salamander: The Story of the Mormon Forgery Murders* (Salt Lake City: Signature Books, 1988), 247.

78. The full text of the blessing can be found in Tanner, *Tracking the White Salamander*, 79.

This document had much larger implications for the church's telling of its history than the Anthon transcript. If the document proved real, this meant that prior to his death, Smith had chosen his son to take over the leadership of the church. The blessing bolstered the truth claims of the church then called the Reorganized Church of Jesus Christ of Latter Day Saints (RLDS), which had, in fact, stayed in the Midwest and made Joseph Smith III its president. The blessing had high historical stakes for both churches.

Many LDS church leaders, including Boyd K. Packer and Gordon B. Hinckley, were involved in the discussions about what to do. In the end, the LDS Church worked with the RLDS Church to confirm the document's veracity and, while there were still concerns about its provenance, the two churches held a joint news conference on March 19, 1981.[79] Perhaps most importantly, though, a talk by Gordon B. Hinckley at his church's general conference the following month illustrated the document's significance to Latter-day Saints.

In that April 4 talk, Hinckley went to great lengths to explain the document and its context, but most importantly he told church members how they should read and understand it. "We determined that we would give full publicity to the discovery," Hinckley stated, "even though we were confident that critics, knowing little of the factual history of the Church, would seize upon it as suggesting a flaw in our line of authority."[80] First, Hinckley established that church authorities were not afraid of new documents and information. They were confident that the history they knew and told was the official history of the true Restoration. Second, he told his listeners that they should not see the document as a challenge to the authority of their line of prophets, but simply as "a father's blessing." Here, he narratively limited the scope of the document, describing it as an expression of fatherly love rather than a divinely ordained statement of fact. He explained that the document had "great sentimental value" for the RLDS, but otherwise not much value at all.

Hinckley then launched into a discussion of the historical context, using it to tame the document's disruptive power. He noted

79. Turley, *Victims*, 54–57.

80. Gordon B. Hinckley, "The Joseph Smith III Document and the Keys of the Kingdom," *Ensign*, May 1981.

that it was the transcript of a blessing and not an ordination to an office. He further softened the document's declarative language by saying that church members should know that a blessing is conditional on two things: "one, the worthiness and faithfulness of the recipient, and two, the overriding will and wisdom of God."[81] Thus he suggested that what Smith's son did and what God wanted could also override the outcome of such a blessing.

After taming the worrisome document, Hinckley turned to historical evidence that supported the story that the Latter-day Saints' Quorum of the Twelve Apostles would take the keys of authority over the church in the absence of Smith. Narrating the events immediately following Smith's murder, when many recalled a vision in which they saw the mantle of the prophet descending on Brigham Young, Hinckley briefly spoke of the subsequent journey westward of those who followed the Twelve and Young to the Salt Lake Valley. From Hinckley's perspective, all the history that came afterwards, the thriving of the church in the desert, was proof that Young was Smith's rightful successor.[82]

Finally returning to the details of the document itself, Hinckley noted that Thomas Bullock, who reportedly recorded the document, had followed the Saints westward and never doubted that Young held the authority to lead the church Smith established. If that was the case, how could believers in the late twentieth century suggest that this one brief document proved wrong an entire history of divinely ordained prosperity?

While Hinckley carefully controlled and tamed the document through his interpretations, he demonstrated that history-telling was the province of church authorities. While professional historians may well have been trained to read and understand documents, church authorities were better suited for the task of narrating a faithful history. This set of arguments would become increasingly important for the purity system upheld by the church authorities who saw its roots in the history of the Restoration. In this one speech Hinckley managed to accept the document as new historical

81. Ibid.
82. Ibid.

information, tame its impact on history-telling, and uphold the purity of the historical narrative told by church leaders.

The Joseph Smith III blessing was not the last document that Hofmann discovered that threatened to upend traditional church narratives about the Restoration. In August 1982, he found another surprising document: a letter written by Joseph Smith's mother, Lucy Mack Smith. Dated January 23, 1829, the letter suggested it was written between the time that Martin Harris had lost the first 116 pages of the transcribed Book of Mormon manuscript and Joseph's later return to the process of translation. In the letter, Lucy described the contents of the 116 pages.[83] While the letter itself did not challenge deeply seeded narratives, it did point to a document that could. The 116-page manuscript that had been lost for more than 150 years always threatened to reappear, its ability to disrupt ever present.[84] And Hofmann was on its trail.

After it had abandoned the practice of polygamy in the late nineteenth and early twentieth century, the church turned to other aspects of the history of Joseph Smith, focusing on and celebrating them to shift attention away from plural marriage as the source of group identity.[85] Because of this shift, the stakes of history-telling about Smith were all the more important to the restoration movement in the twentieth century. In January of 1983, Hofmann met with Gordon B. Hinckley, then counselor to President Spencer W. Kimball, and shared a letter from Joseph Smith to Josiah Stowell dated 1825. Hofmann had already had the letter authenticated. The letter painted Smith as a treasure seeker who used folk magic to find what he sought. This portrayal of Smith was one that the church had spent a long time trying to bury. For many, it seemed that someone interested in treasure seeking for economic gains, who later found gold plates and became a prophet, was clearly a false prophet.

The church wanted to emphasize Smith's spiritual seeking over any other economic activities in order to keep Smith's image pure.

---

83. Tanner, *Tracking the White Salamander*, 100.

84. Turley, *Victims*, 341–45. E. Marshall Brooks, *Disenchanted Lives: Apostasy and Ex-Mormonism among the Latter-day Saints* (New Brunswick, NJ: Rutgers University Press, 2018).

85. Kathleen Flake, *The Politics of American Religious Identity: The Seating of Senator Reed Smoot, Mormon Apostle* (Chapel Hill: University of North Carolina Press, 2004).

After Hinckley read the letter, he made a choice that seemed to contradict the confidence he had exuded in his talk about the Joseph Smith III blessing. He gave Hofmann a $15,000 check and put the letter in his vault. At that time, Hofmann also sold Hinckley a contract that Smith and Martin Harris had signed in order to publish the Book of Mormon. While the latter faith-affirming document went to the Historical Department, the former stayed in the vault, suggesting that church authorities wanted only particular versions of their history to be shared with others.[86]

Yet another of Hofmann's documents appeared in January 1984. Supposedly written on October 23, 1830, what came to be called the "Salamander Letter" was a letter from Martin Harris to W. W. Phelps, a potential convert to the church. In the letter, Harris explained that Smith had used a seerstone to find the gold plates four years earlier than traditional church narratives claimed and that the spot where they were buried was enchanted. Eventually, the letter recounted, Smith was led to the spot by a white salamander and when he took the plates out of the hole, a toad turned into a spirit.[87]

Perhaps more than any other, this document threatened to disrupt LDS narratives of the Restoration. Smith had recounted, and official church histories recalled, that it was an angel named Moroni, a resurrected being who had been one of the authors of the Book of Mormon during his mortal life, who had showed Smith the spot where the plates were buried. The existence of the letter suggested that Smith participated in magical practices, had lied about the origins of the church he founded, and had received the gold plates four years earlier than he later claimed, which would have given him plenty of time to author the Book of Mormon.

The Salamander Letter heightened the suspicions of a number of people about the spectacular documents Hofmann continued to procure, especially as it seemed he had unlimited sources that no

86. Sillitoe and Roberts, *Salamander*, 269–72. While Hinckley certainly made choices about what documents and histories to publicize, it is important to remember, as Richard Turley argues, that church leaders were also victims of Mark Hofmann. See Richard E. Turley Jr., *In the Hands of the Lord: The Life of Dallin H. Oaks* (Salt Lake City: Deseret Books, 2021), 200–1.

87. The full text of the Salamander Letter can be found in Tanner, *Tracking the White Salamander*, 7.

one else had access to. One of the people first concerned was Jerald Tanner. Tanner, along with his wife, Sandra, had set up Utah Lighthouse Ministry in an attempt to challenge the history-telling of the church. The Tanners spent their life's work and earnings publishing church documents that they hoped would shed light on untold church history and disrupt the church's story-telling about itself.

Even so, Jerald Tanner felt that the Hofmann discoveries were too good to be true: All of a sudden one person was finding documents that either supported or challenged the church's early history-telling in multiple ways? When he read the Salamander Letter, Tanner felt confident that it had not been written by Martin Harris, a historical figure he had studied. So Tanner started to speak about his doubts, and at an August 1984 Sunstone Symposium, he presented his concerns. Later Hofmann gave the Salamander letter to Hinckley as a gift, and on April 28, 1985, the LDS-owned *Church News* published the Salamander Letter with a statement from the First Presidency that said there was no evidence that the letter was fraudulent.[88]

In October 1985, three bombs exploded in Salt Lake City, upending the scandals caused by the Hofmann documents. The first two victims, Steve Christensen and Kathy Sheets, were killed on October 15, 1985. Christensen worked in finance and collected historical documents, and Sheets was the wife of Christensen's employer. The third bomb exploded in Hofmann's own car one day later.[89] It first appeared that the three had been perceived by someone else as a threat. Later it was revealed that Hofmann himself had made the bombs. He claimed that the third bomb had been a suicide attempt. Out of desperation, and in order to keep his secrets, Hofmann had turned violent.

---

88. Huggins, *Lighthouse*, 249–57. See also Sillitoe and Roberts, *Salamander*, 292–96. While Hofmann certainly wanted to disrupt the narratives of the church that he had been a member of his whole life, he also wanted to make money. In addition to the church documents, Hofmann forged others, perhaps most well-known was the "Oath of a Freeman," the first document to be printed in the Massachusetts Bay Colony. Historians know of the document from John Winthrop's diary, but a copy has never been found. Hofmann told people that he had purchased the document for $25 and claimed that it was worth $1.5 million. Turley, *Victims*, 313–18. See also, Tanner, *Tracking the White Salamander*, 120.

89. Turley, *Victims*, 160–66.

His most sensational documents had been forged. Along the way, he had made mistakes, even as he could be numbered among fairly successful forgers. As he wrote the texts of his documents, he studied the known writings of the authors to whom he attributed the texts. Thus they would contain words and phrases that were used by the source.[90] He would purchase or steal paper from the time period so that any testing of the paper would indicate the historicity of the document. When he testified in court, he confessed that he had used bug worms to create holes in the documents and heat to brown the paper.[91] What finally exposed him, in addition to the textual evidence Tanner had relied upon, were the cracks in the ink he had used.

Hofmann was charged with a total of 32 felonies. In January 1987, he reached a plea agreement with the court. Hofmann pled guilty to two counts of the second-degree murder of Steven Christensen and Kathy Sheets, a second degree theft-by-deception count for selling Christensen the Salamander Letter, and second-degree fraud for taking money from Alvin Rust for what he called the McClellin collection (a falsified historical collection that did not exist). In return the court dismissed his remaining felonies and prosecution by other bodies including the federal government and the state of New York.[92] He then entered Utah State prison, sentenced for life.

The ripple effects of the Hofmann events on the LDS church hierarchy were profound. In the words of Jerald Tanner, Hofmann had "effected his own 'restoration' of religious documents from the past."[93] And his documents challenged the historical narratives that lay at the foundation of the church's purity system. Even though the documents were later proven false, the events raised serious questions about history-telling in the church.

First, church authorities had made public those documents that reinforced its version of narrating the Restoration or were easily interpreted to do so.[94] This suggested that the church had an interest in keeping its version of history pure from anything that might

90. Huggins, *Lighthouse*, 248.
91. Turley, *Victims*, 319–22.
92. Sillitoe and Roberts, *Salamander*, 474–76.
93. Tanner, *Tracking the Salamander*, 155.
94. Ibid, 52.

challenge or sully its founders. At the same time that it exposed church leaders' willingness to hide undesirable history, it also showed that church leaders who professed to be prophets, seers, and revelators had been unable to discern the true from the false documents, thus suggesting that they may not have been as confident in their version of history as Hinckley and others had suggested. They clearly wanted to manage the story, to ensure that history-tellers' ultimate goal was faith promotion.

On July 31, 1987, the First Presidency released a statement expressing sympathy for the families of the people Hofmann had murdered and gratitude for the law enforcement officials who had worked to investigate the crime. Noting that the church had emphasized record-keeping as a divine mandate since its inception on April 6, 1830, church leaders said that they had been asked if the Hofmann scandals had "rocked the foundations" of the church. To that they replied a hearty no. Now knowing that the documents were forged, they declared that "the events of the last two years have in no way undermined the traditional history of the Church."[95]

Public discourse about the documents, they claimed, had been written primarily by people who did not believe in the miraculous events of the Restoration. The church leaders then doubled down on their own approach to history-telling. "Any accurate, objective history" of the church "requires an understanding of the spiritual powers attending this divine work." And so they claimed history-telling as the province of believers and church authorities. Objectivity, then, included accepting God's work in history as an underlying premise. No longer would they allow the outside world and its expectations to challenge their narrative of the Restoration.

On August 6 of that same year, Apostle Dallin H. Oaks gave a talk titled "Church History and Recent Forgeries" at BYU. In that talk, Oaks set the pattern for how the church would officially narrate the Hofmann scandal. He said, "What interested me most was the fact that these forgeries and their associated lies grew out of their author's deliberate attempt to rewrite the early history of The Church of Jesus Christ of Latter-day Saints and that so many persons and

95. "Church Releases Statement on Mark Hofmann Interviews," *Ensign*, October 1987.

organizations seized on this episode to attempt to discredit the Church and its leaders."[96] In his speech, Oaks portrayed the church as an oppressed institution; outsiders were consistently challenging its history and Hofmann was merely one of the many who had tried to sully its good name. Throughout the decades church members had endured attempts to "blacken the reputation of faithful persons, living and dead."

Oaks then went on to counter several specific charges. First, the argument that the church had made public certain documents while hiding others. To this accusation, he said: "Are documents ever acquired by the Church and then closed to the public? Of course. This is true of most large archives, as any well-informed person should be aware."[97] Second, he responded to the question about how it was that church leaders were duped by Hofmann. Oaks declared that "in order to perform their personal ministries, Church leaders cannot be suspicious and questioning of each of the hundreds of people they meet each year. Ministers of the gospel function best in an atmosphere of trust and love." It was Hofmann who had ill intentions. Church officials should choose trust and love when interacting with others.

While he enumerated many details of the case and the church's response to several challenges, the messages of Oaks's talk were clear: Outsiders had always sought to take down the church; this was simply another reiteration of that long history. Oaks expressed that one lesson everyone should learn from the Hofmann events was caution.

Oaks and many others in the church's highest bodies believed that everyone should be cautious about new documents and histories that disrupted the tried and true narratives told in Sunday school. They warned that new narratives were risky. Professional historians who peddled "objective" histories without any acknowledgement that those histories may come at the cost of faith were even more dangerous. The church's version of history—its own, "There once was a time…"—should be trusted and retold, inspiring faith and solidifying group identity along the way. Church leaders ought to

96. Dallin H. Oaks, "Church History and Recent Forgeries," BYU Address, August 6, 1987.

97. Ibid.

be the only trusted story-tellers and their goal was to maintain the foundation of the purity system by exorcizing unauthorized stories and their tellers. While it had little to do with history as a discipline and profession, the Hofmann case cemented church leaders' commitment to narrating, policing, and claiming ownership of the history of the Restoration.

2: DOCTRINAL PURITY

"The apostates ... were a problem needing to be taken care of."
—Malcolm Jeppsen

In October 1993, just a few weeks after the September Six disciplinary councils, the First Presidency and the Quorum of the Twelve issued a statement responding to the "extensive publicity given to six recent Church disciplinary councils in Utah." The purpose of the statement was to clarify the church leaders' perspective on the events that had happened, suggesting that believers may have heard a lot of misinformation from the media and other sources and that outsiders fundamentally misunderstood how the church worked. First, they articulated that they "deeply regret the loss of Church membership on the part of anyone." With these words, they set the somber tone.

What culminated in the disciplinary actions against six church members was framed as a sad and unfortunate, if necessary, series of events. In order to better clarify institutional structure and process, the statement explained the division between general authorities and local disciplinary councils—the first did not direct the latter. This statement seemed crafted not only to help outsiders understand, but also to indirectly address swirling rumors that members of the highest church bodies were inserting themselves into local affairs.

In addition, the statement explained that it was impossible to publicly discuss these councils properly because such matters were confidential and private, and thus church leaders would not provide the perspective of the local church officials involved. They felt confident that faithful members would understand and be able to tell the difference between simple disagreements about matters of opinion and charges of apostasy. The statement referenced the *General Church Handbook*'s definition of apostasy. This reference made clear that they were not hiding their definition but that church members could have ready access to it:

> Church members were apostate if they: "(1) repeatedly act in clear, open and deliberate public opposition to the Church or its leaders; or (2) persist in teaching as Church doctrine information that is not doctrine after being corrected by their bishops or higher authority, or (3) continue to follow the teachings of apostate cults (such as those that advocate plural marriage) after being corrected by their bishops or higher authority."[1]

Finally, the leaders insisted that they had "the responsibility to *preserve the doctrinal purity* of the Church. We are united in this objective."[2]

And so the church hierarchy named the issue that had and would continue to play a central role in their actions: purity. When a religious institution emphasizes purity as a core value, its actions flow from there. The institution's goal will be to maintain and police the boundaries of purity, to ward off impurity. Of highest priority to a religious institution focusing on purity are the twinned principles of orthodoxy (correct thinking) and orthopraxy (correct practice). In the late twentieth century the church hierarchy grew increasingly concerned with what was happening at the local level. Church leaders felt they had to monitor and discipline wayward members in order to maintain the power to define what would and would not be considered pure.

Strengthening Church Members Committee

Eugene England encountered institutional expectations about doctrinal purity throughout his adulthood. He had come up against the church hierarchy's standards of loyalty and obedience particularly during his time teaching at Brigham Young University from 1977 to 1998. As a church institution, BYU was supervised by church leadership on its board of directors. Even though he knew this, England wanted to teach at the church's university, firmly believing that academic freedom and faith could both be embraced as ideals.[3] England

1. "Statement by the Council of the First Presidency and the Quorum of the Twelve Apostles of the Church of Jesus Christ of Latter-day Saints," *Deseret News*, October 16, 1993.
2. Ibid, 72. Emphasis added.
3. Terryl L. Givens, *Stretching the Heavens: The Life of Eugene England and the Crisis of Modern Mormonism* (Chapel Hill: University of North Carolina Press, 2021), 150.

thought of himself as both a liberal and a conservative church member: the conservative side was tied to his belief that prophets and apostles spoke directly to God and therefore had been vested with divine authority. The liberal side differed from the church hierarchy and many believers on the social issues of the day.[4] Perhaps more than anything, England understood his faith tradition as one that embraced dialogue and discussion. He enjoyed theological exploration and saw in the early church echoes of this kind of theological questioning and investigation.

England wanted to maintain open inquiry and robust dialogue in the church. It was part of how he understood the Restoration. Because of this, he had been one of the founders of *Dialogue: A Journal of Mormon Thought* in 1966.[5] He and four others, Wes Johnson (a Stanford professor), Joseph Jeppson (professor at the College of San Matteo), Paul Salisbury (an architect), and Frances Menlove (a psychologist) founded the journal, describing it as a forum "established to express Mormon culture and examine the relevance of religion in secular life.... The journal encourages a variety of viewpoints."[6] The new journal along with the founding of the Mormon History Association as a place for scholarship around the Mormon tradition, seemed to promise that the late twentieth century was a time for inaugurating a new approach to inquiry and questions in the LDS faith. The church hierarchy was not so sure.

England's open theological curiosity received pushback from the church hierarchy in 1979. At that time he had begun to examine the potentially contradictory claims within the Mormon tradition about whether or not God progressed. Joseph Smith had suggested that God progressed from one capacity or level of greatness to an even higher one. Taken with this idea, England presented his own analysis at an honors lecture for BYU's series on education. Directly after that, he heard from Joseph McConkie, a member of BYU's religion faculty and the son of Apostle Bruce R. McConkie. Joseph McConkie declared that England had been teaching false doctrine.

4. Kristine L. Haglund, *Eugene England: A Mormon Liberal* (Urbana: University of Illinois Press, 2021), 3.

5. For ease of reading, I will simply use *Dialogue* to refer to this journal from here on.

6. Qtd. in Givens, *Stretching the Heavens*, 66.

England, interested in discussion and dialogue, invited the younger McConkie to offer a rebuttal the next time England gave a talk, which would be at the University's Varsity Theater.[7]

McConkie accepted the invitation but did not engage in open dialogue. Instead his rebuttal was harsh and full of venom. He questioned England's logic, suggesting he had none. He invoked his relationship to the Smith family (his grandfather was Joseph Fielding Smith, a president of the church and great-nephew of Joseph Smith, the founder) and to his own apostle father. His church royalty bloodlines provided him with the authority, he asserted, to determine that England's claims were pure heresy.[8]

Then, in 1980, Apostle Bruce R. McConkie gave a talk at BYU titled "Seven Deadly Heresies," which clearly deemed England's ideas heretical. At the next general conference the elder McConkie also gave a talk challenging anyone who argued that God progressed. McConkie never named England. In the pursuit of purity and orthodoxy he addressed the idea or claim rather than the person. In addition to the public debate, England and Bruce R. McConkie exchanged letters about the issue that resulted in England choosing not to speak about it again during McConkie's lifetime.[9]

In February 1981, Apostle McConkie wrote England a letter that he claimed "may well be the most important letter you have or will receive." Perhaps most tellingly, McConkie wrote that "because I do not engage in controversy or discussion of divergent views, either orally or in writing," he had tried to ignore England's letter and his document titled "The Perfection and Progression of God: Two Spheres of Existence and Two Modes of Discourse." In that paper, England had done what the title suggested, reconciling God's perfection with the idea that God was also progressing. McConkie, however, was not persuaded: "I want you to know that I am extending to you the hand of fellowship though I hold over you at the same time, the scepter of judgment." Here McConkie framed his actions as coming out of kindness and concern while he reminded England of the institutional power he held.[10]

7. Ibid, 162–63.
8. Ibid, 163–64.
9. Haglund, *Eugene England*, 69–70.
10. McConkie to England, February 19, 1981. Copy in author's possession.

For several pages McConkie then went on to explain his argument and the error of England's ways. To make his argument, McConkie acknowledged that all people, even prophets, err sometimes. "No single individual all the time is in tune with the Holy Spirit," he explained. For this reason, he declared that the scriptures were set forth, providing believers with what he characterized as a stable measuring stick against which to judge other truth claims.

Even as he acknowledged leaders might make mistakes, McConkie used his power to police the boundaries of doctrinal purity. He explained, "Those at the head of the Church have the obligation to teach that which is in harmony with the standard works." But even so, he made a distinction between himself and England. "I advise you to take my counsel on the matters here.... If I err, that is my problem," he wrote, "but in your case if you ... end up being wrong, you will lose your soul."[11]

Teaching something that went against the church hierarchy put a person in great social and spiritual peril. If England persisted in writing and speaking contrary to the hierarchy, McConkie cautioned that England would have "a spirit of rebellion" growing in his heart that would injure his soul, his faith, and his standing in the church. He told England that, after speaking with another general authority about what was happening, that leader said, "Oh dear, haven't we rescued [England] enough times already?" Here McConkie suggested to England that he was on the hierarchy's list as a problem, someone who was possibly in a state of rebellion. McConkie ended his letter directing that England "remain silent on those [topics] where differences exist between you and the Brethren." If he chose to speak rather than be silent, "perils lie ahead."[12] In no uncertain terms, McConkie told England that his difference of opinion was unacceptable. His soul was in peril and his status in the church was on the line. If England persisted, it was clear he would become an outsider.

The struggle between England and McConkie pointed to a larger struggle over doctrinal purity. As an intellectual, England wanted dialogue and felt as though he ought to be an equal participant in the discussion. But that felt like a direct challenge to the church

11. Ibid.
12. Ibid.

hierarchy, which had dug its feet in on the concept that it was those at the top who determined truth through their positions tied to divine authority.[13] That meant individuals below them could not question or explore those arguments. They were expected to fall in line. England and others continued to operate as the object lesson for this message. The church hierarchy felt it had to protect the organization from impurity and draw firm boundaries around its understanding of the Restoration. And Eugene England had still not learned the lesson.

Under Benson's leadership in the mid-1980s, and in the spirit of achieving a hands-on approach to managing doctrinal purity, the church hierarchy created a new group called the Strengthening the Church Members Committee (SCMC). In the words of church spokesperson Don LeFevre, the committee "provides local Church leadership with information designed to help them counsel with members who, however well-meaning, may hinder the progress of the Church through public criticism."[14] LeFevre's comments reveal the institution's concerns. In the tradition of the correlation process, the church was centralizing and shoring up power, putting what had been localized and diverse under greater observation. The new SCMC addressed not only what individual people believed, but primarily what they were saying publicly, reinforcing the insular expectations of the institution: to believe what the institution defined as heresy was one thing, but to share it with others was simply unacceptable. Airing dirty laundry both inside and outside the church walls was a betrayal.

The institution put great stock in the SCMC, appointing Apostles James E. Faust and Russell M. Nelson to head the committee. "Generally, The Church of Jesus Christ of Latter-day Saints does not respond to criticism levied against its work," the official announcement read. It also explained that the church had a democratic, non-professional clergy, which meant that local leaders may or may not have the backgrounds necessary to address all the issues they faced in their communities. The SCMC was created to "help fulfill this need" of local church leaders and would serve "as a resource to

13. Haglund, *Eugene England*, 69–70.

14. "Church Defends Keeping Files on Members," *Sunstone* 16, no. 2 (August 1992): 63–64.

priesthood leaders throughout the world who may desire assistance on a wide variety of topics."[15] And so the creation of the SCMC exemplified the move to centralize what had once been intentionally localized. Church leaders claimed orthodoxy as a matter for the highest leaders to monitor.

The announcement enforced the institution's purity system, one that required fidelity, silence in the face of criticism, and only private disagreement. It offered scriptural justification for the committee's existence, citing Doctrine and Covenants 123: "In this section the Lord instructs Joseph Smith to gather information concerning the Church's enemies and make it public to the world."[16] While the argument for the SCMC was a new interpretation of that passage, suggesting that the "enemies" could be within and embodied in well-intentioned church members, the new interpretation provided the hierarchy with scriptural justification for gathering information on members.

At the same time, critics saw the committee as a problem and, in the words of *Dialogue* editor F. Ross Peterson, "a strange carryover from a paranoia that resembles McCarthyism."[17] Dean May, a historian teaching at the University of Utah and a Latter-day Saint, felt as though the SCMC went against the nature of the church in which he grew up. He explained that in the church of his youth, "local bishops and stake presidents know their members most intimately" and no person who doesn't know them personally "has ecclesiastical rights to make judgment as to [their] worthiness." Because of this, May argued instead that the policy created "garbled files" that led to potential misunderstandings about who believers actually were as individuals and as community members.[18]

May's comments and the creation of the SCMC demonstrate two tensions in the church: First, the church was growing at a rapid pace

15. "First Presidency Statement Cites Scriptural Mandate for Church Committee" *Sunstone* 16, no. 2 (August 1992): 63.

16. The Doctrine and Covenants is a collection of canonized revelations accepted by the Church of Jesus Christ of Latter-day Saints. For a discussion of the church's justifications of the SCMC, see "Church Defends Keeping Files," 63–64.

17. Ibid.

18. Dean L. May, "Dissent and Authority in Two Latter-day Saint Traditions," *Sunstone* 15, no. 1 (June 1994): 18.

and so the distance between the First Presidency and local believers was an ever-widening gap that could no longer be fully spanned. Second, while it illustrates on one hand that local bishops and stake presidents may not be well-suited to understand, counter, and respond to the academic arguments and scholarship of intellectuals in the church, on the other hand, it demonstrates a strong strain of anti-intellectualism, a distrust that scholars who were also believers would be working for the best interests of the church as an institution.

With the SCMC at work, it felt as though anything anyone said might be reported to the committee and that it would then be sent to a local bishop. And that's precisely what happened. When Lavina Fielding Anderson spoke at the 1992 Sunstone conference in a presentation where she referred to the SCMC as an "internal espionage committee," England, still a professor of English at BYU, stood up and protested its existence saying, "I accuse the committee of undermining the Church."[19] He felt the SCMC went against the spirit of his faith and the spirit of dialogue. His comments were caught on camera and then aired on the national news.[20]

In March 1993, England issued an apology published in the *Sunstone* newsletter. The apology tells us a lot about the culture of politeness in the church and also the high stakes of disagreement. Perhaps England had been encouraged to issue the apology. "I am sorry that I spoke out so rashly and angrily," he wrote, "and before I learned more about the Committee or spoke privately to its members about my concerns."[21]

Clearly it was the *public* nature of the outburst rather than the critique itself that he knew his audience needed him to address. In the apology he also acknowledged that he had not fully understood the nature or process of the committee and that he did "regret what I said and the spirit in which I said it." Tellingly, England went on to "invite all of us to find ways to deal with our differences of opinions, even our offenses, directly and privately—in such a way that both offended and offender can express fully their concerns and hear full explanations." Again emphasizing the public nature as the problem, he encouraged

19. "Church Defends Keeping Files," 64.

20. Haglund, *Eugene England*, 19.

21. Eugene England, "An Apology," *Sunstone* 16, no. 4 (March 1993): 2.

faculty at BYU and his fellow believers "to refrain from criticizing our leaders and each other in ways that violate that ideal."[22]

England had laid it on the table: criticizing leaders and doing so publicly was the problem. And he understood that those actions had consequences: they offended the insularity of the purity culture expected of church members. In this moment England aligned himself with the values of the church hierarchy that expected unity, respecting those above you, and following their counsel.[23] Finally, England suggested that people who were affected by the SCMC should report those effects to the committee, "so they can assess those results."[24]

England's efforts to embrace theological curiosity and engage in dialogue surfaced throughout his career and his 1992 outcry about the SCMC signaled his frustration over church leaders' attempts to silence open inquiry and the free exchange of ideas. His apology represented his acquiescence, at least on this topic, to the hierarchy's authority to monitor the public statements of its membership. Even a full decade after he received McConkie's letter, England was still smarting at the actions the church hierarchy took to police discussion and enforce orthodoxy.

Battles Over Purity

When people describe September 1993, one way that the disciplinary councils are framed is with a narrative that pairs the September Six with the excommunications around the same time of several right-wing, apocalyptic—sometimes called ultraconservative—church members. Excommunicated in the 1990s, ultraconservative believers were hosting regional meetings that often centered around apocalyptic thinking and pushing back against the federal government, including refusing to pay income taxes and, at times, practicing polygamy.

This narratival pairing of liberal and ultraconservative disciplinary actions, a "middle-of-the-road" narrative, implies that as the church was globalizing, the church hierarchy needed to move to the center

22. Ibid.

23. For a discussion of these issues in England's life, see Haglund, *Eugene England* and Givens, *Stretching the Heavens*.

24. England, "An Apology," 3.

in order to appeal to and include as many people as possible. Thus the hierarchy had to cut off those who were extreme on either side.[25] Historian D. Michael Quinn, one of the September Six, used this narrative nearly a year before he was excommunicated. He said, "The church used to attack liberals and now it's attacking conservatives.... It's not inconsistent at all. The leadership just wants everybody to be in the center."[26] Similarly, Lavina Fielding Anderson, another member of the Six, wrote, "During the month of September 1993 six Mormon scholars in Utah, representing both liberal and conservative ends of the spectrum, were served notices by ecclesiastical leaders to appear before church courts."[27] Even the simple act of pairing two sets of excommunications implies the "middle-of-the-road" approach.

While the middle-of-the-road narrative is alluring, especially when set against the increasing globalization that meant increasing diversity in the church's fold, it is also problematic. First, it allows the church hierarchy to appear to be neutral, simply charting the course of least resistance, rather than what it was actually doing: actively defining what the church would look like as it entered the twenty-first century. That active definition included aligning the institution with the Religious Right, a blend of conservative Christianity and politics. For this reason, church authorities would also find the middle-of-the-road narrative appealing—it portrayed them as moderates, masking their own political and theological leanings. Second, it places both groups of excommunicants on the extreme fringe, rather than acknowledging the ways that the experiences of the September Six represented broader changes in the culture and within the church. And finally, it forces variant stories into the same frame, making it difficult to see what is actually at work in the story of the September Six. The middle-of-the-road thesis simply does not hold up: the church disciplinary councils of right-wing

---

25. For another example, see J. B. Haws, "LDS Church Presidency Years, 1985–1994," in Matthew L. Harris, ed., *Thunder from the Right* (Urbana: University of Illinois Press, 2019), 208–38, esp. 216–19.

26. Dirk Johns, "Seeking a Moderate Image, Mormons Expel Extremists," *New York Times* December 21, 1992.

27. Lavina Fielding Anderson, "The September Six," in George D. Smith, *Religion, Feminism, and Freedom of Conscience* (Salt Lake City: Signature Books, 2014), 3.

ultraconservative believers were about the nature of the purity system, whereas the September Six were arguing for an alternative to the purity system itself. For this reason, I'd like to explore the ultraconservative excommunicants separately, suggesting that while the two groups were chronologically contemporaneous, they were not part of the same impulse.

The church could be conservative socially, theologically, and politically, and still define right-wing apocalypticism as a threat to social order. These ultraconservatives saw common cause with church president Ezra Taft Benson.[28] As a church leader Benson had long been adamant that large government was a problem and injured the ability of individuals to make free choices. Because of this, he yearned for a romanticized past where he imagined that small and less centralized government allowed the individual to flourish. He was concerned about communism and socialism, which, he believed, strangled individual choice.[29]

Benson spent forty-two years, from 1943 to 1985 (when he then became president of the church), as an apostle and he was well-known for his anti-communist position. His theological worldview provided the structure for his conservative politics. Benson served as US President Dwight D. Eisenhower's secretary of agriculture from 1953 to 1961, and his activism in politics led to his connection to the All-American Society and the Freemen Institute (both politically conservative movements) and the John Birch Society (a right-wing extremist conspiracy organization).[30] Benson's connection to the Birch Society helped move him from a politically conservative libertarian to a more right-wing extremist.[31] Benson believed the world

28. Matthew L. Harris, *Watchman on the Tower: Ezra Taft Benson and the Making of the Mormon Right* (Salt Lake City: University of Utah Press, 2020), 125, and Haws, "LDS Church Presidency," 216–17. See also Christopher Smith, "Ultraconservative Gritz Remains as Bold as Ever," *Salt Lake Tribune*, December 7, 1992.

29. Matthew Bowman, "The Bundys are Stuck in Mormonism's Past," *Time Magazine*, January 7, 2016. Matthew Harris, "Ezra Taft Benson, Dwight D. Eisenhower, and the Emergence of a Conspiracy Culture within the Mormon Church," *John Whitmer Historical Association Journal* 37, no. 1 (Spring/Summer 2017): 5.

30. Harris, *Watchman on the Tower*, 1–3; Harris, "Conspiracy Culture," 55–56.

31. Patrick Mason, "'A Conservative Conservative': Era Taft Benson's Pre-John Birch Political Ideology," paper given at Mormon History Association Conference, Rochester, New York, June 2023.

was experiencing a cosmic battle between good and evil and viewed communism and liberalism as sinful movements. He saw evidence of the quickly approaching end times—of the culmination of that cosmic battle—in the world around him.[32]

During his tenure as an apostle and as church president, Benson contributed to the maintenance of the purity culture in numerous ways. In February 1980, he gave a talk at BYU titled "Fourteen Fundamentals in Following the Prophet." In it he spoke about how God would ensure that the church president could never lead the church astray. In addition, he argued that the living prophet was more important as a spokesperson for the church and God's will than a past one.[33] He declared that a prophet did not need to be trained in any particular area of study in order to be able to speak the final word about that topic. In so doing, he, like Boyd Packer, placed the mantle of the prophet above intellectuals who had been trained to inquire about and study various different disciplines.

Blurring the lines between simply speaking as a human with a particular perspective and revelatory speech, Benson argued that a prophet does not need to say "Thus saith the Lord" for his speech to be revelatory in nature. That same prophet could have revelation about any topic and his word would become the church's stance.[34] From Benson's perspective, it was perfectly acceptable for the prophet to speak on civic matters, and church members could expect that when that happened, worldly outsiders would despise their leader. Those who did not follow the prophet did so at their own peril and the refusal to follow, he claimed, was most often tied to pride.[35]

Because of his dualistic thinking and reactionary tendencies, other members of the church hierarchy felt that they had to keep Benson in line. Sometimes rebuking him, sometimes taking behind-the-scenes actions to rein him in, his cohorts saw him as someone who at times did not seem likely to succeed Spencer W. Kimball as prophet when Kimball died. When in November 1985 Benson rose to the position of church president, his selection of Thomas S.

32. Harris, *Watchman on the Tower*, 7, 90.

33. Ezra Taft Benson, "Fourteen Fundamentals in Following the Prophet," address given at Brigham Young University, February 26, 1980.

34. Ibid.

35. Ibid.

Monson and Gordon B. Hinckley as his two counselors in the First Presidency helped to assuage any concerns in that area.[36] While conservative, the two were less reactionary and extreme than Benson.

Ultraconservatives in the church came to see Benson's beliefs and statements on politics and theology as prophecy. When he became president of the church it simply confirmed that they were in the right place, members of a community on God's narrow path. In 1989 when George H. W. Bush gave Benson the Presidential Citizens Medal for service to his country, they understood the action as government sanction of his views.[37] For a time, God and country seemed in line. What they did not notice, though, was that Benson's most extreme and conservative thinking and preaching receded in his time as prophet.

Through much of the twentieth century, the church hierarchy had become a "gerontocracy," or rule by the elderly. After Joseph Smith's death, the LDS Church began a practice that became set policy: when a church president dies, he is succeeded by the man who has been serving longest as an apostle of the church. This approach meant that the ages of the highest officials were quite high. And it meant that prophets were not always capable of performing the entirety of their positions. This was especially true of Benson.

At the time of the September 1993 events, Benson was ninety-four. He had been mentally incapacitated for several years and was in a wheelchair with twenty-four-hour nursing care.[38] In the last year of his life, he had cerebral hemorrhages that made him unable to speak at meetings and also caused dizziness and memory loss.[39] Benson's struggle with health concerns came on the heels of Spencer W. Kimball's tenure as church president, which ended at the age of ninety after several years of declining health. To mediate this aging problem in the upper echelons of the church hierarchy, the church leadership subtly shifted from emphasizing the power of the prophet alone to emphasizing the power vested in the prophet, his two counselors in the First Presidency, and the Quorum of the Twelve. This

36. Harris, *Watchman on the Tower*, 104–5.

37. Harris, "Conspiracy Culture," 76.

38. William Hamilton, "Elders Banish Dissidents in Struggle over Mormon Practice" *Washington Post*, November 26, 1993.

39. Harris, "Conspiracy Culture," 78–79, and Harris, *Watchman on the Tower*, 114–15.

diffusion of power at the top allowed other church leaders to speak on behalf of the highest office of the church when the church president could not.[40]

Benson's first counselor, Gordon B. Hinckley, had already been serving as counselor to Kimball when Kimball was incapacitated, and so knew how to lead during Benson's increasing absence.[41] But the partial vacuum in the First Presidency meant that junior apostle Boyd K. Packer, intent on disciplining wayward members of the church, particularly those on the left, had less of a check on his power. Benson's two counselors, Hinckley and Monson, as well as the president of the Quorum of the Twelve, Howard W. Hunter, could have done more to restrain him, but they chose not to in the interest of collegiality.[42] As Apostle Dallin H. Oaks said of Packer, "You can't stage manage a grizzly bear," meaning that other apostles felt it easier to go along with his vision than to stand in his way.[43] Thus when Packer spoke, he could often control the narrative for the entire body.

Even though several church leaders were speaking for the church, right-wing ultraconservatives believed that Benson's ideals were foundational to the institution and they harkened back to a time when they claimed that the church had not given itself over to the broader culture. They called for a purity that "returned" to an imagined idyllic past. They argued that other church leaders were taking the institution off its narrow and godly path. From their perspective, the church had accommodated too much to the "worldly" ways of the broader culture in order to become respectable and mainstream, that it was becoming impure. And when US President H.W. Bush gave a speech in 1990 saying that the country would be part of a "new world order," they came to believe the nation had also stumbled off its path and fallen prey to a conspiracy for global domination.[44] In response, many of them retreated to the mountains, both physically

40. Gustav Niebuhr, "New Leader of Mormons Takes Joy in Changes" *New York Times*, July 23, 1995.

41. Haws, "LDS Church Presidency," 215–16.

42. Paul Toscano, *The Sacrament of Doubt* (Salt Lake City: Signature Books, 2007), 14–15.

43. Qtd in Matthew S. Brown, "Elder Oaks Says News Story 'Seriously Distorted' Facts," *Deseret News*, October 16, 1993.

44. John Charles Duffy, "The Making of Immanuel: Brian David Mitchell and the Mormon Fringe," *Sunstone*, October 2003, 36–38; Johns, "Seeking a Moderate Image."

and metaphorically, feeling that the church and the nation were corrupt and the only reaction was to retreat and close themselves off from the world and its end.[45]

One of the most well-known of the ultraconservatives was Bo Gritz, a Vietnam War veteran who had led Cambodian mercenaries on an attack of dozens of Viet Cong camps and even spent time in a Laotian jail. While searching for American prisoners of war in the jungles of Southeast Asia, Gritz had a spiritual experience that later led him to join the LDS Church in 1984. In the church he found great appeal in the teachings about personal revelation and believed that a church with Benson as its leader would support his political views. Gritz was known for pushing back against the problems he saw in the government, including his beliefs that the government was part of the drug trade, allowed constitutional rights to be slowly eroded, and unjustly collected income taxes. In 1992, Gritz ran for president, winning 28,000 votes on an ultraconservative platform with the slogan, "God, Guns, and Gritz." He preached that the apocalypse was at hand, evidenced by a growing global conspiracy to have a single government system—the "new world order." He taught that if the United States did not return to its Christian roots, it would become part of a global government that would literally place bar codes on citizens' foreheads in order to track them.[46]

In the 1990s, Gritz promoted American isolationism, abolishing federal income taxes, and declaring the United States a Christian nation. He believed the church had given in to the broader culture, largely to keep its charitable status with the IRS. Because of his beliefs, Gritz preached that it was better to be right with God than with the institution. The church, in the end, would not be the one that would judge someone's soul.[47] Church discipline started when Gritz was first told he could no longer speak in any church gatherings or church buildings. The discipline smarted. But it was not until

45. Hugh Dellios, "Doomsday Mormons Say Church Rejects Them," *Chicago Tribune*, January 3, 1993.

46. Duffy, "Making of Immanuel"; Dellios, "Doomsday Mormons"; Smith, "Ultraconservative Gritz"; and Matthew Bowman, "Conspiracy Theory and the Idea of Freedom: The Lessons of Bo Gritz, *By Common Consent* (blog), August 25, 2021, bycommonconsent.com.

47. Smith, "Ultraconservative Gritz."

1994, when he refused to file his income taxes and his stake president denied him his temple recommend because of it, that Gritz decided to resign from the church.[48] From Gritz's perspective, the church had gone too far, settled too much, and given away its authority in a bid to fit in.

Unlike Gritz, Sterling Allan had been a lifelong member of the church when, in 1990, at age twenty-six, he founded the American Study Group (ASG) in Provo, Utah. The ASG was rooted in conservativism, survivalism, and the politics of Bo Gritz.[49] Allan had been driven to carefully read the Book of Mormon by Benson's call for believers to do so. From his reading he produced his own method of using the text to predict how the end times would happen. Allan imagined ASG as a crossroads for the John Birch Society, the Eagle Forum (a politically conservative organization founded in 1972 by Phyllis Schlafly), and conservatives of many ilks. Group members believed that the end of the world was at hand and saw the signs in current events. They foretold that there would be economic collapse, then chaos accompanied by the suspension of constitutional rights, with an eventual nuclear war. Survivors would be captured by Soviets, but ultimately would congregate in Independence, Missouri, a site that Joseph Smith claimed would be the origin of Second Coming events.[50]

The group grew rapidly in popularity, numbering about 5,000 members and thirty-five to forty chapters at its height. V. Dennis Wardle, a member of the LDS Church and the ASG advisory board, recounted that the group had four rules: 1) Supporting the key values of the church; 2) Acknowledging the existence of global conspiracies; 3) Believing that "Latter-day Saints will triumph"; and 4) Being loyal to the United States.[51] Even as the group declared loyalty to church and nation, it argued that both had gone astray. The church had become so accommodating of the broader culture that its main goal was to keep its tax-exempt status.

48. Bowman, "Conspiracy Theory."

49. Duffy, "Making of Immanuel."

50. Duffy, "Making of Immanuel"; Dawn House, "Group Studying Apocalypse Calls it Quits," *Salt Lake Tribune*, October 29, 1991; Peggy Fletcher Stack, "World Events Prove End Is Near, Group Says," *Salt Lake Tribune*, September 3, 1991.

51. Stack, "World Events."

The demise of ASG came in 1992, when the church intervened and Allan chose to close the group down rather than face disciplinary proceedings. That same year, Allan attempted to take the podium during general conference, the church's biannual meeting, in order to warn members that the institution had gone astray, that it was turning to apostasy. He wanted to revive the purity of the teachings of church president Benson and the politics of ultraconservatism. After the group collapsed, Allan ran to the mountains, believing that a nuclear war was coming. When he returned to Manti in January 1993, he was excommunicated, in part for his teachings tied to the work of biblical scholar Avraham Gileadi, one of the September Six. Allan first tried to submit to church authority and return to church membership, but eventually gave up and embraced his departure from the church.[52]

Jim and Elaine Harmston were also drawn in by the teachings of Ezra Taft Benson. Even as they appreciated what he had taught, they thought they saw other church leaders "who speak 180 degrees against him."[53] They were concerned when, after reading the Book of Mormon, they thought the institutional church had turned away from its true and godly path. They began hosting a scripture study in their home, encouraging members of their study group to stockpile goods and homeschool their children. They also had been teaching about prayer circles, a sacred prayer form that church leaders had prohibited outside of temples. In 1978, the First Presidency announced that all prayer circles were to be stopped except for those happening during the endowment ceremony in the temple.[54] But the Harmstons' study group still embraced the practice.

The Harmstons' network continued to grow and included Mormon fundamentalists who practiced polygamy, raising concerns from church leaders who started to seek out which church members were participating. First, their stake president told them that they could not discuss the gospel with anyone except for family members. When they refused to stop their study groups, they were

52. Duffy, "Making of Immanuel."

53. Chris Jorgensen and Peggy Fletcher Stack, "It's Judgment Day for Far Right," *Salt Lake Tribune*, November 29, 1992.

54. For a history of this practice, see D. Michael Quinn, "Latter-day Saint Prayer Circles," *BYU Studies Quarterly* 19, no. 1 (Fall 1978): 79–105.

excommunicated in October 1992. Two years later Jim Harmston founded the True and Living Church of Jesus Christ of Saints of the Last Days, claiming that he had received the keys of the true church through revelation, and was returning to the original goals of the Restoration, including polygamy.[55]

The church's response to these ultraconservative right-wing apocalypticists was swift and clear, some calling it a "purge" of hundreds, though the church never publicly confirmed the numbers.[56] Church spokesperson Don LeFevre explained that excommunications were rare, arguing that the church was neutral on the politics of its believers, "but the church doesn't get into predicting the end of the world. And if somebody is doing that, they're off base."[57] While the church said that there was no official policy in response to survivalists and ultraconservatives, it was clear in church leaders' speeches that they were concerned about members who were too patriotic, too committed to survivalist tendencies, and too open to the practice of polygamy.[58]

Malcolm Jeppsen, who had served as a bishop, stake president, and regional stake president, was called to the Second Quorum of the Seventy in 1989 and to be president of the Utah South region of the church (in the church Utah is divided into three regions: Utah North, Salt Lake City, and Utah South). In January 1988, on a visit to the Manti and St. George temples, these ultraconservative groups first came across his radar and quickly became a focus of his leadership. On that trip, Jeppsen and his wife met with Robert Rice, a stake president in the area. Rice "mentioned that he had been having people in his stake who were imbued with the philosophy of the end of the world coming up very soon. This in spite of his preachments that this was false doctrine. Several had sold their homes, cashed in their insurance and other savings to get money to go out to northwest Utah by Snowville."[59] In Snowville, their plan was to prepare for the return of the Ten Lost Tribes, which would be one step in bringing about the Second Coming.

---

55. Dellios, "Doomsday Mormons"; Duffy, "Making of Immanuel."

56. Johns, "Seeking a Moderate Image."

57. Qtd in ibid.

58. Smith, "Ultraconservative Gritz."

59. Malcolm Seth Jeppsen and Marian Davis Jeppsen, *Up Close and Personal: The Life History of Malcolm Seth and Marian Jeppsen* (N.p.: by the authors, 2003), 397.

In order to help call people back to an orthodox position, Jeppsen went to speak to the stake. "I warned about fringe groups who taught these things as teachers of false doctrine, and pleaded that each and every one would resolve to follow the First Presidency and Twelve in matters of Church doctrine and policy."[60] Jeppsen wanted the ultraconservative groups to stop of their own accord. To help Rice, he left a copy of his speech with him, asking him not to circulate it. Even though he made the request, Jeppsen soon realized that copies of the speech got out. In his position in the Second Quorum of Seventy, he received copies of his speech along with commentary from ultraconservatives: "They really took me to task, mostly by taking quotes of President Benson out of context and saying that I was speaking contrary to him."[61] And so, there was a battle of doctrinal orthodoxy, with each side arguing that theirs was the pure form of the church. Benson's words were used by the ultraconservatives to shore up their claim that they were on the narrow path and that the church had gone astray. They believed they were the watchdogs of institutional purity.

In his role as president of Utah South, Jeppsen continued to do battle with these groups where he proved himself to be a fixer for the institution. He understood that part of his work was "cleaning up the apostate groups that were forming in Southern Utah, and Eastern Utah."[62] When he received the assignment, "One or two of the Twelve gave me some hints ... to the effect that the apostates in the Utah South area were a problem needing to be taken care of."[63] With his charge from the church hierarchy clear, Jeppsen called a meeting of the stake presidents, mission presidents, and temple presidents in the area.

There he outlined for the group a profile of what church members of concern might look like, and from that outline, regional stake presidents created a list of problematic activities. Though not an official list, the profile included home schooling, study groups and other splinter meetings, preoccupation with food storage, reading apocalyptic texts,

60. Ibid, 398.
61. Ibid.
62. Ibid, 423.
63. Ibid.

preaching about the end of times, participating in temple rituals outside of the temple, a desire to know the exact moment of the Second Coming, and membership in the John Birch Society.[64]

Jeppsen instructed the local leaders to "point out that they can believe anything they want and remain a member of the Church, but cannot teach false doctrine and do so as a Church member. The thrust of their teachings was that we were being led into apostasy as a Church because President Benson was infirm."[65] These local groups were calling upon the authority of the prophet, one who had preached that those following a prophet would never be led astray. They argued that it was other church leaders like Jeppsen who were pulling the church away from its foundation and toward more worldly ways, taking advantage of Benson's incapacity to lead.

Jeppsen set up a system to try to cut them off at the roots. In Manti, where Harmston was located, "The apostates ... were doing much of their own teaching in the temple celestial room.... They would even trade recommends around to get inside the temple."[66] For many church leaders, this was a particular insult, as it was the temple that was a symbol of their institutional authority and represented all that was pure and good. Hinckley called Jeppsen in to inquire about Harmston, concerned about Harmston's group and its practices. Jeppsen explained what had been happening: "I told him that having talked extensively to [Harmston's] stake president about his activities, I was assured by the president that he would be excommunicated the following Sunday. Whereupon President Hinckley seemed reassured and encouraged me to continue what was planned."[67] In addition to reprimanding Harmston, Jeppsen had bishops send him weekly reports of the progress they were making in their local communities on addressing ultraconservative and apocalyptically-oriented members. Eventually he recorded that about forty to fifty people in Manti were excommunicated, while one hundred were "guided back into the church's folds."[68]

---

64. Jorgensen and Stack, "It's Judgment Day for Far Right"; Dellios, "Doomsday Mormons."

65. Jeppsen and Jeppsen, *Up Close and Personal*, 423.

66. Ibid, 427.

67. Ibid, 428.

68. Ibid.

Jeppsen recalled that those who had been disciplined in southern Utah spoke to the media "and told the TV audiences that I was behind a big purging." At a local football game people placed leaflets on cars telling the football fans to contact the First Presidency and tell them that Jeppsen was out of line and they needed to call in their watchdog. Even though he hated the publicity, Jeppsen wryly replied to the pamphleteers: "It was so inane since I wasn't doing anything that I wasn't instructed by that very First Presidency to do."[69]

This entire process showed that the church wanted to rid itself of members who were on the fringe and who were preaching that the Second Coming was at hand. Those members, though, were not critiquing the *fact* of the purity system present in the church. Rather, based on their readings of the Book of Mormon, the writings of Avraham Gileadi, the teachings of Ezra Taft Benson, and their interpretations of current events, they concluded that the church had gone astray. One of the ultraconservative community members put it this way: "But it's the church that has changed from early doctrine, not us."[70]

Avraham Gileadi and The Last Days

Fundamentalist Brian David Mitchell, the Salt Lake City man who kidnapped, repeatedly raped, and held teenaged Elizabeth Smart captive from June 2002 to March 2003, read a lot of apocalyptic texts. Mitchell felt nostalgia for a church past rooted in purity and polygamy, one that had not succumbed to the broader culture. This was a sentiment he shared with other ultraconservatives. He felt called to separate himself from the corrupting ways of society, choosing to embrace an apocalyptic worldview that taught the Second Coming was imminent.[71]

Like other Mormon fundamentalists, some of the writings in which Mitchell found inspiration included biblical scholar Avraham Gileadi's about the Book of Isaiah, writings that had become popular in the Latter-day Saint community and were even published and sold by church-owned Deseret Book. In the 1990s, Mitchell said that he had a revelation in the Salt Lake Temple where he learned

69. Ibid, 427.
70. Johns, "Seeking a Moderate Image."
71. Duffy, "Making of Immanuel."

that the church had lost its way and was under admonishment for not taking Benson's teachings on the Book of Mormon seriously.[72] Mitchell believed there were eight testaments to Jesus Christ that included the Bible and Book of Mormon, but also the works of modern writers, including Avraham Gileadi.[73] Because of his reading of Gileadi, Mitchell anticipated a leader who was "mighty and strong" and who would appear to inaugurate the Second Coming. Mitchell understood himself as the Davidic Servant who would restore Israel prior to the event.[74]

Avraham Gileadi, one of Mitchell's influences, was the least Six-ish of all of the September Six. He was an academic and intellectual, but his inclusion in the alliterative "September Six" happened only because he was excommunicated in the same month. Gileadi has always been at right angles to the others. He was excommunicated for writing and promoting his book, *The Last Days*, a book that was popular in the Latter-day Saint community. Even so, Gileadi had his critics. Some were BYU professors who accused him of heresy, making claims about the events leading up to Jesus's Second Coming that were simply untrue.[75] Though Gileadi was disciplined for reasons different from the other September Six, there is much to learn from his case about how the institution used discipline to address those perceived as stepping outside the bounds of the purity system. First, it shows the amount of power behind the church's choice to discipline its members and second, it shows how the institution would like for the process to work. In the end, Gileadi followed the counsel of his priesthood holders and did not speak outside of the family about the dirty laundry he experienced within it, and so he was soon rebaptized into the church. For the institution and its purity system, his process could be considered a success.

Gileadi was born in the Netherlands in 1940 but grew up in New

72. Harris, "Conspiracy Culture," 78.

73. Duffy, "Making of Immanuel."

74. The anticipated leader who was "mighty and strong" refers to an 1832 prophecy made by Joseph Smith, who declared that a leader would come to prepare the church and "steady the ark." Since the prophecy, a number of individuals have declared that they are the "mighty and strong" leader. Harris, *Watchman on the Tower*, 113–14; Duffy, "Making of Immanuel."

75. Peggy Fletcher Stack, "Gileadi: 'I Feel Like I'm Home Again, and It Is a Good Feeling," *Salt Lake Tribune*, March 2, 1996.

Zealand. His Catholic family included some priests, a testament to the importance of their faith. Gileadi attended a Catholic school for part of his education and especially loved the study of the Christian Old and New Testaments.[76] He embraced his spiritual life, but did not always feel a strong commitment to it. Just when he felt like he was losing his spirituality, Gileadi was introduced to a growing new art form: rock music. He put together a rock and jazz group and became a professional musician for a time. But as he played he began to realize his career's negative effects on his spirituality and on society. In his continued examination of scripture, Gileadi had an epiphany. According to his reading of the New Testament, it was "music that ravished the soul" that caused the people of the covenant to turn from God. And the connection for him was obvious: "I myself, I realized, was playing that kind of music, so I decided to give it up and go back to my spiritual roots."[77]

At the time, that meant that he decided to go to a Catholic seminary in order to become a priest. But for him, the seminary life was "stifling spiritually," and so he quickly moved away from the faith and turned to other spiritual pursuits. This eventually led him to convert to Judaism because he "felt that in Israel the Jews were fulfilling prophecy as recorded in the Old Testament."[78] His fascination with Judaism and the study of scripture took him to Israel to further his education. It was there that he received his Hebrew name and became an Israeli citizen. Gileadi was a rabbinical student in Jerusalem in 1972 when he came across a copy of the Book of Mormon and decided to convert to the LDS Church. He was baptized in the Pool of Siloam. After that decision, the next ones seemed easy. He moved to Utah where he attended BYU and earned a doctorate in Ancient Studies. After his studies he worked for the church doing translations, teaching, and giving lectures and seminars.[79]

It was his best-selling book, *The Last Days: Types and Shadows from the Bible and the Book of Mormon*, published by Deseret Book

76. Paul Rawlins, "An Interview with Avraham Gileadi," *Student Review*, January 22, 1992.

77. Ibid.

78. Ibid.

79. Steve Fidel, "Excommunicated Scholar Re-Enters LDS Church," *Deseret News*, March 7–8, 1996.

in 1991, that got him into trouble. The topic, of course, was the "last days," or the "time before the millennial reign of Jesus Christ." In it Gileadi identified what he argued were problematic positions in the church. On the one hand, there were those who "cling to the idea that the Prophet Joseph Smith told us all we need to know about the last days—and everything else." This camp believed that the exodus of believers who followed Brigham Young west to the Salt Lake Valley (which they understood as Zion) had fulfilled the prophecies and that Jesus's Second Coming was off in a distant future. On the other hand, there were those who "detect apostasy throughout the Church" and believed that the Second Coming was at hand. Gileadi argued that both groups injured the church because they were not grounded in scripture. The first group, he declared, failed to see the current church's role in bringing about the kingdom of God, choosing instead a "comfort zone," while the second group "sees gross defects in all but its own self."[80]

Gileadi argued instead for a "middle course," suggesting that many church members were experiencing a spiritual awakening. In an argument that inspired fundamentalist readers at the time, Gileadi explained that, "Two latter-day servants of God, one righteous, the other wicked, will typify the attitudes of the people."[81] When that happened, the righteous would understand the calamities that were about to ensue and would help one another, turning to God in an uncertain time. They would have prepared for the end times and would be ready to do what was necessary. Gileadi declared that there would be a political Messiah who would come, one who had been prophesied in Jewish scriptures. While he did not claim that this idea of a "Davidic servant" was church doctrine, he did understand that he was challenging some church leaders' interpretations of the Book of Isaiah, especially Bruce R. McConkie.[82]

Gileadi argued that his unique contribution to the discourse about the last days was tied to his distinct personal history. Because his

---

80. Avraham Gileadi, *The Last Days: Types and Shadows from the Bible and the Book of Mormon* (Salt Lake City: Deseret Book Company, 1991), 1–2.

81. Ibid, 3.

82. Bruce D. Porter, review of *The Book of Isaiah: A New Translation with Interpretive Keys from the Book of Mormon*, by Avraham Gileadi, *Review of Books on the Book of Mormon* 4, no. 1 (1992): 40–57, and Rawlins, "Interview with Avraham Gileadi."

religious seeking had led him in several directions, he believed that he could "use the [research] manner of the Jews, information from the Book of Mormon and the Doctrine and Covenants, and this covenant theology that scholars have researched, tying it back to ancient Near Eastern parallels."[83] The center for Gileadi was his training in reading and understanding Jewish scripture. He felt this training could apply to the Book of Mormon because it, too, claimed to be Jewish scripture. He knew that Latter-day Saints had had the Book of Mormon for a long time, but they were just assuming they understood it well.[84] And it was through an analysis of the book of Isaiah that they could come to read the restoration scriptures with new eyes.

Gileadi explained that he had carefully studied the scriptures and knew that the Book of Mormon could "hold up under scrutiny."[85] He affirmed that his studies included a process of studying the Book of Mormon alongside other scriptures but also letting the Spirit guide him. He encouraged his readers to do the same because "we have yet to understand much of that message and that much hinges on whether we understand it."[86]

While he cautioned readers to be mindful of the times, he also stated that he drew on the teachings of the general authorities and also had Hugh Nibley, a well-respected scriptural scholar at BYU, as his guide.[87] In his reading of the Jewish prophets, Gileadi reminded readers that "Israel has always jeopardized her status as a chosen people by adopting the customs of the Gentiles."[88] This was a powerful argument for those who felt that the church was losing its orthodoxy in its bid for cultural acceptance.

His book then turned to an exploration of the ancient prophecies while also seeing examples of what those prophecies foretold in the culture of the 1980s and 1990s. Gileadi pointed to: television (which, he argued, taught a "false social code"), the "immoral music" of the times, organized sports (as "predominantly idolatrous in nature"), the worship of money, expansive militarism, and nature cults

83. Rawlins, "Interview with Avraham Gileadi."
84. Ibid.
85. Gileadi, *Last Days*, 5–7.
86. Ibid, 7.
87. Ibid, 8–9.
88. Ibid, 10.

(or environmental spirituality) as evidence of what the prophecies foretold.[89] Gileadi portrayed all of these aspects of 1980s and 1990s culture as signs of the last days.

He warned that while Latter-day Saints would play an important "saving mission" in the final days, "the great day of the earth's judgment will catch most people unawares."[90] Arguing that the restoration scriptures of Joseph Smith shared the same vision and worldview of the Jewish prophets, Gileadi explained that "temporal salvation, spiritual salvation, and exaltation, each associated with a covenant, are at the heart of the revealed gospel." Jesus had prepared the way, he finished, and now believers just had to follow: "the only path to the celestial kingdom lies through him; he employs no keeper at its gates."[91] While nothing in his work explicitly encouraged fundamentalist thinking, Gileadi tapped into themes and questions that were powerful for many fundamentalists and ultraconservatives. He saw evidence of the end times prophesied in scriptures and linked them directly to events, practices, and people in the current day—all readers had to do was look around them to see confirmation of what he taught.

Gileadi's book was popular. In part because it was supported by well-known and beloved scholars like BYU professor Hugh Nibley and was endorsed by the Foundation for Ancient Research and Mormon Studies (FARMS). Founded in 1979, by lawyer and scholar John Welch, FARMS began as an informal network of scholars in scriptural studies. Eventually, in the late 1990s, FARMS became an official part of BYU. Operating primarily as a faith organization, FARMS argued that "Mormon scriptures are compatible with pre-Columbian history." Daniel C. Peterson, a professor at BYU wrote: "The idea is not to prove Mormonism, but, by assuming scripture is what it claims to be, showing that this assumption can help us better understand it."[92] Thus FARMS scholarship started with the assumption that the Restoration is founded on ancient scriptural sources. From there believing scholars endeavored to explore other

89. Ibid, 18–19, 25, 30.

90. Ibid, 177.

91. Ibid, 257, 259.

92. Peter Scarlet, "Grow Gathering Data to Support Book of Mormon," *Salt Lake Tribune*, March 19, 1994.

ancient sources in order to help shed light on the texts' ancient context and meaning.[93]

In the midst of the rising popularity of *The Last Days*'s, some in the church raised concerns. First, there were several professors in BYU's religion department who felt the book contradicted teachings by several modern apostles. Second, when the *Ensign* wanted to include portions of Gileadi's chapter on modern idolatry in its pages, the committee in charge of correlation, on which Malcolm Jeppsen served, caught wind. They disapproved of its inclusion because the chapter "was obvious false doctrine."[94] They made sure that the chapter was not reprinted and went even further to try to stop the book's popularity.

Their concern was heightened because the book was gaining popularity with ultraconservative fundamentalist-leaning believers who saw in it interpretations that supported their theories about the end of times. Those believers were "making dramatic career changes and had moved to remote locales because of the book's apocalyptic tone."[95] Thus it was fostering interpretations that the apocalypse was at hand and that people should go into preparation mode. Because of these two things, Deseret Book decided "to stop carrying its *own* briskly selling book." Some even reported that removal from the shelves was not enough and the press was considering shredding the text. Instead of that option, though, Deseret Book sold Gileadi the remaining copies, which he then resold to Seagull Book and Tape. It sold its entire supply within days.[96] Thus the church hierarchy's concerns about Gileadi came both from his unorthodox arguments *and* how readers were interpreting those same arguments.

While Gileadi's book surely raised specific concerns, it also raised questions about the church hierarchy's need to place limitations and boundaries on scriptural interpretation. Writing for the *Student Review*, an off-campus newspaper in Provo, Paul Rawlins tried to imagine the church's perspective. He argued that the world was watching the church and so there was "a curtailing of dialogue, in

93. Terryl L. Givens, *By the Hand of Mormon: The American Scripture that Launched a New World Religion* (New York: Oxford University Press, 2002), 124–25.

94. Jeppsen and Jeppsen, *Up Close and Personal*, 435.

95. "The Bomb of Gileadi" *Sunstone* 15, no. 3 (September 1991), 72.

96. Ibid.

an effort to preserve the community."[97] Rawlins asked why, rather than engaging the book and offering a counter-argument, detractors instead avoided debate altogether, choosing to censor the book by having it removed from Deseret Book's shelves. Rawlins was concerned: Gileadi had not presented his perspective as doctrine, instead he presented it as his own interpretation. And Rawlins wondered, why would church authorities not speak to the interpretation in response? While he pondered the above, Rawlins asked Gileadi about his thoughts on the issue. Gileadi felt pretty confident that it was his chapter on "modern idolatry" that caused all of the hullaballoo, because "it just touches a lot of nerves." When Rawlins asked him why, Gileadi's answer was simple: "the idea that we are idolaters."[98] In the context of growing apocalypticism and ultraconservatism, Gileadi was claiming that most had fallen off the narrow path.

Whatever the precise concern, church leaders viewed Gileadi as a problem in need of fixing. Gileadi's case bolsters accusations that general authorities were putting their hands into the local matters of disciplinary councils. In October 1992, Gileadi's stake president, Randall Gibb, counseled him to stop publishing and speaking about the Book of Isaiah and predictions about the Second Coming. Gileadi followed those instructions and Gibb felt as though he had adequately complied. However, Malcolm Jeppsen, the Utah South Area President, wanted actions against Gileadi to proceed further than Gibb was willing to take them.[99] He called Gibb in to give him a report outlining the false doctrines that Gileadi was teaching. After their first meeting, Jeppsen told Gibb to discipline Gileadi several times. In their final meeting, when Jeppsen sensed Gibb's resistance to any further action, he put his arm around him and said, "We're short on counsel in this office but long on direction. I'm directing you to take action to correct or else excommunicate this man. He cannot be allowed to be teaching what he is teaching and remain a member of the Church."[100]

---

97. Paul Rawlins, "The Last Days of Avraham Gileadi," *Student Review*, September 18, 1991.

98. Rawlins, "Interview with Avraham Gileadi."

99. Peggy Fletcher Stack, "More Stories Point to LDS Leaders as Source of Dissident Crackdown," *Salt Lake Tribune*, October 16, 1993.

100. Jeppsen and Jeppsen, *Up Close and Personal*, 435.

"Still nothing happened," Jeppsen wrote in his journal, "so [Gibb] was released as a stake president."[101] Boyd K. Packer selected the new stake president, Leaun G. Otten. Some found this choice odd because Otten had been installed as the stake patriarch just a few months before. But to others, the choice made perfect sense. Otten was a professor in BYU's religion faculty and had been a vocal opponent of Gileadi's work.[102] Jeppsen wrote in his journal that Otten "was appraised of the problem, and moved to correct it quickly."[103] Gileadi was excommunicated. The verdict of Gileadi's council, "was read from the pulpit in every ward in [Gileadi's] Salem stake, both in Relief Society meetings for the women and Priesthood meetings for the men."[104] This was not a common practice in modern excommunications, and so the message was clear. His church leaders wanted Gileadi silenced and also wanted his community members to see him as a threat. Orthodoxy and purity had won the day.

While it may seem like an abrupt turn of events, just a few years after his excommunication in September 1993, Gileadi was rebaptized into the church. At the same time as his baptism, church officials lifted the ban that had been placed on his writing and speaking. Even as they did, they recommended that he not veer far from the counsel of church leaders. Each of these steps is important in demonstrating how the disciplinary process ideally worked from the institution's perspective. Gileadi expressed contrition, then promised not to speak about similar topics in public and to always seek church authorities' approval of what he published.

Jeppsen put it this way: "The brother was excommunicated, and immediately the next day other [dissidents] who heard about it came to him wanting him to sign on to a full page ad in the *[Salt Lake] Tribune* blasting what they were calling religious freedom. He would have none of it. Telling them he had made a mistake, but he still loved the Church immensely and would stop his seminars, etc., and do whatever he needed to do to get his membership restored."[105] From Jeppsen's

101. Ibid.

102. Stack, "More Stories Point to LDS Leaders." See also, Toscano, *Sacrament of Doubt*, 14–15.

103. Jeppsen and Jeppsen, *Up Close and Personal*, 435.

104. Stack, "More Stories Point to LDS Leaders."

105. Jeppsen and Jeppsen, *Up Close and Personal*, 437.

point of view, the disciplinary council had effected precisely the kind of change needed. Gileadi learned the error of his ways, worked to get in line, and came back into the church. At least from Jeppsen's perspective, Gileadi was better off for having gone through it.

In return for his obedience to church authority, Gileadi was welcomed back into the fold. According to Latter-day Saint teachings, he once again had access to the constant presence of the Holy Ghost, the authority of the priesthood, access to the temple, and potential exaltation in the afterlife. Gileadi had demonstrated his allegiance to the institution in his commitment to not speak to external bodies about his excommunication. In addition, he always framed his disciplinary council as a series of misunderstandings, rather than an issue where church authorities had been wrong. Because he willingly bowed to the authority of the hierarchy, he gained admittance back into the ranks.

"My baptism was a sweet experience," Gileadi stated, "I feel like I'm home again and it is a good feeling."[106] The same local leaders who had excommunicated Gileadi were at his re-baptism, offering those who were there a sense of reconciliation. A repentant Gileadi acknowledged that the years since his excommunication had been financially difficult. His livelihood came from sales of his books and the seminars he offered. During that time he had to turn to his savings to support his wife and nine children.

His return to full membership was emotionally powerful. "I've grown so much," he said. "I have learned to love my leaders unconditionally."[107] And so he re-entered the church. Unlike the other five, Gileadi's return was relatively immediate and happened in virtually the same climate in which he had left the church. In that regard, too, his excommunication had been different.

Gileadi also explained that his excommunication drove his sons to fully commit themselves to the church. His second son performed his re-baptism shortly before leaving for his full-time LDS mission, while his eldest was successfully completing his mission. From the beginning it seemed that Gileadi's goal was to just get back into the church. "In my heart I've never felt like I've had an apostate spirit,"

106. Stack, "I Feel like I'm Home Again."
107. Ibid.

he explained. "I will repent of whatever was wrong with me and forgive whoever wronged me."[108]

Ever since 1993, Gileadi wanted to mark himself as separate from the September Six in a number of ways. In June 2012 he wrote an online statement responding to what he saw as continuous inaccuracies about himself written on Wikipedia. First, he did not believe that there was any evidence to support the charges against him. And, because he was rebaptized, that meant that "all record of it was expunged from the church's records nearly a decade ago in a tacit admission that the church had made a mistake." It was therefore a "non event," from his perspective.[109] In that response twenty years after the fact, he spoke of the events in the breeziest of fashions. He was just as active in the church as ever and he continued to publish books, even another one about Isaiah. He told the *Salt Lake Tribune,* "I hope for the day that zealous Mormons will no longer be treated as anti-Mormons."[110]

Gileadi also distanced himself from the other five because the others "pleaded their cause in the media at that time and thus embarrassed the church, I never did so."[111] This description portrayed the other five as looking for a type of fame and attention that could only come by publicly denouncing the church. Gileadi saw himself as upholding the purity culture of the church and following the expectation that one be humble and silent about church leaders in the public realm. He therefore did not see himself as one of the September Six. While his criteria were one-sided, the claim is nonetheless accurate. He conformed to the rules of the purity system. He had not publicized his excommunication nor did he turn to the press or the pulpit to defend himself. While his writings may have been a challenge to notions of orthodoxy, they did not claim to be orthodoxy. Instead, he had offered his contribution to the conversation and, when disciplined, he had promised to stop his inquiry and his discussion. He

108. Fidel, "Excommunicated Scholar."

109. Avraham Gileadi, "Responses to Wikipedia Article Dated June 12, 2012," Avraham Gileadi Testimony, June 14, 2012, avrahamgileaditestimony.blogspot.com, accessed October 4, 2022.

110. Peggy Fletcher Stack, "He's Outside the Faith but the Faith Is Still inside Him," *Salt Lake Tribune,* September 28, 2013.

111. Gileadi, "Responses to Wikipedia."

followed the rules. He did not want to be remembered as one of the September Six, believing that the only thing that tied him to the others was a clever alliteration. In many ways, he was right.

3: FAMILIAL PURITY

"The rights of a woman to be a woman, a feminine, female woman; a wife and mother."
—Boyd K. Packer

In June 1970, about ten educated women met in the Boston area to discuss their lives as women in the church. One of those women, sociologist and historian Claudia Bushman, described those early meetings as ones in which "we try to speak honestly and openly, but otherwise the scene resembles a Primary preparation meeting or morning brunch with ladies chatting together while toddlers trip over their feet and infants demand attention."[1] For the women involved, the meetings felt like a breath of fresh air. They valued their labor in the home and as mothers while also knowing that they wanted lives that extended beyond those roles. To know that someone else felt that way too, in a church where they had been taught that being a wife and a mother was the "measure of their creation," was invigorating.

While they pushed back against the images of womanhood that conjured only "the imaginative homemaker and the diligent Church worker" alongside other domestic chores, they spent "no time railing at men." They wanted partnerships with their husbands and they wanted to raise their children well.[2] And they wanted more. They spoke about their own circumstances and discussed feminist thinkers like Kate Millet and Betty Friedan, author of the groundbreaking *The Feminine Mystique* (1963) that challenged women to use their

1. Claudia Lauper Bushman, "Women in *Dialogue*: An Introduction," in Joanna Brooks, Rachel Hunt Steenblik, and Hannah Wheelwright, eds., *Mormon Feminism: Essential Writings* (New York: Oxford University Press, 2016), 36.

2. Ibid, 36.

education to seek occupations beyond their roles in the home. Historian Laurel Thatcher Ulrich, another member of the group, wished she could remember the exact date they started meeting so that a plaque could be placed at the site: "Here…in this ordinary looking, gambrel-roofed house, the second generation of Mormon feminists was born."[3] Recalling that time, Ulrich described Mormon feminism this way: "A feminist is a person who believes in equality between the sexes, who recognizes discrimination against women and who is willing to work to overcome it. A Mormon feminist believes that these principles are compatible not only with the gospel of Jesus Christ but with the mission of the [LDS] Church."[4]

Not long after these budding feminist moments, *Dialogue* published an issue addressing women's lives and the social and religious expectations they faced. Created at the prompting and participation of the Boston collective, and remembered as "The Pink Issue" (because it had a bright pink cover and because it was dedicated to addressing women), the issue contained essays from many Latter-day Saint perspectives. Bushman later pinpointed her favorite sentence in the introduction to that edition: "Does it undercut the celestial dream to admit that there are occasional Japanese beetles in the roses covering our cottages?"[5] Here Bushman drew upon the theology of the family set forth by Joseph Smith in Doctrine and Covenants 132.[6] The revelation made a distinction between marriages "for time" (which would end when this life ended) and marriages in the temple, overseen by a priesthood holder "for time and eternity." The promise was that together a heterosexual couple could achieve exaltation in the next life, reaching the highest level of heaven, called the celestial realm. It was there that: "They be gods, because they have no end; therefore shall they be from everlasting to everlasting, because they continue; then shall they be above all, because all things are subject unto them." And

3. Laurel Thatcher Ulrich, "The Pink *Dialogue* and Beyond," in Brooks, Steenblik, and Wheelwright, eds., *Mormon Feminism*, 113.

4. Ibid.

5. Claudia L. Bushman, "Mormon Feminism after 1970," in Amy Hoyt and Taylor G. Petrey, eds., *The Routledge Handbook of Mormonism and Gender* (New York: Routledge, 2020), 159.

6. D&C 132 is a revelation dated 1843, though there is evidence that Smith taught many of the principles over the prior decade.

so Bushman was imagining the greatest goal of her co-religionists as a place where women had more room. She expressed in her analogy the reform feminism that many Mormon women imagined. They were not asking to change everything, to re-imagine the tradition or the heavens; rather they were asking for small changes, more room for motherhood and career, home and public life.

Bushman saw that women in the church also needed more connection. One of the ways that they could achieve this was through gathering informally in circles where they knew that they could express their feelings, just like the Boston collective had. As well, she acknowledged that new publications focusing on women's experiences offered a sense of connection to other like-minded believers while they "provided a voice for Mormons exploring new ideas."[7] In 1972, *Exponent II* appeared on the publication scene. It was "a modest but sincere newspaper which … [meant to] bring Mormon women into closer friendship."[8] Billed as "faithful but frank," the publication allowed for discussions about current events and the lives of believers. It had two goals: "to strengthen the Church of Jesus Christ of Latter-day Saints" and "to encourage and develop the talents of Mormon women."[9] These early publications brought hope to feminists in the church that there was room for them to navigate the intersections of the two identities.

Many Latter-day Saint feminists in the 1970s looked to women in the nineteenth-century church as models of how to embrace their power as women while also being active in faith and church community. Jill Mulvay Derr, a historian of Latter-day Saint women who worked for the LDS Church History Department, expressed this position quite clearly. Derr "felt a kinship with these [nineteenth-century] sisters." For Derr history was not just about recalling the facts, but "the experiences of other women's lives gave meaning to my own—meaning I had missed in my own experience until I began examining and gaining respect for their experiences."[10] Mormon feminism in these years

7. Bushman, "Mormon Feminism after 1970," 159.

8. Claudia Lauper Bushman, "Exponent II Born," in Brooks, Steenblik, and Wheelwright, eds., *Mormon Feminism*, 113.

9. Ibid, 40.

10. Jill Mulvay Derr, "Missing and Restoring Meaning," *Dialogue: A Journal of Mormon Thought* 55, no. 2 (Summer 2022): 57–76.

explored history, encouraged robust lives for women in the church, and primarily stayed on the reformist end of the feminist spectrum.

What happened to Mormon feminism, then, was a surprise to everyone. What once seemed to be a budding and powerful movement helping to create larger roles for women in the church quickly met a blockade called the Equal Rights Amendment. With the growing interest in the ERA, the institutional church cemented a vision of womanhood that locked women into their roles as mothers and as wives. The familial pillar of the purity system came to center around a complementary gender system—where men and women took on complementary but opposing gender roles—each group was limited in the scope of how to inhabit those genders. Women who attempted to expand their roles were portrayed by the institution's purity system as disruptive, stepping out of line. Their resistance to the limitations placed on their gender was read as a challenge to the institution itself and those who refused to step back in line suffered the consequences.

Sonia Johnson and the ERA

Just as twentieth-century Mormon feminism was developing out of its infancy, the Equal Rights Amendment came along and complicated matters. "Suddenly in 1978 Mormonism and feminism seemed incompatible," Ulrich recalled.[11] And it was in this context that Sonia Johnson came to the party. Even though she awakened to her feminism later in life, Johnson "had unconsciously known for a very long time that something was wrong with patriarchy." While she experienced it in her church, she knew that her experiences there were simply a symptom of the larger culture, and something that she had not yet been able to face. Johnson recognized that within her church "patriarchy is sacred; it is held to be the principle of organization by which a male God created and governs the world through other males like himself." She finally saw that it "is the masculine glue that holds the world together."[12]

11. Ulrich, "Pink *Dialogue* and Beyond," 14. For a discussion of the tensions surrounding the ERA and LDS feminism, see Colleen McDannell, *Sister Saints: Mormon Women since the End of Polygamy* (New York: Oxford University Press, 2018), 105–12.

12. Sonia Johnson, *From Housewife to Heretic: One Woman's Spiritual Awakening and Her Excommunication from the Mormon Church* (Garden City, NY: Anchor Books, 1983), 29, 94–95.

It was in her ward community that Johnson first learned about the ERA. Living in Virginia, she likely would have found out about it anyway. Virginia was one of the states that took some time to consider the amendment. First proposed to Congress by famed suffragist Alice Paul in 1923, the amendment came up yearly until Congress finally passed it in March 1972. The amendment then required ratification by thirty-eight states (or ¾ of all states) within seven years for it to become constitutional law. By the end of 1974, thirty-three states had ratified the amendment, but neither Virginia (Johnson's home state) nor Utah (the center of the church) had. Before Phyllis Schlafly mobilized conservative groups, including the LDS Church, in opposition to the ERA, the legislation was moving towards ratification.[13]

After 1973, when the ratification deadline was extended for nine years, only five more states ratified the ERA, while at the same time five states rescinded their ratification. In Utah the amendment was first defeated in 1973, but when there was an effort to reconsider, the church decided to speak out. Relief Society leaders like Belle Spafford and Barbara B. Smith were central to the institution's firm stance against the amendment. One of the first public statements heralding the institution's commitment to defeating the ERA came from Smith, the general president of the Relief Society, the women's auxiliary of the church. For Smith, the existence of the Relief Society was all the evidence necessary to show that God believed women were special and equal and vital to the inner workings of the church.[14] Speaking at the University of Utah LDS Religious Institute on December 13, 1974, Smith made the case that God had created two sexes intended to complement one another so that families could be sturdy and children well cared for.[15] Smith's speech, along with editorials in the news, shifted the weight of state legislators and church believers against the ERA.[16]

13. Neil J. Young, "'The ERA Is a Moral Issue': The Mormon Church, LDS Women, and the Defeat of the Equal Rights Amendment," *American Quarterly* 59 (2007): 626–27.

14. Martha S. Bradley-Evans, *Pedestals and Podiums: Utah Women, Religious Authority, and Equal Rights* (Salt Lake City: Signature Books, 2005), 96.

15. Lori Winder Stromberg, "LDS Position on the ERA," *Exponent II* 6 (Winter 1980).

16. O. Kendall White Jr., "Mormonism and the Equal Rights Amendment," *Journal of Church and State* 31, no. 2 (Spring 1989): 249–67.

The debates about the ERA had been happening for years when Johnson first heard about them. In her ward's Sacrament Meeting, her bishopric read a letter from the church hierarchy that declared the amendment both unnecessary and a threat to the family.[17] Johnson could not help but wonder why the church was opposing something "with a name as beautiful as the *Equal Rights Amendment*."[18] She learned about the church's opposition at the same time that she came to realize how important the ERA was to her own life and the lives of all women in the United States. She spent the next several months in a "state of shock," because she felt certain that what the leaders had read to her ward was not right or true. She believed she could be faithful to the church *and* to the ERA as a feminist cause. When they read that letter in her ward meeting, "The whole women's movement just fell on me. That letter railroaded me into feminism."[19]

Johnson saw that the teachings of the early nineteenth-century church and its doctrine were compatible with Mormon feminism. She made her own restoration argument of sorts. Where she saw support of women's activities and the independence of the Relief Society in early Mormonism, she believed the modern church had changed. In it she observed that "women are supported in word only, not in deed, a practice which confuses and blinds many church members."[20]

In addition to her sense that support of women had become hollow teaching rather than substantive practice, Johnson also noted that the church was moving toward preaching that the living prophet was infallible.[21] If those two strands came together without any push back, she believed that the outcome would be a church that claimed divine sanction for its social practices of restricting women's roles. Further, it would imply that if the prophet made any political

---

17. Karen De Witt, "The Pain of Being a Mormon Family," *New York Times*, November 27, 1979.

18. Johnson, *From Housewife to Heretic*, 102.

19. De Witt, "Pain of Being a Mormon Family."

20. Sonia Johnson, "The Church Was Once in the Forefront of the Women's Movement," in Brooks, Steenblik, and Wheelwright, eds., *Mormon Feminism*, 70.

21. Sonia Johnson, "Patriarchal Panic: Sexual Politics in the Mormon Church," in Brooks, Steenblik, and Wheelwright, eds., *Mormon Feminism*, 74.

statement, many in the church would take that to be a stamp of God's approval of the political stance.

During this period the church was facing a crisis of sorts, and Johnson became the face of that crisis and the shadow of its worst fears. She had butted up against the purity system of the institutional church. She was an example of a woman who had broken the familial purity structure by questioning the patriarchal order. Her story reflects the institutional anxiety around the second pillar of the purity system: a nuclear family in which everybody had their place. When Johnson challenged the familial purity of the church, she exposed the expectations for women in the system. They were to remain in the home and provide the labor for the upkeep of family, the basic unit of church culture. When women like Johnson wanted something else, those in power sometimes felt as though the entire edifice might crumble.

At the same time that Johnson was making her own transformation into feminism, the church was further developing its anti-ERA stance. This came on the tail of the correlation process that made the Relief Society no longer an independent organization, but an auxiliary organization under the direction of the priesthood. The Relief Society could not collect dues or engage in fundraising; its funding, planning, and activities would now come through and be overseen by its male counterparts.[22] The correlation process consolidated power in the hands of the male priesthood, affirming their roles as decision makers even while also making claims for a complementary gender system.[23]

Just as the church hierarchy stressed the importance of correlation to strengthening the family, it also emphasized the importance of the patriarchal order, the foundational concept of the second pillar of the purity system. Men were to lead and provide for the family with their priesthood authority and their careers, while women were to focus their attention on homemaking and child rearing. The father was to operate as the patriarch who would ensure the family's purity.

22. Bushman, "Mormon Feminism after 1970," 158.

23. Maureen Ursenbach Beecher, Janath Russell Cannon, and Jill Mulvay Derr, *Women of Covenant: The Story of Relief Society* (Salt Lake City: Deseret Book, 2010), 342. See also Robert Gottlieb and Peter Wiley, *American Saints: The Rise of Mormon Power* (San Diego: Harcourt Brace Jovanovich, Publishers, 1986), 195–99.

He was the institution's representative in the home. This power was embodied in the centralization of Family Home Evening, where the family would gather, pray, learn a religious lesson, and do activities together.[24] The identification of an evening that was set apart for the family and church activities demonstrated that the church was not just an institution people visited on Sunday, but an integral part of everyday family life.[25]

It was not until October 22, 1976, that the First Presidency issued its first public statement about the ERA. In it, the leadership made its own style of restoration argument: "From its beginnings, [the church] has affirmed the exalted role of woman in our society." Collapsing the past 150 years of changing stances on women, the hierarchy suggested that Joseph Smith had established the Relief Society to be a "companion body" to the priesthood and that it had continued in that same function throughout its existence, "strengthening motherhood and broadening women's learning and involvement in religious, compassionate, cultural, educational, and community pursuits."[26] Crafting the argument that would become central to the church's activism against the ERA, the First Presidency suggested that the ERA would harm the family and "even stifle many God-given feminine instincts." They asserted those instincts were rooted in fundamental and essential differences between men and women that were both divinely ordained and biologically given. The ERA, they argued, "does not recognize these differences."[27] The core logic went: men and women were fundamentally different, and those differences needed to be enshrined in the law, not collapsed by it.

That statement started the ball rolling and the ERA became the topic of many a speech by general authorities. For example, several anti-ERA organizations asked Boyd K. Packer to speak in Pocatello, Idaho. In his speech, which was later published in the church's *Ensign*

24. Bradley-Evans, *Pedestals and Podiums*, 111–13.

25. Bushman, "Mormon Feminism after 1970," 158. At the same time that these correlation changes were happening, the church also moved to restrict women's participation in church meetings by declaring that opening and closing prayers—the bookends of the weekly rituals—must be led by priesthood holders.

26. First Presidency Statement on the ERA, October 22, 1976.

27. Ibid.

magazine in 1977, Packer first attempted to depoliticize the issue by framing the church's concern as "basically moral and spiritual." Then Packer moved to re-package opposition to the ERA as being about purity. He told a story about a contagious disease he had once learned about in a health class. In the story, children came home one day and told their mother that a neighbor child had the chicken pox. One child in the neighborhood would catch the chicken pox and then another would catch it, and so on down the line. The frustrated mother decided "this could be resolved in another way" and so she called the neighbors: "I'm sending my children over.... They might just as well all get the chicken pox at once and then we'll be done with it.... I wouldn't even care if they ate off the same dishes."[28] Several days later, it seemed the plan had worked, all of her children had a fever and signs of infection.

"That afternoon word was sent to her that things had not gone well at the neighbors," Packer warned. "It was not chicken pox at all ... it was smallpox. That night the neighbor youngster died."[29] What was the moral of this story and how did it tie to the church's stance on the ERA? "How often it is that our solutions become problems," he cautioned. Big government represented in new legislation meant the loss of individuality and the ability to act according to personal conscience.

The work to cure the chicken pox (meaning women's lower status in society) "may once again see us exposed, dangerously exposed, to a virulent and deadly smallpox" (meaning the confusion of gender identities and the downfall of the patriarchal family).[30] "A man," Packer argued, "needs to feel protective, and yes, dominant, if you will, in leading his family." On the opposite end of the spectrum, "A woman needs to feel protected, in the bearing of children and the nurturing of them." The feminist movement was not going to end up looking out for the best interest of women, he preached; the church and its anti-ERA activism would. It would protect believers from "a smallpox of a most lethal kind."[31] The answer to women's lesser status

28. Boyd K. Packer, "The Equal Rights Amendment," *Ensign*, March 1977.
29. Ibid.
30. Ibid.
31. Ibid.

was the "strength and stability of the American home in the spiritual and moral and emotional health of families."

Packer counseled against making a hasty diagnosis of the problem because doing so could further weaken the family. Instead, he claimed that he wanted to protect "the rights of a woman to be a woman, a feminine, female woman; a wife and a mother." And in a complementary fashion, he was for "protecting the rights of a man to be a man, a masculine, male man; a husband and a father."[32] By doing so he argued that children would be best protected and nurtured.

As he laid out his argument, Packer participated in what theorist Lee Edelman has called a heterosexual reproductive futurism that centers the "Child" as the goad and goal for the future: "That figural Child alone embodies the citizen as an ideal, entitled to claim full rights to its future share in the nation's good, though always at the cost of limiting the rights 'real' citizens are allowed."[33] Further, Edelman describes "the pervasive invocation of the Child as the emblem of futurity's unquestioned value."[34] This rhetorical process allows for the demand of a heterosexual construction of society and its understandings of time. It operates by "enacting a logic of repetition that fixes identity through identification with the future of the social order."[35] Thus Packer's invocation of the health of the future Child served the function of reifying the nuclear family as the proper structure to oversee the welfare of society.

It certainly was not just the men in the church who were anti-ERA. Like Relief Society President Barbara B. Smith, many faithful women saw the value of a complementary gender system and felt feminism negatively critiqued their way of life. In 1977, pro-ERA advocates organized conferences around the country and in other nations to celebrate what the United Nations called the International Women's Year. The women of Utah were no different. In Salt Lake City the organizers expected 3,000–4,000 attendees. They got 13,000. It was the largest state conference in the country. Church officials, including Relief Society leadership, had spread the word

32. Ibid.

33. Lee Edelman, *No Future: Queer Theory and the Death Drive* (Durham, NC: Duke University Press, 2004), 11.

34. Ibid, 3–4.

35. Ibid, 26.

that each ward should recruit at least ten women to attend and vote against proposals tied to the ERA. Because of the issuance of this charge, anti-ERA Latter-day Saint women flooded the conference and voted down the resolutions offered by the conference organizers, even those that had nothing to do with the ERA.[36]

In these years, LDS women became some of the most ferocious anti-ERA activists. Opposition to the ERA was a means for them to perform their faith and obedience to the all-male hierarchy. They could prove their piety and also demonstrate their commitment to the complementary gender system.[37] One such anti-ERA leader was Elaine Cannon, general president of the Young Women's auxiliary. In an October 1978 general conference speech, Cannon argued that there was a great "joy of being a woman" because women were helping to bring the "fulness of time." She offered several wives of general authorities as models of womanhood: "They live close to the Lord. They follow the Prophet implicitly. They contribute to society meaningfully, and in turn they have endured difficult circumstances which bring beauty into life."[38] Cannon insisted that these women modeled femininity, in part, by hailing the authority of the all-male hierarchy, especially the prophet, Spencer W. Kimball. She noted that he was speaking to the women that same evening and that "it is as if the Lord Jesus Christ himself were addressing us sisters."[39] Here Cannon conflated femininity with obedience to the authority of the institutional structure.

In order to illustrate the point, Cannon told a story about waiting for the elevator in the lobby of the Church Office Building a few years earlier. When the elevator arrived, she moved out of the way for some security officers only later to see that it was President Kimball himself getting on the elevator. When he turned around and saw her, he said, "Aren't you going to get on?" She was unsure about whether

36. Gottlieb and Wiley, *America's Saints*, 202; Young, "ERA is a Moral Issue," 623–44; Lori Motzkus Wilkinson, "Buttons, Banners, and Pie: Mormon Women's Grassroots Movements: 'Equality Yes, ERA No' versus 'Another Mormon for the ERA,'" *Journal of Mormon History* 44, no. 4 (October 2018): 112–37; J. B. Haws, *The Mormon Image in the American Mind: Fifty Years of Public Perception* (New York: Oxford University Press, 2013), 91.

37. Young, "ERA is a Moral Issue," 624–25.

38. Elaine Cannon, "If We Want to Go Up, We Have to Get On," *Ensign*, November 1978.

39. Ibid.

she should get on the elevator with the prophet. He asked, "Aren't you going up?" and she said "Yes." He replied "Well, tell me, how do you intend to get there?" and then insisted she "come along."[40] Here again Cannon suggested that women needed to "get on" to "go up," meaning that their own spiritual well-being required them to get on board with the church hierarchy and especially the prophet if they wanted spiritual progress: "He is our leader, in all the world of would-be leaders, who can guide us back to the presence of God."[41]

"[W]hat is our part as women in all of this?" Cannon asked her listeners. First, the role of mother. "The girl is the future mother of the man." Second, the role of wife. "The woman is companion to the priesthood." Women were made to influence society and men for good, Cannon claimed, and to work toward the will and desires of God, not their own. "When the prophet speaks, sisters, the debate is over," Cannon declared, suggesting that discussions surrounding the ERA had already been settled. Their role as women was to be obedient and to help others to be obedient as well. In this way Cannon argued that the role of women was to be the gatekeepers and laborers of the institution's purity system. By policing their homes and keeping their place within it, they would ensure the future of church and society.

In these official statements and public speeches, the church was much like the leaders of the Religious Right with whom they had started to identify and who would eventually help support the strategy of affirming their status as *truly American.* Evangelical church leaders helped model how to turn the combination of theological beliefs and social commitments into partisan politics. It was a practice for which they had already been training for decades. It was in the middle decades of the twentieth century that theologically conservative Protestants came to see the GOP as a party that supported their understanding of a moral society while it also fought communism. In the 1960s and '70s, conservative Protestants began to single out sympathetic politicians, making alliances and merging their own goals with the platform of the party.[42]

40. Ibid.

41. Ibid; McDannell, *Sister Saints,* 105.

42. Daniel K. Williams, *God's Own Party: The Making of the Christian Right* (New York: Oxford University Press, 2010), 1–3.

Feminism in the 1960s and '70s helped solidify the commitment of conservative Christian believers, even if it had not yet brought them to see their common cause. Conservative Christians believed in a strong nuclear family with clearly gendered roles as the foundation that had withstood the communist threat.[43] The movement in the 1960s to become a more diverse and more egalitarian nation in terms of ethnicity, immigration, sexuality, and gender felt like it was moving too quickly, changing in directions that seemed secular and dangerous.[44] Part of the conservative Christian construction of the family emphasized patriarchy, a patriarchy that was reflected in the divine realm—a male God who wanted to support the male oversight of the family and society.[45]

From the perspective of conservative Christians, the family was coming apart at the seams. Between 1965 and 1976, the divorce rate doubled. More women were giving birth out of wedlock while at the same time the number of abortions was increasing.[46] The 1973 Supreme Court decision in Roe v. Wade, which forced many states to relax their abortion laws, made it feel as though the highest levels of government were helping to undermine the role of mother in society.[47]

At the same time the 1972 Title IX legislation made it seem as if the complementary gender system the Religious Right embraced was going to collapse with both Congress and institutions of higher education actively chipping away at the foundations of society. Those same colleges and universities—which religious conservatives believed were becoming increasingly secular—were starting to get rid of curfews and single-gender housing. While they felt the top governmental bodies were changing the very nature of gender and family in the country, churches on the right saw, too, that many of the activists who were pro-ERA were the same people who supported abortion rights, broad-scale women's rights, and gay and

43. Matthew Avery Sutton, *Jerry Falwell and the Rise of the Religious Right* (Boston: Bedford/St. Martin's, 2013), 14–17.

44. Andrew Hartman, *A War for the Soul of America: a History of the Culture Wars* (Chicago: University of Chicago Press, 2015), 2–6.

45. Kristin Kobes Du Mez, *Jesus and John Wayne: How White Evangelicals Corrupted a Faith and Fractured a Nation* (New York: Liveright Publishing Corporation, 2021), 272.

46. Williams, *God's Own Party*, 106–7.

47. Hartman, *A War for the Soul of America*, 92–93.

lesbian rights.[48] Public discussions of civil rights for marginalized groups seemed to evidence that things were going to change, and that conservative Christians were going to be pushed out of the centers of power.

It was in 1979 that Baptist pastor and conservative activist Jerry Falwell launched the Moral Majority. The alliance of evangelicals, Catholics, and Latter-day Saints, was hard won. Prior to the 1980s, even though they may have shared some common cause with conservative evangelicals and Catholics, especially surrounding images of the ideal family and the "breakdown" of Christian values in the face of what they believed was a growing secularism, theological differences kept Latter-day Saints from being included with these groups. In particular, the divisions between Latter-day Saints and evangelical Christians, who often portrayed the LDS Church as a dangerous cult posing as Christianity, were strained and contentious throughout the early and middle decades of the twentieth century. It was not until Jerry Falwell acknowledged that the three groups—Catholics, evangelicals, and Latter-day Saints—would have to join forces to increase their political power, that religious leaders began to downplay their real theological difference in hopes of succeeding politically. All three groups saw Ronald Reagan's 1980 presidential campaign as a chance to help the nation change its course and believed that his presidency would grant them moral oversight of the country.[49] These coalitions continued to focus their energies on reinforcing power and hierarchies in the public realm just as they sought to foster hierarchies of power in the private realm.

---

48. Beecher, Cannon, and Derr, *Women of the Covenant*, 368. See also, Hartman, *A War for the Soul of America*, 95, 135. Today we use the LGBTQ+ designation to name and encapsulate the diversity in the LGBTQ+ community. At the time, though, the focus was primarily on lesbian and gay rights.

49. Neil J. Young, *We Gather Together: The Religious Right and the Problem of Interfaith Politics* (New York: Oxford University Press, 2016), 2–7, 68, 174–77. See also, Haws, *Mormon Image*, 97–101. Megan Goodwin also offers an important corrective to many narratives of the right by noting that "Catholic sexual morality directly informs the New Christian Right's weaponization of concepts like 'the family' and 'normal sex.'" See Goodwin, *Abusing Religion: Literary Persecution, Sex Scandals, and American Minority Religions* (New Brunswick, NJ: Rutgers University Press, 2020), 8–25. Kristin Kobes Du Mez has added that Reagan "didn't just speak the language of the Right, he looked the part." He was a manly man who could operate as an image of patriarchal power. See Du Mez, *Jesus and John Wayne*, 101–4.

Perhaps it was the church's internal struggle over the ERA that best embodies its encounter with feminist ideals in the 1970s and '80s. During the ERA years the LDS Church promoted anti-ERA politicians and worked to raise money for candidates. In addition, the institution joined in coalitions with other anti-ERA organizations. When church members worked for these organizations they sometimes portrayed themselves as interested citizens rather than Latter-day Saints being driven by their faith. The media picked up on this and some coverage of the church's anti-ERA activism portrayed the institution in a negative light because of its under-the-radar approach to activism.[50]

Like their evangelical counterparts on the Right, the church chose to frame the ERA not as a political issue, but as a moral one. In fact, the church's official statement in March 1980 said just that in its title: "The Church and the Proposed Equal Rights Amendment: A Moral Issue." The statement appeared as an insert to the *Ensign*. Quoting a September 1962 statement by the First Presidency, the document read: "Strictly political matters should be left in the field of politics where they belong. However, on moral issues, the Church and its members take a positive stand." Thus the church hierarchy saw its political action against the ERA as defending the morality of the church that they knew to be divinely ordained. Further, they explained that, "Only the First Presidency and the Twelve can declare a particular issue to be a moral issue worthy of full institutional involvement."[51]

In framing the ERA as a moral issue, the church created a platform on which it could officially make arguments about the amendment while still maintaining that it was a politically neutral institution. The church also framed the ERA as being about the family, and it could claim a vested interest in the family precisely because of the theology of the Plan of Salvation. This, too, aligned it with its evangelical counterparts. The argument went something

50. "While describing the LDS Church's crusade as subterranean may not entirely capture its essence," historian Martha Bradley-Evans writes, "it was nevertheless a campaign functioning just beneath the horizon of visibility and was primarily a grass-roots effort by church members." See Bradley-Evans, *Pedestals and Podiums*, 285–89. Haws, *Mormon Image*, 94–95.

51. "The Church and the Proposed Equal Rights Amendment: A Moral Issue," *Ensign*, March 1980.

like this: The ERA would make it difficult for women to be mothers because it would force them into the workforce and into the military. When women stopped acting like women, they were not in line with their own nature and would cause men to quit taking on the roles and responsibilities that were theirs: protecting and providing for the family. As women refused their prescribed role as mothers and nurturers, they would also feel more comfortable having abortions.[52]

Then, if complementarism collapsed, men might turn to relationships outside of marriage, including adultery and even same-sex attraction. Divorce might follow and both the immediate and temporal needs of children would not be met nor would their spiritual needs. In addition, the hierarchy argued that the ERA could force states to recognize gay marriages and that children brought into the home might be raised by gay parents.[53] And so the church set up a framework for arguing that the issue of same-sex sexuality was simply an outgrowth of its stance on gender roles, marriage, and family. It claimed that there were those in the United States who sought "a unisex society" and "an increase in the practice of homosexual and lesbian activities, and other concepts which could alter the natural, God-given relationship of men and women."[54]

The 1980 statement argued that the ERA was a moral issue because "women will be treated less favorably in many fundamental regards." The "family unit—in the Mormon sense of a sacred and eternal relation—will be denigrated, cause great and substantial damage to not only the Church but also the nation."[55] The family needed to be kept together—and the answer was to defeat the ERA. In order to support the image of the ideal family, the church upheld particular women as the ideal: homemakers, mothers, and especially supporters of priesthood holders. For this reason, it was often general authorities' wives and other female relatives who were lifted up as models of womanhood.[56] The model was always about serving a

52. Ibid.

53. Ibid.

54. Ibid.

55. Ibid. In this portion the church quoted a letter from Keith Petty, a California attorney.

56. Claudia L. Bushman, *Contemporary Mormonism: Latter-day Saints in Modern America* (Westport, CT: Praeger, 2006), 114.

supportive role to priesthood-holding men, maintaining the purity of the home and church.

Finally, in the statement the church hierarchy indicated that it may be the case that individual church members might believe that they felt a spiritual guidance to espouse a political position other than the one taught by the First Presidency. If that were the case, it would not be considered apostasy. But the expectation was that such individuals would keep their thoughts to themselves: "[W]e could not conceive of a man publishing those differences of opinion, and seeking by arguments, sophistry and special pleading to enforce upon the people to produce division and strife, and to place the acts and counsels of the authorities of the Church, if possible, in a wrong light."[57]

Sonia Johnson was going to be in trouble. While her church family was speaking out on behalf of the church's official anti-ERA stance, she was having a crisis of conscience. Her experiences told her that the ERA was exactly what she and other women needed and that she should become an activist for the cause. As she continued in her thinking, she read Mary Daly, a theologian who had been raised and educated in the Catholic tradition and had come to critique it as a patriarchal church. Daly famously said, "If God is male, then the male is God." And that statement spoke to a truth that Johnson knew well.

She began to see and understand the importance of Heavenly Mother in the Latter-day Saint tradition. She came to understand that, "With Mother on her throne as a model for me in heaven, I felt wonderful...knowing that femaleness is as divine, as desirable, as powerful as maleness."[58] With the understanding that both Daly and other feminist Christian (and post-Christian) theologians had offered, Johnson realized that the way communities imagined the divine realm shaped and structured the hierarchies of the social realm. She came to believe that the feminine divine was important not only to her own faith, but also the faith of every religious person.

As she continued to study the ERA and the broader feminist movement, Johnson came to realize its importance to her life. This

57. Here they quoted George Q. Cannon writing in the Deseret News in 1869. "Church and Proposed Equal Rights Amendment."

58. Johnson, *From Housewife to Heretic*, 119.

was true in her family life where she shared responsibility for nurturing and providing for her children with her husband. It was also true in her public life. She committed herself to the movement broadly and also to her work with Mormons for the ERA (MERA), a group founded in Washington, DC, three years after the Utah legislature did not ratify the amendment. As a spokesperson for the group, Johnson testified before a senate subcommittee in 1978 on behalf of the move to extend the deadline for ratification to 1982. In her discussion she attempted to assuage concerns that Latter-day Saint and other Christian leaders might have. She insisted that "the ERA does not threaten the family unit," while at the same time suggesting that it may "encourage more conscious personal definitions of the shared responsibilities and commitments undertaken at the time of marriage."[59] She added that legal equality would ensure greater stability as the partners in the marriage would be equal in the eyes of the law and therefore more easily partners in everything.

In that subcommittee meeting, Johnson went toe-to-toe with Utah senator Orrin Hatch. The two were on fire, each representing their shared faith in front of a national audience. Each one was confident; both had something to prove. As Johnson testified, Hatch became increasingly uncomfortable. In her journal she recalled that Hatch said, "It's implied by your testimony that you're more intelligent than other Mormon women, and that if they were all as intelligent as you, they would all support the Equal Rights Amendment.' And then he banged his fist on the table in angry emphasis and shouted, 'Now that's an insult to my wife.'"[60] While Hatch's sense of personal insult may have been tied to a defensiveness about his faith community and its public persona, it was also tied to an important division: many Latter-day Saint women simply did not support the ERA. While the extension passed, the debate between Johnson and Hatch made public the internal divisions in the LDS community over the issue.[61]

Johnson and the members of MERA continued to promote their

59. Quoted in Bradley-Evans, *Pedestals and Podiums*, 335.
60. Johnson, *From Housewife to Heretic*, 135.
61. McDannell, *Sister Saints*, 106.

cause even as they were accused of improper womanhood and discipleship. Under the leadership of Johnson, Hazel Davis Rigby, Maida Rust Withers and Teddie Wood, the group that had begun informally in 1978 became an official nonprofit organization in 1980.[62] MERA was one small part of a broad movement in support of the amendment and their members' reasons for participation varied.[63] In the fall of 1979, MERA hired planes to fly banners over Washington, DC, during the church's area conference and Salt Lake City during general conference. The banners read "Mother in Heaven loves Mormons for ERA."[64] For the church hierarchy, of course, this would be seen as doubly heretical: the banners were calling upon a theology of Heavenly Mother (who was rarely discussed) to argue against a political view embraced and taught by the institutional church. In addition to making public arguments that were rooted in Latter-day Saint theology, MERA also sought support for its position within Latter-day Saint history. Here they made their own type of restoration argument, seeing in Joseph Smith an early proponent of women's rights.[65]

Sonia Johnson and MERA were not alone. There were other people in the church who were troubled by its anti-ERA stance. In March 1979, members of the Alice Louise Reynolds Forum, a group of feminists in Provo, Utah, wrote to President Spencer Kimball of their concerns:

> Dear President Kimball: We speak for a sizeable minority of LDS women whose pain is so acute that they must try to be heard. Does the First Presidency really know of our plight? We cannot believe that anyone deliberately seeks to destroy us; nevertheless that is the signal we are receiving. We feel that we are the victims of a deliberate and punishing ultra-conservative squeeze to force us out of fellowship.... We desperately need to know whether, after serious consideration, soul-searching, and prayer, you indeed and in fact find us unworthy, a minority open to attack, and ultimately expendable. If not can the word get out that Mormon feminists are not to be subjected to intimidations, rejection for Church assignments, loss of employment, and

62. Bradley-Evans, *Pedestals and Podiums*, 332.
63. Ibid, 89.
64. Johnson, *From Housewife to Heretic*, 158.
65. Bradley-Evans, *Pedestals and Podiums*, 1–3.

> psychological excommunication? Every difference of opinion or sincere question should not be answered with a threatening indictment of one's testimony. We are women who love the Lord, the Gospel, and the Church; we have served, tithed, and raised righteous children in Zion. We plead for the opportunity to continue to do so in an atmosphere of respect and justice. For decades we have been part of the solution, whatever the need has been; we are saddened to be now considered part of the problem.[66]

These women, too, felt the sting of the church's new political stances, a sting that told them they were "unworthy" and "expendable."

And it was not just the ERA that made them feel the church was not ready for Mormon feminism. On August 19, 1979, a woman named Ann Kenney was called to serve as Sunday School president in the University of Utah's Second Stake. When her stake president initially spoke with her about the role, Kenney's response was to laugh because she thought he was joking. She knew that asking a woman to take on that role was an unusual choice. He assured her that it was no joke "and that he had been strongly impressed to ask her to the position."[67] Kenney's first task was to find two counselors, which she promptly did, selecting two women to accompany her. On September 24, 1979, just one month later, she was "released" from the presidency, meaning that her services in that role were no longer needed. "The official statement was that in areas where there were worthy priesthood holders available, they should serve in the Sunday School," she recalled. Months later, the church issued a priesthood bulletin that included a "reminder" of the church's position that women should not be called as Sunday School presidents.[68] For those paying attention, this seemed like a dangerous precedent. What was once simply an unwritten tradition had become institutionalized policy in the blink of an eye. The institution was ensuring that women's roles would continue to be circumscribed.

These issues within the church only provided greater motivation for Sonia Johnson. As she worked, Johnson observed that "the

66. Qtd in Joanna Brooks, "Mormon Feminism: The Next Forty Years," *Dialogue: A Journal of Mormon Thought* 47, no. 4 (Winter 2014): 2–3.

67. "Church Tradition Now a Policy" *Sunstone* 10 (February 1985): 32.

68. Ibid, 34.

church belongs to its hierarchy, which is men in power. Those outside the hierarchy, and especially women, are at best only renters and at worst squatters in religious territory."[69] Johnson, who had earned both a Master of Arts and an EdD from Rutgers College, knew that Mormonism was not the only tradition with patriarchy in its structures. Women were squatters everywhere. And so perhaps it was no surprise that her testimony before the Senate (or the "Hatch debacle" in Johnson's terms) led to her first official meeting with her bishop, Jeff Willis.[70] While she assured Willis that she would not teach or speak about Heavenly Mother in public and that her private beliefs were just that, Willis remained concerned. Later he reported to her that Gordon B. Hinckley "had advised him to warn me about my activities." Willis ominously cautioned Johnson: "If they tell me to excommunicate you, Sonia, you know I'll have to do it."[71]

At another meeting with Willis on November 17, 1979, they discussed her now foregone disciplinary council. In her notes from that meeting, Johnson wrote that the charges against her were "evil speaking of the Lord's anointed; the law of consecration; [and] your general attitude and expression."[72] In addition to not acting in an obedient manner and speaking against those with authority in the church, Johnson was told that she was not using her gifts well—she needed to offer them to the work of the church, not to politics. As they continued to talk, Johnson asked Willis who her accuser was, he told her that he was. When she asked who her judge was, he told her that he was. She recalled telling him, "For heaven's sake, Jeff, I've been an American too long to feel comfortable with that." In response he said, "Don't worry, Sonia ... I will receive the correct decision through inspiration from our Heavenly Father."[73]

As her disciplinary council approached, Johnson was anxious about what would happen. She knew the likely outcome, but that did not make it any easier. When the bishop told her that she was not to talk to the press about her council because it was a "private, sacred matter," she responded: "This may be a private, sacred matter

69. Johnson, *From Housewife to Heretic*, 160.
70. Ibid, 240.
71. Ibid, 247.
72. Ibid, 279.
73. Ibid.

to you, but it is *my* trial and to me it is neither private nor sacred." For her the council was solely about the fact that she had taken a different political stance than the church. It had nothing to do with her faith, which made it a "public, political matter."[74]

But Johnson had already broken the insular code of promising not to air her dirty laundry to outsiders. She knew full well that the church did not want attention called to what was happening. Even observers could see that publicity would be a problem. Historian Leonard Arrington wrote in his journal: "The Church cannot gain from this entire incident. If the bishop should excommunicate or discipline her, she will become a martyr among pro-ERA women, both Mormon and non-Mormon.... On the other hand, if the bishop should not excommunicate her or discipline her, Sonia herself will be the first to say that she has been justified all along in her activities."[75] Arrington pinpointed the crux of the Johnson problem for the church. The institution was in a double bind and any decision would make for negative results.

In the time between her council and hearing the outcome that she had been excommunicated, Johnson wanted to go to church one more time to bear her testimony—and it just so happened to be fast and testimony Sunday, a monthly meeting where speakers and topics are not assigned, but church members are invited to stand and share their testimony with their congregation. On that Sunday, Johnson "felt a great desire to speak one last time as a Mormon to other Mormons," and to tell them "how much they had meant to me."[76] But as she tried to offer her testimony, others in the community worked to ensure that she could not. They filled in ahead of her. And one man even stood up in front of her and then offered a "filibuster"-style testimony running out time so that she was not able to speak one last time as one Mormon to others.

Looking back on her excommunication, Johnson explained that many people in the Latter-day Saint community had to do gymnastics in order to narrate her case, so that they could "keep church

74. Ibid, 300.
75. LJIA, December 3, 1979.
76. Johnson, *From Housewife to Heretic*, 347.

leaders perfect and infallible."[77] When she later appeared on the Phil Donahue show on December 13, 1979, and even after, Johnson noticed that church members speaking publicly about her case often intimated that they had special, secret "insider" information that no one else had access to. In so doing, they could suggest that her excommunication was actually for other and much worse reasons, without ever providing any evidence for the claim. Eventually, she realized that the Latter-day Saint community would not offer her exoneration, or a welcome back for that matter, but she also realized that she could endure "because I exonerate myself."[78]

For a year after her excommunication, Sonia Johnson continued to attend her local ward meetings because she still identified as a Mormon. She wanted her community to see that she had not chosen excommunication, that what had happened was not right. She wanted them to know that she was appealing the excommunication and that she still wanted to be a member of their tribe. "The Mormons are my people and I am theirs," she recalled, "whether we like it or not, whether we are comfortable with one another or not."[79] Even as she imagined an expansive notion of community that would encompass both her own family and her fellow ward members, Johnson also understood she attended because she had a rebellious streak. In addition to sending the message that she was still a part of the community and still maintained her faith, she also wanted "to alert Mormons that the church is sitting on a time bomb labeled *women*."[80]

While Johnson may well have made peace with her own excommunication, the event signaled to anyone in the church with feminist leanings that they had better toe the line. Their work would be monitored and questioned. The institution had expectations of its female members, and public denunciation of its decisions was not going to end well for individual believers. A woman's role was in the home, as laborers on behalf of the institution's purity system. In the 1980s, even as the dream of passing the ERA died, publications continued to appear, if only at a trickle, on Mormon women's history

77. Ibid, 352.
78. Ibid, 353–60.
79. Ibid, 391.
80. Ibid, 393.

and considerations about the place of women and the feminine in Latter-day Saint cosmology. Those who wrote and published knew the dangers and yet continued to doggedly pursue their questions even as Johnson's excommunication haunted their every move.

Feminism at BYU

Johnson's experience gave Latter-day Saint women a clear map of what not to do. Any woman who upset the familial pillar of the purity system would lose her good standing—and perhaps membership—in the church. Feminists learned this lesson again and again, particularly at Brigham Young University, the church's flagship institution. It was often on college campuses that debates swirling in the larger culture played out. BYU was no different and served as a flashpoint for all of the broader institutional and cultural concerns about feminism. Dallin H. Oaks oversaw BYU as president from 1971 to 1980, a time roughly paralleling the infancy of modern Latter-day Saint feminism and the legislative blossoming of feminism on the national scene. While certain aspects of the campus culture offered opportunities for women, Oaks was not interested in having feminism, which he saw as a foreign and unwelcome import to campus, shape the community. He was especially concerned about how legislation might affect the university. For this reason, he put together an ad hoc committee on the Status of Women, chaired by Professor Margaret Hoopes, in order to ensure that he was made aware of and could speak to changes in the broader culture.

While Oaks was fretting about feminist inroads, there were feminist faculty members who worked hard to ensure that the strides made on campus did not devolve out of a reactionary climate to broader cultural change.[81] These faculty worked hard not only because they were passionate about the issues, but also because they understood Oaks's concern about legislative changes.[82] He was likely to frown upon any movement toward women's equality that did not appear indigenous to the campus and church culture.

In 1975 Oaks issued an official "statement on the education of

81. Bryan Waterman and Brian Kagel, *The Lord's University: Freedom and Authority at BYU* (Salt Lake City: Signature Books, 1998), 41–42.

82. Ibid, 42.

women at Brigham Young University" before campus community members at his BYU President's assembly. In his talk he explained that, "Our young women at Brigham Young University properly aspire to and prepare themselves for the experiences and blessings of motherhood, which is their highest calling and opportunity for service."[83] While the church had often emphasized motherhood as a goal for women, Oaks argued that education was central to women's lives both during and after motherhood: "Our young women should in all events aspire to and prepare themselves for the most effective use of their talents, first in the family, for that is the number one priority for male and female, but also in the wider world of service and accomplishment."[84]

In addition to encouraging women to see their nurturing tendencies extending beyond the home and toward society more broadly, Oaks also quoted Harold B. Lee's address to the Relief Society general meeting in October 1964: "When you teach a boy, you are just teaching another individual, but when you teach a woman or a girl, you are teaching a whole family."[85] Quoting Lee functioned to make a point about women's roles, but also to help ensure a sense of tradition in the church's teaching on women just as ideas about femininity and women's roles were being called into question. This is what we have consistently taught, he suggested, it is the way of the Restoration.

Oaks certainly was not keeping his ideas about the women's movement and feminist causes to himself or even within the confines of the campus. In 1975 he testified in congressional hearings against Title IX and explained BYU's official opposition to it. He was concerned that the proposed bill would harm athletics and collapse the gender complementarity system at the heart of so many of BYU's policies, particularly gender-segregated housing. In addition, and at the behest of Ezra Taft Benson, he hosted well-known anti-feminist Phyllis Schlafly on campus where she spoke against the ERA.

83. Dallin Harris Oaks, "Statement on the Education of Women at Brigham Young University," made at BYU President's assembly, September 9, 1975. Copy available in Church History Library, Salt Lake City, Utah, under call number M243.8 O11s 1975.

84. Ibid.

85. Ibid.

President Oaks also helped enshrine the Honor Code as a central aspect of the institution's identity. When it was first established in the 1950s, the Honor Code focused on academic issues and concerns, but in the 1960s, it grew under the oversight of Oaks's predecessor, Ernest L. Wilkinson, to include much more, especially how students acted and dressed. During Oaks's tenure, under the perceived challenge of the "unisex threat," the school began to search out and expel gay students, going to such lengths as having undercover officers pose as gay students and taking down license plates at gay bars.[86]

Even after Oaks returned to the court system as a Utah Supreme Court Justice and Jeffrey R. Holland took over as president of BYU in 1980, feminism was still not particularly welcomed on campus. Throughout that decade, church leaders continued to preach that women's primary calling was motherhood, and that calling was tied to the role of nurturing. In April 1990, Apostle Gordon B. Hinckley told a conference on working women that young women should pursue education and training, but that they should primarily seek to take care of children at home and halt "a tragic and widespread breakdown in family life."[87] Placing the responsibility for the preservation or breakdown of the nation on the backs of women, Hinckley went on to detail the problems facing the nation: abuse of children, abandonment of wives, and crimes against women. "It is my opinion that the very situation of an ever-increasing number of mothers out of the home and in the workplace is the root cause of many of the problems of delinquency, drugs, and gangs, both male and female."[88] Echoing the Religious Right and Republican platforms, Hinckley articulated the heart of the problem: women were stepping out of their place.

In 1989, Rex E. Lee, who had served as a legal advisor to the church on its stance on the ERA, became president of BYU, where he served until 1995. That same year, a feminist group named VOICE began on BYU's campus after a discussion about Carol Gilligan's *In a Different Voice*.[89] One of the group's advisors described its members

86. Waterman and Kagel, *Lord's University*, 125, 161–62.

87. Qtd. in "Journalist Ellerbee and President Hinckley Differ," *Sunstone* 14 (April 1990): 54.

88. Ibid.

89. This group formed out of what had previously been called the Committee to Promote the Status of Women. Waterman and Kagel, *Lord's University*, 59.

as being "so insistent on being treated fairly and not at all shy at demanding that. And so there was just some really good activism. And there was so much joy in it. Everybody was so excited to have found one another."[90]

Even as they experienced the joy of discovering community, they faced a campus culture pushing back at every turn because of a "really fierce conservative backlash." Part of this pushback was from a group of students drawn to Rush Limbaugh, a politically conservative radio talk show host, who called themselves "dittoheads." They would attend VOICE meetings with the goal of being disruptive and rude.[91] Much like feminist student organizations at colleges and universities all over the country, VOICE's primary activities centered around conversations about issues facing women. Topics advertised in flyers about regular meetings in the late 1980s and early 1990s included body image, the representation of women in advertising, home-making, women and work, and biology versus cultural conditioning. The group also invited speakers to campus. In 1992, those speakers included Lavina Fielding Anderson, Maxine Hanks, and Paul Toscano.[92] In addition, VOICE studied the political, economic, and social conditions facing women in cultures all over the world.[93] They were an educational group, a support group, and an activist group all rolled into one.

As feminists struggled to push forward their goals on BYU's campus, their activism inspired small steps that represented the work of countless faculty and students, including VOICE members. One result of all of this behind-the-scenes labor appeared in March 1991 when BYU issued its first sexual harassment policy, stating "BYU is committed to assuring an environment for all employees and students where the dignity of each individual is recognized and respected."[94] This came on the heels of the 1991 Violence Against Women Act which helped to bring the issue of gender-based

90. Cecilia Konchar Farr, oral history with author, February 7, 2023.

91. Konchar Farr, oral history with author. Tomi-Ann Roberts (a professor in the Psychology department) and Cecilia Konchar Farr (in the English department) were the co-advisors to the group during this time. This description is Farr's.

92. Waterman and Kagel, *Lord's University*, 59.

93. VOICE documents, Signature Books Collection.

94. BYU Sexual Harassment Policy, March 1, 1991. Signature Books Collection.

violence more centrally into the public eye. While the institution put the words to paper in an official capacity, that did not mean that women's safety on campus was guaranteed. Members of VOICE understood that all too well.

Their focus in late 1991 came to center on women's safety in the context of rape culture on BYU's campus, an issue that, when brought to light, upset many. People imagined BYU as immune in many ways to the issues facing the larger culture, as a space set apart because of its religious mission. So to accept that rape happened on campus was to accept that the issues facing the world existed at BYU as well. The event that inspired VOICE to greater action was an attack on a female student walking on the campus's Maeser Hill at 9:20 in the morning. She was struck on the head several times (which required stitches) but eventually was able to fend off her attacker. "There is a reason they call it 'rape hill,'" said Mary Ellen Robertson, a member of VOICE.[95] VOICE acted by first organizing a rally in the tradition of "Take Back the Night," a vigil and protest happening on college campuses around the country. Founded in the late 1970s, Take Back the Night sought to point out the issue of sexual assault on college campuses and push to make campuses safer by raising awareness and forcing institutions to reckon with what was happening in their spaces.

Wanting to do even more, VOICE put up flyers all over campus declaring a curfew for all male students. "NOTICE," it read, "Due to the increase in violence against women on BYU campus, a new curfew has been instated. Beginning Wednesday, November 20, men will no longer be allowed to walk alone or in all-male groups from 10 p.m. until 6 a.m." Meant to highlight the fact that men move through spaces without having to think about their safety but that women always do, the notice went on to say, "Those men who must travel on or through campus during curfew hours must be accompanied by two women in order to demonstrate that they are not threatening."[96] In addition to highlighting men's relative safety in public spaces, the flyer also emphasized the fact that women often

95. Dallas Scholes, "Y. 'Curfew' for Men Aims to Curb Attacks on Women," *Deseret News*, November 20, 1991.

96. VOICE flyer, Signature Books Collection.

need to travel in packs in order to ensure their safety, especially on Maeser Hill. A member of VOICE explained, "We wanted to shock the males on campus and make them realize how it feels to have their freedom restricted."[97]

"If the curfew proposal increases awareness of the problem, then it has served its purpose," the director of Public Relations for BYU said, yet the administration would not actually put the curfew into practice "because it is impractical and infringes on the rights of students as well as being impossible to enforce."[98] This PR argument was interesting precisely because BYU had institutional policies about gendered curfews in the past. As Carolyn G. Owen brought up in a letter to the editor of *The Daily Herald*, "When I was a freshman at BYU in the early 1960's, women living in campus housing were required to observe a 10:30 p.m. curfew.... There was no corresponding curfew for men."[99] Owen noted that no one had suggested that those limitations on women's behavior had infringed on the rights of women, ending, "Hell hath no fury like a man curfewed."[100]

While Owen found the curfew reasonable and understood that the flyer was trying to make a point rather than change policy, campus and local newspapers were overwhelmed with letters that found the idea stupid. Those letters did not recognize the intended irony of the ban, but rather declared it sexist and an example of radical feminists "crying wolf."[101] In response VOICE issued a flyer titled "Another Attempt to Explain..." On it the group acknowledged that people had been caught up in the practical curfew questions rather than addressing the larger questions VOICE wanted to raise. The new flyer explained that the imagined curfew was an attempt to institute "*real* change," and to focus attention "on the sexual abusers not the victims." Focusing on the victim often allowed people to ignore the fact that most sexual violence happens from "people we know and trust." Knowing that people did not want to hear that

97. Cheri Padfield, "VOICE Protests Advice to Women about Attack," *Daily Universe* November 21, 1991.

98. Ibid.

99. Carolyn G. Owen, letter to the editor, *Daily Herald*, November 26, 1991.

100. Ibid.

101. VOICE documents, Signature Books Collection.

BYU students may well be rapists, VOICE encouraged men "to take responsibility for how they treat women."[102]

While VOICE tried to address a systemic problem, it was continuously met with people trying to frame the problem on an individual level. Why punish all men when it was just a few? Why suggest that the problem was male students when it must be outsiders? And so the campaign fell flat. Yet the questions and issues were raised in new ways on the campus, a ball dropped on the field for future feminists to pick up and carry.

It was not just student feminism that had the administration of both the church and the university concerned. It was also the intersections of feminism and intellectualism on BYU's campus. At the same time that VOICE felt the weight of patriarchy, church authority, and anti-feminism on campus, so too did academics. Even Colleen McDannell, professor of history and religious studies at the University of Utah who was not a church member, knew that something was different and that the climate felt more hostile to academics. In 1991 as part of her research on Mormonism and material culture, she presented a paper on priesthood garments at a Sunstone conference. "In spite of my careful attention to Mormon sensibilities," McDannell recalled, "my paper and several others by Latter-day Saints were deemed to be offensive."[103] McDannell's presentation was not the only one that raised concerns. Sunstone conferences often had panels discussing women's issues in the church and the divine feminine. In addition to feeling as though that which was sacred was discussed publicly, casually, and perhaps even irreverently, members of the church hierarchy felt several recent presentations at conferences (including those on the status of women) seemed to challenge the teachings of the prophets both historically and in the present day, and so they sought to curtail such projects by showing disapproval for the gatherings where these issues were discussed.

It may seem as though symposia are not worth prohibiting. But for the church hierarchy of the early 1990s, they were an instance of the dangerous scholarship and activism that were taking place in

102. "Another Attempt to Explain..." and "Another Open Letter to the BYU Community," from VOICE, in VOICE documents, Signature Books Collection.

103. McDannell, *Sister Saints*, x.

the church and on BYU's campus. On August 31, 1991, the First Presidency issued an official statement: "Recent symposia sponsored and attended by some members have included some presentations relating to the House of the Lord, the holy temples, that are offensive," they wrote. "We deplore the bad taste and sensitivity of these public discussions of things we hold sacred."[104] The church leaders then took an interesting stance toward controversial issues. "There are times when it is better to have the Church without representation than to have implications of Church participation used to promote a program that contains some (though admittedly not all) presentations that result in sacred things or injuring [the Church] ... detracting from its mission, or jeopardizing the well-being of its members."[105]

While Sunstone was not the only group hosting forums for such discussions, it was an important one. Begun as a magazine in 1974 by students at BYU and University of California–Berkeley, *Sunstone* was initially seen as a place where students could be published on important Mormon-related issues of the day. Under the leadership of Orson Scott Card as editor, it changed into a magazine with a broad readership. As the organization began hosting events, it became a community where believers could discuss issues in the LDS Church and Mormonism more broadly without being under the umbrella of any religious organization. This allowed a freedom of thought and discussion that many people enjoyed. Elbert Peck, the executive director of Sunstone in the 1990s, understood that the church was experiencing growing pains at the time, attempting to embrace new levels of diversity in its ever-increasing membership. He explained that discussions happening at Sunstone were healthy and necessary explorations.[106] From Peck's perspective this was natural and while there may be some tension, the discussions of increasing diversity were vital to the life of the church.

Yet Peck understood that the general authorities felt differently. From their perspective Sunstone symposia were a place where people

104. "Statement from the First Presidency," *Church News*, August 31, 1991.

105. Ibid.

106. "There is Sunstone in My Heart Today: An Interview with Elbert Eugene Peck, Executive Director of the Sunstone Foundation," *Student Review*, August 1993.

felt comfortable enough to question church doctrine and policy and even challenge the church hierarchy.[107] While the hierarchy could not crack down on everyone, it could control the situation at BYU. In 1992, Sunstone held its first conference in Utah since the church had issued its statement about symposia. The evidence was clear: prohibiting symposia made general attendance skyrocket while at the same time participating BYU faculty declined by half.[108] Many experienced the ban on symposia as a crackdown on the freedom of thought and exploration within the church and at BYU.

It was into this milieu that Cecilia Konchar Farr walked in 1990. The English department hired her because a number of faculty in the department understood that if their students were going to be successful applicants to graduate programs in their field, they would have to know something of cutting-edge theories, including feminist theory. Not only was Farr a feminist trained in feminist theory, she was also a practicing Latter-day Saint. She valued what the church had to offer to people's lives. She grew up in a working-class family that converted while they were in Alaska for her father's construction job: "We were very poor and a Mormon woman came over with a box full of those giant Alaskan vegetables."[109] The woman and her mother connected and that was the family's first contact with the church. They were quickly invited to a church meeting in someone's home. Farr, her siblings, and her mother were baptized two years later. While her mother was drawn to the supportive community, Farr remembers loving the stories of the early church.

Farr held that the differences between men and women were not essential or biological or divinely ordained but were the result of a culture that told men and women they were different and then put them in a hierarchical relationship.[110] She called herself a radical feminist. For her that meant she was not willing to accept the same systems with only small changes. And so she was focused on "re-thinking social structures." But she did so from the stance of literature and theory, not activism. Even while she claimed radical

107. Ibid.

108. Waterman and Kagel, *Lord's University*, 259–63.

109. Konchar Farr, oral history with author.

110. Waterman and Kagel, *Lord's University*, 205.

feminism, she knew her life choices were not like those of a lot of other radical feminists: "I sat in my office and thought about feminism.... So a radical feminist? I mean heterosexual, monogamous, two kids, still very much a Mormon. That is not the M.O. of a radical feminist!"[111] That Farr could hold onto her faith and her radical feminism was a sign, she later understood, of her ability to compartmentalize and live with dissonance in the 1990s. She did not apply the feminist questions she asked about the literary canon and the study of literature to her church. She was not a theologian. And maybe somewhere in the back of her mind she felt that if she applied her feminist questions and lens to the church, something would have to give. But, for a time, she was a radical feminist *and* a faithful Latter-day Saint.

As part of her work as an advisor to VOICE, Farr attended a pro-choice rally in January 1992. The story of her path to that rally started in a class she was teaching. The small class on modernist literature, filled with senior students, was reading Ernest Hemingway's four-page short story "Hills Like White Elephants." The story, a perfect example of the modernist genre, is entirely in dialogue and the two characters discuss abortion without ever naming it. One character wants the other to have an abortion, while the other resists. In the context of the class discussion, the students asked Farr what she thought about abortion. She replied "You know, this isn't the church's position. I'm not representing the church, but I think that women need to make these decisions for themselves."[112]

One of her students in the class was connected to someone in Salt Lake City organizing a pro-choice rally in response to proposed state legislation that would restrict access to abortion. After the class discussion, the student asked Farr if she would attend the rally and if she would speak. She was a BYU professor who held a pro-choice stance; Farr understood why they wanted her. Her participation would be a significant sign of the complexity of feelings on the topic within the church community.

Farr took some time to consider the request. She spoke with friends and family, trying to decide what to do. She knew there were

111. Konchar Farr, oral history with author.

112. Ibid.

high stakes. Because of that, she spoke with her bishop and showed him the speech she planned to make. She also spoke with her stake president and said, "I just think that you ought to know that I'm going to do this. It might make waves, but you know me. You know I'm a faithful Mormon. This matters to me. I'm only speaking out because I'm also politically engaged and this concerns me." He told her, "There is nothing wrong with that."[113]

And so Farr gave the speech. She made clear that the views she expressed were her own and not the institution's. She believed that the best route forward was for society to improve its treatment of women and children and educate everyone about their choices.[114] At the rally she gave the speech while bouncing her baby daughter on her hip. Farr said, "Listen to me. I am a Mormon and I am for choice."[115] The rally "was all full of people and they were screaming and cheering," but "I understood Mormon culture enough to know that people would see this as transgressive." As she guessed, the speech caused a stir. Clips played on the nightly news. The response was swift and angry. Farr received furious letters from other church members who felt she had betrayed the church. She even received death threats in her campus mailbox.

In the midst of the backlash against the speech, Farr was called in to meet with her department chair. He said, "What you did was wrong…[it] was against the church and no one who teaches at BYU is allowed to have a pro-choice position." The two disagreed about whether or not the university could dictate what Farr could and could not say publicly. After their talk, a feminist newspaper in Salt Lake City asked Farr if it could reprint her talk. She agreed. "And then I got called back in [to the chair's office]," she recalled. "And now they didn't need any reason to critique me except that I had been disobedient. That he had told me never to say it again and I had done it. And so now I'm disobedient. And disobedience, that's grounds for whatever they want."[116]

Farr was one of fifty faculty members undergoing review that same year. The possible outcomes in each case were threefold: the

113. Ibid.

114. Waterman and Kagel, *Lord's University*, 207.

115. Qtd. in ibid, 207.

116. Konchar Farr, oral history with author.

person's candidacy could be recommended for continuing status, they could be assigned provisional candidacy (where requirements for improvement would be outlined), or they would be assigned non-candidacy (which meant they would teach for one more year before being terminated). Farr, along with five others were not granted candidacy for continuing status. Even as Farr determined to fight back, the cards were stacked against her. Provost Bruce Hafen inserted an official anti-choice statement from BYU into her file after the fact, suggesting that she had known the potential fallout of her statements in Salt Lake City all along.[117]

In response to these and other growing concerns about the campus climate, BYU issued a statement on "Academic Freedom" in September 1992. In it, the school asserted that academic freedom extended to individuals' ability to "ask hard questions," while it also insisted that faculty members could not "seriously and adversely affect the university mission or the church."[118] Thus the statement focused on the religious nature of the institution that had to be protected from secularism.[119]

In her discussion of the new climate at BYU, journalist Peggy Fletcher Stack noted that a shift took place in the church in the 1970s. The church began to "isolate its intellectuals at universities," while rarely calling them to church leadership in the hierarchy or in the production of educational materials.[120] In doing so, the church put its own intellectuals at arm's length and in very controlled situations where their ability to engage church laity would be under control. In May 1992, Stack noted, Phi Beta Kappa had rejected BYU's third attempt to create a chapter "because of the lack of perceived academic freedom."[121] In October 1992, the administration issued a series of policies that would be tied to the new academic freedom statement. Then President of BYU, Rex E. Lee, explained that there was

117. Waterman and Kagel, *Lord's University*, 212.

118. Peggy Fletcher Stack, "The Mind May Know No Boundaries, but Intellectual Pursuit Does at BYU," *Salt Lake Tribune*, October 24, 1992.

119. John-Charles Duffy, "Can Deconstruction Save the Day? 'Faithful Scholarship' and the Uses of Postmodernism," *Dialogue: A Journal of Mormon Thought* 41, no. 1 (Spring 2008): 16–18.

120. Stack, "Mind May Know No Boundaries."

121. Stack, "Mind May Know No Boundaries." See also Kagel and Waterman, *Lord's University*, 190–91.

a "long-standing expectation" that all faculty members were active members of the church and considered in good standing.[122]

The letter that Farr received from the Faculty Council on Rank and Status asserted that her scholarship was not careful, that it did not adequately address other scholarship, and that it lacked a critical lens and sufficient rigor.[123] Not long after she received her letter announcing her dismissal, an article in the *Salt Lake Tribune* suggested that while the focus of the controversy centered around academic freedom, some students were upset that their courses were being politicized by professors with feminist commitments. The students argued that those same professors were attempting to indoctrinate them and that the classroom had become a hostile environment to their own interests.[124] Not realizing that their own positions were also political, those same students declared that feminist professors were bringing "worldly wisdom and philosophies" into the "spiritual atmosphere" of the university.[125]

Farr was not the only intellectual at BYU experiencing the crackdown of the institution on what was becoming unorthodox belief. David Knowlton, too, was assigned non-candidacy. Knowlton had served his mission for the church in Bolivia and then studied South America as an anthropologist. In 1991 he gave a paper at Sunstone that discussed anti-LDS terrorism in South America. He suggested that the attacks would continue unless the church addressed its "Yankee imperialist" image.[126] After the talk Knowlton was called in to speak with his bishop. Soon thereafter he learned about his own termination from BYU. Knowlton submitted a 1,000-page response in the appeals process and made a collateral claim that the Council of Rank and Status had fired him for reasons not stated in their official decision, but he was eventually denied. He said of his process of appeal: "I'm going against the walls of Troy, and I don't have

122. Kagel and Waterman, *Lord's University*, 190–95.

123. Ibid, 222.

124. Associated Press, "BYU Teachers with Feminist Leanings Politicizing Courses, Some Students Say," *Salt Lake Tribune*, July 28, 1993.

125. Michael Morris, "Ideological Battle Rages at BYU," *Utah County Journal*, July 27, 1993, 1.

126. Waterman and Kagel, *Lord's University*, 216–17.

a Trojan horse."[127] In addition to Farr and Knowlton, Gail Houston, an English professor who also worked closely with VOICE was given provisional status, meaning that her future at BYU was undetermined.

As knowledge about BYU's treatment of Farr, Knowlton and other professors grew, several sympathetic protests took place in Provo. In the end, and after the appeal process period had passed, Knowlton was denied continuing status. Farr was also denied continuing status but negotiated a monetary settlement with the university. In the settlement she received an additional year's salary.[128]

But it was not just their jobs and economic security that were in peril. Their membership in the church was too. Later, Farr remembered that her bishop told her he was pressured by church leaders above him in the hierarchy to call a disciplinary council. He refused. Both he and her stake president said she was being mischaracterized and refused to call a council. Thirty years later, she explained that their refusal "still really touches me to this day because that's hard for a Mormon man to do.... But it's also very sad that the only reason that I survived [as a church member] ... was because I had two good guys in the way."[129] Because she won the "bishop roulette," Farr left Provo, Utah, with her temple recommend in hand.

Before she left BYU and went to teach at Saint Catherine University in Minnesota, Farr wrote a piece in which she called herself a radical feminist, "meaning that I imagine huge changes, not just reformative or cosmetic changes, are going to be necessary to alter women's oppressed situation in our world."[130] While she framed her feminism as recognizing or even demanding a radical change in how things operated, Farr was still immersed in her faith life: "I stay because Mormonism means something to me at the deepest levels of my being," she contended. Farr noted that when she

127. Susanne Wendt, "Knowlton Makes His Pleas," *Daily Universe*, (clipping with n.d.) and Rommyn Skipper, "Meeting of Dismissed Educator and Y. Panel Yields No Decision," *Deseret News*, September 28, 1993.

128. Waterman and Kagel, *Lord's University*, 223–41, and Konchar Farr, oral history with author.

129. Konchar Farr, oral history with author.

130. Cecilia Konchar Farr, "Dancing through the Doctrine: Observations on Religion and Feminism," in George D. Smith, ed., *Religion, Feminism, and Freedom of Conscience* (Salt Lake City: Signature Books, 2014), 147–48.

attended Pilgrimage—an annual meeting of a group of faithful feminists—in the spring of 1993, she grew concerned about what was happening with feminism in the church. What she saw was "a feminism based on individual liberation ... a homogenous feminism that seemed ... comfortable in its familiar surroundings." This type of feminism merely sought to get male leaders of the church to understand women. It was an apolitical feminism that fit itself inside the institution rather than demanding institutional change.[131] Even as she believed feminism in the church was shrinking in light of the hostile climate and context, she encouraged her fellow feminists to keep working. There was much to do, and "we feminists must be about our Father's business."[132]

As she critiqued Latter-day Saint feminism and encouraged those same feminists to do the work that they knew was necessary, she also thought about the issues facing BYU. She hoped that the institution could support its faculty, expecting them to be faithful and follow the Honor Code, but then to trust them. From Farr's perspective, the issue was simple. Everyone taught from a particular value system, but those who taught from a "conservative, Republican, traditional perspective," claimed to have an objective, scientific, and divinely inspired perspective. What they needed was to realize that *every* person came from a particular perspective and offered their own unique contributions. For Farr, the goal was that the church would be changed by "revelation and not by revolution."[133]

---

131. Ibid, 150.

132. Ibid.

133. Kelli Potter, "An Interview with Cecilia Konchar Farr," *Student Review* (n.d.). After leaving BYU, Farr moved to Minnesota and taught at Saint Catherine's University. For ten more years, she remained a member of the church with a temple recommend. It was not until she saw that attending church was a problem for her daughter, who also faced tension and dissonance, that Farr decided to stop: "She was 13 and we went to a gay pride parade in the morning and then to Mormon Church in the afternoon and at Mormon Church they started preaching against pride. They started telling her, they literally said to a 13-year-old girl, 'the most important decision you'll ever make is who you'll marry. So you need to start thinking about that now and making good choices.' She said 'What if I didn't want to marry a man? What if I love a woman?'... She got in the car on the way home and she just burst into tears and we started talking and I realized what I'd been trying to negotiate all those years.... The values that I wanted her to have were being not just undermined but opposed when I took her to church. So we both decided to stop going to church just like that. It was so good for both of us." Konchar Farr, oral history with author.

Later, even though Farr did not receive ecclesiastical discipline, many would mis-remember her as one of the September Six, illustrating the space she inhabited in Mormon memory. She was remembered as the rebel in a Viking helmet shaking her fist at the institution, as characterized in editorial cartoons at the time. She recalled that she was "seen as a kind of Sonia Johnson figure who was rebellious and disobedient and challenging Mormonism." For Farr, this was difficult, "because really I wasn't challenging Mormonism."[134]

The aftermath of the BYU dismissals was far-reaching and included a crackdown on scholarship. From the institution's perspective, the question of feminism's role at BYU and in church was simple. How much and how well could it serve the ends of the Restoration? If it was deemed to be at odds with that aim, it was not necessary. And BYU administrators felt that their call was to further the aims of the Restoration. As Apostle Neal A. Maxwell put it in a speech in late August 1993, "There is no reason for the tithe payers of the church to fund another secular university since, as taxpayers, they are already helping to fund useful systems of public higher education." Because the church subsidized the school, Maxwell argued that it had every right to inquire about and be concerned about what happened there. Along similar lines as Boyd K. Packer had, Maxwell described the ideal faculty member as "bilingual," someone who could speak "both the language of scholarship and also of faith." This meant that the school should look for employees who were openly willing to seek the Spirit and bear testimonies of their faith even as they excelled in their scholarly work. "Such individuals," Maxwell insisted, "need never look anxiously over either shoulder."[135]

Just a few days later BYU President Rex E. Lee made similar arguments. He said that the idea that BYU would have to choose between being intellectually or faithfully driven was "borderline nonsense." Instead he argued for a "Church university" as a place "that combines faith in God with the pursuit of the highest in academic achievement." From Lee's perspective the combination of both

134. Konchar Farr, oral history with author.

135. Qtd. in Associated Press, "BYU Must Pay Dividends to the Faith to Justify Its Existence, Says Mormon Church Apostle," August 27, 1993.

pursuits was BYU's "unique contribution to the restored kingdom and also our unique contribution to American higher education."[136]

Calling upon the mission of the Restoration as the primary goal of the university, Lee placed all other controversies and debates under that umbrella. If church leaders saw faculty getting in the way of the hierarchy's vision of the Restoration, they would be dismissed. The faculty at BYU, Lee asserted, "are now and always will be drawn from persons of unshakable faith in the reality of the Restoration."[137] And so women in the 1990s received the same messages that Sonia Johnson had the decade before. Public challenges to the patriarchal order of things, which the institution declared central to the Restoration, would cost them. At the very least, they could lose their place in the community of believers. Reform feminism that focused on individual relationships and private matters might still be tolerated, but feminists who spoke publicly or sought to change the institution, especially in ways that would distance it from its growing ties to the Religious Right, would be expelled.

136. Tad Walch, "President Lee Defends Idea of Academic Freedom at BYU," *Daily Universe* August 30, 1993.

137. Ibid.

4: BODILY PURITY

"Avoid sexual transgression as you would the plague."
—Gordon B. Hinckley

In 1983, Affirmation, at that time a group of primarily gay and lesbian Mormons, published a document titled "All About Excommunication."[1] The document prepared group members for the likely possibility of excommunication if they were outed in their religious community.[2] "If you are an active member and are homosexual," the document warned, "then the probability of excommunication is very real."[3] The authors were two leaders from the Los Angeles chapter, Robert Axelson and Paul Mortensen, who warned their readers that they did not believe the disciplinary process would be fair. In fact, they argued that "the excommunication process itself is entirely foreign to Christ." Even as they declared it foreign to the true church, they recognized that Affirmation members needed to be prepared for what might come. They counseled their readers that "your soul is NOT on trial; only your membership in the temporal Church. They

1. Over its fifty-year existence Affirmation has changed its name to reflect a growing attempt at inclusion. First its name only included "Gays and Lesbians," and then it grew to include other members of the LGBTQ+ community before finally adding families and friends of LGBTQ+ folk. For ease, I will simply use the name Affirmation.

2. In this chapter I will use the terms "gay-lesbian movement" or "gay-lesbian rights movement" to refer to this community. These are imperfect phrases that capture the fact that trans- and bi-erasures happened frequently in the queer community and the broader culture during these decades. Today LGBTQ+ or a version of it is used widely, but the phrase "gay-lesbian movement" better captures what was happening in this time period. Even so, and as I argue in this chapter, the primary concern of the church was gay members.

3. Robert Axelson and L. Paul Mortensen, "All About Excommunication: For the Gay & Lesbian Mormon," December 1983, in Affirmation Records, 1977–2010, ACCN 1867, box 8, fd. 18, Special Collections, Marriott Library, University of Utah (hereafter, Affirmation Records).

cannot take away your salvation, your testimony, your faith, your life or your God."[4]

After reassuring their readership that the process did not change their spiritual status, only their membership in the church, the authors turned to offering practical advice. First, during group members' disciplinary hearings, they would not be able to record the proceedings even though church leaders might. And they should not expect what happened to be confidential; it would be likely that others in their ward would know why they were excommunicated. For the institution, they wrote, "excommunication means that they don't have to deal with you anymore," and "the exercise of priesthood authority [for gay men] no longer has the sanction of the Church."[5] The document's focus on priesthood status shows that its authors were primarily concerned with the experiences of male members. It also demonstrates that Affirmation members understood well how the purity system worked.

The church viewed sexually non-conforming bodies as impure, unclean. But it was male bodies in particular with which the institution was concerned. And the institution worked to draw a clear boundary between insiders and outsiders. The purity system embraced by the LDS Church hierarchy during the late twentieth century seemed to always be exposing people's private lives and condemning them for their sexual identities and activities. The Affirmation authors counseled readers not to accept the way their stories were told by the institution and, most importantly, not to believe what the church taught about excommunication: "[T]he Spirit does not withdraw."[6] And so however bereft and adrift the excommunicant might feel, the Spirit which had counseled them to join the church would also stay with them even if they were declared unclean by church leaders.

In 1988, five years after Affirmation's publication of "All About Excommunication," Denise Szekely, a trans woman who had been a member of Affirmation for just a few years, told her story about attending a local ward meeting for the first time as a woman. "Was I nervous? What do you think?" she asked. Not long after that visit

4. Ibid.
5. Ibid.
6. Ibid.

she received a letter from her ex-spouse's bishop and learned that her former spouse had requested a cancellation of their temple marriage sealing. Whenever a former spouse requests a cancellation, the other spouse is invited to write a letter to the First Presidency stating how they feel about the request. Though Szekely no longer accepted the authority of the institution, she did write a letter to the First Presidency and she also published it in an Affirmation newsletter.

Szekely wrote, "As a child of God, I maintain a testimony that the Church is true. I also maintain that there is a place for me in God's great plan." Even as she affirmed the truth of the church, she also confirmed her understanding of her place in the Plan of Salvation even if the hierarchy sought to deny her such a place. "Whether I'm a member of your Church is not important for me to obtain eternal life," Szekely told church leaders. When she formerly presented as male, she had done all that the church had taught her, even as the incongruity between who she knew she was and how people perceived her was heartbreaking.

Because of this incongruity, she considered suicide, and when she shared her struggles with a church leader he counseled her to "do manly things" as an antidote to her questions about gender. Szekely eventually chose to embrace her true identity and she ended her letter with a testimony, following the pattern that she had learned in the church: "My testimony to you and the world, Brethren, is: that all who come to a separation of mind, body, or spirit, need to know that they are still loved by our Creator. I testify to you that I've received personal revelation as to my purpose in life. I am a child of God."[7]

Here Szekely pushed back against the narrative that the church had told about her life and her identity. She testified to the existence of the God that the church had taught her about while also arguing against the purity system that infused every level of the institution. Szekely saw her life as evidence that the purity system, which drew boundaries around insiders and outsiders, was a system constructed by fallible humans. It was not inherent to the Restoration or to God.

The purity system promoted by the church taught that the institution had a stake in the bodily purity of its members, the third

7. Denise Szekely, Letter to the Editor, *Affinity*, October 1988, in Affirmation Records, box 11, fd. 5.

pillar of that purity system. In particular, it sought to manage what believers consumed and their sexual practices. Just as the last decades of the twentieth century saw a rise in institutional anti-feminist political activity, policing women who were stepping outside the boundaries of family and proper femininity, church leaders were becoming increasingly concerned with male sexual purity. And they framed sexuality in terms of morality in order to inspire political activism against gay and lesbian rights.

The Priesthood and Purity

The late nineteenth-century church had aligned itself with those who wanted to pass anti-miscegenation laws in its bid for the power that came with whiteness and as part of its attempts to distance itself from Blackness. These teachings worked together with the temple and priesthood racial bans to enforce a system rooted in racial hierarchy. The notion of purity, then, was part of how the church protected whiteness.[8] In the latter part of the twentieth century, though, the church gave up its rhetorical and doctrinal, if not its cultural, prohibitions against interracial marriage. To be clear, the church did not give up the practice of racial separation, but rather gave up messages from the pulpit calling for racial separation.[9] In its place, the church focused its attention on same-sex sexuality as a deviant sexual practice that would pollute, in particular, the male priesthood holders' body. Thus the purity system that spoke out against interracial marriages and families, while it did not disappear, receded in the discourse while the church's stance against same-sex sexuality moved to the center of discussions about purity.

Modern purity projects in the United States are often moments in which Christians claim the role of savior to the nation state, positioning themselves as the moral fabric of society. Evangelical Christians use the rhetoric of purity in order to secure their ties to conservative politics, suggesting that their ideas about family, gender, and sexuality

---

8. W. Paul Reeve, *Religion of a Different Color: Race and the Mormon Struggle for Whiteness* (New York: Oxford University Press, 2015), 171–87.

9. K. Mohrman, *Exceptionally Queer: Mormon Peculiarity and U.S. Nationalism* (Minneapolis: University of Minnesota Press, 2022), 257, and Taylor G. Petrey, *Tabernacles of Clay: Sexuality and Gender in Modern Mormonism* (Chapel Hill: University of North Carolina Press, 2020).

are the only ones that can keep society from crumbling.[10] Part of evangelical cultural purity work is to perpetuate a religion of fear so that evangelical leaders can explain how only one form of sexuality—heterosexual, monogamous marriage—can keep the individual safe and the state secure.[11] These observations hold true for Latter-day Saints in the late twentieth and early twenty-first centuries as well. Most certainly church leaders preached that individual choices affected the broader religious community and the nation.

Take for example, Ezra Taft Benson's 1986 general conference speech titled "Cleansing the Inner Vessel." In the speech Benson identified bodily purity, or in his words "sexual impurity" as one of the great threats that the church faced. Relying on teachings of Joseph F. Smith, Benson explained that sexual impurity "permeates our society." Benson's talk, though, recognized that purity was not just an issue for the individual body, but was a structural issue facing church and society, thus linking the individual to the larger whole. He argued for a system of purity which he framed as the need to "cleanse the inner vessel." "We must cleanse the inner vessel," he preached, "beginning first with ourselves, then with our families, and finally with the Church."[12] Benson went on to call his community to change, saying that to cleanse themselves, "we must forsake immorality and be clean," (again, the language of purity) beginning with their personal lives, but then radiating their cleansing work outwards to their families, and finally the entire church. This, he declared, would help church members to repent and to help build Zion.

While the LDS Church participated in the rhetoric of sexual purity, it did so by drawing from its own theological sources. This included the idea that following the Law of Chastity was part of an individual's journey toward exaltation.[13] These arguments allowed the institution to help create a public sphere that reinforced the church's theology.

10. Sara Moslener, *Virgin Nation: Sexual Purity and American Adolescence* (New York: Oxford University Press, 2015), 1–2; Megan Goodwin, *Abusing Religion: Literary Persecution, Sex Scandals, and American Minority Religions* (New Brunswick, NJ: Rutgers University Press, 2020), 11–15.

11. Moslener, *Virgin Nation*, 10–15.

12. Ezra Taft Benson, "Cleansing the Inner Vessel," *Ensign*, May 1986.

13. Sara Moslener, "Sexual Purity and its Discontents in Mormonism," in Amy K. Hoyt and Taylor Petrey, eds. *The Routledge Handbook of Mormonism and Gender* (New York: Routledge, 2020), 271–74.

At the same time that the church preached chastity outside of marriage as a requirement to achieve heaven, it also participated in the rhetoric of fear surrounding gay and lesbian identities and their supposed dangers for the nation. In this way, the institutional church could police the activities of individual bodies under the framework of faith while also aligning itself with the Religious Right. Participating in the policing of non-conforming bodies meant the church could participate in the making of the nation and it could do all of these activities while promoting an image of ecumenical participation in the interest of the state.

It is around the priesthood role that the LDS Church has constructed masculinity. In Latter-day Saint parlance, the priesthood is the "power to act in God's name." Because of the importance of the priesthood in the tradition, priesthood-holding males have been imagined as "the carriers of religious piety," meaning that it was the male body that was the primary concern of the institution.[14] While the church did join other types of Christianity in fretting over female sexual purity, that project was largely tied to the familial pillar of the purity system and the construction of future wifehood and motherhood, the roles the church held for women. Young women were taught that they were to abstain from sexual activity, therefore maintaining their purity until marriage, and that they were responsible for helping priesthood holders do the same. Young men, on the other hand, were priesthood holders first and the patriarchal priesthood meant that the purity of the male body was the project of the church hierarchy. A man polluting his body was particularly grievous: it was a pollution of himself as a priesthood holder and also, therefore, a pollution of the institution.

Over the course of the twentieth century the priesthood was offered to younger and younger males and used to train the male body to conform to the bodily and behavioral expectations of the institution. To hold the priesthood, one had to be male, but one also had to

14. Amy K. Hoyt and Sara M. Patterson, "Mormon Masculinity: Changing Gender Expectations in the Era of Transition from Polygamy to Monogamy, 1890–1920," *Gender & History* 23, no. 1 (April 2011): 72–91; Gregory A. Prince, *Gay Rights and the Mormon Church: Intended Actions, Unintended Consequences* (Salt Lake City: University of Utah Press, 2019), 120.

be pure, or worthy.[15] To train male bodies to be carriers of the power to act in God's name, the church sought connections with other organizations that could contribute to male worthiness. The Boy Scouts of America seemed the ideal fit and in 1913 the church adopted the program into its ecclesiastical structures. The Boy Scouts offered a perfect blend of patriotism and stories about the frontier that allowed white Latter-day Saints to celebrate their own history of westward expansion.[16] In addition, the church began to promote recreational activities that were designed for lessons tied to team building, morality, physical control and discipline, and socialization. From the institution's perspective, athletics kept young men busy and gave them motivation to keep their bodies pure; sports were the perfect blend of masculine ideals and faith.[17]

Prior to the twentieth century, LDS masculinity revolved around the priesthood and the practice of polygamy. Plural marriage marked Latter-day Saints as a distinct community, separate from others and called by God to be different. After the church gave up the practice of polygamy, a gradual process that took several decades, it shifted masculinity away from sexual practices and identities that went against the norms of heterosexual monogamy, and towards other markers of distinction.

The priesthood was and is central to the church's understanding of the Restoration and what made the LDS Church distinct from other churches. Over the course of the twentieth century, the church sought to assimilate into American norms, aligning itself with white, and increasingly conservative, identities to gain acceptance. In the decades following the 1890 Manifesto that publicly declared the end of polygamy, the church began to ignore and sanitize its polygamous past, instead turning its focus to the early history of Joseph Smith's restoration movement to guide it into the twentieth century.[18] The restoration claim it made focused on priesthood leadership and the importance of the family. The emphasis on family allowed the church

15. Hoyt and Patterson, "Mormon Masculinity," 72–91.

16. Ibid, 76–78.

17. Richard Ian Kimball, *Sports in Zion: Mormon Recreation, 1890–1940* (Urbana: University of Illinois Press, 2003), 3–4.

18. Kathleen Flake, *The Politics of American Religious Identity: The Seating of Senator Reed Smoot, Mormon Apostle* (Chapel Hill: University of North Carolina Press, 2004).

to continue its communal and theological value systems while changing its understanding of what the ideal family looked like: rather than the polygamous extended kinship networks of the nineteenth century, the church came to increasingly focus on the immediate family constructed around heterosexual monogamy. In essence, through its emphasis on family, the church publicly covered over its nonconforming past in an effort to enter into the American mainstream.

In the late twentieth century, though, as the church further aligned itself with the conservative, evangelical right, the church's polygamous past reared its head. This was one of the sites of debates over history-telling where church leaders felt identity was at stake. In the 1980s, especially, the institution's past polygamous doctrines haunted the church as it was trying to assimilate. Polygamous branches that had separated from the LDS Church at various times since 1890 made national headlines. In 1981, two popular books were published about polygamy, Peter Bart's *Thy Kingdom Come* (Linden Press), which explored the past practice of polygamy in the church hierarchy, and *Prophet of Blood: The Untold Story of Ervil LeBaron and Lambs of God* (Putnam Publishing) which examined one of the fundamentalist branches that had broken from the LDS Church to continue the practice of polygamy. This latter book arrived just as Ervil LeBaron appeared on national most-wanted lists for having his rival leaders killed.

In 1984, Ron and Dan Lafferty (who had begun to embrace the doctrines of polygamy) murdered their brother's wife and infant daughter because they perceived the wife to be too modern in relation to the doctrines they embraced. They claimed they had received revelations instructing them to do so.[19] Even though the LDS Church had pinned its future to monogamous heterosexuality for almost a century, most Americans did not distinguish between the mainstream church and its fundamentalist Mormon siblings. They were one and the same in the American mind. And the church's past kept following it around like an unwanted shadow. Though church

19. Jan Shipps, *Sojourner in the Promised Land: Forty Years Among the Mormons* (Urbana: University of Illinois Press, 2000), 104. J. B. Haws, *The Mormon Image in the American Mind: Fifty Years of Public Perception* (New York: Oxford University Press, 2013), 148–49.

leaders wanted to lay the institution's polygamous history to rest, historians like D. Michael Quinn, who in 1985 published "LDS Church Authority and New Plural Marriages, 1890–1904" in *Dialogue*, were unearthing that same past, including the church's secret, underground continuance of polygamy after 1890. For some church leaders, these historians were just as cumbersome as Ervil LeBaron or the Lafferty brothers: they were all reminders of a past that the institution would rather forget.

Throughout the twentieth century the institution continued to offer a new masculinity and sexuality that would help it fit into the mainstream. The new masculinity focused on missionary work, monogamous heterosexual purity, and adherence to the Word of Wisdom (a dietary code that prohibited the consumption of coffee, tea, tobacco, and alcohol).[20] In the early decades of the twentieth century, church members were encouraged to see the Word of Wisdom as a divine mandate and at the same time to imagine it as a code of health, able to keep their bodies pure.[21] Whether or not a church member followed the Word of Wisdom became one of the questions that would determine their worthiness to enter the temple. The new LDS construction of masculinity portrayed the LDS man as a person set apart; he was the ideal American citizen, one who was economically savvy, a provider for his family, sexually monogamous, worthy to enter the temple, and willing to stand for his faith in the face of any opposition.[22]

Spencer Kimball's Miracle of Forgiveness

After World War II, general authorities joined their voices with other religious and political conservatives who believed that American culture should rest on patriarchal authority. Men needed to be men, and their role in the home was as provider and leader. For many Latter-day Saint believers, these teachings seemed ideal.[23] At the same time that church authorities were preaching gender hierarchy and complementarism in a bid to conform to American norms,

20. Hoyt and Patterson, "Mormon Masculinity," 72–73.

21. Thomas G. Alexander, "The Word of Wisdom: From Principle to Requirement," *Dialogue: A Journal of Mormon Thought* 14, no. 3 (Fall 1981): 78–88.

22. Hoyt and Patterson, "Mormon Masculinity," 73.

23. Petrey, *Tabernacles of Clay*, 32–35.

there was also a shift in thinking about gay sex. During the 1950s and 1960s, cultural focus turned away from strictly moral claims about same-sex attraction and sexuality and added new layers of psychological explanations that began to appear in many Christian churches' discourse, including Latter-day Saints. The growth of the field of psychology in these decades enabled religious explanations to merge with scientific ones.[24]

"Homosexuality" was a term first coined in the late nineteenth century. It appeared in the American Psychological Association's Diagnostic and Statistic Manual I (DSM-I) published in 1952, demonstrating that the field of psychology had claimed sexuality as its domain. The first volume attempted to standardize nomenclature and diagnoses for mental health issues. It classified homosexuality as a "sociopathic personality disturbance." In the next edition the classification shifted to a "personality disorder." Then it changed again in 1973, with the DSM-III, which called homosexuality a "sexual orientation disturbance." This focused on the individual struggling within an unaccepting culture rather than on the identity itself. Because of the countless work of LGBTQ+ activists and scholars, homosexuality did not appear as any kind of disorder in the DSM-IV of 1987.[25] While the inclusion of homosexuality in the DSM helped transform the discourse around homosexuality from a moral and theological one to a scientific and psychological one, it did little to change the negative connotations surrounding the identity. It was not until the American Psychological Association (APA) decided in 1987 to take the term out of the DSM entirely that the field began to make greater changes to the discourse. The APA came to embrace therapeutic practices that helped people accept their identities in a hostile world.

Perhaps nowhere can the third pillar of bodily purity, and the changing definitions of same-sex attraction, be seen better than in the person of Spencer W. Kimball, president of the church from 1973 to 1985. Kimball had long been concerned about non-conforming sex. In 1946 and 1947 he had two apostolic assignments. One of those was to supervise the church's relationship with Native

24. Ibid, 53–62.

25. Ira Glass, "81 Words," *This American Life*, January 18, 2002, thisamericanlife.org.

American groups. The other was to oversee how people engaging in serious sexual transgression were counseled by church leaders. Kimball thought he knew the path to addressing this sin. Repentance after the fact was important, but he wanted to avoid sexual sin in the first place. He believed the key to prevention was to teach men and women to take their gender roles seriously and to prevent themselves from being in any situation where they might be tempted.[26] In the 1960s and 1970s, Kimball led the charge in developing the church's approach to same-sex attraction specifically and sexual sin more broadly.[27]

In 1969, just a few years before he became church president, Kimball published *The Miracle of Forgiveness*, a book that articulated the theology he had developed around sin, repentance, and forgiveness. The book was popular, selling 500,000 copies in seventeen languages between 1969 and his death in 1985.[28]

Kimball began the book by admonishing his readers, explaining that the text was not for entertainment value, but for calling people to repentance for their sins.[29] In its preface, he acknowledged that he spent quite a bit of time focusing his attention on sexual sin. His explanation for that focus was three-fold: First, "men and women are human and normally carnally minded," and so he understood his project as fighting against what may be part of human drives and temptations. Second, he wrote that he came in regular contact with "broken homes, delinquent children, corrupt governments and apostate groups," all of which were the result of sin, particularly of a sexual nature. Here he tied the project of policing sexuality with the preservation of the nation. And, finally, he saw that sin had a snowball effect that quickly went from temptation to indiscretion to "major transgressions which bring heavy penalties."[30]

While Kimball's goal was to invite people back onto a path of righteousness and close relationship with God, he discussed sin in

26. Petrey, *Tabernacles of Clay*, 19–20.

27. Ibid, 66–68.

28. Edward L. Kimball, *Lengthen Your Stride: The Presidency of Spencer W. Kimball* (Salt Lake City: Deseret Book, 2005), 79.

29. Spencer W. Kimball, *The Miracle of Forgiveness* (Salt Lake City: Deseret Book, 1969), ix.

30. Ibid, x–xi.

much greater depth and detail than he did forgiveness. In the end, though, his message was that purity was "essential to eternal life." He explained that in the Latter-day Saint worldview, "purity must be our constant aim." Living a valiant life would mean that the person would achieve perfection; they would become "as a god" in the afterlife. And so the ultimate goal of the Plan of Salvation was to attain a level of purity that meant one lived with command over their physical body and with their eyes on God.[31] In order to reach exaltation, one had to control sexual impulses and participate in sexual activity only within the confines of a monogamous heterosexual marriage.

While sexual sin was his focus, Kimball identified other sins that could disrupt a righteous life: idolatry, rebellion, Sabbath-breaking, the love of money, and vulgarity. In Kimball's hands these sins seemed fairly harmless, though, because he talked about other sins that "are so serious that we know of no forgiveness for them." Those sins were the "diabolical crimes of sexual impurity."[32] Sexual impurities could run the gamut from masturbation to adultery, which "the Lord apparently rates … close to premeditated murder."[33] Even as he likened adultery to murder, Kimball saved his greatest condemnation for same-sex encounters. From his perspective, homosexuality was "unnatural," a serious offense to the way that God had ordered the natural world. That unnaturalness was rooted in Kimball's belief that the procreative act was at the center of an "honorable marriage" and family system. Gay and lesbian sex did not multiply and replenish the earth, as he argued God had commanded. It did not create more bodies for future humans. It therefore was "hostile to God's purpose."[34]

Kimball declared that the US legal system had become slack in its perspective about gay sex; he saw this as "another evidence of the deterioration of society."[35] He then counseled believers not to fall for the idea that because society seemed more accepting of same-sex attraction that they should be as well. God should be their focus. Here he called believers to be the moral watchdogs of a society that was falling into sin. The God Kimball described was loving and forgiving,

31. Ibid, 26–27.
32. Ibid, 61–62.
33. Ibid, 62.
34. Ibid, 79–83.
35. Ibid, 79.

but also spent time monitoring people's lives. "There are no corners so dark, no deserts so uninhabited, no canyons so remote, no automobiles so hidden," he cautioned, "but that the all-seeing One can penetrate and observe."[36] Kimball's model of God was of a judge whose all-seeing eyes sought out people who were acting in impure ways. His God was one who would hold people accountable.[37]

While Kimball's discussion of same-sex sexuality focused almost exclusively on men, women did appear in his discussion of purity. Women were to keep their bodies pure for their husbands and bore the responsibility for maintaining heterosexual boundaries. In an especially dangerous passage, he maintained that even when someone experienced rape or incest, chastity was lost. He recognized that if the actions were not voluntary, the person should not be condemned, but added that, "It is better to die in defending one's virtue than to live having lost it without a struggle."[38]

Also under Kimball's oversight, in 1974 the Church Welfare Services published a pamphlet called "Homosexuality" that was to be used by local church leaders to counsel gay church members. The pamphlet is an excellent example of the merging of religious and psychological explanations for same-sex attraction. The pamphlet first defined homosexuality as a sin that "violates the Lord's eternal plan for man's progress."[39] Even as it described homosexuality as a sin, it also offered several explanations for what the origins of same-sex attraction may be: molestation as a child, experimentation in youth, and having a "domineering mother and a passive father."[40] The explanations for origins are not rooted in scientific facts or arguments, but they do represent an attempt to provide psychological explanations. The pamphlet, too, insisted that homosexuality was a learned behavior (and therefore could be categorized as a sin) rather than an inborn trait.

The pamphlet turned to the individual's relationship to the church and it demonstrated well the precarity of any member who was gay

36. Ibid, 110.

37. Ibid, 140.

38. Ibid, 196.

39. Welfare Services, *Homosexuality* (Salt Lake City: The Church of Jesus Christ of Latter-day Saints, 1973), 3.

40. Ibid, 5.

or lesbian, even if the person was not acting on same-sex desire. First it said that it was acceptable for a "repentant homosexual" (meaning one who had accepted their same-sex attraction as a problem and was committed to avoiding what was framed as temptation) to serve in "safe" callings. In effect, that meant that gay members could not receive a calling in which they would work with children. Here it conflated homosexuality and pedophilia, a false claim that was and is popular in homophobic discourse.

Second, unless someone was repentant, they could not be an employee of the church. If the person was not repentant, the pamphlet explained that disfellowshipment or excommunication could be the outcome. Disfellowshipment meant the temporary suspension of the individual's relationship to the church that would last until the individual changed. In a telling passage, the pamphlet also talked about excommunication as a permanent end of the individual's relationship to the church. "Excommunication cleanses the Church," it said, "and releases the person from the blessings of baptism and, when applicable, the endowment."[41] While a repentant person could potentially be reinstated, the use of the term "cleanses" speaks to how the primary concern of the church was the purity of its members. But individual purity was also about institutional purity as Kimball made clear. The church had constructed an understanding of the Restoration that relied on purity: If the church did not remain pure, it would lose its status as the 'true church' and its ability to remain pure relied on the bodily purity of its members. If an individual believer would not get in line, then they would be expelled in order to preserve the church's holiness.

All of this was not just talk, it was laying the groundwork for church action. At the same time that the LDS Church experienced these shifting trends in theology and psychology, it also sought to discipline members who practiced non-conforming sex. With its particular focus on men and maintaining the purity of the priesthood, the church worked with law enforcement in Utah to have men who were arrested for "vice charges" (referring to gay sex) sent to bishops for counseling. The church also used strategies it learned from police

41. Ibid, 16.

and military organizations to find gay church members through surveillance, informants, and forced confessions.[42] At BYU, the church supported the use of conversion therapy, electroshock and aversion techniques, arguing that same sex attraction could be "cured."

Affirmation Pushes Back

In 1977, a group of gay Latter-day Saints attending BYU started to meet secretly, grieving over the effects of the church's position on gay sexuality. This group initially called itself Affirmation: Gay Mormons United. Word spread and affiliate groups began to develop in Salt Lake City, Denver, and Dallas. In 1978 a branch of Affirmation formed in Los Angeles that became the hub of Affirmation as a national organization for several years.[43] In those early years, the group changed its name to Affirmation: Gay and Lesbian Mormons. The name Affirmation was "chosen to indicate the participants affirmed their identity as children of God and their right to simply talk to each other." Some of their earliest meetings were called Family Home Evenings; the name echoed what was a familiar ritual for all members of the church, one that indicated just how much the correlation project had shaped believers' daily lives. In addition, it showed that Affirmation members, along with their non-conforming siblings everywhere, were redefining the notion of family.[44]

A 1996 version of Affirmation's mission statement, which captured the heart of the organization's vision, described Affirmation as "a non-profit educational fellowship group serving gay, lesbian and bisexual Latter-day Saints, their families and friends since 1977. It is a place for open, honest dialogue, friendship and support. All are welcome regardless of gender, sexual orientation or religious affiliation."[45]

Affirmation was vital for many Mormons because it provided a safe place with people who understood the religious worldviews that had shaped members' perspectives. James Kent, a leader at both the

42. Neil J. Young, "Homosexuality and Politics in Mormonism," in Hoyt and Petrey, eds. *Routledge Handbook*, 208.

43. Dwight Cook, "A Brief History of Affirmation," n.d., Affirmation Records, box 10, fd. 4.

44. *Affinity* 19, no. 4, April 1997, copy in Affirmation Records.

45. Statement read at 1996 Palm Springs Affirmation International Conference, October 11–13, 1996, Affirmation Records, box 1, fd. 6.

local and national level in the late twentieth century, put it this way: "Growing up as Latter-day Saints, we were taught that in order to be 'worthy' so that we could eventually become Gods and Goddesses of our own worlds, we had to 'be ye therefore perfect, as your Father in Heaven is perfect.' How hard we tried to be the best little boy or best little girl in the world . . . but we knew that it was all a front and a sham to cover up how unworthy we were."[46]

Here the power of the purity system in the lives of gay and lesbian members is apparent. Because they understood not only the social but also the theological ramifications of their sexuality, they struggled in every way that they could to live up to the purity standards that they had been taught were divinely created. Elsewhere Joshua S. Smith and I call this a struggle against the "covenantal hetero-captivity" of the Latter-day Saint institution. Gay and lesbian members were told by the church that not only were their sexual identities wrong in this life, but they were also wrong in the next. They could never achieve the exaltation that had been promised to all worthy members who strove for it unless they surrendered to a heterosexual framing of faithful life.[47]

Even as Affirmation sought to comfort members who felt that their sexual identities would be rejected by their families, their church, and their God, the organization chose not to comment on church policy. In doing so, Affirmation challenged the go-along-to-get-along approach of many of their fellow co-religionists. While they would not support the Latter-day Saint hierarchy, they also would not disavow its teachings. They wanted to be an expansive and inclusive group, unlike Evergreen, another group for gay and lesbian Latter-day Saints. Founded in 1989 by a dozen Mormon men who felt they were struggling with their same-sex desires, Evergreen International taught that one could overcome homosexuality through prayerful acceptance of God's will and through therapeutic intervention.[48] Affirmation was different.

Affirmation members wanted to be diverse at the same time that they wanted to model a different type of behavior than the institutional

---

46. *Affinity* 21, no. 1, January 1999, copy in Affirmation Records.

47. Joshua S. Smith and Sara M. Patterson, "For Time and Eternity: Feeling the Spirit in the Lives of LGBTQ+ Mormons," *Culture and Religion*, April 2023.

48. Prince, *Gay Rights and the Mormon Church*, 94.

church: "[W]e feel that each person's opinions and feelings are valuable and important and should be heard, whether we agree or disagree with each other or the Church leaders."[49] The group sought to acknowledge that their membership might feel differently about various topics and wanted, in a more egalitarian approach, to model how organizations might survive disagreement and dissent.

But even as they embraced these democratic ideals in the last decades of the twentieth century, Affirmation did not prove to be particularly concerned about lesbians, making it difficult for women who wanted community with people who understood Mormonism. In a 1991 letter from Linda in Las Vegas that appeared in Affinity for Women (a newsletter created by Ina Mae Murray, a national Affirmation leader, to speak to women's needs in Affirmation), Linda expressed this concern. She had gone to the local Affirmation meeting seeking community but felt as though she "had stepped back 5 years in time." For her it seemed that the men present "had not left Mormonism at all." Instead it appeared that, "They were just waiting for the church to come around. Mentally they were no different from the men I had left behind. They were still white and bright, and privileged because of it. They hadn't even begun to question patriarchal rule." This made Linda feel unwelcome. The men were replicating the patriarchal authority of the church. They were hoping for simple reform that would allow them to return to the church, whereas Linda and many other women saw that sexism and homophobia ran throughout the entire system and needed radical change.[50]

Suzie Ripperton said many similar statements in the Affinity newsletter in June 1995. She acknowledged that Affirmation's membership was predominantly male, but that it went much farther than that. Lesbian Mormons "are understandably repelled by any organization that even resembles the patriarchal structure of the Mormon Church," she wrote. "Why would they seek solace and support in an

49. Mel Barber to "Dear Chapter Director," February 17, 1987, Affirmation Records, box 8, fd. 9.

50. *Affinity for Women—A publication of Affirmation for Lesbian Mormons*, March 1991, Ina Mae Murri Papers, ACCN 2887, Special Collections, Marriott Library, University of Utah. For a full discussion of women's experiences within Affirmation, see Joshua S. Smith "'Where Have All the Women Gone???' Erasure and Marginalization in the Lesbian Mormon Experience," Senior Thesis, Hanover College, 2020.

organization that mirrors the very institution that has not only repressed them as lesbians, but as women?"[51] Women who loved other women faced a seemingly unchangeable patriarchal structure in Affirmation just as they had in the church.

The Church Hierarchy's Political Activism

In the 1980s a number of forces came together and began to again shift the Latter-day Saint discourse about gay and lesbian identities. Even so, the foundation that Kimball had set in place still proved relatively firm. The church began to focus even more attention on the nuclear family. Along with other conservative religious and political groups, church leaders saw the disintegration of the family as causing the downfall of society and their activism grew as they fought the passage of the Equal Rights Amendment.[52] As the 1980s continued, another issue came to represent the downfall of American society: the AIDS epidemic. The Reagan Administration was slow to respond to the health crisis, and the growing epidemic gave conservative Christians, including LDS church leaders, more fuel for political action. They chose to read the medical epidemic as a moral one. The moral panic that they promulgated provided them with further evidence that abstinence and heterosexual monogamy were the defining features of a godly society. In this way they tied sexual control to nationalism and argued that their views of Christian morality would help to keep the nation healthy.[53]

At the same time, the 1984 LDS Church Handbook declared that disciplinary courts could be convened to address same-sex activity, but only in instances where the priesthood holder held a "prominent church position" was a disciplinary council mandated.[54] Also that year, newly ordained apostle and former Utah Supreme Court justice Dallin H. Oaks wrote a white paper titled "Principles to Govern Possible Statement on Legislation Affecting Rights of Homosexuals." The document advised the church hierarchy on how it might take political action in civic matters pertaining to same-sex

51. *Affinity*, 17, no. 4, June 1995, copy in Affirmation Records, box 2, fd. 5.

52. Petrey, *Tabernacles of Clay*, 107–9.

53. Anthony M. Petro, *After the Wrath of God: AIDS, Sexuality and American Religion* (New York: Oxford University Press, 2015), 2, 7–9.

54. Prince, *Gay Rights and the Mormon Church*, 17.

marriage. In the paper Oaks portrayed gay rights advocates as crafty manipulators who were "skillfully appropriating the rhetoric and tactics of civil rights activists." They did so, he argued, to claim that they were an "oppressed minority who should be protected by anti-discrimination laws." Oaks painted gay rights proponents as nefarious individuals who wanted public approval of their actions and "the right to proselyte their lifestyle."

For this reason, he argued that the church needed to be careful in the causes it took up. If it fought wide-scale anti-discrimination laws, it would look "like a religious effort to use secular law to penalize one kind of sinner." Basically, if people saw the church actively fighting anti-discrimination laws that were about equality, the church would be in a public relations nightmare. Instead he suggested two alternate approaches: 1) only support "well-reasoned exceptions" to any anti-discrimination legislation and 2) have a formal position if a law was proposed to legalize same-sex marriage. The church's explanation should be, "We speak in defense of the family," except in the case of "homosexual marriages," which "are wholly deviant to the patriarchal family."

In a move that aligned his own reasoning with conservative Christians, Oaks argued that opposition to same-sex marriage would protect the purity of the family, the church, and the nation. "One generation of homosexual 'marriages' would depopulate a nation, and, if sufficiently widespread, would extinguish a people. Our marriage laws should not abet national suicide," he wrote.[55] While his language was hyperbolic, it matched the intensity and tenor of other conservative Christians about the danger of widescale acceptance of non-heterosexual citizens.

This fear could be seen everywhere. Even though C. Everett Koop published the 1986 Surgeon General's Report on AIDS, a report that argued the best route forward was education about condoms and healthy sexual activity, conservative Christians did not take up the message. At the forefront of joining their messages about morality with Christian nationalism was President Ronald Reagan, who argued instead for the moral system of much of his Christian base.

55. Dallin H. Oaks, "Principles to Govern Possible Public Statement on Legislation Affecting Rights of Homosexuals," August 7, 1984, unpublished paper.

His project was rooted in abstinence-only education. The AIDS epidemic came at precisely the right time for the Christian right, a group with which the Latter-day Saint hierarchy was working to align itself. They could declare the epidemic was the result of loosening public morality in the 1960s and 1970s. This gave them the perfect platform to argue for an across-the-board shift to embrace conservative Christian morality—about same-sex attraction, patriarchal order, chastity, and divorce—as the morality of the nation.[56]

In a 1987 general conference talk titled "Reverence and Morality," Gordon B. Hinckley addressed the issue of AIDS. The talk itself juxtaposed two seemingly distinct topics: comportment in sacrament meetings and sexual morality. The first part of the talk, surrounding the issue of comportment and reverence, focused on cultivating a "beautiful spirit of worship" and "increased reverence" in Sunday meetings and within ward buildings. Hinckley declared that church meetinghouses were "holy ground" and church members should act accordingly.[57] Hinckley's talk then transitioned to sexual morality. While it seems to be an abrupt shift in focus, almost as though there were two topics smashed into one talk, it makes sense in a framing that addresses bodily behaviors. Admonishing church leaders to have members act respectfully in meetinghouses is part of training the body to act in a faithful way, to keep what was sacred pure. Hinckley's transition, then, to sexual morality should be understood as training the body to act faithfully in sexual choices as well.

Displaying a reluctance to discuss sexual issues at the general conference, Hinckley suggested that the danger was so grave, that he simply had to. "There is a plague of fearsome dimensions moving across the world," he discussed. "Public health officials are greatly concerned, and everyone else should be."[58] Citing the statistic from Koop's office of a predicted American death toll of 170,000 in four years (and with the death rates growing even more rapidly in other areas of the world), Hinckley spoke about his concern about the AIDS epidemic in which "innocent people also become victims." He ended by warning against the "sexual adventurism which is

56. Petro, *After the Wrath of God*, 190.
57. Gordon Hinckley, "Reverence and Morality," *Ensign*, May 1987.
58. Ibid.

spreading like another plague across the world." From Hinckley's perspective, Koop was wrong about his harm-reduction approach to the epidemic. Hinckley made the case for abstinence-only education, emphasizing the purity system rooted in the Latter-day Saint hierarchy and its depictions of God. He told his audience that in order to achieve happiness for themselves and future generations, they should "avoid sexual transgression as you would the plague."[59] Thus he couched sexual activity outside of marriage in a negative framework, suggesting that it was dangerous and could pollute the body, the entire church, and even the nation.

Also in 1987, Dallin H. Oaks gave a talk at BYU titled "Free Agency and Freedom." In Oaks's talk, the Plan of Salvation was key. He began by outlining the progression of spirit beings, noting that humans had free agency in the premortal existence because God had rejected Satan's plan to take it away. In human bodies Satan would continue to offer temptations to people, trying to encourage them to use their free agency to choose the evil option. If not thwarted, Satan could ultimately hold humans captive. From Oaks's perspective, this was part of the important knowledge shared through the Restoration, foundational to the church's expectations about members' activities.[60] Because God had not chosen Satan's plan, humans had free agency and "no person or organization can take away our free agency in mortality." But, what could be diminished or taken away was human freedom, "the power to act upon our choices." Oaks claimed that "free agency is absolute, but in the circumstances of mortality freedom is always qualified."[61]

This argument provided the framework for the heart of Oaks's point. He was not talking about freedom and agency in the abstract alone. He was responding to the argument that gay and lesbian people were "born that way." Did it mean that people with same-sex desires had no choice or agency? No, he declared, "Our doctrine teaches us otherwise." Free agency is "unfettered," it was freedom that might be qualified.[62] In this he found it appropriate to liken same-sex

59. Ibid.

60. Dallin H. Oaks, "Free Agency and Freedom," Speech at Brigham Young University, October 11, 1987.

61. Ibid.

62. Ibid.

desires to addiction, an argument that would echo for some time in Latter-day Saint discussions. In the comparison, Oaks suggested that some might be more biologically prone to addictive behavior, but that did not mean that they did not have free agency. Their freedom was simply limited. And, likewise, he declared that gay and lesbian people, while maybe limited, still had the agency to choose otherwise as part of their moral decision making. Thus Oaks laid the groundwork for future church arguments to respond to 'born this way' claims by asserting that while some may be born predisposed to certain choices, they could still choose purity through abstinence.

The 1990s saw another subtle shift in church teachings about same-sex desire and sexuality as the hierarchy grew increasingly concerned about the general social acceptance of queer identities and behaviors. Just as Latter-day Saints were struggling with the role of women and arguing for a patriarchal order rooted in a heterosexual masculinity that embraced fatherhood, providing and protecting, so too did other conservative Christians on the right. Groups like James Dobson's Focus on the Family abounded. A group known as the "Promise Keepers" had its first rally in 1991. Founded by Bill McCartney, the head football coach at the University of Colorado, the goal of the movement was to return men's focus to their familial roles and to reinforce a type of masculinity rooted in patriarchal order. McCartney started the movement after finding out that his daughter was pregnant because she had sex with one of his football players.[63] McCartney felt he was partially responsible for not being present to his family—his daughter having sex out of wedlock was a symbol that his family—and one of his football players—had not maintained the strict standards of purity on his watch.

That same year the First Presidency issued a statement about same-sex sexuality. The statement began by calling upon church members to re-establish their commitments to moral conduct. "Parents should teach their children the sacred nature of procreative powers," they wrote, "and instill in them a desire to be chaste in thought and deed."[64] At the same time that they emphasized procreation, they

63. Kristen Kobes Du Mez, *Jesus and John Wayne: How White Evangelicals Corrupted a Faith and Fractured a Nation* (New York: Liveright, 2020), 150.

64. First Presidency Statement, November 14, 1991.

also acknowledged that there were "divinely appointed roles of men and women." Just as they warned against same-sex love, they re-emphasized firm gender boundaries. Without changing their teachings about same-sex attraction, and in concert with their political work against same-sex marriage, they softened their discussion of how gay and lesbian members should be treated, encouraging bishops and stake presidents to reach out to people "struggling" with these issues to let them know that they were welcome to return to the church.[65] At the very same time, the church softened its language about patriarchal authority in heterosexual marriages. And yet because of the patriarchal structure of the church, with men holding every position of authority and leadership over every position held by women, both softenings masked structural patriarchy and heterosexism. While the discourses changed, the arguments that there were only two genders and they were distinct, opposite, and perfectly paired in a heterosexual relationship remained.

In 1993, Hawai'i's court case Baehr v. Lewin made it seem that Hawai'i might be the first state in the U.S. to legalize same-sex marriages. The LDS Church, with about 50,000 members in the state who made up five percent of its total population, stepped into the public fray, working in an organized fashion to provide economic, political, and social power to defeat that possibility. The church's public and political anti-LGBT work stretched back to its activism against the ERA; in fact, the anti-ERA political work served as training for how to combat the legalization of same-sex marriage. Church leaders believed both would upset binary gender roles in the family. Just as it was embracing a more compassionate stance towards those experiencing same-sex attraction, the church began to increase its political fight against same-sex marriage.[66]

In 1995, Dallin H. Oaks offered counsel to people on "same-gender attraction." In his talk he argued again that God had placed heterosexual attraction in humans so that they could have families and raise children. Choosing a life different from the one prescribed

65. Ibid.

66. Neil J. Young, "Mormons and Same-Sex Marriage: From ERA to Prop 8," in Patrick Q. Mason and John G. Turner, eds., *Out of Obscurity: Mormonism since 1945* (New York: Oxford University Press, 2016), 145–54. See also Young, "Homosexuality and Politics in Mormonism," 208.

by the Plan of Salvation was a grave sin.[67] Oaks then outlined how believers should respond when a family member told them that they had same-sex desire and what they should say in response to the idea that people were "born that way." First, he enumerated the portions of the Plan of Salvation that declared gender was an essential characteristic of all spirits prior to their being born into a physical body. Second, spirit bodies took on physical bodies in order to prepare them to be like their heavenly parents. The goal, in the end, was exaltation in the celestial kingdom, "and [exaltation] is only available to a man and a woman who have entered into and been faithful to the covenants of an eternal marriage in a temple of God."[68]

This speech exemplifies covenantal hetero-captivity in the LDS tradition.[69] In other Christian traditions that frown upon same-sex attraction and sexuality, believers are subject to that teaching only for their mortal lives; sexuality and gender are not often seen as inherent to identity in the afterlife. In the Latter-day Saint tradition, though, LGBT believers are locked into a heteronormative and cisgender framework from their pre-mortal through their post-mortal existence, thus making their earthly sexual identity a topic of infinite concern.

Oaks argued that Satan constantly sought to disrupt human progression to godhood. To do that Satan attempts "to persuade us to misuse our sacred powers of procreation, to discourage marriage and childbearing by worthy men and women, and to confuse what it means to be male or female."[70] Oaks encouraged believers to maintain a strict gender boundary and to see heterosexual marriage and procreation as the goal of human existence. At the same time, he expressed the "softer" side of the church's position—that it was unacceptable to participate in "gay bashing," which included both verbal and physical attacks. In addition, he taught that compassion should be the response to people who have HIV or AIDS, moving away from the church's earlier language of plague and punishment. Finally, Oaks distinguished between "thoughts and feelings" (which

67. Oaks, "Same-Gender Attraction," *Ensign*, October 1995, 7–14.

68. Ibid.

69. Smith and Patterson, "For Time and Eternity."

70. Ibid.

could be resisted) and "homosexual behavior" (which he defined as a serious sin). He again turned to the comparison between same-sex attraction and addiction, arguing that while biology may limit a person's freedom, it did not limit agency. In the end, he promised that the church would not discipline people for thoughts or feelings, but continued sin (especially if it encouraged others to partake in it), could bring church discipline.[71]

In September 1995, as part of the same meeting where Oaks gave his address, church president Gordon B. Hinckley announced, "The Family: A Proclamation to the World," as official church doctrine. The Quorum of the Twelve had been discussing the document since the fall of 1994. Boyd K. Packer, then Acting President, encouraged the group to make a doctrinal statement about the family that followed the strategic suggestions Oaks first made in his 1984 white paper. The Family Proclamation could be used in cases like Baehr v. Lewin to draft amicus briefs against the legalization of same-sex marriage.[72] In this way the church could join other churches that had similar official statements. The Family Proclamation would be a tool to make arguments against legalizing same-sex marriage and for religious freedom protections for those who did not want to provide services for such ceremonies based on their faith systems.

The Family Proclamation stood as the culmination of many of the teachings about gender roles and sexuality that general authorities had taught for several decades. Having reached an almost scriptural status since it was issued, the Proclamation confirmed that the Plan of Salvation was built upon an understanding of heterosexuality as the center of the family structure.

The Family Proclamation also emphasized gender complementarity. Marriage was between a man and a woman. Men and women were to raise children and provide for both their physical and spiritual needs. According to divine intentions "fathers are to preside over their families in love and righteousness and are responsible to provide the necessities of life and protection for their families." Mothers "are primarily responsible for the nurture of their children." Thus the

71. Ibid.

72. Richard E. Turley Jr., *In the Hands of the Lord: The Life of Dallin H. Oaks* (Salt Lake City: Deseret Books, 2021), 215.

document limited women to their role as mothers and created a hierarchical relationship, with men presiding over the family. This it did even as it couched its description in the language of gender equality.[73]

While the document acknowledged that circumstance might require other familial structures, it set up the nuclear family with a heterosexual marriage as the norm and the ideal. It ended with a warning that the disintegration of the family would cause the breakdown of communities and nations. But it was not just a simple warning. The end of the Proclamation is also a call to church members, "responsible citizens," and government officials to be politically active, to defend the morality of the nation by protecting the family based on a heterosexual monogamous marriage as the foundation of a moral and thriving society.

The Family Proclamation was a declaration that firmly aligned the LDS Church with other conservative religious organizations. In the face of perceived threats about a society that was becoming increasingly more permissible and liberal, the church staked its claim. Men and women were different. Men presided over women. The two were meant to be in a procreative, heterosexual, monogamous union for eternity. All would be measured against that ideal and that norm. The preservation of the nuclear family would be part and parcel of how the institution would understand the purity system and how it would determine who was worthy and who was not. The policing of gender and sexuality enabled the church to firmly stake its claim at the center of what was then mainstream American life.

73. Caroline Kline, "Saying Goodbye to the Final Say: The Softening and Reimagining of Mormon Male Headship Ideologies," in Mason and Turner, eds., *Out of Obscurity*, 214–15.

PART II
DISSENTING VOICES

"Well, this isn't Kansas, there's no yellow brick road, or emerald city, or real wizard or magic slippers, but there are wicked witches, a lot of scarecrows with straw for brains, and quite a few cowardly lions."
—D. Michael Quinn

In the April 6, 1988, edition of the student-run, off-campus newspaper called the *Student Review*, D. Michael Quinn, a professor in BYU's history department, wrote an essay about the marketplace of ideas. He began with the argument that a "true" university should be a vibrant, bustling marketplace. "As in any free marketplace, the goods have various uses, shapes, sizes, colors, and qualities," he wrote. "One size does not fit all." Various merchandise options would appeal to different people, some would be made to last a lifetime and others would be shoddily crafted. The key was that people could try them out to see if they worked. Vendors would display their wares, arguing for their own and not those from the next stall. They did not need permission to be there. They just had to make their best sell. For Quinn, an open university was just such a marketplace: "boisterous, unruly, energetic, exciting, multidimensional, fluid, and structured only enough to maintain the integrity of that orderly chaos of the mind."[1] Quinn's envisioned marketplace was a lively space where free inquiry meant questions could be asked and answers weighed for their relative value.

Quinn then described what he called the House of Faith. While

1. Mike Quinn, "The Marketplace of Ideas, the House of Faith, and the Prison of Conformity," *BYU Student Review*, April 6, 1988, 11–13.

the marketplace was cacophonous, the House of Faith was "calmer, more secure, and heavily structured." Those who enter "move through corridors through which countless others have passed in orderly procession." Even though the experience of the House of Faith was more disciplined and sedate, it did not want for adventure, "because you may chance upon a room so long in disuse that even the custodians ... have forgotten it." Those custodians were there to ensure people's safety "in the house they did not build, whose floor plans they do not know precisely."[2] And so they may caution people away from particular rooms, noting that they are not well lit or are in disarray. The custodians did not want anyone to fall or wander around lost. Perhaps at this point in their reading of Quinn's essay, readers would believe that he was juxtaposing the "open university" with the Church of Jesus Christ of Latter-day Saints, recognizing their differences while also showing their overlap. The custodians in the House of Faith, after all, were concerned for the safety and well-being of all.

But one other place occupied a spot in Quinn's exploration, one that had not been created by God. This place was not open to new or diverse ideas. It did not allow for the freedom to choose or ask questions. People there viewed vulnerability as a weakness and questioning as a dangerous liability. Quinn called this place the Prison of Conformity. "Convinced that regular members of the culture would only be confused by unrestricted inquiry," Quinn explained, "the authorities of the Prison of Conformity have adopted several methods of inhibiting freedom." First, the authorities speak exclusively about positive aspects of the culture. Anyone who criticizes or tries to point out flaws is swiftly punished by wardens who want to ensure that only a rosy picture of things shapes people's worldview. Next, those in charge close off access to any documents or other evidence that does not support their version of history and belief, seeking to sanitize the information that prisoners can know. If people find information to the contrary, they are portrayed as "renegades who are seeking to disturb the happiness and loyalty of the rest of the culture." In addition to being depicted as rebels, authorities teach

2. Ibid.

prisoners that those who share different knowledge betray the culture and must be expelled because the culture would be "actually better off without the presence or influence of these independent people." Finally, the wardens use "instruments of power" to "harass, isolate, silence, expel, or force into exile those who do not conform sufficiently."[3] By this point in the essay, readers surely would have begun to see that Quinn might be suggesting that Brigham Young University and the LDS Church were Prisons of Conformity rather than Houses of Faith, squashing any forms of independent thinking or diversity.

But then he announced that, "This particular Prison of Conformity, of course, is the Soviet Union," catching his readers who had been thinking about their own communities by surprise. He used this writing technique to warn about what he saw as traits of the Prison of Conformity seeping into BYU. "There is a danger that BYU's slogans may be more accurate in their inverted form," he cautioned. "Instead of 'The World Is Our Campus,' the reality may be that 'The Campus Is Our World.'"[4] Quinn believed that the campus where he had been teaching was closing itself off, perhaps had already closed itself off, from the excitement created by the exchange of ideas, the benefits of diverse perspectives, and the freedom of conscience.

By the time he wrote that article, Quinn had determined to leave BYU, feeling that he was being pushed out. In fact, he had asked his friend and mentor, Leonard Arrington, to write letters of recommendation for him. Quinn gave up his continuing-status position at the university for a one-year research fellowship at the Huntington Library in Southern California, one of the positions for which Arrington wrote a letter of support. Arrington told Martin Ridge, the head of research at the Huntington, that Quinn "is a fine lecturer—is able to enthuse students and colleagues with the excitement and meaning of history. Although I regretted his decision to resign from Brigham Young University, I fully understand it; it was probably inevitable." Further, Arrington told Ridge, "[Quinn] is a first-rate scholar and a first-rate person."[5]

3. Ibid.
4. Ibid.
5. Leonard Arrington to Martin Ridge, February 3, 1988, Signature Books Collection.

In February 1988, Arrington had hosted a gathering of BYU history professors at his home, paid for by the school's history department, to honor Quinn upon his leaving. There, Quinn explained to his colleagues that he had been feeling pressured for a number of years to make professional changes. He knew, for both stated and unstated reasons, that he did not have a future at BYU: "And while no one had suggested to him that his job was on the line, it had become increasingly clear the last couple of years that his future opportunities at BYU would be limited." When Quinn spoke to his peers that evening, he thanked them for their community and support at the same time that he gave a rather pessimistic view of the field of Mormon history, one surely reflective of his experiences of rejection and church discipline. In response to his comments, fellow BYU historian Ronald W. Walker asked: "Can we have professional history written in the church today?"[6] Walker's question echoed the sentiment of many in the 1970s, 1980s and 1990s. How could historians, including believers who were trained as professional historians, operate in the context of a church that closely guarded its archives? To Walker, Arrington responded in his ever-optimistic way that all present had to keep trying—that they would succeed; that they must.[7]

Two months after his article appeared in the *Student Review*, Quinn wrote to Arrington about his decision to leave the university. He explained his "departure from BYU was as cold at the university administration level as one might expect." He described going to do his official exit interview with the associate academic vice president, who took the form, looked at Quinn, and then signed the form without saying a thing. "That was the best farewell BYU's administration could cough up after my eleven years on the faculty," Quinn wrote. "There's no love lost on either side."[8] Unsurprisingly, after years of BYU's board of directors seeing Quinn as a thorn in the side of the institution, the administration was glad to see him go, perhaps

6. Joseph Fielding Smith Institute, Minutes of Gathering with Mike Quinn, Arrington home, Salt Lake City, February 17, 1988, Signature Books Collection.

7. Ibid.

8. D. Michael Quinn to Leonard Arrington, June 21, 1988, Signature Books Collection.

even glad that he was choosing to leave so that they would not have to deal with any publicity that might come with his ouster.

Quinn went on to tell Arrington that he had always lived with a strong sense of mission and believed he was called to use his gifts to bless the church and its membership. It had always been his dream. "Well, I've come to the end of dreams," he wrote. Now, "walking away from the ruins has been a relief." He felt that if people had not already been assigning him bad motivations in his historical work, then they would now. But he told Arrington that "I have felt that Mormonism is truer than the laws in its human leaders and people." Quinn was writing to tell Arrington goodbye, in a way. He did not expect to continue on in Mormon-related endeavors in the manner he once had. He had chosen to leave Utah. His life story had not gone as planned: "Well, this isn't Kansas, there's no yellow brick road, or emerald city, or real wizard or magic slippers, but there are wicked witches, a lot of scare-crows with straw for brains, and quite a few cowardly lions. My dream was satisfying in its way, but only in anticipation of a greater fulfillment."[9]

As he expressed his disillusionment with how his life had gone, Quinn also explained his belief that he had held since childhood, confirmed by several personal religious experiences, that he would one day become an apostle in the church. He wanted to serve people and build up a thriving ministry.

Even as he had these powerful dreams of what the future might hold, he knew that his identifying as a gay man, which at the time he still regarded as a problem that needed to be overcome, might stand in the way. At the age of twelve, he had determined he "would give up every other preference in the effort to fulfill this mission for God and His children on earth."[10] Willing to suppress his sexual desire for what he considered loftier goals and a divine calling, he soldiered into the life the church had set out for him, participating in a heterosexual marriage and nuclear family. In 1988 Quinn told Arrington of a previous encounter with Apostle Spencer W. Kimball, in which he hoped Kimball would tell him to walk away from his lifelong dream of becoming an apostle, that it was never meant

9. Ibid.
10. Ibid.

to be. Instead, Quinn recalled that Kimball suggested that God may well call him as an apostle. Confessing these things to Arrington symbolized Quinn's "abandonment of the dream." He knew that his sexuality and his scholarship had stood in the way of his ability to flourish at BYU and would continue to stand in the way of his relationship to the institutional church. In the end he acknowledged that he continued to struggle with the ambiguities in his own life, but he was setting off to find a new path and a new sense of his relationship to his scholarship, his sexuality, and his faith life.[11]

Quinn was but one person who would feel the weight of church expectations on those who dissented in the last decades of the twentieth century. As one of the September Six, he was someone who would be immortalized. His struggles with the church hierarchy defined his life long after 1993, precisely because he could not, and perhaps did not want to, change his image as a rebel shaking his fist at an unforgiving and unmoving institution.

The individuals who came to be dubbed the September Six were not working in concert. They were not the only dissenters in the church. They did not have a master plan to challenge the purity system. Yet what they did—their community building, their scholarship, their activism, and their beliefs—amounted to a challenge. That challenge, though, was heterogeneous, offered in fits and starts, and never unified. Rather, it demonstrated the diversity that in reality had been part of the church all along, even as the institution sought to unify, standardize, and correlate.

The disciplinary actions of 1993 were a distillation of decades of institutional labor on behalf of the purity system. Each individual's story is distinct and worthy of attention. It is important to remember that while what happened to the Six in September 1993 was extreme and chronologically compact, it was part of a much larger movement by the institution to define and police the purity system. The church hierarchy sought to manage diversity of thought and identity with a standard of purity in a rapidly growing church. What happened in September 1993 was simply the most extreme moment in a decades-long process. For this reason, this book has and will

11. Ibid.

continue to discuss the September Six alongside others disciplined by the church outside of that month.

While the challenges made to the purity system varied widely, they do bear some striking similarities. Perhaps most pronounced was the claim that religious life was not a rigid system focused on rules and requirements.[12] As the institution called upon the notion of tradition rooted in history to make its claims about the nature of the Restoration, the Six focused more on experience and personal conscience as important and authoritative sources of knowledge. Yet their claims, too, were rooted in history. History-telling was often the battleground on which these disagreements about the Restoration's meaning played out. In different ways, each dissenter talked about spiritual experiences that led them to believe that the road the institution was taking was not in line with God's will. They argued instead for a God concerned not with purity, but with openness, inclusion, truth-seeking and telling, and personal relationship.

Part of what the dissenters attempted to expose was the intersection between history and "tradition," defined here as the accrual of certain narratives and experiences, whether rooted in fact or not, that over time form the impression that things have always been a certain way. The Six typically worked in scholarly and activist ways to make public the idea that church leaders of their day operated in a historical context and that their biases affected their perceptions and actions. They did this while acknowledging that revelation could be at work in history, but the relationship between revelation and context was complicated. In addition, their work sought to deconstruct the notion of "tradition" by showing that things were not as they had always been. The restoration movement changed over time and tradition was simply the narrative told by those with power about how they came to have power and why they should continue to be in power. Tradition is the accumulation of experiences of those at the top, imbued with so much hierarchical privilege that certain aspects of history are forgotten, and others overemphasized. Like Lester Bush, dissenters

12. Marcus Borg notes that the challenge to the purity system of ancient Israel also had this characteristic. Borg, *Meeting Jesus Again for the First Time: The Historical Jesus and the Heart of Contemporary Faith* (New York: HarperCollins, 1995), 82.

wanted to expose that those who called upon the weight of tradition were often just demonstrating their power.

At the same time as there were disagreements even about the nature of God and the nature of the Restoration, the institution and its dissenters quarreled about how disagreements should be discussed. The nonconformists often argued that public dissent was a critical part of institutional health. Without hearing alternative voices, they maintained, believers would not be able to make informed decisions for themselves and the institution would not be able to acknowledge its problem areas, name its mistakes of the past and the present, and move toward a better future.

Individual dissenters were not the only ones making these arguments. Another notable example was the Sunstone Foundation, one of the groups that hosted the symposia the church found problematic. Elbert Peck, executive director of the Sunstone Foundation in 1993, argued that the Foundation existed "because the independent discussion of Mormon issues is healthy for Mormonism. There are things which should not be talked about under the auspices of the sponsorship of the Church, because that would convey the official sanction of the Church." Believers needed a venue for discussing their questions, Peck argued, ones that should be explored rather than quashed. Those conversations also happened in church hallways, he observed: "They are sometimes speculative, sometimes irreverent, but they are essential to social bonding."[13] Peck suggested that informal conversations about faith were vital to the life of the church. Many struggling with the purity system felt that the exploration of such questions fostered a healthy dialogue, one that would allow all Latter-day Saints to stake their claim as members of the church while feeling ownership over their faith lives and spiritual paths.

But while the institution may have had room for private individual dissent, it did not make room for public dissent. Repeatedly during this time, church leaders explained that apostasy was not about differences of opinion per se, but about discussing those differences publicly or in ways that might lead other church members away from orthodoxy and orthopraxy. They framed authority as they

13. "There Is Sunstone in My Heart Today: An Interview with Elbert Eugene Peck," *Student Review*, August 1993.

framed revelatory experiences. One could disagree on a personal level, but to take that disagreement to others, especially those over whom one did not have priesthood authority, was simply unacceptable in the eyes of the church hierarchy.

Some of the Six showed a naivete about how institutions worked; they were surprised that the church responded the way that it did. They genuinely believed that their own quest for truth would be welcomed as soon as other believers could see things as they did. At times, this meant that they argued for a kind of conforming non-conformity—a desire to do some policing of their own about how the Restoration should be understood.

Several dissenters also showed some anxiety. And this anxiety may have stemmed from membership in an institution that sought to be a "record-keeping people." They were pushing back against the ways the institution had hidden and sanitized its history. They were pushing back against forgetfulness. In their realization about how the institutional church was shaping its history-telling to undergird its purity system, some feared that alternative voices would be stamped out. It seemed that the interest of a singular, correlated narrative told by those with power would eventually overpower any record of another narrative. They feared that the *one* narrative would be carved in stone. Because of this anxiety, these dissenters at times worked tirelessly to write pages and pages of alternative narratives, perhaps subconsciously believing that sheer volume of pages could counter the tradition-making and correlated version of institutional history.

As they pushed back against the seemingly immoveable institution, they drew hope from the idea that things in the church had not always been the way that they were. If that was the case, then there was a possibility of a different future. They looked to ancient history and the history of Joseph Smith's Restoration for the egalitarianism on which they argued the church should be patterned. They wrote and spoke, having faith in the idea that dissent and dialogue would ultimately strengthen the church. They pointed to a different path the institution could take into the future, a path they believed led to the "true church."

5: SEPTEMBER 14

"Leaving Mormonism was like taking off a really tight shoe."
—Lynne Kanavel Whitesides

When she heard that the LDS Church had excommunicated fellow feminist Janice Allred in 1995, it did not really surprise Lynne Kanavel Whitesides. After her own disfellowshipment on September 14, 1993, nothing much could. She was the only one in the September Six who was not excommunicated. Instead, Whitesides was disfellowshipped, a more murky category that did not revoke her membership in the church but did severely limit her role in it. In that status, she could not publicly speak, teach, or pray at church, enter the temple, or take on any official public roles in the community.

When she heard about Allred, Whitesides shared her belief that the LDS Church always reacted to women, intellectuals, and particularly women intellectuals that way. To the press, she likened it to a witch hunt. "When women come to the waters of baptism from now on, we could add one step: See if they float, then we can save all of us a lot of time and heartache."[1] Whitesides saw a pattern—if a woman had something to say, if she was unhappy or questioning in any way, she would be viewed as a witch. "We would have been burned, those of us who were doing what we did back then."[2] Two years after her own disciplinary proceedings, Whitesides framed what had happened to Allred as a religious institution cleansing itself of what it could not stand.[3]

1. Lynne Kanavel Whitesides, interview with Philip Lindholm, in Philip Lindholm, *Latter-day Dissent: At the Crossroads of Intellectual Inquiry and Ecclesiastical Authority* (Salt Lake City: Greg Kofford Books, 2011), 14. Hereafter Whitesides Interview.
2. Ibid.
3. Lynne Kanavel Whitesides, oral history with the author, August 17, 2022.

In the *New York Times* on October 2, 1993, just two weeks after she was disfellowshipped, Whitesides made her own prediction about the future: "If you excommunicate one of us there will be 10 more to step up and take her place," she foretold. "Excommunicate those 10 and there will be 100 to take their places."[4] Whitesides's interpretation of that prediction ten years later proved to be more accurate: "I think I was right, not so much that women are getting excommunicated by the tens of hundreds, but rather that women are leaving [the church]."[5]

While her prediction may have had its accuracies and inaccuracies, one thing is clear. What happened in September 1993 had a chilling effect on Mormon feminism. Mormon feminism continued, transforming over the decades, but it also remained a beleaguered movement. Many women in the church were afraid of taking on the moniker because it had gained such a bad reputation among church members. The disfellowshipment of Lynne Whitesides, along with the later excommunication of Janice Allred in 1995, made clear that the purity system of the church depended on women keeping their place. Outspoken women who felt free to publicly criticize the church and its leaders would be punished for their choices. Both Whitesides and Allred knew this. They had challenged the patriarchal order of the church, both theologically and practically, offering instead a vision of egalitarianism, both human and divine.

No one may have anticipated that Lynne Whitesides would become one of the faces of Mormon feminism in the late twentieth century. She was a convert who had been raised Lutheran, the granddaughter of Germans and Italians. Her father had fought in World War II and then returned to marry her mother when he was nineteen and she only sixteen. Whitesides always joked "that being raised by them was like being raised by the babysitters." Throughout her childhood, her family struggled against poverty. Her father had only an eighth-grade education and her mother did not graduate from high school. "They were very bright people," she recalled, but they were "busy all the time just trying to make ends meet."

4. Dirk Johnson, "As Mormon Church Grows, So Does Dissent from Feminists and Scholars," *New York Times*, October 2, 1993.

5. Whitesides Interview, 15.

In addition to always scrambling to survive financially, her family moved around a lot. Whitesides was often working to make a community of her own. Each year from seventh grade through her senior year in high school they moved to a new town.[6]

During her time as a Lutheran and well into her experiences with the LDS Church, Whitesides had a central desire: "Ever since I was a little girl, I have wanted to experience God."[7] That desire was so strong that she would imagine God while she was going to sleep. She "wanted not to understand the meaning of life (or God), but to experience being alive. To me, this means to experience or to merge with God."[8] When their Lutheran pastor who was also a family friend suddenly died, causing a lot of grief for her and her family, Whitesides began to seek out other relationships and answers.

In her junior year of high school, she began to investigate the LDS Church. It provided her with the supportive community she was looking for. They "just kind of surrounded me and made me feel welcome" and offered an immediate community that took her into their care. That new community had an even better bonus to a rebellious Whitesides: "[M]y parents didn't like the church. They didn't like the church at all!"[9] Even though her parents were concerned, perhaps *because* her parents were concerned, she forged ahead and was baptized one week after her eighteenth birthday. She wanted to embrace the community that had welcomed her when she did not feel particularly rooted anywhere else.

Then something happened that surprised everyone—perhaps her concerned parents the most. When they attended her baptism, her parents had profound spiritual experiences of their own and decided to join the LDS Church just three months later. They eventually converted about thirty of her relatives.[10] Looking back, Whitesides remembered that what appealed to her about the church was not only a sense of community and feel for God that she had not had before, but also "the ability to question."[11]

6. Whitesides, oral history with the author.

7. Lynne Kanavel Whitesides, "The Dance of Love," *Sunstone*, December 2003, 14.

8. Ibid.

9. Whitesides, oral history with the author.

10. Philip Lindholm, "Introduction," in Lindholm, *Latter-day Dissent*, 2, and Whitesides, oral history with the author.

11. Whitesides Interview, 18.

Even as she felt that the church spoke to her desire to connect with the divine, she began to observe the different gendered messages that were given to boys and girls. Those differences gave her pause. "When I became a member of the Church," she recalled, "girls were being told to shine the shoes of their brothers so they could make it to priesthood meetings on time."[12] Young women were also taught that they should be sexually pure, that no suitable husband would want to marry "a chewed-up piece of gum." Boys were taught the same lesson, but the focus was not on their own sexual purity but rather that they should desire only un-chewed sticks of gum (meaning virgins) for their wives. In addition, while girls were being taught the importance of their purity and their beauty, Whitesides felt that the boys were receiving practical lessons like learning to operate a compass.[13]

Nonetheless Whitesides was excited to head off to college at Brigham Young University in 1970. As soon as she arrived, though, and her entire time there, she did not feel like she fit in. She never felt like she got the knack of the culture. But she had fun during her brief time on the campus, remembering it as a time when "her major was dating."[14] While she enjoyed some of her classes, she most embraced the social life and the newfound freedoms.

What began as questions about why boys learned more practical lessons than girls turned into questions about why men held priesthood authority over everyone else. Whitesides was becoming a feminist. The questions she asked about the church were questions that she asked about the broader culture as well. She lived in the tension of trying to find answers. Her negative experiences at BYU, of feeling out of place and mistreated for her differences and her gender, ended with her leaving before finishing her degree.

From there she went to California where in 1977, she married Alan Whitesides, who was studying to be a doctor. Together they had three children. Early in their marriage, the Whitesides spent two years living in Mexico. There Lynne continued to ask the same questions about gender inequality in a new culture. She concluded

12. Ibid, 9.

13. Ibid, 8–9.

14. Whitesides, oral history with the author.

that the culture of Mexico was misogynist and treated women poorly, just as she had noticed in her experiences of the United States. Patriarchy was everywhere. She was in her late twenties and "beginning to ask all those questions that [church leaders] don't like you to ask [and so] I got a little bit of a reputation for asking those questions."[15]

After Whitesides's family moved to Chicago, her feminism continued to grow, nurtured by the liberal ward they were a part of at the University of Chicago. There she befriended Lori Stromberg, another Mormon feminist. When she heard a rumor that Stromberg had stood in the priesthood blessing circle when Stromberg's son was confirmed a church member after his baptism, she decided to go find out for herself. "I went and said to her 'Did you do that?' and she said 'Yeah,' and I said, 'Oh, let's get to know each other!'"[16]

As Whitesides made friends with similar feminist leanings, she was also raising three children and active in the church community. One of her roles was to support the Cub Scouts and one of her duties was to attend a meeting with the male scout leader in what people considered to be a dangerous part of Chicago. People in the ward told her that she could not be in a car alone with her fellow scout leader because it was against the rules of the church. Her response was to say, "Really? Because, well you know me … if I get in a car with him his pants are going to be off in a minute!" What surprised Whitesides most in that moment was that no one laughed. They had not appreciated her humor or the fact that she had called out communal expectations.[17]

After this happened, Whitesides noted that she was not asked to speak at ward meetings for quite some time. She attributed the pause to ward members understanding how much she was juggling: her husband was in his medical residency, she was the mother of three young children, and they did not have much money to live on. It was not until sometime later, when she was talking to friends, that one of them told her that she was not invited to speak in church because of her reputation as a firebrand. She had a hard time believing that her joke would make her undesirable in that way, but when she

15. Ibid.
16. Ibid.
17. Ibid.

went in for her temple recommend interview the bishop told her she was "kind of a troublemaker."[18]

Lynne was beginning to understand that the questions that seemed natural and obvious to her made others view her as a rabble-rouser. She asked questions like: Why was it inappropriate for a woman to be in a car with a man? Why can't a mother participate equally in the ritual life of her children? Why would the community offer very different educations to boys and girls? And in the midst of this Whitesides and her family moved back to Utah, the heart of LDS orthodoxy.

During that period of transition from Chicago to Salt Lake City, her feminism continued to grow and she developed new and broader networks of community. In Utah she took graduate classes in feminist thought where she devoured the writings of deconstructionist and feminist theorists like Derrida, Cixous, and Kristeva. She chaired the B. H. Roberts Society (a group named after one of the church's intellectuals at the turn of the twentieth century), a group that investigated current issues in the church. She worked for, chaired, and attended panels at Sunstone symposiums, where standing-room-only crowds talked about how feminism and faith intersected.[19] She fostered the relationships and community that nurtured the critical lens she was fine tuning, the one she had carried her entire life.

As she planned and put together panels for each conference, she made sure that every session included a feminist and an LGBT voice, knowing these voices would raise the issues that people most needed to discuss. Later, she would note that all of the groups she was a part of at the time were ones that helped church members address their questions and concerns. "If the Church had just left all of them alone," she argued, "then most of [the people in those groups] would have worked through these issues and, mostly, been able to stay in the Church."[20]

Mother on Earth, Mother in Heaven

In some ways, Whitesides should have seen the writing on the wall. She knew what had happened to feminist and ERA supporter Sonia

18. Ibid.
19. Lindholm, "Introduction," 2.
20. Whitesides Interview, 16.

Johnson in December 1979. Johnson's excommunication warded off Mormon feminists for years, demonstrating that the church's stance on a political issue, one of *the* political issues of the day, was going to determine not only the politics of the state of Utah, but the culture there and throughout the church.[21] But Whitesides did not heed the warning. She was both naive about the consequences and ready for a fight.

As her concerns continued to grow about how the church was treating women, she pointed to a talk Ezra Taft Benson gave as a prime example of what she saw as the church's problematic teachings about gender. In a fireside address on February 22, 1987, titled "To the Mothers of Zion," Benson spoke about the importance of family and home to the LDS theology and understandings of exaltation. But family was not his central theme; instead, it was motherhood. He argued that mothers were "the very heart and soul of the family."[22] For Benson, "No more sacred word exists in secular or holy writ than that of *mother*. There is not more noble work than that of a good and God-fearing mother."[23]

Benson's talk was a direct response to the arguments made by mainstream American feminism that women could fulfill more than only the role of mother and that they, too, should have equal access to meaningful work and equal pay. Benson instead encouraged women to have children as early as they could, noting that their goal as co-creators was to have the largest families possible, so that they could help their Heavenly Father continue in his project. He counseled that women should not listen to the "reasoning of the world," which told them to wait to have children: "Do not curtail the number of your children for personal or selfish reasons."[24] He encouraged women to eschew the teachings of "conventional wisdom" and realize that "a mother's calling is in the home, not in the marketplace." While some women might find themselves infertile, single, divorced or widowed, Benson counseled church members to see those as the exceptions. They may not be able to control their situations entirely,

21. Peggy Fletcher Stack, "Where Have All the Mormon Feminists Gone?" *Salt Lake Tribune*, October 4, 2003.

22. Ezra Taft Benson, "To the Mothers of Zion," Fireside address, February 22, 1987, churchofjesuschrist.org.

23. Ibid.

24. Ibid.

but "in a home where there is an able-bodied husband, he is expected to be the breadwinner."[25]

Then Benson listed ten ways that mothers could fulfill their "God-given roles" that were "vital to your own exaltation and to the salvation and exaltation of your family."[26] Thus he enforced the idea that motherhood was the measure of a woman's salvation. A woman was her relationships. Her ability to achieve exaltation in the next life was bound to her ability to do her gender right.

Whitesides thought Benson's talk was patriarchal hogwash. She embraced the idea that women could have more expansive roles. Women did not need to be celebrated, they needed to be treated as equals. She understood the talk to be indicative of the problem: "They put women on a pedestal in the Church like they're great, and yet there is this patriarchal hierarchy."[27]

Writing a retrospective for the *Salt Lake Tribune* sixteen years later about the ripple effects of Benson's talk and the disciplinary actions of the 1990s, titled "Where Have All the Mormon Feminists Gone?," Peggy Fletcher Stack noted that the talk had "an immediate and overwhelming impact," in that "dozens if not hundreds of Mormon women quit their jobs, believed that was what their prophet wanted, while others felt guilty for ignoring that mandate." Later church policies would attempt to institutionalize and regularize the role of motherhood by further limiting the leadership roles of women who had children under the age of eighteen.[28]

Not only was she frustrated by the fact that women were taught that their primary worth was tied to their ability to mother and nurture, but Whitesides also had concerns about how the institution itself worked. She recalled that she once invited a member of the Relief Society general presidency to come to her house to give a talk to a gathering of women. That speaker explained that the church president had not met with the Relief Society presidency for five years.[29] From Whitesides's perspective, this was an outcome of the correlation process. And it was an indication that women did not

25. Ibid.
26. Ibid.
27. Whitesides Interview, 9.
28. Stack, "Where Have All the Mormon Feminists Gone?"
29. Whitesides Interview, 9.

have any real power. She believed these Relief Society leaders had no independence and that they were not even respected in the positions they did hold.

Mormon feminists at the time had all kinds of influences from the broader culture's feminism, and these were connections that Whitesides cherished. The Mormon Women's Forum (MWF) was founded in 1988 and Gloria Steinem came to speak at the group's first Counterpoint Conference. In addition to feminists of all ilks, group members were influenced by the feminist theology going on in Judaism and other branches of Christianity. These feminist theologians were scrutinizing the theology, ritual life, and ecclesiology of their religious communities and exposing sexism and misogyny wherever they found it. Rosemary Radford Reuther, author of *Sexism and God-Talk*, spoke to a MWF audience about the position of women in the church and the role of the feminine divine.

Phyllis Trible, author of *Texts of Terror: Literary-Feminist Readings of Biblical Narratives* (1984), a book that focused on and analyzed all of the biblical texts that contain violence against women, spoke at another MWF conference. Trible's visit was particularly important for Whitesides. Thirty years later she remembered well what Trible said to her at that conference: "Lynne, you guys can do all this. Liberal women will take all of the arrows and the conservative women will waltz in. Just know that." And for Whitesides that was an accurate prophecy of what happened: she witnessed that the women she made community with, those excommunicated and those disciplined in less auspicious ways, "widened the envelope" in the church. They forced men to pay attention to women's voices, but in the end it was conservative women's voices the church amplified.[30]

In addition to the practical matters of church governance, Whitesides argued that women were being marginalized by the theological worldview of the institution. She saw this especially in church attempts to silence discussion of Heavenly Mother. In LDS theology, Heavenly Father has a wife, Heavenly Mother, who is an important, if not often discussed figure. In 1845 Eliza R. Snow, a polygamous wife of Joseph Smith, wrote a hymn titled "O My Father":

30. Whitesides, oral history with the author.

I had learned to call thee Father,
Thru thy Spirit from on high,
But, until the key of knowledge
Was restored, I knew not why.
In the heav'ns are parents single?
No, the thought makes reason stare!
Truth is reason; truth eternal
Tells me I've a mother there.

When I leave this frail existence,
When I lay this mortal by,
Father, Mother, may I meet you
In your royal courts on high?

The hymn is the best-known mention of Heavenly Mother in the early church. Even though it was written after Joseph Smith's death, the hymn indicates that Smith also taught about Heavenly Mother, even if that may have only been to a select group of people.[31]

Heavenly Mother surfaced in the interests and discussions of Mormon feminists in the 1980s. Like Catholic, Protestant, and Jewish feminist theologians, they could see the importance of having a feminine divine figure for the flourishing of women in the church. As their interest grew, so did concern within the church hierarchy. At the church's October 1991 general conference, Gordon B. Hinckley (then counselor in the First Presidency) spoke to the general women's meeting about Heavenly Father and Heavenly Mother. He began by assuring women that they were God's daughters, "precious to Him, loved by Him, very important to Him." Further, he argued that women were going to take part in the highest degree of glory, the celestial kingdom, because "the man cannot enter without the woman, neither can the woman enter without the man."[32]

Hinckley then reasoned that if humans had a Heavenly Father, they also had a divine Mother. Yet "the fact that we do not pray to our Mother in Heaven in no way belittles or denigrates her.... None of us can add to or diminish the glory of her of whom we have no

31. David L. Paulsen and Martin Pulido, "'A Mother There': A Survey of Historical Teachings about Mother in Heaven," *BYU Studies Quarterly* 50, no. 1 (2011): 71.

32. Gordon B. Hinckley, "Daughters of God" *Ensign*, November 1991, 1, 4.

revealed knowledge."[33] In one breath Hinckley acknowledged the existence and importance of Heavenly Mother while also stating that the church had had no revelations about her. She was an unknown fact. Church members knew nothing and therefore should not be praying to or hypothesizing about who she was. He then added the weight of scripture to his assertions by mentioning that in the Sermon on the Mount, Jesus only instructed people to pray to "Our Father," in what Christians often refer to as the Lord's Prayer.[34]

For Whitesides, the exclusive focus on Heavenly Father was not fulfilling. "The absence of the feminine not only makes a home lonely," she later wrote, "but it also damages everybody in the house."[35] As a seeker of religious truths, she wanted the church to feel like a home base and have the kind of comfort and warmth that an ideal home had. But she did not feel she could find it with a church that was "full of the masculine with the feminine somewhere out in the margins."[36] She continued to struggle, feeling marginalized by her religious community at the same time that she was a leading voice of LDS feminism.

Disciplinary Action

Not always anticipating the far-reaching consequences of her words, Whitesides felt comfortable "saying anything I wanted to. And [I] knew the Church was getting upset, but not *that* upset." She simply felt compelled to speak when she thought something was wrong. Early in 1993 she had been asked to pray at a ward meeting, but even as she was asked, the bishop inquired about who would be the focus of her prayer, Heavenly Father or Heavenly Mother. She made a joke of it in her reply to him but felt the continued sting of being labeled a troublemaker. The day she was to pray, the stake president gave a talk. She recalled that in it he asked the audience to imagine how they were going to feel when they were in heaven standing behind Ezra Taft Benson, the prophet of the church, when Heavenly Father says to him, "You didn't work hard enough." The stake

33. Ibid, 9–10.

34. Ibid. For a discussion of church teachings on Heavenly Mother, see Paulsen and Pulido, "A Mother There."

35. Whitesides, "Dance of Love."

36. Ibid.

president then chided the community to work harder and to spend more time on their church callings.[37]

When she got up to pray after the talk, Whitesides was angry, angry that her working-class ward had to hear a call by a privileged stake president to work harder. And so she prayed, "Heavenly Father, please forgive him because he doesn't know what he is talking about."[38] Afterwards, she remembered, everyone was quiet. Even as people came to quietly thank her, she knew that it was no longer a place she could tolerate or one that could tolerate her. She quickly made a decision to stop attending regularly.

Then, just after Boyd K. Packer's talk to the ACCC in May 1993, Whitesides appeared on Utah television on a Sunday morning, talking about Mormon feminism. It was that show that was the impetus for her disciplinary process. When the host Chris Vanocur, a KXVX-TV Salt Lake City correspondent, asked her, "Are you demanding change?" Whitesides responded by saying, "We're asking. I mean, what can we demand? We don't have any power at this point, but we can say, 'Listen to us. We have something to say that you need to hear.'"[39]

As the interview continued, two things happened. First, Vanocur asked about Whitesides's reaction to Packer's talk. She remembered questioning Packer's relationship to Christ in her response, arguing that a true Christian would not have declared intellectualism, feminism, and the gay-lesbian rights movement as enemies. When Vanocur asked if she had any plans for nonviolent action and protest, she quipped, "Well, we're thinking about toilet-papering the temple."[40] That was just like Whitesides. She took sacred symbols and played with them. She willingly called out what she thought was problematic, no matter who said it. She thought, "Well, I can do an interview on a Sunday morning. Who's going to be watching? They're all going to be at church! And, yeah, many people were watching!"[41]

Shortly after her appearance on television, her bishop called to ask for a meeting. Whitesides thought he wanted to address her discomfort, and the reason for her Sunday absences so she went to

37. Ibid.
38. Ibid.
39. Dear Friend Letter, September 13, 1993. Signature Books Collection.
40. Ibid.
41. Ibid.

meet with him in summer 1993. His two counselors were there and rather than talking about her discomfort, her bishop told her that he had called her in "to meet with you to see if we need to take any ecclesiastical action against you."[42]

Whitesides felt blindsided. Even so, she left the meeting feeling as though they had had a nice discussion. She was surprised, then, when she later received a notification about disciplinary proceedings. She immediately called her friend Lavina Fielding Anderson, who arrived at her house with bread and jam and an offer to help her come up with a plan. After her time with Anderson, Whitesides wrote a letter to the bishop "saying that if he went through with the Church court, then we were going to let the media know."[43]

When she arrived at her disciplinary council on September 14, there were about two hundred people outside holding candles and singing as part of a vigil. In addition to the crowd of supporters, there were TV stations and newspapers. Whitesides knew the local media would attend, but she was surprised to see that CNN and the *New York Times* were also there. In fact, her story made it to the front page of the *New York Times*. Before her council, Whitesides had called her previous Social Movements professor and asked him what he suggested she say to the media. He told her, "The attention span of a reporter is very limited, so if you are going to make any points, just make three and make them really count." So she prepared her comments and was ready for the cameras.

The day before the council, Whitesides asked herself if she was in the wrong. After some self-scrutiny, her answer was "No, I am not. This is really, really bullshit. Really. What they're doing, just everything about it is ridiculous." And so she went to her council feeling good about where she stood and warmed by the signs that said "Lynne is not a heretic!"[44]

Her local church leaders told her that she could not have anybody stay with her throughout the proceedings as a sign of support. Her bishop, Virgil Merrill, for whom she had a lot of sympathy because she knew how much he hated publicity, would not even allow her

42. Whitesides Interview, 3.

43. Ibid, 4.

44. Whitesides, oral history with the author.

husband, her priesthood holder, to attend.[45] At the beginning of the council, she learned that there had been a letter-writing campaign on her behalf. "It's not about whether you are a good person," Whitesides remembered Merrill saying. "I get that you are a good person. What's not being judged here is if you are a good person."[46]

After establishing that Whitesides's goodness was not up for debate, the council's grueling questions began. "The bishop started by asking why I thought it was all right to pray to a female deity—a god who is not male. I said that people like my Chinese sister-in-law could not relate to a white, male God, which made the secretary mad. He yelled, 'We know what God looks like. Joseph Smith told us.' I just looked at him and said, 'Which one of his accounts are you talking about?'"[47] Over the course of the next several hours, Whitesides did have the opportunity to call in six witnesses to come in, speak on her behalf, and then leave. This group included Lavina Fielding Anderson and Margaret Toscano, both of whom would later be excommunicated. While Whitesides was not yet aware of all of the tactics of the Strengthening Church Members Committee, she observed that the stake council had transcripts of interviews she had given, with highlighted passages pointing out areas of concern.

After the deliberations, her bishop told her that she was disfellowshipped, meaning that she retained her church membership but would be severely restricted in what she could do. And there were conditions for her re-entry to full fellowship. "One was that I could no longer speak evil of the Lord's anointed by saying anything derogatory about the Church or its leaders. Also, I was not allowed to talk about Mother in Heaven or how women should hold the priesthood." Whitesides was thankful at the time that she was not excommunicated. She told the *New York Times*, "I don't want to be excommunicated.... I love the church, it's part of my being. I also have to consider my children, who would be greatly affected."[48] Even though she felt sure that she would be socially ostracized, she

45. Ibid.
46. Whitesides Interview, 5, and Whitesides, oral history with the author.
47. Whitesides Interview, 5.
48. "Mormons Penalize Dissident Members," *New York Times*, September 19, 1993.

thought, "At least I'm still sealed to my husband and kids," echoing a fear that others in the coming weeks would share.[49]

Whitesides would later remember the events as the church's attempt to silence her for being her authentic self. She argued that, "The fact that I was thinking does not seem like apostasy to me."[50] She followed all of the stated rules and behavioral expectations for the Saints, except for publicly criticizing a church leader, namely Boyd K. Packer. Even though it hurt, Whitesides also understood that "leaving Mormonism was like taking off a really tight shoe."[51] There had been pain and the pain was not yet over. But there was also *relief.* The most painful part of the disciplinary process was the rift it caused between her and her parents, especially her father. "For me, it was 'I can't believe that you would … choose Boyd Packer and not me,'" she recounted. "For them, it was 'Well, we believe the church.'"[52]

Whitesides also felt a lot of anger, even rage. She realized later that she was blaming others for things that happened to her, while not looking internally. Besides feeling rejected by the church community, her marriage dissolved not long after the disfellowshipment for reasons unrelated to the church. "About this time, two things happened," she recalled. "I found an incredible therapist, and I began doing Native American ceremonies." For Whitesides, both were gifts from God that allowed her to explore her spiritual and mental well-being.[53]

As she began to understand herself better, she also felt like she was able to better understand and approach God. But her understanding of who God was and how God worked had shifted. It was no longer the God she imagined in her time in the LDS Church, a God who was "looking at us through the barrel of a shotgun, just waiting for us to slip up so he can punish us." That was a God who supported purity as the focus of theology and church discipline. Instead, she came to see God as "a loving presence who feels definitely personal."[54]

---

49. There was a fear and a generally held belief, even if it was not actual LDS doctrine, that sealings to people disciplined by the church were severed. Whitesides Interview, 6.
50. Ibid, 7.
51. Whitesides, "Dance of Love."
52. Whitesides, oral history with the author.
53. Whitesides, "Dance of Love."
54. Ibid, 15.

Whitesides discovered this more mystical God, one that has an I-Thou relationship with people, in multiple religious traditions. She had an intense experience with that God in 2001, while sitting by a fire and praying in the middle of the desert. She had a vision and came to understand "how amazingly beautiful God is" and that she herself "was a part of that incredible beauty … because I am made from it."[55] Leaving the "tight shoe" of the church allowed Whitesides to experience a more expansive vision of who God was to her and what God was concerned about. She felt as though the church as an institution had made God into a military, law-and-order figure, and it had locked Christ into a very small box as well. When she returned to reading Christian scriptures with her new and more expansive lens, she saw a Christ who was much bigger than she had been taught by the institution.[56]

Whitesides's experiences with new teachers led her down a spiritually enlightening path. She began to practice a more experientially based and fully embodied kind of religious practice. She "finally realized we are on a ball that spins and doesn't knock us off and sprouts food." Such an observation allowed her to feel awe and wonder. She chose to embrace a type of panentheism—a vision of divine spirit enlivening the world. This shift helped her see that things were much more expansive than she had imagined at any other time in her life. "It is the thing that changed my life in such a beautiful way," she recalled.

The journey had only begun. She continued on with other teachers and seekers of wisdom. Recalling her childhood desire to experience the divine in a new way, this time she learned that, "There is not some guy between you and the experience," between you and the "consciousness that has created the universe and all it contains." Her spiritual journeys made her believe that an institution cannot contain or claim ownership of the divine.[57] Her new teachers also helped her feminism blossom. She came to believe that patriarchy was leading to the environmental decimation of the earth that sustained humanity. And she maintained that patriarchy had a "sell by" date, and that the date was long past due.[58]

55. Ibid, 15–16.
56. Whitesides Interview, 7.
57. Whitesides, oral history with the author.
58. Ibid.

For Whitesides, then, it was the institution and its patriarchal structures that bound believers into a narrow vision of God and the world. She recalled that a few years after her disciplinary council, she wrote a letter to the general authorities apologizing. She apologized for her anger at them, for thinking they could grant her power as a woman in the church. She had come to learn that she already had power as a woman and that "you could not give me what I already possessed."[59] Later she felt thankful for the process she had gone through, realizing that "standing up to them in the way that it happened, without me even needing to do that, was such a powerful experience of me finding my own self."[60] She reported that she received a response that asked her to return to the church, but she did not feel she needed to because she now knew that she could access the divine anywhere at any time, all on her own. And she was no longer sure that those in the church hierarchy could.[61]

When asked if she was still Mormon ten years after her disciplinary council, she declared, "Maybe a little. The lens is still there, and I can't remove it because I was Mormon for twenty years, but I don't feel Mormon."[62] When asked thirty years later, she had shifted dramatically. She understood that when she wrote the letter to the church she was still in a "patriarchal weird world" that held her in relationship to it. While the others dubbed part of the September Six were all still in some kind of relationship with the church—whether through re-baptism, research, or participating in the community as a non-member—Whitesides did not want any kind of relationship with the church and its patriarchy. She had worked to create a loving and complex community that had nothing to do with the LDS Church.[63]

Janice Allred

Janice Allred was called into her own disciplinary council two years after Whitesides. Allred had been a leader of the MWF and she joined the Mormon Alliance, a group working to stop clergy abuse, shortly after it was formed. Though Allred was living in Mexico with

59. Whitesides Interview, 10.
60. Whitesides, oral history with the author.
61. Whitesides Interview, 10.
62. Ibid, 17.
63. Whitesides, oral history with the author.

her family during the September 1993 excommunications, she felt like she was intimately involved. Besides her participation in the two groups that were identified as problematic by church leaders, her brother-in-law was Paul Toscano, one of the September Six. During that month, she felt thousands of miles away yet immediately present.

One night in September 1993, she had a dream "that I received my own invitation to a Church court. It was a beautiful invitation on exquisite white paper, embossed with white roses. The handwriting was elegant, the language formal and polite," she remembered. But when she opened the invitation, she saw that the inside did not match the outside. Inside the card was "a crudely drawn mimeographed map showing the homes where all those who would attend my court lived; the Stake President, his counselors, and the twelve men who were members of the high council."[64] Later, when she faced numerous exchanges and interviews that eventually led to her own disciplinary council and excommunication, Allred concluded that the dream was prophetic and symbolic: "Those who asked me to come and be judged by them were polite and correct on the surface," she recalled, "but underneath, where they lived, they were as crude and violent as a military weapon."[65] During the process, she felt like she was shot with a weapon discharged by men with smiling faces who told her that they cared about her.

Allred's interest in feminism had grown as she raised her nine children. Reading Sunstone newsletters and *Dialogue* heightened her awareness of the sexism that existed in the church and in the broader culture. She had followed the Sonia Johnson case and was shocked to read Johnson had been disciplined for her feminist commitments. What happened to Johnson made her see the high stakes that she was dealing with.[66]

At the 1992 Sunstone Symposium, Allred presented a paper on Heavenly Mother, in which she argued that if female and male are truly equal, then God must also be male and female. In her analysis,

64. Janice Allred, "My Controversy with the Church," *Mormon Women's Forum* 6, no. 1, 1.

65. Ibid.

66. Ibid, 2–3.

"The Father becomes the Son, Jesus Christ, who redeems us from our sins, and the Mother becomes the Holy Ghost, who is with us to comfort us, teach us the truth and sanctify us. They both sacrifice to be with us, they both play a vital part in our salvation."[67] Allred's argument encapsulated gender equality while also hinting that there was gender complementarity, different roles for different genders, both necessary.

Not long after she gave the paper, her stake president, Carl Bacon, asked her to visit his office. That meeting and subsequent ones resulted in Bacon telling her she must not publish her Sunstone paper. She responded that she was not planning to publish it but might one day in the future. She promised she would let him know before she did. In 1993, Allred decided to submit her essay to *Dialogue*. Based on her Sunstone talk, her article provided "a reinterpretation of the Godhead based on my readings and pondering of the scriptures."[68] Allred intended to fulfill the letter, if not the spirit, of her pledge to Bacon. She planned to tell him right before the essay appeared in print so that any attempt to stop her would not work.

But Bacon found out the publication was coming before then and felt betrayed. During their next meeting, Allred defended her faith and made it clear that "I would always try to follow what I felt the Spirit inspired me to do, even if it contradicted what a leader said." At the end of a long discussion, the bishop and stake president signed the temple recommends for both Allred and her husband. But the couple left believing that Bacon saw them as "dissenters who had connections with 'those apostates' who were giving the Church so much trouble in the press."[69]

Allred and her husband, David, very quickly felt the effects of being labeled dissenters. Their bishop told them that they would not be allowed to speak at the sacrament meeting sending off one of their sons to his full-time mission and welcoming home another son from his mission. David had not been given a calling in the local

67. Ibid, 3.

68. Janice M. Allred, "Toward a Mormon Theology of God the Mother," *Dialogue: A Journal of Mormon Thought* 27, no. 2 (Summer 1994): 15–40. See also, Janice Allred, interview with Philip Lindholm, in Lindholm, *Latter-day Dissent*, 134, 146. Hereafter Allred Interview.

69. Allred, "My Controversy," 4–5.

ward, even though he was in good standing. All of this raised some concerns for both the Allreds because David was a professor at BYU. Together they decided that he would stop attending any meetings that Janice had with local leaders so as to ensure that they did not get lumped together in the leaders' minds.[70]

Some people wondered if Gordon B. Hinckley was involved in Allred's case. He may have experienced her work as a direct critique and defiance of his 1991 speech on Heavenly Mother. In addition to that talk, Hinckley gave a talk in October 1993 titled "Bring Up a Child in the Way He Should Go."[71] In it Hinckley preached, "This church is established on principles that are divine. From the day of its organization, it has been led by prophets, and I solemnly testify that the Lord Jesus Christ, whose church it is and whose name it bears, will never let any man or group of men lead it astray. His is the power to remove them if they should ever be found taking the wrong turn." Hinckley asserted that if church leaders were ever wrong, the responsibility was not on believers, but on God to take care of it. To Allred and others this seemed like a dangerous claim to infallibility, one that told believers to lean back from their responsibility to reflect on and consider the teachings of their leaders via their personal conscience.

In response to Hinckley, Allred wrote her own talk titled "Him Shall Ye Hear." In it, she articulated what she had been saying to her local leaders all along. The idea that the prophet could not lead the church astray was wrong, she thought, and it was causing two big problems. First, the church was becoming increasingly authoritarian. Second, and in relation to the first, believers were being taught that passive acceptance of whatever church leaders said and did was what faith looked like. She wanted believers to think critically so that they could take greater ownership of their faith.[72]

When her bishop eventually scheduled a disciplinary council for her, Allred chose to speak to reporters. She knew that doing so might anger and frustrate church authorities—she had witnessed what happened to the September Six after all—but she believed

70. Ibid, 7–8.

71. Gordon Hinckley, "Bring Up a Child in the Way He Should Go," *Ensign*, November 1993.

72. Allred, "My Controversy," 7.

it would help bring about "a more open Church." Allred ended up having two disciplinary courts, the first of which took place October 12–13, 1994. Just before the council, Hinckley gave a speech in Idaho in which he mentioned her Sunstone speech. He said, "She can present her paper until doomsday, but God will see to it that the Church will not be led astray."[73]

The October 12 meeting began at 7:00 p.m. and lasted eight hours. In it, the bishop told her she could not publish any article "challenging prophetic infallibility." Allred refused the instruction, "because I believe that a person should be free to follow truth and his or her conscience wherever they lead."[74] Allred read her twelve-page statement, which noted that disobedience to church leaders was not listed as an offense worthy of church discipline in the church's Handbook of Instructions. She argued that no one could be forced to believe something simply because they had been told to by someone else.[75]

At one point, Allred remembered that she started to cry. In response, her bishop said, "No matter what happens we'll still be your friends."[76] For her, this was the type of false kindness that she had come to expect. It was the stuff she had seen in her prophetic dream. Finally, after long hours of discussion and deliberation and even though she refused to back down, Allred was not excommunicated, but rather placed on probation. Formal probation is similar to disfellowshipment but the conditions and restrictions put upon the member are left up to local leaders. She was told that she could not teach, speak or pray publicly, serve in an official position, partake of the sacrament in weekly church meetings, or visit the temple.[77]

To Allred, not being allowed to teach in church meant being denied a role that was central to her identity. She maintained that she had never brought up any of these potentially controversial issues at church, she spoke about them exclusively at Sunstone symposia and in feminist circles.[78] How she would navigate her new place, role, and relationships while under church discipline seemed insurmountable.

73. Allred Interview, 141.
74. Ibid, 141–42.
75. Allred, "My Controversy," 15.
76. Ibid.
77. Allred Interview, 141–42.
78. Ibid, 237.

She decided to write an open letter to her bishop, in which she argued that probation was an unfair decision. She reasoned that the council had chosen a milder punishment so that they could feel better about their decision. But it still injured her the same way. In addition, Allred told him that she was going to set some boundaries about what she was and was not going to do in the future. She argued that the leaders had set up an "unequal arena where you have the power to judge and punish but are unwilling or unable to engage in an honest and open discussion of ideas and issues." She vowed that going forward she would follow God and her conscience, denying that church leaders had any authority over her personal decisions.[79]

After the council, Allred continued to meet with media outlets, making public how the church treated intellectuals and feminists in its fold. Her story gained attention, in part because the press "loved the irony in the church's disciplining a mother of nine for talking about the Mother in Heaven."[80] It seemed that each time a new article appeared in the press, her bishop grew angrier. In November 1994 she gave a speech at Counterpoint, a meeting of the MWF, called "My Controversy with the Church." When the bishop asked to see a copy of the speech, she refused to give him one, believing that he should not have access to something that was outside his jurisdiction.[81] Her second disciplinary council came just months later, in May 1995. It was then that she was excommunicated.

When she wrote her appeal to the First Presidency, Allred received word of their response from her new stake president. He did not allow her to see the actual communication but explained that they all still loved her. The First Presidency sustained the decision to excommunicate but hoped she would work with her bishop to foster a good result from all of the pain and difficulty. During that meeting, the stake president said he had not heard anything about her from the outgoing bishopric and he wondered how things were going for her in her ward. "People are friendly," she told him. "They say 'hello' to me, but it's difficult for me because I don't know where I stand."[82]

79. Allred, "My Controversy," 15–16.

80. Allred Interview, 142.

81. Ibid.

82. Janice Merrill Allred, "White Bird Flying: My Struggle for a More Loving, Tolerant, and Egalitarian Church," *Case Reports of the Mormon Alliance* 2 (1997): 235.

Later she talked to the bishop about feeling disconnected. He told her that people did not know how to talk to her. "They see you in church, but the only other thing they know about you is that you appeared on TV and on the front page of the newspaper publicly attacking the thing they care most about."[83] In addition to being labeled a dissenter, she had also been labeled a betrayer. She was a dissenter, a betrayer, and a rule-breaker in an institution that preached orthodoxy, purity, and loyalty. The community was not able or ready to talk to her about it, so she had only to intuit that her relationships with them had changed, possibly irrevocably.

In an oral history interview on June 26, 1995, Allred shared that "Mormons are nice people and they're not rude and nobody has been rude to my face." Most people would not talk to her about what happened, fearing perhaps that they would be led astray. But those who breached that social discomfort told her that she had broken the rules. She would ask them which rules and she always came to the same conclusion: "I broke the unwritten rule. And the rule is unwritten because it's indefensible. There is no way you can defend the rule that you have to do whatever your priesthood leader says."[84]

Representing the perspective of following the priesthood leadership unapologetically, Louis Midgely, a professor of political science at BYU, argued that Allred was trying to embarrass the church to the public: "It's unseemly, disgusting and reprehensible for Latter-day Saints. The church can't say anything. It is bound to keep quiet, but I'm just an ordinary member and am not so bound," Midgely said. "The dissidents say these are private opinions she doesn't teach in church but the church is not a building."[85] Midgely surely expressed what many thought. Allred had seen it in her own relationships. She was airing the dirty laundry rather than keeping it in the family and challenging the patriarchal authority of the church hierarchy.

After her excommunication on May 9, 1995, Allred still felt Mormon in many ways, but understood it differently: "I'm Mormon, but I would also say that I'm a Christian and a seeker of truth.

83. Ibid, 241.

84. Ibid.

85. Qtd. in Peter Scarlet, "Mormon Leaders Give Feminist 2-Week Reprieve," *Salt Lake Tribune*, October 15, 1994.

I guess I'm a Christian in the Mormon tradition."[86] She still had a testimony, though, even if it looked different from the testimonies of many other church members. "To me the voice of the Spirit is a clarity of thought, a sudden understanding, a radiating love, an abiding peace, an encompassing fire," she declared. And she had always been genuinely seeking to understand "the mind and will of God," feeling confident that "God has spoken to me."[87]

In her wistful 2003 retrospective, "Where Have All the Mormon Feminists Gone?," *Salt Lake Tribune* reporter Peggy Fletcher Stack explored why the feminism of the 1980s and 1990s, the one that Lynne Whitesides and Janice Allred had helped to lead, was no longer present within the LDS Church. No one was picketing general conference. No one was talking about Heavenly Mother. No one was demanding the priesthood for women. It seemed that feminism was "dead or dying" within Mormonism.[88] Many in the church felt that feminism carried "too many negative connotations derived from past battles and is synonymous with a confrontational style or hostility to motherhood," Stack wrote. "Or ... it has been co-opted by those who define it solely in terms of reproductive rights or competition with men."[89] The MWF, which Whitesides and Allred helped lead in the early 1990s and that eventually led to their disciplinary councils, "can scarcely draw a crowd to its annual fall conference." For a time, at least, it seemed that the institutional church had succeeded in convincing its membership that feminism was a foreign, external threat attempting to infiltrate the church body.

86. Allred Interview, 152.

87. Allred, "White Bird Flying," 276.

88. Claudia Bushman, qtd in Stack, "Where Have All the Mormon Feminists Gone?"

89. Ibid.

6: SEPTEMBER 19

"We were pariahs, we were rock stars, and we were projection screens."
—Maxine Hanks

The Ordain Women movement, with its first public meeting in April 2013, sought equality between the sexes in the Church of Jesus Christ of Latter-day Saints. In an effort to attain priesthood ordination for more than half of the church's members aged twelve and older, the group staged peaceful protests by trying to attend the male-only priesthood meetings at general conference. Ordain Women describes itself as aspiring "to create a space for Mormons to articulate issues of gender inequality they may be hesitant to raise alone. As a group we intend to put ourselves in the public eye and call attention to the need for the ordination of Mormon women to the priesthood."[1] One might well have expected to see Maxine Hanks on the front lines of active leadership in the protests of the Ordain Women movement. After all, she was excommunicated on September 19, 1993, for her feminist writings, particularly in relationship to women and the priesthood. So why wasn't Hanks there in April 2013 and then again in October 2013, when the group went to general conference and stood in line to attend the priesthood meeting? Why wasn't she there at the symbolic moments when dozens of women, one by one, were politely hugged by a woman from the church's public affairs office and then gently turned away at the door?

The day of the second protest, October 5, 2013, was the thirty-fifth anniversary of Hanks receiving her endowment, one of the ordinances bestowed in Latter-day Saint temples. And Hanks wanted to go to

1. ordainwomen.org, accessed July 22, 2022.

the temple again. She had decided to be re-baptized into the church in 2012, nearly twenty years following her excommunication and had purchased her temple garments in anticipation. October 5th would have been the perfect day to return because it was the anniversary of that special time so many years ago. But she could not go to the temple that day because it was closed for general conference.

Hanks still believed there was a place for her in the LDS community. Her journey away from and her return to the church highlights the way the purity system functioned in the 1990s. Hanks disrupted the institution's expectations for women in every way possible. She never married, never mothered in a nuclear family, and publicly argued that women ought to hold the priesthood. Because of this belief, she published *Women and Authority*, an edited collection that sought to make the argument that Joseph Smith and the early restoration church had granted women the priesthood and that it had subsequently been taken away. Echoing the structure of Lester Bush's argument about racial bans, Hanks and her fellow essayists wanted to return the church to what they argued were its egalitarian origins. Even though she did not participate in the Ordain Women protests happening as she was returning to church membership, Hanks maintained that she had not given up her feminist ideals. She simply understood them differently. She felt as though she had learned a lot on her twenty-year journey and taken her spirituality into her own hands. Even if she did not agree with the church's teachings about women and the priesthood, she had come to terms with them.

Finding Her Spirituality

Hanks had had a strong sense of calling toward the priesthood and ministerial roles ever since she was a small child. Even though all sixteen of her great-great-grandparents "were Mormon pioneers who joined the church and migrated to Utah between 1847 and 1869," Hanks's immediate family was not particularly orthodox. They were working class, and Hanks always felt a bit out of place as an intellectual and a mystic in their midst. When she told her family she wanted to go to Harvard, her parents laughed. When she had an active spiritual life, she kept it quiet because it felt as though they were focused mainly on material things. "I was a mystic. I felt like the magic kid in the family of Muggles," she recalled, drawing on a Harry Potter analogy, "They didn't understand me. So I relied on God for help."[2]

Even so, Hanks's relationship to the church was distinct. She always felt like she was an independent thinker with a direct connection to God, so she did not feel that she needed a mediator for her relationship with the divine. At the same time, though, church gave her a bit of familiarity when she felt at odds with the rest of her family. "Because I was magic and my family was Muggle, they didn't understand me." The church felt familiar because it, too, was magic. "It was like going to Hogwarts. Mormon church was my Hogwarts as a child."[3] It was the church that nourished Hanks's spirituality as well as her drive to be a leader. Living in a small ward in Sunnyside, Washington, where Latter-day Saints were vastly outnumbered by other religious traditions, she was able to take on numerous leadership roles in her church, roles that were not necessarily gender-bound. The ward needed anyone who wanted to help lead. For Hanks, who grew up feeling androgynous, this was perfect. She never felt bound by rules about what boys and girls and later men and women should do.

All that changed when Hanks decided to go on a mission and she began to interact more with the institutional center of purity and orthodoxy. Before leaving on her mission, she got to experience the temple, the heart of the magic she longed for, and she could not have been more excited. "[W]hen I first entered the temple in 1978," she recalled, "I was surprised to discover that it wasn't about marriage."[4] She dreamed of the chance to further her own religious experiences and to get to know her inner spiritual core. She wanted to know her own identity rather than understanding herself only in relationship to others, particularly men.

The temple ceremony suited that drive for her to know who she was. For her, it "was about our individual relationship with God, not about couples."[5] And that impulse to walk alone and define her own place in the world continued throughout her life. She did not want to

2. Maxine Hanks, oral history with author, August 18, 2022.

3. Ibid.

4. Maxine Hanks, "LDS Women's Authority and the Temple," *Dialogue: A Journal of Mormon Thought* 52, no. 1 (Spring 2019): 49.

5. Ibid.

be a wife or a mother, even though both were expectations. In church she learned that motherhood was a woman's "duty," her "sacred obligation," and the "full measure of creation," meaning that motherhood would allow her to progress to heaven. But Hanks did not want that life. "From age 18, I knew that I didn't want to experience pregnancy," she remembered, "and decided then that if I ever became pregnant I'd have an abortion."[6] Hanks chose to buck the system. People were constantly asking her why she chose not to get married and the answer was simple: "I wanted to find my own path."[7]

Part of that path was going on a mission. After attending the church-owned Ricks College (today BYU–Idaho), in Rexburg, Idaho, for two years, Hanks saved money for her mission by working on a project that collected Mormon music history in the Snake River Valley. In preparation she found herself in the temple on October 5th right before departing; she was there because she had chosen to be a missionary at a time when women were not being encouraged to go on missions. She yearned to participate fully in the church. She needed to speak to others about it with authority. Being a missionary seemed like the only avenue for women to play a leadership role and she wanted to allow that side of herself to flourish.[8]

The same week in 1978 that she submitted her paperwork for her mission, the church hierarchy announced President Kimball's revelation that lifted the racial bans, a change that signaled that the church might be moving toward a greater egalitarianism for its membership. It was an exciting time for the church as an institution and for her as an individual. She saw the institution she loved taking inclusive strides and celebrated it imagining greater inclusivity lay ahead.

At that exciting time, she had several intense personal experiences. When she was set apart as a missionary through the customary priesthood blessing, she "felt something tangible conferred on me, a spiritual authority or mantle that stayed with me throughout my

6. Maxine Hanks, "Compulsory Pregnancy," *Mormon Women's Forum* 3, no. 1, 9.

7. Hanks, oral history with author.

8. Fiona Givens, Maxine Hanks, Margaret Young, and Neylan McBaine, interview with John Dehlin, "Alternative Feminist Approaches to Ordain Women," *Mormon Stories* podcast, eps. 443 and 444, October 16, 2013, mormonstories.org. Hereafter *Mormon Stories* interview.

mission experience."[9] As she went through the initiatory and endowment rituals in the temple, she had an even more profound experience. "I felt a bigger spiritual mantle descend on me, of the priesthood," she remembered. "I had no idea what type of priesthood it was, but I knew spiritually that I had just received priesthood in some form."[10] Those experiences of *knowing* that she had received the priesthood drove Hanks throughout her mission. The experience was so powerful that the memory of it and the surety of its truthfulness would never leave her. She was called to be there and she was confident in her competence.

But others on her mission did not see it that way. While she felt sure that she "had the same mantle that the elders had," those male missionaries treated her as second class.[11] It was on her mission that she learned that the church had gender inequality baked into its structure and she would not be able to hold any leadership role that she sought. And that realization led to heartbreak: "Suddenly the church no longer felt like Hogwarts. It felt like Umbrage or Voldemort had taken over."[12] She felt frustrated by the negative treatment of sister missionaries. "That was really hard on me," she wrote. "I came back a little disillusioned, even though I had a very successful mission, enjoyed myself, and made great friendships while I was out there." Women were not even considered for certain roles even if they may have been the best person for the job and she felt like she "encountered this brick wall kind of inequality."[13] And the brick wall would not move. It was always there marking a boundary that she could not cross.

Just as Hanks confronted the patriarchal structure of the church on her mission, Sonia Johnson was making arguments about the Equal Rights Amendment that were angering church leaders. While Johnson was taking center stage, Hanks was serving her mission in Florida, which, along with Utah and Virginia, was an important state in the ERA battle. And the church expected its missionaries

9. Hanks, "Women's Authority and the Temple," 50.

10. Ibid.

11. *Mormon Stories* interview.

12. Hanks, oral history with author.

13. Don Bradley, Janet L. Eyring, and Maxine Hanks, "The Loss and Rekindling of Faith," panel at the 2013 FairMormon Conference, edited transcript at fairlatterdaysaints.org, full panel at youtube.com. Hereafter "Loss and Rekindling."

to do political work against the ERA. Mission leaders gave the missionaries pamphlets and wanted them to speak against Johnson, to see their opposition to her and the ERA as part of their religious duty. But Hanks was not having it. "I had to work for two years to save up money to come on this mission," she told them. "I am not doing political work. I'm not doing this for you guys."[14]

Because she felt she had to stand up to the patriarchal structure and defend her role as a missionary, Hanks decided that she was going to leave her mission early. But a spiritual experience, just the kind she had been looking for, kept her there. As she and her companion were out proselytizing, she felt the Spirit move her to visit a "hippie camp." She was confident that she and her companion should knock on a particular door, and when they did a woman answered, rolled her eyes, and said "Oh, not the *Mormons*." But she invited them in to talk anyway and revealed to Hanks and her companion that she had just prayed for the first time since her mother died, "I knelt down and prayed and you two showed up!" After talking for a while, the two missionaries returned home, and Hanks continued to work on her secret plan to leave her mission. But the evening that she was going to do so, the woman from the camp and her partner showed up. They said, "We don't know why, but God told us to come see you." They had driven to find Hanks. She told them that she was planning to leave that night and they encouraged her to stay. "They never joined the church," Hanks recalled. "They were just these really cool people who I connected with spiritually."[15] And so she stayed and she completed her mission even as she faced the mixed bag of intense spiritual experiences combined with a hierarchical and patriarchal institution.

When she finished her mission, Hanks thought she might be able to help improve the institution's missionary program and so she went to work at the Missionary Training Center (MTC) in Provo, Utah, while she started taking classes at BYU. The MTC was in the process of shifting from a program where missionaries memorized a dialogue and recited it verbatim, to having an outline for interactions that would allow missionaries the freedom to both internalize the

14. Hanks, oral history with author.
15. Ibid.

teachings and personalize them.[16] Even as she labored to improve the program, her experiences at the MTC "completed my process of unraveling and disassociation from the LDS Church," a time that ended up being "a costly evolution to a benevolent disillusionment."[17]

"Before my mission I believed completely in the church," Hanks remembered. "After teaching at the MTC, I didn't even believe in the church enough to be disillusioned by it anymore." Falling away from her faith took Maxine on a path away from the church that coincided with her work for a new newspaper in Provo called *Seventh East Press.* Just as she started to think that BYU and Provo held nothing for her, she had read about this newspaper and recognized that several like-minded people she had met were involved. The paper quickly became known for its critiques of BYU and the church.[18] Even though *Seventh East* was a progressive press that critiqued the institutional church, she still experienced sexism as the only woman on the team. She felt confident that she could do any of the work that the others could, but that did not mean that they recognized that in her or appreciated her contributions.

In May 1982, in what Hanks later called the "mini-purge" or a prequel to the events of September 1993, local church leaders questioned and released from their callings a handful of people who wrote for *Sunstone*, *Dialogue*, and *Seventh East Press.* Hanks was one of them. She was also dismissed from the MTC.[19] It was then that she went to work for BYU's College of Humanities, helping faculty members prepare their work for publication from 1983 to 1986. While there, she "realized that I'm a writer. I'm an editor. And I'm a scholar."[20]

Attending and working at BYU, allowed Hanks to investigate the historical roots of the patriarchal brick wall she had encountered on her mission. She wondered what had contributed to the church's immobility on questions of gender, priesthood, and authority. Working for the College of Humanities, she had another of what she later would call a "crisis of faith." She came to realize that humans

16. Ibid.

17. Maxine Hanks, "Teaching at the Missionary Training Center: Awakening to Disillusionment," *Case Reports of the Mormon Alliance* 3 (1998): 189–91.

18. Ibid, 195.

19. Ibid, 195–96.

20. Hanks, oral history with author.

had created God in their own image. The perspective that she developed in contrast was of a divine realm that was not human-like but fully transcendent. In human story-telling about God, she noted the divine feminine had been obscured, diminished, and erased.[21] Put another way, even though Hanks was estranged from the religion of her youth, she still understood the power of religious stories and symbols. And she saw and was able to especially critique the stories, symbols, and silences within the Mormon tradition. Just as Heavenly Mother had been downplayed, silenced, made invisible to believers of all genders, so too had Hanks been downplayed and silenced in relationship to her talents and callings.

In 1986, Hanks moved to Salt Lake City and attended the University of Utah where she continued to study and work for the next two years.[22] While she was there she began to call herself an agnostic. She realized that she could not fully discount the possibility of the divine and spiritual realm, but that she was not entirely sure. Her profound spiritual experiences in her youth had a powerful pull on her. At the same time, her research into the church's history became its own kind of calling. She described it as both her motivation and something that "inhabited" her. Her historical research into the history of Joseph Smith's Restoration confirmed the spiritual experience she had known in the temple.[23] Women *could* hold the priesthood. It was human men who had decided they could not, not God.

As she was writing, a new wave of Mormon feminism was brewing and Hanks was inspired by its activism and its scholarship. Even so, few women felt comfortable claiming the label feminist. The excommunication of Sonia Johnson in 1979 still made the stakes feel too high. Johnson's excommunication resulted in creating "an invisible boundary or veil of fear."[24] Hanks and others felt that it was time to push through the veil—cross the boundary—and reclaim what they saw as inherent to their religious tradition.

21. Maxine Hanks, interview with Philip Lindholm, in Philip Lindholm, *Latter-day Dissent: At the Crossroads of Intellectual Inquiry and Ecclesiastical Authority* (Salt Lake City, UT: Greg Kofford Books, 2011), 61. Hereafter Hanks Interview.

22. Ibid, 54.

23. *Mormon Stories* interview.

24. Maxine Hanks, "Shifting Boundaries of Feminist Theology," *Dialogue: A Journal of Mormon Thought* 50, no. 1 (Spring 2017): 173.

Mormon feminism was not some external ideology being imported into the traditional church. They believed that it had been part of the restoration movement all along, even though a male church hierarchy sought to silence it.[25] Hanks began to make an argument that she would press for years to come: "There is a strong tradition in Mormon feminism for women to exercise the priesthood," she claimed, "so a lot of what Mormon feminists are trying to do is recapture authority and privilege in feminism that was lost."[26] Hanks was making her own restorationist argument. "Feminism helped build this church," she argued, and it was time for the church to remember that.

In 1989 Hanks authored poems that expressed some of her frustrations with women's second class status in the church. One, called "Patriarchal Blessing," claimed authority for women—authority that did not have to be drawn from a male-structured church where only men had gifts of the spirit:

> I'll predict my purpose,
> Divine my destiny;
> I'd rather have my own
> Limits haunting me.[27]

Hanks began to embrace that sense of priesthood and calling that she had had since her childhood. Even as she was not exactly sure what the spiritual or divine realm might look like, she still embraced her spirituality. She claimed her own power to "predict her purpose" and chose her own limitations over those placed upon her by a patriarchal hierarchy. That same year a second poem imagined a utopian future in the church where women were understood and treated differently. In "The Marmalade Feminist Ward," she wrote:

> Priestesses stroll the streets, bless
> The residents, serve the sacrament
> Of wine, bread and poetry, fill the empty
> Halls with universal worship sung in
> Silent songs, hymns of humble dignity…

25. Colleen McDannell, *Sister Saints: Mormon Women Since the End of Polygamy* (New York: Oxford University Press, 2019), 128.

26. Maxine Hanks interview, March 31, 1993, KTKK radio, copy in Church History Library, Salt Lake City.

27. Maxine Hanks, "Patriarchal Blessing," *Mormon Women's Forum* 1, no. 3, 3.

Here, fraternity and sorority mend archaic
Dichotomy, find original complicity
In a peculiar community without The Authority.[28]

It was a world where women could lead and inhabit the *true* measure of their creation and tradition.

Unearthing Women's History

Hanks saw 1990 as an important year for women in the church. Elaine Jack, Chieko Okazaki, and Aileen Clyde had been called to the Relief Society presidency. Dubbed the "Dream Team" by some, the three were active, modern, and sought to centralize women's voices. Many LDS women believed that this leadership of the Relief Society represented a new era. As part of their presidency, the three outlined the priorities for the Relief Society in a way that reflects just how much the emphasis on gender complementarity and the nuclear family—the familial pillar of the purity system—had pervaded the ethos of the church. The first priority focused on the personal testimony of faith for each individual, seeking to build and strengthen it. Second, they wanted the Relief Society to bless the lives of every woman. Third, they chose to highlight the charitable aspects of the Relief Society. Finally, Jack, Okazaki, and Clyde wanted to strengthen the family unit and to foster sisterhood amongst women.[29]

Hanks thought that the Dream Team "modeled authentic voice and position" and were "doing 'feminism' and 'feminist theology' without using the labels."[30] In addition to her desire to foster and affirm feminism within the church, Hanks wanted to create a textbook, a set of essays by different authors, that would serve as a collection that she could use in a Women's Studies course. She had served as a Teaching Assistant for the course at University of Utah under Dr. Vella Evans.[31] Because she thought that it was time for women in the church to re-embrace feminism and its power for framing the issues, and because

28. Maxine Hanks, "The Marmalade Feminist Ward," *Mormon Women's Forum* 1, no. 3, 6.

29. Jill Mulvay Derr, Janath Russell Cannon, and Maureen Ursenbach Beecher, *Women of the Covenant: The Story of Relief Society* (Salt Lake City: Deseret Book, 1992), 401–2.

30. Hanks, "Shifting Boundaries," 173.

31. Hanks Interview, 55

she wanted to expose students to a variety of voices about Mormon women's past and present status, Hanks began to pull together the essayists who would eventually contribute to the work for which she was later excommunicated: *Women and Authority: Re-Emerging Mormon Feminism,* published by Signature Books in 1992. She imagined the book as a collection of voices, not as a singular statement about what the status of women in the church was or ought to be. It was apologetic in a sense, she later reflected, "because it valued and validated Mormon women's voices, history, heritage, and authority."[32]

Hanks was not the only one working on women's history in the church. At the same time that some Mormon feminists were arguing that women had always held the priesthood, there were historians who were offering a tamer version of the history of Mormon women. These scholars were publishing the history in a way that offered factual information most Mormon women had not been taught in their Sunday lessons but that also did not challenge current gender norms and roles. In 1992, Maureen Ursenbach Beecher, Janath Russell Cannon, and Jill Mulvay Derr, published *Women of the Covenant: The Story of Relief Society.* This work was important because it made documents public and accessible that had not been previously available to the masses. Reading the book is a lesson on the careful work required to explore this history while still pleasing the institution. The authors were cautious in their language, writing of the Relief Society: (1) that [Joseph Smith] organized the Relief Society according to the same pattern as he did the priesthood quorums; (2) that he taught Relief Society members the same "doctrine of the priesthood" he had taught the priesthood quorums; (3) that he delegated to the Relief Society certain "keys," or authority; and (4) that the inclusion of women within the structure of the church organization reflected the divine pattern of the perfect union of man and woman, a pattern emphasized in the highest priesthood ordinances administered in the temple and essential to the restoration of the fullness of the priesthood.[33]

Just as the authors offered the words of Joseph Smith about women and the priesthood, they also were clear that they did not

32. Ibid.

33. Derr, Cannon, and Beecher, *Women of the Covenant,* 42.

interpret his actions as granting the priesthood to women. From their perspective, Smith "opened to women channels for service and learning hitherto closed to them." In addition, they made clear that their interpretation of the historical documents reinforced patriarchal authority. "Only through his authority, and by power of his priesthood," they wrote, "could he grant Relief Society the authority to act in all things within the scope of its commission."[34] While sharing the documents that empowered women, they were also clear that women's power derived from the male priesthood. The widely ranging arguments about Joseph Smith also bled into their framing of Emma, Smith's first wife.

The authors surely understood that story-telling about Emma Smith was a treacherous landscape to navigate. The church had a lot at stake in how her story was told, especially because Smith had not followed Brigham Young and the Twelve westward after the murder of her husband. Instead, she stayed in the Midwest, eventually joining the Reorganized Church of Jesus Christ of Latter Day Saints around the leadership of her son, Joseph Smith III. The authors knew that women who had already attempted to tell Emma's story had been reined in by the church.

In 1984 Linda King Newell and Valeen Tippetts Avery had published a biography of Emma titled *Mormon Enigma*. They explored the ways that Emma had been written out of or sidelined in Latter-day Saint histories because she had not followed the movement west to Utah. In their biography they portrayed Emma as a strong woman who acted in complicated ways, unwilling to always do what the male leaders of the church expected of her.[35] At times she supported the institution and at others she was unwilling to be tamed in the service of the needs of the men in the hierarchy. In 1985, the *Los Angeles Times* reported that church authorities had instructed the bishops of Newell's and Avery's wards to prevent them from speaking about Emma Smith at church events. The ban lasted for ten months.[36] In the hierarchy's actions other scholars could see that they needed to toe the line in how they narrated the church's past.

34. Ibid, 47–48.
35. McDannell, *Sister Saints*, 121–24.
36. Ibid, 123–42.

While discussing Emma Smith's response to her husband's introduction of polygamy, the authors of *Women of the Covenant* wrote, "In pitting her authority against that of the prophet through whom her authority had come, and in planting disorder and disunity among the sisters, Emma Smith had erred egregiously."[37] In this one sentence, the church-employed historians made clear the line they would walk. Emma was challenging the authority of Smith, the font of her own authority. She would never be successful if that were the case. Even as the authors' interpretation reinforced a patriarchal order in the church, it still subtly subverted it. They portrayed Emma's power in challenging what her husband taught, a story that many LDS women would never have known. Thus employment by the church certainly affected the way LDS historians narrated history. Often working with the same sources and the same words as the authors in Hanks's collection, the narratives that both groups told operated in service of broader arguments about the present and where the source of authority lay.

Jill Mulvay Derr, one of the authors of *Women of the Covenant,* later reflected that "while stories of women's faith were always welcomed [by church leaders], questions about precedents for Latter-day Saint women's religious authority were not." Historians who worked for the church understood that building up the archive of knowledge about women in the church's history would help to strengthen the faith of women in the church, providing a foundation and usable past of strong women navigating the intersections of faith and gender. At the same time, they knew that challenges to the notion of the Restoration rooted in the purity system would not be tolerated. Derr presented her research and, where others could or would not, found a way to "be true to the scholarship as I understood it while speaking 'within the bounds' that would keep me from contradicting what General Authorities had taught." For Derr, the work to "not only restore a record but revive experience and meaning that have been missing" was fulfilling and satisfying work.[38] For Hanks, the challenge was not only to recover women's

37. Derr, Cannon, and Beecher, *Women of the Covenant*, 62.

38. Jill Mulvay Derr, "Missing and Restoring Meaning," *Dialogue: A Journal of Mormon Thought* 55, no. 2 (Summer 2022): 57–76.

history in the church but to show that "tradition" had taken the church far from its egalitarian restoration roots.

There were practical, everyday reasons why Hanks decided to collect and edit the essays for her book, but there were spiritual reasons as well. She had arrived at a period of renewed spirituality and had a profound experience that helped her discern her path. In November 1987, she had a "waking vision of a divine feminine figure … who I learned was Sophia." Sophia is a Greek word for wisdom and has been used to personify wisdom and the divine feminine in the Christian tradition. Even though she was the divine feminine, Hanks noted that the feminine figure she encountered did not match with what she had been told about Heavenly Mother. At the time, Hanks was not exactly sure how to interpret the visitor, but she was sure that in the vision she was told that the need in the world was great and was asked if she would help. Hanks knew she would, of course, and she "knew that the Mormon psyche was damaged and it had repressed its female side … so it needed to be recovered and it needed to be integrated."[39] And so she set out to do just that. Her academic and intellectual interests merged with her desire to help recover and integrate feminine spirit and power with her tradition of origin.

In April 1992, Dallin Oaks and the other advisers to the LDS Museum of Church History and Art made telling changes to the Relief Society's exhibit marking its 150th anniversary.[40] The struggles over history-telling manifested at every level. The *Salt Lake Tribune* reported that a few hours before the exhibit was to open, three quotations were removed because they were, in the words of the church leaders, "just a little too sacred." The quotations referred to the Relief Society as part of the restoration of an ancient priesthood. Where the quotations indicated that Joseph Smith had delivered the keys of the kingdom to the women of the church, the exhibit texts were reworded, so that it appeared that men were serving as middlemen between women and God. They held and turned the keys on women's behalf. Hanks "saw this censorship as part of a larger historical

39. Hanks, oral history with author.

40. Richard E. Turley Jr., *In the Hands of the Lord: The Life of Dallin H. Oaks* (Salt Lake City: Deseret Books, 2021), 201–2.

trend going back 150 years, in which the Relief Society had been diminished, censored, or reinterpreted by male Church leaders."[41]

It was in this context of struggles over how to tell women's history that Hanks received some warnings from the church hierarchy about the work she was doing. But she forged on nonetheless. The first time she encountered attempts to control her behavior happened after August 1991 when she spoke about feminism within the church at the Sunstone Symposium in Salt Lake City. A month later, her stake president, Paul Hanks (a distant relative), urged Hanks to retract certain statements she made at the conference. She declined. Over the course of their conversation, Paul Hanks revealed that while the concerns he expressed were his own, he had read a transcript made available to him by those higher up in the hierarchy who gave him "direction" about their discussion, presumably the Strengthening Church Members Committee (SCMC). In early 1992, Paul Hanks continued to attempt to make contact with her in order to discuss the issues further, but she avoided him for months.[42]

In what she later remembered as an epiphany event, Hanks recalled a January 1993 dream that operated as "a Gethsemane moment" for her, conjuring the story of Jesus in the Garden of Gethsemane who sees the events that are unfolding before him, even his inevitable death, and wonders if it could go any other way. He then realizes that it cannot. "I saw what was coming and longed to avoid it," she remembered. "The answer was clear—that I would be excommunicated and needed to go through that because it would serve a purpose."[43]

During those few years Hanks was trying to name and identify what she had referred to as the brick wall, the boundary, and the veil of fear. When she met with Paul Hanks she was told that she was crossing that line, that "it was okay to be feminist, just not

41. The quotes that were removed included: "the Society should move according to the ancient Priesthood"; "Joseph Smith wanted to make us … a 'kingdom of priestesses'"; and "sisters will be queens of queens and priestesses unto the most high God." Hanks recalled that the three quotes "were removed and replaced by three statements about the Relief Society's potential for service and blessings." Hanks, "Shifting Boundaries," 167–68.

42. Lavina Fielding Anderson, "The LDS Intellectual Community and Church Leadership: A Contemporary Chronology," *Dialogue: A Journal of Mormon Thought* 26, no. 1 (Spring 1993): 7–64.

43. Hanks Interview, 62

in public."[44] No matter what church leaders said, Maxine soldiered on. She later described her book as "a lot of new and bold feminist research in one book at a time when most Mormons didn't even use the word 'feminist' in public."[45] *Women and Authority* collected feminist voices from throughout the church's history. She and her other contributors knew that there was a risk in their publications, they risked the ire of the church and their status in it, but they also wanted to change the culture—to dismantle the wall and to revise the fear that was driving it all.

Even with all the confidence she exuded during this time, the preface and introduction of *Women and Authority* showed that Hanks was walking a tightrope. While she celebrated essays that examined women in relationship to the priesthood and feminist theology, she also maintained that a collection of essays was the best route to this end. "An anthology is a good way to approach a complex and controversial subject. Answers to questions about Mormon women and authority may not be found in one perspective or pronouncement but in many simultaneous views and approaches."[46] The idea that there were many voices and many feminisms represented allowed her to suggest that the book did not have to be understood as the threat that some might imagine. "I want to stress that this discourse is not about a power struggle," she argued, "it is about women finding identity."[47] Framing it as an apolitical search for identity rather than an assertive critique, Hanks also argued that "this feminist theology is not radical discourse; it works within the scope of Mormon theology and history."[48]

The preface and introduction operate to soothe the reader who may be concerned about the orthodoxy of the works that are contained in its pages. In fact, they posit that feminism is not what the reader might think it is. Speaking directly to church members who remembered Sonia Johnson and the battles surrounding the ERA, Hanks warned that feminism should not be equated with

44. Hanks, "Shifting Boundaries," 174.

45. Hanks, "LDS Women's Authority and the Temple," 46.

46. Maxine Hanks, ed., *Women and Authority: Re-emerging Mormon Feminism* (Salt Lake City: Signature Books, 1992), vii.

47. Ibid, vii–viii.

48. Ibid, viii.

or reduced to the fight for the ERA. It was much, much more. The introductory materials to the book are an attempt to walk a fine line and to speak to multiple audiences while offending none. It was a task that was insurmountable.

Yet the arguments made in the book were important and followed a pattern that seemed like the best way forward for feminist arguments. "Feminism has always existed in Mormonism," Hanks wrote, "It makes sense that Mormon women would be feminists: within male-centered religion and discourse, feminism and feminist theology are necessary."[49] She wanted to legitimize feminism but also to place it squarely within the restoration movement: "We have our own feminism. It's homegrown."[50] In hindsight, the hope was clear. Just as Lester Bush's work had inspired the revelation of Spencer Kimball that made priesthood ordination for Black male members of the church possible, the feminist movement could also operate as inspiration for change. Arguing that women had held the priesthood in the early church, that feminist ideals had been there all along and that subsequent church leaders had stamped out those practices and ideas, carried the hope that the church would *restore* those same ideas and practices. The church did not need to embrace some external set of ideas—rather, it had to restore ideas in the early movement.

That overarching resonance, sometimes more implicit than explicit, rang throughout the essays and was present in Hanks's own contribution that focused on priesthood authority and missionary status. "The calling of a full-time missionary is a paradoxical role for Mormon women," she argued. "It grants women some ecclesiastical authority without priesthood authority; it confers the authorization to preach the saving 'principles and ordinances of the gospel' but not to perform or administer them."[51] Exploring women missionaries throughout the church's history, Hanks noted that they had been present ever since Joseph Smith Jr.'s mother, Lucy Mack Smith, participated in proselytizing. Women missionaries had been around

49. Ibid, ix.

50. Hanks, oral history with author.

51. Maxine Hanks, "Sister Missionaries and Authority," in Hanks, ed., *Women and Authority*, 315.

since the beginning. And the rituals for men and for women were often the same. "'Setting apart,' according to the priesthood handbook, is a 'laying on of hands by those who are in authority' to confer a church calling or position. It is a priesthood ordinance similar to ordination."[52] Women in the church were called as missionaries to a role that assumed priesthood power and it was one way that they might have a role that employed that authority. In essence, Hanks wrote, they "have the authority of the church to declare the gospel and the power of the priesthood but are denied permission to exercise fully their priesthood."[53]

Disciplinary Action

It was not long before Hanks learned that what the divine Sophia had told her was true. In a dream, Sophia had said, "They are going to excommunicate you and you need to go through that.... You need to be excommunicated because thousands of people are going to learn from this.... You are destined to play this role."[54]

On September 8, 1993, Hanks received a letter from her stake president, Paul Hanks, that she would have a disciplinary council. "The Salt Lake Stake Presidency is considering formal disciplinary action against you, including the possibility of disfellowshipment or excommunication, because you are reported to have been guilty of apostasy," Hanks wrote.[55] Even though the letter was from her local leader, Maxine felt confident that the whole thing had been orchestrated by those on the top: "[T]he timing of the Church's reaction was obvious: *Women and Authority* hit bookstores in January 1993 and the Associated Press ran a story about the book that highlighted Mike Quinn's essay [in it]. Then, on the first Sunday in February 1993, both Mike and I were contacted by the stake president [Paul Hanks] regarding *Women and Authority*. (We lived in the same stake on Capitol Hill in Salt Lake City.) I doubt that the stake president was browsing brand-new feminist books fresh off the press, barely on store shelves."[56]

52. Ibid, 320.
53. Ibid, 330.
54. Hanks, oral history with author.
55. Paul A. Hanks to Maxine Hanks, September 8, 1993, Signature Books Collection.
56. Hanks Interview, 57

Perhaps the SCMC, which monitored church members' publications about the church, had read about it in the Associated Press. Whatever the process, Maxine felt confident that church leaders had deemed the book heresy before many had even laid eyes on it. Because of their past interactions, when she heard from Paul that she was going to have a disciplinary council it felt "out of the blue" and "in a hurry." She asked him to talk about it and he would not. She asked for more time to prepare, and he gave her just a few days.[57] She felt that he seemed pressed to accomplish the council before the month's end.

It happened on the afternoon of September 19th, the same day as Paul Toscano's council. Because Maxine was a woman and therefore did not hold the priesthood, Paul Hanks did not need to call a high council for her proceedings. He did not need to, but he did anyway. "Although I was flattered to merit a high priests' council of twelve rather than a bishop's court of three," she recalled, "I declined to enter that room."[58] Later, people would wonder if Maxine had demanded a high court because she believed that she held the priesthood, but that was not it. Even though she wanted to avoid the proceedings altogether if she could, she remembered Sophia's warnings and felt like she knew what was coming. Not long before she had asked that the church remove her name from its records, but Paul Hanks put off the request until after the disciplinary council, saying that once disciplinary proceedings had started, individuals could not have their names removed at their own request.

In an attempt to embrace how she thought things *should* work in the church, Hanks wrote a letter in that short time between her notice about a disciplinary council and the council meeting itself. The letter was addressed to the Relief Society Presidency of the Salt Lake Stake and Paul Hanks. In it, she noted that she had requested that her name be removed from church records and that she was denied. "My response to the charge of 'apostasy'," she wrote, "is that I may be in conflict with church policy, but I'm in harmony with god and my conscience." She went on to argue that men and church councils did not have the authority to judge her. "Were I to appeal

57. Ibid, 59.
58. Ibid.

to any church authority or council for assistance or advice," she argued, "it would be female authority, rather than male." As it went on, Hanks's letter made the same historical, restoration argument that appeared in her book. It is perhaps the best distillation of the intersecting arguments made in the collection of essays. She asserted that the Relief Society had been granted equal power with Joseph Smith's Restoration, but that since that time "various male church leaders usurped authority and priesthood that rightfully belonged to women." In doing so they had ensured that Joseph Smith's original message was "buried under 160 years of church structure."[59] Even though she never received a response to her letter, Hanks imagined that it was a shock to the Relief Society leadership—just as it would have been for most women in the church who were not familiar with the arguments in her book.

After a September 19, four-hour high council meeting which Maxine Hanks did not attend, Paul Hanks let her know that she had been excommunicated for "conduct contrary to the laws and order of the Church."[60] Years later Maxine would remember that time as a tense one in which both she and her church leaders were unwilling to listen or bend. She felt torn. "On one hand, I definitely felt divine guidance to compile the book, I felt aided by higher wisdom. On the other hand, I could have navigated the book's relationship to the Church more sensitively."[61] Nonetheless, she experienced her excommunication as a "revelatory 'shattering of vessels,' opening a doorway to new knowledge and realms I had never known."[62] More than anything else, she had been taught that, at least for a time, "the cost of [church] membership was too high."[63]

On the night of her excommunication, Hanks went out and celebrated with her friends. For someone who had not been going to church, who did not affiliate with any one tradition, but rather with a larger spirituality, there was no spiritual heartbreak. Instead, she knew that this was part of Sophia's vision for the book: "The church

59. Maxine Hanks to Relief Society Presidency of Salt Lake Stake and Paul Hanks, September 1993, Signature Books Collection.

60. "Six Intellectuals Disciplined for Apostasy," *Sunstone*, November 1993, 67.

61. Hanks, "LDS Women's Authority and the Temple," 62.

62. Ibid.

63. Hanks Interview, 60.

just did us the biggest favor it could ever do.... It's going to make Mormon feminism famous! The church did exactly the wrong thing if they wanted to suppress [the book]. It put me on *Nightline*, PBS, CNN. It put me on every channel. It made the book famous."[64] In an ironic twist, Hanks's excommunication took an academic book that would have been short-lived and would not have sold many copies and "it gave the book eternal life!"[65]

Even though her excommunication did not hurt in a spiritual or personal way and even though it gave her book life, it was not an easy event. Before the excommunication, Hanks had not felt that she had the time or space to share with her parents what was about to happen. They learned about it on the news. "They were devastated," she recalled. "My mom was so upset she wouldn't talk to me for three months." On the other hand, "my dad was so upset with the church that he gave me his tithing for that year."[66] In both instances the excommunication intensified already strained relationships. It was just hard for her parents to understand.

As a feminist, Hanks felt "feared, misjudged, rejected," and she experienced her excommunication as a series of losses in her social life and in her family. Not only was she going through the effects her excommunication had on her relationships, she also had to navigate the media frenzy that followed. She found herself explaining Mormonism to the outside world and explaining her own feminism to the Mormon community. "Church discipline is fifteen minutes of fame that hijacks your life," she recalled, "Suddenly your place in the world is reversed overnight—from insider to outsider, from ally to enemy. You are an 'apostate.'"[67] She also felt like a media soundbite, the story of a "feminist in a patriarchal religion [who] gets excommunicated."[68] It was formulaic and also mesmerizing to outsiders.

Hanks took every media interview that she could. She believed in the power of public pressure to change things in the church. To outsiders she argued that women in the church were stuck in a kind

64. Hanks, oral history with author.

65. Ibid.

66. Hanks, oral history with author.

67. Maxine Hanks, "Exile and Return: From Gnostic Mormon to Mormon Gnostic," *Sunstone*, December 2003, 21–22.

68. Ibid.

of "spiritual kindergarten."[69] They had been granted authority in the home to obfuscate the fact that they had no authority in the current institution. To insiders she counseled that they should trust their personal conscience. "Something feels wrong here," she said, "And people need to pay attention to that feeling."[70]

In the midst of all of the strain and the attention, Hanks realized that her excommunication was also offering her a freedom of sorts. First, she had to come to terms with her own understanding of who she was, rather than what others thought about her. She realized that finding a sense of belonging meant, in part, moving "beyond the role of the rejected one.... At some point, you have to cease not belonging and start belonging."[71] Part of her journey of finding community and belonging included her work with women as part of an interfaith movement. What she saw in the other women in the movement was something that she wanted more of in her own spirituality—they were "not waiting to receive acceptance or permission from their fellows, but actually living as ministers of God."[72] Among these women Hanks found community and she helped to create Utah Women in Ministry, an interfaith organization of women.

An integral part of her new journey was to explore her spirituality beyond the confines of the church as she had known it. She started to do this in earnest with a group called Sunday Gathering, which was a congregation of Latter-day Saints and post-Mormons who gathered once a month to support Lavina Fielding Anderson, Hanks, and other members of the September Six.[73] When that ended after two years, she decided she wanted even more. She actively pursued a spiritual tradition that would embrace all of her complexity, including her desire and calling to the priesthood. Up until her excommunication, Hanks felt as though she had experienced the authority of the priesthood but had not experienced its power. And so she set off on a journey to find her power.

---

69. Maxine Hanks, interview with Tom Barberi, KALL radio, September 28, 1993, copy in Church History Library.

70. Maxine Hanks interview, September 24, 1993, KTKK radio, copy in Church History Library.

71. Ibid, 23.

72. Ibid.

73. Ibid.

As her relationship with wisdom Sophia deepened, Hanks also started to see echoes between her own life and the life of Mary Magdalene, a powerful figure in early Christianity who was silenced by the male leaders of the early church who wanted to blot her out of history. In 1997, Hanks found a community that valued the feminine divine and the person of Mary Magdalene in the Gnostic community. Modern-day Gnosticism sought to follow in the footsteps of ancient Gnosticism that had overlapped with the early Christian community. The emphasis in Gnosticism was wisdom. Jesus was imagined as a teacher of wisdom, but what he taught was how each individual could find the wisdom and divine spark in themselves. This suited Maxine's spiritual life perfectly.

There were two branches of Gnosticism that she joined, wanting to reap the benefits of both. One, led by Stephen Heller in Los Angeles, was tied to the Catholic line of the apostle Peter and emphasized male leadership. The other, led by Rosamonde Miller, emphasized the authority of Mary Magdalene and female leadership. Hanks wanted to be in both communities: "I want to do both because I'm androgynous Maxine." In those communities she took on several roles and was ordained into minor orders.[74] Gnosticism offered Hanks something that she had been looking for her whole life: legitimization through roles in a religious institution. "I felt like I've had the priesthood since I was five, but [that] nobody will ordain me."[75]

As she experienced all of the appeal Gnosticism offered, Harvard called. Hanks received a fellowship at Harvard Divinity School in 1998, representing the fulfillment of one of her childhood dreams. There, Elisabeth Schussler-Fiorenza, a well-known feminist biblical scholar, asked her an important question. Noting that Hanks had deconstructed Mormonism, Schussler-Fiorenza asked, "Have you deconstructed the Gnostics yet?"[76]

This was an important question for Hanks because she had been starting to notice differences between the way that she understood Gnosticism and the way her primary group in Salt Lake City did. She needed a time-out from them and the Harvard fellowship

74. *Mormon Stories* interview.

75. Hanks, oral history with author.

76. Ibid.

offered her that opportunity. But that did not mean she quit thinking about the feminine divine. At Harvard Hanks began to work on a project that continues to drive her today. She saw that the Christian calendar had virtually erased all celebration or memory of the divine feminine and she wanted to rectify that problem:

> The Christian year doesn't begin at Advent. It begins in September with the birth of Mary [the mother of Jesus] then it comes around to December and she gives birth to the divine within her. Then the logos, Jesus goes through his cycle of redemption at Easter, then He ascends. Then He sends the Spirit to ignite the World Soul, and then the World Soul has to go through its cycle so that the whole world can be redeemed. And the culmination is the last two weeks of August. You have the Assumption of Mary, and you have her Queenship, and then you have on August 29th, the redemption of the World Soul. [77]

And so Hanks worked to balance the masculine and the feminine not only in her spiritual life, but also in the calendar cycles. When she returned to Salt Lake City, she worked at the Holy Cross Chapel to construct a liturgical calendar that would manifest these balances.

Another balance that she continued to manage and consider was that of insider and outsider. After her excommunication, Hanks felt as though she was both an insider and an outsider within the church, but that she approached it as an outsider would. She asserted that she studied Mormonism as an academic and that she saw it as a valuable community that was one option among many types of faith. "I have transcended it personally," she told an interviewer in 2011, "I don't mean I purged it. I have a transcendent perspective."[78] At that time she viewed Mormonism as a set of "limitations and impositions" that cost her too much socially and spiritually. Yet there were things that she missed, including the church's appreciation of bodies and materiality as well as the sense of the entire community being one big family.[79] Even though she had separated from the community, she valued many of its theological teachings that were not often emphasized in church meetings. She began to see many resonances between

77. Hanks, oral history with author.
78. Hanks Interview, 74.
79. Ibid, 78.

the Mormonism that she had turned away from and the Gnosticism that had come to provide new spiritual meaning in her life.

Hanks's journey into and then out of Gnosticism led her to realize that ordination was something that happened internally, not something that was bestowed externally. Sure, one had to have the permission of a particular group to have the authority to practice the priesthood, but the power came from within.[80]

Feeling confident in that internal knowledge and sense of ordination enabled Hanks to have "the most unexpected transition of all … what I call 'the return.' If it was strange or hard to leave Mormonism, it's even stranger to return to it, after all that I've experienced and who I've become."[81] Twenty years after she left, Hanks was ready to come back. She had moved through the various roles in her Gnostic community, "But when I got to the point of priestly ordination, I pulled back. I moved into recognizing the value and power of a lay priesthood.… My searching was complete. I had my answers."[82] She was no longer angry at the LDS Church and she was able to seek out the relationships with the community of her past in a new way.

"My return to the Church, I would have to say, was really prompted by God, and you know larger forces and my own sense of destiny," she remembered, "in recognizing it was time to come back and recognizing the divine had been directing me."[83] Really questioning whether or not it was the right decision, Hanks felt a strong sense that God was telling her that "you need them, and they need you." And she saw that Joseph Smith had also been attempting to unite or balance the same opposites she had. "He was uniting the esoteric, heretical traditions with Christianity. And he was uniting male and female priesthood … they were brought together into a new formula in the temple.… The Relief Society was an Order of female disciples, like the Magadalene."[84] Furthering the restoration arguments she had made in *Women and Authority*, Hanks saw Joseph Smith restoring a Gnostic Christianity that valued wisdom,

80. *Mormon Stories* interview.

81. Hanks, "Exile and Return," 24.

82. Peggy Fletcher Stack, "Excommunicated Mormon to Tell How She Came Back to the Faith," *Salt Lake Tribune*, July 26, 2012.

83. "Loss and Rekindling."

84. Hanks, oral history with author.

materiality, and the masculine and feminine divine. And she argued that it was later leaders, particularly Brigham Young, who "fell back on hegemony and male privilege." Now she saw what she had not been able to see before, that "Mormonism had done the very thing that I was trying to do myself."[85]

Hanks clearly heard the Spirit telling her, "You have to go back to the Mormon church." It said, "You took this on as a karmic task—this feminist theology—and you haven't completed it. You are not complete until you bring it full circle back to Mormonism." In addition to the theology she was supposed to bring to the church, the Spirit told Hanks that she had succeeded at being a loner her whole life, but now she was going to have to live in community.[86] She was both surprised and not surprised at the message. It seemed to resonate with the kind of messages she had been receiving her whole life. And she had been following and trusting the Spirit since she was a child. But she was not quite sure how to make her return happen.

Around that time an old friend from Ricks College came to visit her during general conference. Her friend asked if Hanks thought she would ever return to the church, and Hanks said she did think that she would someday. Without telling Hanks, her friend went home and wrote a letter to President Henry B. Eyring, then first counselor in the First Presidency, who had taught a class they had both attended at Ricks. The friend explained Hanks's situation, leading Eyring to respond within the week with an encouraging message. Not long after, the local bishop reached out to Hanks. She met with the bishop and his counselors and they accepted her immediately. After good conversations at the local level, Hanks wrote a letter to the church's First Presidency. In it she told them that the entire church had lessons to learn from September 1993. She said she stood by what she had written and would not say she was wrong in her feminist message. What she did acknowledge, though, was that "the one mistake I made was that I didn't realize that you guys were my brothers."[87]

She was rebaptized into the church in 2012, but she went back

85. Ibid.
86. Ibid.
87. Ibid.

feeling as though her eyes were open to what it was. She no longer felt she had to convince people to come around to her way of thinking. Instead, she realized that the church was a group of different people looking for a relationship with God together. She did not have to fight or buck against the system because she felt like she could see what she had in common with everyone, even the church leaders who had excommunicated her decades before.[88] She had compassion for them as fellow seekers of relationship and community. "I didn't go *back* to something I left behind," she said. "I went forward to something new."[89]

At the same time that she felt more open to a diversity of perspectives within the church, she also felt that the church seemed more welcoming than it had twenty years earlier. Maybe people might be open to feminist theology a little more. Maybe aspects of feminism had become a part of the church. When she wanted to return, no one asked her to recant what she had said back in 1992 and 1993. Instead, some of it had become mainstream. The brick wall seemed to be slowly coming down, brick by brick, but there was still a need for more education.[90]

Even as she re-entered the church, Hanks continued to feel like an outsider in several communities. She had never truly felt like she was a respected member of the September Six, which she understood as a relatively privileged group. She saw *Sunstone*, *Dialogue*, and Signature Books as elitist organizations and she did not have the privileges of the others. She had never earned her doctorate. She did not have the financial support of a spouse. She had to work in order to support herself throughout her education. She felt like they often left her out. It was only Michael Quinn to whom she felt genuinely connected. With him she felt like she had a shared intellectual journey. And with him she felt like they both were always standing on the outside of things. "We were a power couple of dissent," she recalled.

While she may not have felt accepted by other members of the September Six, Hanks remembered what happened in September 1993 as "the most validating thing that ever happened to me." For

88. Hanks, "LDS Women's Authority and the Temple," 46–47.
89. Ibid, 50–58.
90. Hanks, "Shifting Boundaries of Feminist Theology," 174–75.

her, "it validated that I had a voice and that my voice was heard and that it had reached the highest levels. And that feminism mattered."[91] Her excommunication provided her with a sense of the necessity of her work. Hanks thinks that the time was important and marked a shift in the LDS tradition. When reflecting on her fame as a member of the September Six, she recalled, "We were pariahs, we were rock stars, and we were projection screens."[92] They were pariahs to the orthodox, deemed too impure to be part of the community. They were rock stars to those who saw them as symbols of the 'true' Restoration, the one that valued personal conscience and truth-seeking no matter what. And they were projection screens for everyone, reflecting the fears, anxieties and hopes of the community from which they were expelled. She remembered that everyone understood the Six differently. She said "The Church saw us as enemies. The dissenters saw us as victims. I saw us as shadow workers."

Even though she felt she had edited a central text in Mormon feminism, Hanks did not feel like she had ever been fully included in the LDS feminist community. At the Sunstone symposium in 2012, she spoke twice. One panel was a response to the twenty-year anniversary of *Women and Authority*, the book that had started many conversations and revealed new research to people who would not have heard it elsewhere. The second talk was about why she returned to the church. During that session, she realized that "some feminists were really threatened by my return." Afterwards, she saw the group that was voicing dissent about her return meeting in the hallway. "They decided I had betrayed feminism," she recalled. They thought "I had sold out." She felt that "they hijacked my narrative and re-wrote it."[93] While she thought she was returning to the church to do bridging and healing work, they saw her return as a betrayal of the values she had stood for twenty years prior. But Hanks saw things differently.

She was not standing outside the general conference with other members of the Ordain Women movement during either of their protests in 2013. She did not feel welcome there. While she felt that

91. Hanks, oral history with author.

92. Ibid.

93. Ibid.

her own feminism was broad enough to include many choices, she felt that the movement's feminism was too narrow to include hers. Hanks's story is one that echoes throughout feminist history. How do boundaries get drawn? Who gets to decide who is and is not a feminist? Whose voices are included and whose are dismissed because they are perceived to represent the patriarchy's in a female tenor?

7: SEPTEMBER 19

"Let me speak for myself."
—Margaret Toscano

It should have been Margaret Toscano. She was the primary focus of the church authorities' attention until her husband, Paul, stepped in. She did not need to be rescued. She could speak for herself. When he was excommunicated instead of her, she felt like a "non-person." His personality and the public attention pulled everyone's focus away from the work that she had done. "I felt subordinated to Paul by both the Church and the intellectual community," she remembered. "Yet even though I wasn't excommunicated until 2000, I had essentially been excommunicated with Paul in 1993."[1]

After September 1993 Margaret felt like she was in exile. She had been labeled a bad person. Ostracized in the church, she could have been embraced by the progressive and intellectual communities. But everyone there was focused on the September Six, seeing them as role models who embodied intellectual freedom, the quest for truth, and the demand to follow personal conscience. "Because I wasn't one of the September Six, people forgot about me," she recalled years later.[2] Standing on the outskirts of multiple communities, Margaret felt as though she lost herself for a while. "Nobody asked me to speak anymore, and all my feminist work seemed to be forgotten for several years."[3] Instead of being viewed as pushing against the patriarchal system, she was "robbed of the dignity of being considered

1. Margaret Toscano, interview with Philip Lindholm, in Philip Lindholm, *Latter-day Dissent: At the Crossroads of Intellectual Inquiry and Ecclesiastical Authority* (Salt Lake City: Greg Kofford Books, 2011), 162. Hereafter Margaret Toscano Interview.

2. Ibid.

3. Ibid.

worthy of formal censure, and deprived even of the dubious status of a critic and dissenter on the level with a priesthood holder."[4] Margaret Toscano was without a role. She struggled to find the networks of support that had surrounded her, both her church community and her intellectual and feminist ones.

"If a woman is perceived by church leaders to be equal to or stronger than her husband," Paul Toscano later mused, "she might be viewed as worthy of separate punishment. If she has an outspoken husband, she may be viewed merely as his alter ego."[5] Believing that church leaders saw Margaret as an afterthought after they had dispensed with him, Paul Toscano described what happened to his wife. She was punished because she refused to be an appendage to her husband. Wives, he said, were supposed to behave "derivatively, as if they had no thoughts, interests, rights, or personhood of their own."[6] Church leaders, he argued, found in Paul a "much more deserving target," even though it was Margaret who was most challenging the theology, doctrine, and gender hierarchies of the church. She therefore felt "informally excommunicated" in September 1993, even though it took seven more years for the church to officially excommunicate her on November 30, 2000.

Margaret and Paul Toscano's cases highlight the familial pillar of the purity system at work in the church, in part because of their rebellion against it. They were, in Paul's view, a representation of "the church's rejection of gender equality, or the fullness of the priesthood conferred jointly on men and women, and of the equal divinity and dignity of the Heavenly Father and Mother."[7] Paul and Margaret Toscano, he argued, embodied the kind of couple that challenged the church's understanding of what a heterosexual couple should look like.

Egalitarian relationships that pushed back against gender complementarity felt like they would undermine the very theological underpinnings of the church and its connections that had been made with the Religious Right. While Margaret Toscano may have drawn church leaders' attention because she was a woman who stepped out

4. Paul James Toscano, *The Sacrament of Doubt* (Salt Lake City: Signature Books, 2007), 4.

5. Ibid.

6. Ibid, 11.

7. Ibid, 154.

of bounds, Paul became their focus because of his priesthood status. He was a man who had failed to keep the patriarchal order. Margaret was a woman who stepped out of bounds and Paul was a man who encouraged and defended her. Together they both challenged the power structure—at the local level by refusing local leaders' counsel and at the institutional level by arguing that personal conscience was the site of religious authority, that dissent was a healthy part of any community, and that the church hierarchy was hiding behind a shield of infallibility.

Margaret's Feminism

It was Margaret Toscano's intellectual and feminist work that challenged the theology, practices, and polity of the church. In June 1993 she gave a talk accompanied by a slide show titled "Images of the Female Body, Human and Divine" to VOICE, the student group focused on the status of women on Brigham Young University's Provo campus. About forty students attended the event. The talk examined how femininity and female identity had been depicted in human and divine images. Toscano argued that "God the Female has and will be embodied in history, nevertheless I believe that we must first accept her in metaphor." Noting that embodiment was central to Mormon theology, she argued that the way Heavenly Mother was imagined and depicted in the church *mattered*. "Broadening our perspective about God the Mother not only facilitates our access to her," she said, "but it helps us understand ourselves better too."[8] The next day the front page of BYU's official student newspaper, the *Daily Universe*, had a banner headline reading, "Mother God Repressed, Voice Told." The accompanying article highlighted only the most controversial information that Toscano explored, sensationalizing what was an academic exploration.[9]

The talk was not Toscano's first foray into feminist theology. She had been on a personal quest to better understand the intersections of gender with her faith tradition for a long time. Though she was a BYU graduate with six generations of Mormon ancestors on both

8. Margaret Toscano, "Images of the Female Body: Human and Divine," *Mormon Women's Forum* 5, no. 4, 1–5.

9. Margaret Toscano Interview, 159, and Toscano, *Sacrament of Doubt*, 3.

sides, she had questions that developed throughout her education and her experiences.

While she taught classical languages at BYU from 1975 to 1989, she began to investigate feminism and ponder how it applied to her faith. Her new inquiries initially manifested in a paper titled "The Missing Rib," which analyzed the intersections between the role of priesthood and gender expectations in the Mormon movement. In the essay, Toscano explored the ways that Joseph Smith experienced and explained the priesthood. She argued that "Joseph's companion, Emma Smith, was also anointed and ordained to the highest order of the priesthood ... making her the first woman to receive these ordinances."[10] Not only did she argue that Emma received those ordinances, but also that it was Joseph Smith's intention that all women could. "Women needed the priesthood as much as the men did because the priesthood was not merely a status or fraternity, but a requirement for full salvation."[11]

Having the priesthood would allow women access to spiritual gifts that they had not experienced before: "revelations of greater knowledge and wisdom, including the discernment of spirits, the reception of the ministry of angels, the voice of Jehovah, the visitation of the Father and the Son, and finally, the power of an endless life." This understanding also meant that if priesthood was the key to spiritual gifts and salvation, it should be available to all members of the restored church. The Relief Society was intended to be a "school to prepare women for the holy order."[12] In that order, then, Emma Smith had a lot of power. She received her endowment from Joseph, but once she was endowed a queen and priestess, she could initiate other women in the sacred rites.

Like Maxine Hanks and D. Michael Quinn, Toscano made an argument that reflected the framework of arguments made by other feminists and by LGBTQ+ Latter-day Saints. It was a restoration argument mirroring the claim Joseph Smith made when he declared that Jesus's vision for the church had been corrupted and that he

10. Margaret Toscano, "The Missing Rib: The Forgotten Place of Queens and Priestesses in the Establishment of Zion," *Sunstone* 10, no. 5 (July 1985): 18.

11. Ibid.

12. Ibid.

was restoring the true church. It was the argument that scholars of Black Mormon history like Lester Bush made about the priesthood and temple bans. In her essay, Margaret argued that Brigham Young and other church leaders had taken out and erased from memory the female authority that Joseph Smith had institutionalized, so that women were taught that they had never had the priesthood. After Joseph died, the place of women in the quorum and their role as priestesses were dealt "quick death blows."[13]

The restoration arguments that these scholars made echoed those of Bush and others within the LDS community. At the same time, they also mirrored arguments made by feminist theologians and historians in other branches of Christianity. For example, feminist historians like Karen King, Elaine Pagels and Karen J. Torjesen sought to unearth evidence of women who had been active in church leadership in early Christianity. Works like theirs appealed to Christian feminists precisely because of a similar argument: if women had been priests, prophets, and leaders in early Christianity, why couldn't they be in the twentieth century? And, if Jesus had embraced women as spiritual authorities in their own right, why did subsequent church leaders cover up that fact?

In feminism more broadly, the work of scholars like Marija Gimbutas in the 1970s and 1980s made parallel arguments. Gimbutas used archeology to explore ancient cultures that worshiped goddesses, had matrilineal structures, and generally valued women. This work felt important to some feminists because it spoke to the possibility of a time before modern patriarchy. If that time existed, then why couldn't society return to a more egalitarian vision of the world?[14]

Over the decades and with continued historical forgetfulness about the "true church" practices that Joseph had instituted, Toscano argued, the priesthood had become something that it was not before. Now the priesthood was viewed "as a managerial system for the purpose of correlating and controlling the worldwide Church and as a means of insuring a homogeneous and cost-effective organization."

13. Ibid, 22.

14. These projects were subsequently critiqued by scholars like Cynthia Eller who argued that they were driven by a desire to discover a matriarchal past more than an accurate assessment of evidence. Eller, *The Myth of Matriarchal Prehistory: Why an Invented Past Will Not Give Women a Future* (Boston: Beacon Press, 2000).

And so Toscano maintained that not only had women lost access to any kind of authority, but they had also lost access to the spiritual gifts of the priesthood. She asserted that to Smith the priesthood was "raw spiritual power," but in the late twentieth century, it had transformed into "coercive power" that protected the institution.[15] It was a coercive power that kept women in their place and reinforced the purity system that told believers to stay in line.

Toscano presented this work at a Sunstone symposium and later described it as "trying to pursue an issue that was really important to me personally.... I was just naively pursuing what I thought was the truth."[16] In addition to these activities, and at the intersection of her scholarship and activism, in 1989 Margaret Toscano hosted a panel at a Sunstone symposium titled "Women and the Priesthood." In response to the panel, BYU canceled her entire schedule of classes for the upcoming semester. Margaret decided to throw her energy into completing her PhD at the University of Utah where she also taught after 1996.[17]

As she continued to investigate, her feminism infused her scholarship but also her activism. In 1990, she and her husband Paul co-authored a book titled *Strangers in Paradox: Explorations in Mormon Theology*. In it, they demonstrated their willingness to ask theological questions and participate in theological speculation as they sought out answers. They noted a central tension in the priesthood in the LDS Church that had been around from the beginning: on one hand it was based on the impulse for "hierarchical governance" and on the other hand the search for "individual liberty," and "personal empowerment."[18] In addition to exploring that tension, they joined their voices with others who argued that women had been involved in the priesthood not only in the history of the Restoration, but also with Sarah and Abraham and Jesus and the Marys. Women and priesthood echoed throughout Christian history.[19]

Margaret did not set out to import feminism into Mormonism.

15. Toscano, "Missing Rib," 18, 22.
16. Margaret Toscano Interview, 177.
17. Margaret Toscano Interview, 157–58.
18. Margaret and Paul Toscano, *Strangers in Paradox: Explorations in Mormon Theology* (Salt Lake City: Signature Books, 1990), 143.
19. Ibid, 167.

For her it was an organic set of questions arising from her own faith experiences and therefore grounded in the church and its history. "All the leaders thought I was trying to impose feminist notions on the Church," she remembered, "but my question started out as, 'Does God want me to be subordinate to men? And if so, why would God want that of me?'"[20] As she engaged those questions, Toscano naturally spent some time pondering the priesthood. She saw that the role was not just about leading the church, though it certainly was that. It was also about spirituality and the ability to deploy spiritual gifts. The priesthood had been framed as *the* primary mode for exercising certain spiritual gifts and therefore women were not expected to have or use any gifts. Because of this, they were not full citizens in the Kingdom of God.[21]

In addition to being barred access to the primary roles in the church, women were also denied the ability to see themselves authentically reflected in the divine realm, Toscano argued. Even though the doctrine of Heavenly Mother existed within Mormonism, allowing for the possibility of the feminine divine in ways that seemed impossible in other forms of Christianity, the hierarchy supported a theology often taught in churches that Heavenly Mother was not to be discussed because Heavenly Father wanted to protect her from being misunderstood and mistreated. "I've heard that explanation a thousand times," Margaret recalled, "but it's patronizing and makes God look like a controlling patriarch." Instead she chose to imagine Heavenly Mother as a being who could handle human anger and frustrations, her children's pain and suffering, and even their mistreatment.[22] Heavenly Mother was a complex being and could take it.

And so Margaret Toscano challenged the institution on multiple levels: the social, the ecclesiastical, and the theological. As part of her feminist commitments, Margaret helped found the Mormon Women's Forum in 1988. In 1992 she, along with her husband, Paul, and several trustees, founded the Mormon Alliance, a group dedicated to researching and addressing church leaders' abuse of church members.

20. Ibid, 173.
21. Margaret Toscano Interview, 174.
22. Ibid, 173.

In July 1993, Paul Toscano wrote an article for *Sunstone* explaining the need for the Mormon Alliance and what the group would do. He made a case for the type of Mormonism he thought was the healthiest and the most true to its original intentions. A good faith tradition allowed for dissent, including critique of religious leaders. He asserted that critique could and often did come out of a desire to want a faith tradition to have a stronger future.[23]

Paul pointed to a book titled *The Subtle Power of Spiritual Abuse* written by two Christian authors, David Johnson and Jeff VanVonderen, as the source of much of the group's understanding of spiritual abuse. Nonetheless, the founders of the Mormon Alliance felt they needed a more succinct definition than the authors offered and so they concluded that, "Spiritual abuse is the persistent exploitation by spiritual or ecclesiastical leaders in a religious system of an imbalance of power between the leaders and the followers, whereby the leaders maintain control through the exercise of their authority without adequate accountability." Those leaders took advantage of members' fears, their insecurities, their lack of experience and their ignorance in order to allow their coercive power to flourish.[24]

The authors of *The Subtle Power* named several types of spiritual abuse, which Paul Toscano listed while providing examples from the Latter-day Saint institution. Those were 1) Legalism: "a form of religious perfectionism that focuses on the careful performance of some behaviors and the careful avoidance of others"; 2) Power-posturing: "The watch-cry of modern Mormonism is 'Follow the Brethren'"; 3) Shaming; 4) Secretiveness; 5) Demand for Peace and Unity (without naming and addressing conflict); and 5) the "Can't Talk" rule, where if one names a problem in the institution that person is then identified *as* the problem.[25]

The founders organized the Mormon Alliance on July 4, 1992, with a mission "to uncover, identify, define, name, chronicle, resist, and even combat acts and threats of defamation and spiritual abuse perpetrated on Mormon individuals and institutions by Mormon

---

23. Paul Toscano, "Dealing with Spiritual Abuse: The Role of the Mormon Alliance," *Sunstone*, July 1993, 32–33.
24. Ibid, 34.
25. Ibid, 34–36.

and non-Mormon individuals and institutions."[26] Within the Alliance, there were four divisions, each with its own focus and mission. The reconciliation division was designed to intervene when instances of spiritual abuse happened and to promote justice and support groups for survivors. The defense division would work to address anti-Mormon sentiments and defend the institution from unfair portrayals of it. The Case Reports division would compile, verify, and publish instances of spiritual abuse. And, finally, the Common Consent division would "promote the right of members to participate in church governance and will work to open and maintain a correspondence with the leadership of the Church."[27] And so the Alliance set itself up as a defender of abuse victims, as a research organization, and as a group that stood up against mischaracterization. They imagined that the group would fill a void, drawing attention to instances where church leaders overstepped their bounds.

Disciplinary Action

After Margaret's 1993 "Images of the Female Body, Human and Divine" talk to VOICE, and its subsequent coverage in the *Daily Universe*, Boyd K. Packer met with the Toscanos' stake president, Kerry M. Heinz. Not long thereafter, Heinz called Margaret into his office and told her that she was "not to speak or write about, seek publicity for, or publish any of her religious opinions."[28] What began as a discussion in which Heinz inquired about her theological perspectives and her views on whether or not women should hold the priesthood, eventually shifted. "It seemed he couldn't answer all the issues and evidence I was bringing up," she explained, "so he switched directions and wanted to make it a matter of obedience."[29] Though Heinz fell back on the patriarchal hierarchy that would force Margaret to yield to his authority, she did not feel as though she could accept his assertions.

Framing the things she had been discussing as her "opinions," Heinz did not want to leave anything up for interpretation. He sent

26. Ibid, 38–40.
27. Ibid, 39.
28. Toscano, *Sacrament of Doubt*, 3.
29. Margaret Toscano Interview, 159.

her a follow-up letter, saying, "Please do not misunderstand me. Participation in public discussions, publications or media events, regarding church policy or doctrine, will be seen as apostasy and acting in clear, open and deliberate public opposition to the church and its leaders. I hope you will be able to make this sacrifice because you have been asked."[30]

Heinz's message was clear. Margaret needed to toe the line and understand that her "opinions" were not welcome in the public arena. Yet Margaret understood the matter differently. She shared her own ideas, but did not demand that others agree. Nor did she claim that her assertions represented the church. She wanted to create change through challenging assumptions, not forcing conformity.

Even though Heinz had been clear, Margaret did not feel bound by his restrictions. To her, his authority did not extend to matters of personal conscience and academic research. She told him that she could not be silent, because silence meant acquiescence to the patriarchy, which would be denying her conscience and freedom of speech. "There was a time in my life when I would have submitted or compromised in some way, with my words at least if not with my heart," she recalled. "But it was too late; it was twenty years too late."[31] She did not stop writing her scholarship or sharing her ideas with others. Later that summer in August 1993, she participated on a Sunstone panel with D. Michael Quinn, organized by Maxine Hanks, titled "If Women Have Had the Priesthood since 1843, Why Aren't They Using It?"[32] Margaret's participation in the panel demonstrated to Heinz that she was disobedient, prompting him to call a meeting with Margaret and her husband. It was at this meeting that Heinz shifted his attention to Paul while simultaneously pulling the rug out from beneath Margaret.

In that meeting, the tone of things changed. Both Toscanos had had discussions with church leaders about their ideas in the past. But this time was different. The seriousness with which Heinz and their bishop Wilson Martin were taking things was palpable. Margaret

30. Qtd. in Toscano, *Sacrament of Doubt*, 3.

31. Margaret Toscano, "The Courage to Act, to Speak, to Risk," *Mormon Women's Forum* 4, no. 4, 3.

32. Margaret Toscano Interview, 161.

remembered that Paul, in response, did the "savior thing," seeking to divert the attention away from her.

The stake president and bishop quickly realized that Paul, as the priesthood holder in the Toscano home, was not going to rein Margaret in, but rather supported her choices. In fact, Paul said he "manifested an aggressive determination to support and defend Margaret, peppered with rebukes of … Heinz's spiritual abuse."[33] First, Paul refused to use the title of "President," with Stake President Heinz (as was common practice in the church), but referred to him by his first name. Second, he said "Kerry, what do you know about the scripture? You're a real estate agent. They made you a stake president—so what!? … It's insulting that you're sitting across from us questioning our theology. What's *your* theology? It's a vacant lot!"[34]

Continuing in his battering, Paul accused Heinz of being in Boyd K. Packer's pocket, unwilling or unable to think for himself. Feeling like Heinz was "a bull chasing my wife across a field," Paul intervened, waving a flag to distract him. Being protective of his wife—as he had been taught to do by the church—he placed himself in Heinz's crosshairs. "Margaret has relatives in the Church going back to 1830," he thought to himself. "I, on the other hand, was expendable."[35]

That expendability was something that he had felt the entire time he was a church member. A convert at age sixteen, Paul Toscano doggedly committed himself to the church, eventually getting permission from his parents to be baptized two years later, in 1963. As he was welcomed into the church, he noticed that his Italian identity seemed like a stumbling block for some in the Latter-day Saint community. Just the way they looked at him indicated that "there was something subterranean about my being Mediterranean."[36]

Having no pioneer ancestors, he was taught that he would be the pioneer for his family and future generations. This was an example of the church's attempt in an increasingly globalized church to connect international believers to the story of the pioneers' nineteenth-century

33. Toscano, *Sacrament of Doubt*, 3–4.

34. Paul Toscano, interview with Philip Lindholm, in Lindholm, *Latter-day Dissent*, 23. Hereafter Paul Toscano Interview.

35. Ibid, 23–24.

36. Toscano, *Sacrament of Doubt*, 5–6.

trek westward to the Salt Lake Valley.[37] To Paul it felt like a "consolation prize" and an example of how he would always be a second-class citizen in the church community. Even as he wanted to call out the ethnocentrism and racism he was experiencing, he felt he could not because it was all shrouded in a politeness and courtesy that felt impenetrable. Though social cues told him he would always be second tier, he decided that theologically it was "better late in the lifeboat of Mormonism than not at all."[38]

Even though church leaders' attention had initially been on Margaret, Paul Toscano had not been quiet in his critique of the church hierarchy or his exploration of Mormon theology. He, too, had questions about how the church enforced its patriarchal structure and its hierarchical power.

When the contracts of two professors at BYU, David Knowlton and Cecilia Konchar Farr, were not renewed after their third-year reviews in 1992, Paul gave a talk in support of them on June 16, at the Seven Peaks Resort Hotel in Provo. In it he encouraged BYU students to see themselves as the victims of what was happening. "The school can ill afford the backlash following the suppression of academic freedom," he argued. Students' diplomas were being devalued. In addition, he warned that the church culture was toxic. "Beware those who compel purity, coerce righteousness, or force Zion," he counseled. "Beware those who attempt to bring about goodness by compulsory means."[39]

In the July 1992 issue of *Mormon Women's Forum* (the journal of the group with the same name), Paul had engaged Rodney Turner, a Professor Emeritus of Ancient Scripture from BYU, over the issue of women, Heavenly Mother, and the priesthood. Turner argued that God the Father had not authorized the worship of God the Mother, citing President Gordon B. Hinckley's 1991 speech as evidence while attempting to intellectualize and give scriptural backing to Hinckley's

37. Eric Alden Eliason, "Celebrating Zion: Pioneers in Mormon Popular Historical Expression" (PhD diss., University of Texas at Austin, 1998), 96–109. See also Eric A. Eliason, "Pioneers and Recapitulation in Mormon Popular Historical Expression," in Eric A. Eliason and Tom Mould, eds., *Latter-day Lore: Mormon Folklore Studies* (Salt Lake City: University of Utah Press, 2013), 174–211.

38. Toscano, *Sacrament of Doubt*, 6–9.

39. Toscano, *Sacrament of Doubt*, 32–33.

comments. "This does not mean that the mother of spirits is undeserving of honor and admiration," Turner wrote. "To the contrary, she merits more esteem than we are presently capable of rendering."[40] Second, he argued that Heavenly Mother's realm was heavenly, and this "fallen world" was not her immediate responsibility. Third, he argued that goddess worship was very old in human history, but that goddesses were usually tied to sex, fertility, and "sacred prostitution." He argued that "LDS men and women praying to and otherwise invoking a female deity for blessings and healings is not without precedent in heathen and apostate religions."[41] In his discussion Turner participated in the discourse of Orientalism, a colonial discourse that sexualized goddess worship in order to set it firmly outside of the bounds of Mormonism, making interest in Heavenly Mother an import "advocated by non-Mormons."[42] Finally, Turner put Mormon women on pedestals (and Heavenly Mother, as well) in order to undermine their claim to equality within the priesthood and to effectively silence any attempts to discuss or explore relationships with the female divine.

Paul Toscano was not having it. In his response in the same issue, he took on Turner point by point, offering his own intellectual response rooted in scripture. Noting that Turner was particularly concerned with contamination, impurity, and the trinity, Toscano responded arguing that Latter-day Saints had never been trinitarian. Inspired by Joseph Smith's first vision, they believed that Father, Son, and Holy Ghost were three separate entities, not three-in-one. In addition, he argued that the heavenly realm did not reflect the social inequalities found on earth. Only the earthly *institution* had fostered sexism and made claims that Heavenly Mother was lesser than the Father. "The picture of a submissive and powerless Heavenly Mother is used in Mormonism to reinforce conventional patriarchal power structures that continue to repress women. For if the Goddess is powerless in heaven, then her daughters must content themselves with that same status on earth," Paul Toscano wrote.[43] Perhaps God

40. Rodney Turner, *Mormon Women's Forum* 3, no. 2, 6.

41. Ibid, 4–5.

42. For a discussion about such discourses that demonstrate colonialism and racism, see Edward Said's, *Orientalism* (New York: Vintage, 2014).

43. Paul Toscano, "How Shall We Worship God the Mother?" *Mormon Women's Forum* 3, no. 2, 8.

had not yet communicated in certain ways about Heavenly Mother because humans had not yet proven themselves mature and worthy enough to receive revelations about her.[44] Paul noted that women had prayed, witnessed, and prophesied in the early Christian church, so those roles could be theirs in the Restoration as well. Last, he argued that Heavenly Mother was part of a co-equal relationship with Heavenly Father.

Debating ideas about the divine feminine and women's roles in the church was not Paul Toscano's only concern. In the Spring 1993 issue of *Dialogue*, Paul doled out a biting critique of the church hierarchy in an essay titled, "A Plea to the Leadership of the Church: Choose Love Not Power." He held nothing back. His first accusation was that the authorities had divided the church "into leaders and followers, intellectuals and mainstream members, believers and liberals, true voices and alternate voices, active Mormons and inactive Mormons."[45] Those divisions would eventually harm the community, he wrote, dividing people who should work as one unit. He warned about what church leaders had been teaching recently and wanted to call them to account and remind them about their own humanity. He explained "that prophets do not always speak as prophets. They can be wrong. This means that you cannot lay claim to infallibility."[46]

Further, Toscano argued that the Brethren were acting out of fear, a fear that made their actions less than loving. They feared anyone who asked questions, pushed back, and disagreed. He counseled that their response should not be to excommunicate those people. "Do not hold secret councils or keep secret files," he argued. "Do not look for scapegoats or resort to the silent treatment."[47] He insisted that church leaders were using power to control rather than fostering community trust and encouraging questions about faith. The article was a direct challenge to their power and a critique of their leadership styles and structures. Perhaps even a critique of how they understood God.

Even without the outburst in the meeting with Heinz, Paul Toscano's articles and work on the Mormon Alliance would have

44. Ibid.

45. Paul Toscano, "A Plea to the Leadership of the Church: Choose Love Not Power," *Dialogue: A Journal of Mormon Thought* 26, no. 1 (Spring 1993): 97.

46. Ibid, 98.

47. Ibid, 105.

eventually drawn the ire of church leaders. That same spring of 1993, Paul responded to Boyd K. Packer's May 1993 speech to the ACCC in which the apostle identified intellectuals, feminists, and the gay-lesbian rights movement as the enemies of the church. He articulated a position that echoed throughout his writing and his speeches. The reason these three groups were Packer's focus, Toscano wrote, "is because each of these groups asks church members to question the competence of their leaders ... [they] insist on distinguishing authority from competence." Reminding people that just being a church authority, did not make someone an expert on everything, Paul argued that intellectuals were precisely the antidote needed to challenge authoritarianism.[48]

Even though he was bound to bring the hierarchy's disciplinary weight to himself eventually, Paul's distraction strategy in the meeting between the Toscanos and their church leaders worked. He became the target of Heinz's attention. Though he gladly diverted the attention from Margaret, he realized things would not go as he hoped. He had wanted to have conversations and debate about the ideas he and Margaret had been discussing. Yet the charges against him quickly revolved not around ideas, but his refusal to obey men who were above him in the church hierarchy.[49]

While his immediate crime had clearly been disobedience to Heinz, a talk Paul had given at the 1993 Sunstone symposium, titled "All Is Not Well In Zion: False Teachings of the True Church," was also identified as part of the problem. In the speech, Paul began with a quotation from 2 Nephi 28:4–5 in the Book of Mormon: "Wo be unto him that is at ease in Zion! Wo be unto him that crieth: All is well!" Paul used this passage to suggest that while things might seem like they were going well in the church, there were problems roiling just under the surface.

The Mormon Alliance, of which he was a founder and a trustee, had documented dozens of cases of spiritual abuse. The Strengthening Church Members Committee was keeping secret files on church members. And worst of all, "I believe that in Mormonism our chief idol is a false concept of God," Paul argued, "a heresy which I call

48. Toscano, *Sacrament of Doubt*, 66–68.
49. Paul Toscano Interview, 25.

'patriolatry.' It is the idolatry of God the Father."[50] This particular form of pernicious idolatry, he maintained, set the church up as a patriarchy, demanded the absence of any feminine divine figures, and infantilized believers. "Because God is pictured as patriarch, some church leaders believe they are justified in hammering us into subordination, in making us eternal children who must live forever under a patriarchal control we can neither outgrow nor outlive."[51] Patriolatry required unthinking acceptance of church leaders, who were leaders simply because of their gender identity. The structure enforced a culture of silence and reprimanded those who asked questions. From Paul's perspective, the only solution was for church members to take Nephi's counsel and to be uncomfortable: to seek out the shortcomings of Zion and to acknowledge that all was not well.

The church's charges against Paul Toscano shifted like grains of sand: first, they focused on teaching false doctrine and leading people away from their faith. Then they charged him with not being obedient. He received a summons to a disciplinary council on September 12. Earlier that morning he woke up from an important dream. "I had what seemed like a remnant of a dream of four individuals standing at the foot of my bed, two males and two females, who were dressed peculiarly.... They gave me a message, and I woke up Margaret and told her, 'I'm going to be excommunicated, and I'm going to receive my summons today. It will be soon, but I'm not supposed to worry about it because everything will be alright.'"[52] Just as dreams had done for other dissenters, Paul's dream confirmed for him the rightness of his path, the knowledge of its outcome, and the certainty that things would be fine.

The council that convened on September 19, 1993, "made no effort to demonstrate the error of anything I had said," but focused its attention on Paul "being critical and mocking of church leaders."[53] During the proceedings, they listened to a recording of his Sunstone speech, then asked him questions. Next they heard testimony from

50. Paul Toscano, "All Is Not Well in Zion: False Teachings of the True Church," paper given at Sunstone Theological Symposium, August 1993. Reprinted in Paul Toscano, *The Sanctity of Dissent* (Salt Lake City: Signature Books, 1994), 156.

51. Toscano, "All Is Not Well in Zion," 161–62.

52. Paul Toscano Interview, 26.

53. Toscano, *Sacrament of Doubt*, 23.

his character witnesses, including Margaret and their friend Lavina Fielding Anderson. After the council's deliberations, the stake president informed him that he had been excommunicated. "It was like a wrecking ball hit me in the chest," he said. "Even though I knew they were going to say this, when they uttered those words, it hurt, and I knew then that I had expected some miracle would happen."[54]

The official letter of excommunication he later received from his stake president stated, "You have spent many years writing and speaking 'speculative theology,' which has thrown you into the spotlight. [Your choices indicate] that you have gone too far, become too critical of the Lord's anointed and have expressed too strongly personal beliefs that cannot be supported by scripture."[55]

Paul did not really disagree with the charges per se. He acknowledged that out of anger he had been disrespectful to Heinz, even though he felt that disobedience to a church authority should not bring about excommunication. And he knew that he engaged in speculative theology, but he had only done so at Sunstone symposiums—where people went to engage in such conversations—never in church. Despite the charges against him, Paul wrote, "I do not believe my excommunication was sealed by the holy spirit of promise.... Of course, I am here and now an excommunicant. But I am not an apostate, not a heretic."[56] Even so, he remembered that "excommunication, like revenge, is best served cold. Mine was—cold and quick on a clear autumn day."[57]

For Paul, Boyd K. Packer represented the unchecked power of the church hierarchy. He believed that Packer was behind his excommunication and Packer certainly loomed large in his thinking about the problems he saw in the church hierarchy. Packer even appeared in a series of Paul's dreams during this time. In one, Paul remembered that

> I am in a cavern that had the inverted shape of the Salt Lake Temple, as if someone had turned the entire temple upside down and pressed it

54. Paul Toscano Interview, 29
55. Toscano, *Sacrament of Doubt*, 23.
56. Ibid, 29.
57. Paul Toscano, *Road to Exile: Memoir of a Mormon Excommunicant* (Salt Lake City: Merrill and Toscano, 2006), 1.

> into soft clay … I stood in a small elevator-like cabin that dangled above the deep recess of this cavern.… I was standing in this contraption with my back to one of the two openings facing Boyd K. Packer. He was dressed in a black suit with a black tie. His face was expressionless. He stood with his back perilously close to the other opening. The tension between us was palpable. Neither of us said a word. Then, suddenly, he took a step back into the void and plummeted to the bottom of the heaven.… I gasped and awoke. It was several years before I suspected that the Boyd Packer of my dream was not really him, it was that part of me that was ambitious, controlling and authoritarian as he. The dream was about how my excommunication would permanently destroy this part of me in order, perhaps, to save my soul from the religion the LDS Church leaders had turned inside out and upside down.[58]

As this dream shows, Paul's feelings about Packer were complicated. In many ways, following Packer came to represent the path of least resistance, one Paul could have taken if he accepted the patriarchal hierarchy and his place in it. For Paul, Packer symbolized an easy hierarchy that did not require questions or further thinking. Packer's hierarchy was one in which believers could lean back, allowing others to do the theological and social heavy lifting.

Paul Toscano's excommunication had ripple effects. According to his recollections, Heinz told him that once he was severed from the church community, his temple marriage to Margaret was considered void along with his sealings to their children. This contradicted the *Church Handbook*, which frames excommunication as "a suspension of blessings that can be restored in the event of repentance."[59] But it felt like an additional threat, showing the power of lay folklore to define how church members understand their theology and community. What happened during earthly life would have implications for his entire family in the next life.

Even in this life, the ramifications for the Toscano family were great. Paul came to learn that he was not welcome in many Salt Lake City social and business circles any longer.[60] Margaret also experienced the loss of social connections. While she initially continued

58. Ibid, 313.
59. Toscano, *Sacrament of Doubt*, 4.
60. Toscano, *Road to Exile*, 1.

to attend ward meetings, their daughter Sarah, only nine years old, accused Margaret of betraying the family by attending church. So she stopped going, in part because of Sarah, but also because the religion and the community had stopped feeling like a home for her.[61] The Toscano children continued to feel a sense of alienation from the religious community, recognizing the deep hurt that the excommunication had caused their family.

In the months following his excommunication, speculation circulated about the role of Boyd K. Packer in Paul's excommunication. Part of the controversy arose around an interview that Apostle Dallin H. Oaks gave to the *Arizona Republic*. In that interview, a reporter asked Oaks if Packer had had anything to do with the Toscano excommunication. Oaks responded that he did not know whether Packer and Heinz had met to discuss it but that if they had, that meeting would be inappropriate because a general authority should not be involved in the inner workings of a disciplinary council at the local level. "So," Oaks said, "if Elder Packer is having any conversation with Kerry Heinz, it is outside the normal channel."

Once a reporter demonstrated that evidence existed of Oaks's previous knowledge of that exact meeting between Heinz and Packer, Oaks admitted the mistake and explained that it was tied to "inadvertence" or "forgetfulness," stating that he had not intentionally misled anyone.[62] What Oaks framed as simple error, others, including Toscano, felt demonstrated the lengths the church hierarchy would go to police the boundaries of orthodoxy and hide its tracks.

Even as information came to light that Packer played a role in Toscano's excommunication through his influence on Heinz, Paul initially challenged his excommunication. He immediately wrote an appeal to the church hierarchy. In December 1993, Heinz called both Toscanos into his office to read them the letter denying Paul's appeal. Margaret remembered that as they were leaving, Heinz turned to her and said, "'I really should do something about your situation, too. It's something I need to take care of but haven't gotten

61. Margaret Toscano Interview, 163.

62. See Steve Benson, "Oaks Dissembled Packer's Role in Toscano Excommunication," *Sunstone*, December 1993, 69, and Paul Toscano, "Partial Transcription of Oaks Interview," *Sunstone*, November 1993, 73.

around to it yet.'"[63] The threat seemed clear—Margaret was not off the hook for what she had done.

A year later Paul Toscano tried to return to church membership again when Howard W. Hunter became church president on June 6, 1994. Hunter gave a speech that seemed to be open to and welcoming of those who had found themselves outside the boundaries of the church. In the statement Hunter later issued to the press, he said: "To those who have transgressed or been offended, we say come back. To those who are hurt and struggling and afraid, we say let us stand with you and dry your tears. To those who are confused and assailed by error on every side, we say come to the God of all truth and the Church of continuing revelation. Come back. Stand with us. Carry on. Be believing. All is well, and all will be well."[64]

Paul wrote to Hunter, "We would like to accept your generous offer of reconciliation with the church and the Brethren. But we do not know how to do this. We are unsure how the damage can be undone, the stigma removed, and confidence restored."[65] Even so, the Toscanos offered the hope and the vulnerability of possible reconnection with their community.

That they heard no reply indicated to Paul that the break was irrevocable and that the church was not, in fact, open to critique and questions. Lavina Fielding Anderson later noted that Hunter's inaugural speech was edited several times in the months that followed so that the "conciliatory tone was made more strident."[66] Paul Toscano saw in the institution a desire to squash personal gifts of spirit and intellect in support of the institution's power. He felt he understood that the institution itself had dug its feet into a position of infallibility, one that would leave it particularly vulnerable in the future.

After that, Paul started on a journey of asking questions and coming to increasingly doubt his past spiritual experiences, the scriptures, and even Jesus. Distinctly Mormon theologies of a three-layered heaven, its understanding of prophets, and its exclusive claims, started to "seem threadbare, tribal, and inadequate."[67] As the years

63. Margaret Toscano Interview, 162.
64. Qtd. in Toscano, *Road to Exile,* 317.
65. Toscano, *Sacrament of Doubt,* 18.
66. Toscano, *Road to Exile,* 319.
67. Toscano, *Sacrament of Doubt,* xi–xii.

passed he felt that he was no longer a Mormon in any way, unlike other members of the September Six. "I am not a cultural Mormon because Mormon culture holds no fascination for me," he wrote. "I do not view the Mormon past with any real affection."[68]

His sense of an identity tied to the church and its community had dissolved. "I lost my faith. I didn't renounce it," he remembered, "I just lost it—like losing your eyesight after an accident."[69] Later he described it in another way, showing the profound emotional loss that came with his excommunication. "Losing your faith is not like denying what you knew once," he explained to an interviewer. "It's like losing your sense of sight or smell. I used to be able to taste Jesus in my mouth. I can't now."[70] Describing it as a loss of an integral aspect of himself, Toscano continued to experience the effects of the church's decision long after 1993. After that, he viewed the church with a mixture of pity and sympathy, "It is like a cherished old relative with advanced Alzheimer's disease.... The LDS Church is preoccupied with exteriorities. It prizes righteousness over holiness, image over inspiration."[71]

Margaret's Excommunication

A few years after Paul's excommunication, Margaret decided to take off her temple garments. For those intervening years, she had continued to wear them, telling herself that they were an object representing her relationship with God rather than the church. But even that began to feel too restrictive.[72] She knew that she was still connected to the church in multiple ways, even as her church community was treating her differently and slowly moving her to the margins.

And Heinz's threat that he would get around to excommunicating her seemed to loom. In 1995 her sister, Janice Allred, was excommunicated because of her feminist activism and her theological explorations of Heavenly Mother. Like Paul Toscano, Allred had questioned the sense of infallibility surrounding the role of prophet.[73]

68. Ibid, 61–62.
69. Ibid, 148.
70. Paul Toscano Interview, 43.
71. Toscano, *Sacrament of Doubt*, 148.
72. Margaret Toscano Interview, 164.
73. Janice Allred, interview with Philip Lindholm, in Lindholm, *Latter-day Dissent*, 142–46.

In November 1999, Dale Blake, Margaret Toscano's new stake president whom she had never met, called her into his office. They talked about her work and her experiences. Then, a year later in November 2000, without any explanation as to why, she was suddenly told about her own disciplinary council that would be held four days later. Margaret did not know how she felt about it. She had not been going to church. She had stopped wearing her temple garments. She knew the effects that Paul's excommunication had had on her family. But the idea of the disciplinary council still brought her anxiety. She decided she did not want to make a big deal about it. She was not going to call in the press. Knowing that the end result would be her excommunication, she did not want to put her children through another round of emotional upset. She wanted to protect them, as well as her own energies, which were going toward finishing her doctorate.[74]

She did, however, decide to attend the council: "For some reason, I wanted them to have to face me."[75] She did not bring any witnesses on her behalf. She had been told that she could bring two, but they had to be members in good standing. When she arrived at the building, it was dark. Someone let her in because the door was locked. They told her they were afraid the press and her husband were going to show up, "along with a big crowd of supporters." They could not believe that she came by herself, without witnesses and without support. She was led into a room and seated in a chair that faced the twelve high councilors who were seated in a semicircle. Just as in a courtroom, the stake president and his two counselors sat to her right facing the council as well. Rather than the "happy-go-lucky guy" she had encountered previously, stake president Blake acted like a "hard-hitting prosecuting attorney." Part of his prosecutorial strategy was to bring in a surprise witness: Kerry Heinz.[76]

Heinz spoke and then left. Blake worked through Margaret's writings, discussing how they were dangerous, "focusing mostly on the issues of Heavenly Mother and women in the priesthood." In addition, he discussed how she had failed to obey her stake president's order to be silent. As she went to defend herself, he stopped

74. Margaret Toscano Interview, 167.

75. Ibid, 168.

76. Ibid, 168–69.

her and said, "You will only speak if I give you permission. We will not allow you to lecture us."[77]

When Blake was done, he finally let Margaret speak. "I knew it wasn't going to do any good to argue doctrine because he had shown that was not his main concern," she remembered, "so I talked about the importance of free agency for moral choice and how it is vital to a healthy spiritual community[,] basically the notion that we can disagree and still love each other."[78] Arguing for her vision of a different community, Margaret knew that her cause would not be won in this room. But she was finally getting a chance to speak for herself.

Because the council had focused primarily on her disobedience, she knew that, from their perspective, the accusation of disobedience was persuasive. Even so, the official letter she received days after the three-and-a-half-hour council included another count to the accusation: She "had promoted pernicious doctrine and damaged the testimonies of Church members." This charge was included even though "evidence of [it] had never been given in council."[79] Once she was done with the proceedings, she first felt relief. "The mercy killing was over," she recalled. But the next day, after she taught her Latin class, she broke down and cried for several days.[80] She felt the weight of the final act even though it had been such a long time coming.

After her excommunication, Margaret worked hard to break her generations-long ties to Mormonism. She stood in front of a mirror practicing "saying the word 'fuck' without choking. I wanted to distance myself from that veneer of niceness that often characterizes Mormon culture." It was that niceness and polite veneer that halted discussions about "very real problems that need to be worked on for healing."[81] In many ways, she still felt Mormon. It was her heritage, in her blood. It was good people with whom she felt connected. She loved some of the theology and a number of the practices.[82] The excommunication was simply another level of breaking the ties. She felt like she had been through a divorce after a "really bad marriage,"

77. Ibid, 169.
78. Ibid.
79. Ibid, 170.
80. Ibid, 171–72.
81. Ibid, 176.
82. Ibid, 172.

and she did not want to try another relationship with another tradition. She felt harmed by her previous relationship and needed to find a new way of being.

Even if she wanted to, Margaret could not go back. She disagreed with the anti-intellectualism, the racism, the homophobia, and the teachings about women's roles and status.[83] After considering all of that, though, she still felt she was somehow Mormon. Not Latter-day Saint, in that she was no longer a member of the church and could not see how she could be. But she *was Mormon*, tied to the culture and community that had been a part of her life for so long.

83. Ibid.

8: SEPTEMBER 23

"Masks casting hideous shadows
have been placed over our real faces."
—Lavina Fielding Anderson

On June 25, 1981, after eight years of successful employment, Lavina Fielding Anderson was fired from her job at the *Ensign*, the monthly magazine for adult church members of the Church of Jesus Christ of Latter-day Saints. The correlated magazine offered artwork, poetry, and a variety of articles written by church leaders and members, including news of the institutional church. Every October and May, it also published all of the talks given at the church's twice-yearly general conferences.

Anderson was well-qualified for her job. After serving a Swiss French mission, she received a BA and MA from Brigham Young University in English and then a PhD in English from the University of Washington. Despite her qualifications and years of service, Anderson was dismissed when she tried to share a copy of a general conference speech given by Hartman Rector, a general authority, with *Sunstone* magazine, which took a more progressive and liberal approach to the faith and was of concern to many church leaders.

Most general conference speeches required First Presidency approval before they were given and then again before they were published. When Rector gave his talk, it contained a list of sins that would mark the last days, including "abortion, homosexuality, birth control, and sterilization, among other things." Peggy Fletcher, who was the editor of *Sunstone* at the time, wanted to publish both the original speech and the revised-for-publication version, which did not include the list and a number of other more controversial statements. Anderson offered to give Fletcher the original text, which was a breach of the *Ensign's* confidentiality policy. She justified her choice by noting that it had been a public speech and therefore heard by thousands of people. Because of this, she did not think confidentially extended after the fact. She copied the speech, placed it in an interoffice envelope, and addressed it to a church history employee who happened to be on his way to Sunstone for another matter and had offered to bring it to Fletcher.

Gary Bergera, an undergraduate student at BYU at the time, wrote to Rector to inquire why the published version of the speech was different than the spoken one. "Sometimes it is not expedient to make people angry by telling them in plain terms what their problems are," Rector wrote back. "I presume a combination of things made the First Presidency decide to eliminate certain portions of my remarks even tho' they had received and cleared the talk before it was given. It is O.K. They know best. However, what was said is still true."[1]

Anderson was soon called into a meeting with the *Ensign*'s managing editor, who told her that he saw the interoffice envelope she had addressed to someone in the church's history department and "felt inspired to open it."[2] He said that her action warranted immediate dismissal, that she was being "terminated for distributing confidential material to unauthorized personnel." He and someone from the church's personnel department escorted her to her office, where she was instructed to pack up her possessions. Then they walked her to her car. Anderson "expected to feel traumatized by being fired," she recalled. But to her surprise, she did not. Instead she "felt cheerful."[3]

When her friend and fellow feminist Linda Sillitoe, a *Deseret News* reporter, sent her a poem after she was fired, Anderson knew that it encapsulated her feelings exactly:

> One by one
> they throw us from the tower.

1. Qtd. in Lavina Fielding Anderson, "The LDS Intellectual Community and Church Leadership: A Contemporary Chronology," *Dialogue: A Journal of Mormon Thought* 26, no. 1 (Spring 1993): 15n19.

2. Anderson, "LDS Intellectual Community," 16.

3. Ibid. See also Levi S. Peterson, "Lavina Fielding Anderson and the Power of the Church in Exile" *Dialogue: A Journal of Mormon Thought* 29, no. 4 (Winter 1996): 170. Hereafter "Church in Exile."

And we spread our wings
and fly.[4]

Anderson suspected that her boss had not just fired her because of the Rector incident. She believed he felt "that my value as an employee was marginal." Just three months earlier, she had given birth to her son Christian, and, at that time, she felt that her boss "strongly disapproved of working mothers," that he was uncomfortable with her attendance at academic conferences, and that he disliked her calls to be more open with the editorial process.[5] After her dismissal, Anderson took charge of her professional life while mothering, setting herself up to be self-employed under Editing, Inc, becoming the editor for the *Journal of Mormon History*, and editing microhistories.[6] But the intersections of institutional authority, personal conscience, and feminism continued to dog her.

Though Anderson's faith, work, and feminist commitments intersected easily in her personal life, they did not flourish at those intersections when she interacted with the institutional church. Instead the institution insisted that those identities could not intersect, at least not in the way she configured them. Because her feminism led her to question the authority of many church leaders and the way that they wielded that authority and because it led her to break the code of silence expected by the institution, Anderson challenged the very heart of the doctrinal and familial purity of the church.

Naming Ecclesiastical Abuse

In the Letters to the Editor section of the spring 1993 edition of *Dialogue*, Anderson and Janice Allred, two trustees of the Mormon Alliance, announced the formation and intention of the new organization, a group with the express purpose of documenting and addressing cases of "ecclesiastical or spiritual abuse within the context of the Latter-day Saint church.... We are not interested in church-bashing," the authors wrote, instead their goals were "to listen nonjudgmentally and confidentially ... document accurately and responsibly the events that occurred ... and to heal breaches of trust

4. Anderson, "LDS Intellectual Community," 16.
5. Ibid.
6. "Church in Exile," 170.

within the Mormon community."[7] While not characterizing their work as "church bashing" felt important to Anderson and Allred, the very process that they were putting into play challenged fundamental assumptions in the purity system, including that those in authority had been called by God and therefore would not misuse that power.

Prior to writing the letter to the editor, Anderson had been working on a number of publications throughout the years. Perhaps most important was *Sisters in Spirit: Mormon Women in Historical and Cultural Perspective*, a work she co-edited with Maureen Ursenbach Beecher in 1987. The book, which included essays that explored women and the priesthood, women and scriptural interpretation, women's role in the temple and in their communities, and women as mothers and wives, had received funding from the National Endowment for the Humanities (NEH) and was published by University of Illinois Press, demonstrating that there was great outsider interest in the work of feminism within the church.[8]

The collection came out of a group of women who met for lunch on Wednesdays in the 1970s outside the Church Office Building. Their discussions over lunch were candid. They had heard outsiders accuse the church of misogyny, often with cause. And they had heard insiders vehemently defend the faith without question. Neither position seemed quite right. "So we talked, until our talking led to further researching and to discover some of the routes by which Mormon women arrived at the point where we found ourselves," members of the group remembered. And while they did not always agree with each other, they valued the conversations, the diversity of perspectives, and the contradictions.[9] They decided to share their conversations, inspirations, and research with others in order to spark conversations about the status of women in the church.

When Anderson worked in the Church Office Building she came to make friends with several historians. She learned from them that

---

7. Lavina Fielding Anderson and Janice Allred, letter to the Editor, *Dialogue: A Journal of Mormon Thought* 26, no. 1 (Spring 1993): ix.

8. See Colleen McDannell, *Sister Saints: Mormon Women Since the End of Polygamy* (New York: Oxford University Press, 2019), 123–28.

9. Maureen Ursenbach Beecher and Lavina Fielding Anderson, eds., *Sisters in Spirit: Mormon Women in Historical and Cultural Perspective* (Urbana: University of Illinois Press, 1987), xiii–xv.

nineteenth-century Mormon women had played important leadership roles in the institution *and* that they had exercised spiritual gifts, gifts that they could no longer use. She was shocked to find out that women's use and knowledge of those gifts had ended over the course of one generation.[10]

Lavina came to believe that the all-male church hierarchy had covered up women's spiritual power in the past, forcing a kind of forgetfulness, in order to bring about complacency toward women's current status. She saw that feminism and rescuing history through historical research went hand in hand. Erasing history, the enforced historical forgetfulness perpetrated by the church hierarchy, she believed, was its own type of ecclesiastical abuse. And it was one that happened at the systemic and structural level of the institution.

While she helped feminist arguments find their way to publication, Anderson also worked to address other forms of ecclesiastical abuse. As her critique of the church's enforced silence developed, her research and writing led her to ask questions about the abuse of authority in the church's purity system. Just as believers were hearing more and more messages from the hierarchy about prophetic infallibility and the patriarchal authority of the priesthood, she was unearthing instances of clerical abuse, showing that unquestioned authority had a dangerous side.

Anderson was addressing ecclesiastical abuse in a time when people throughout the United States were becoming more aware of it. In 1985, a Catholic priest in Louisiana pled guilty to eleven counts of molestation.[11] In 1992, the Fall River Diocese (part of the Boston Archdiocese) saw 100 victims of a former priest named James Porter come forward. He was charged with abusing over twenty children.[12] This set of charges was the beginning of what would become an even larger sex abuse scandal in Boston, then the United States, and later around the globe. While sexual abuse was only one of the types of abuse Anderson investigated, and clearly not the primary one in her research, she was part of a much broader movement to break

10. "Church in Exile," 171.

11. Corey Flintoff, "Priest Abuse Claims Date Back Decades" *NPR*, April 26, 2010.

12. Michael Rezendes, "Church Allowed Abuse by Priest for Years," *Boston Globe*, January 6, 2002.

the silence about how people to whom institutions granted spiritual authority could abuse that power for their own personal ends.

Anderson understood that ecclesiastical abuse was an umbrella concept that had an aspect of spiritual abuse, "Since the Church leader or policy replaced the gospel principles of love, joy, peace, and service with an insistence on obedience to authority." When that happened, "the member got the clear message that God was displeased…and that there was no place in Christ's church for [that person]."[13] She sought to expose those abusers in her church and bring them under public scrutiny so that the abuse could be addressed. As she uncovered them, though, Lavina challenged the patriarchal order, the infallibility of church leaders, and the mandate not to air dirty laundry outside of the church family.

In January of 1992, Anderson had an important dream that defined her work. "I saw a stick figure on a blackboard and something was erasing it," she recalled. "For me the meaning was clear: By being silent I was being erased."[14] The dream encouraged her not just to collect information, but to speak and write publicly about the abuses she was recording and so she began to present to several audiences.

In those presentations she expounded upon her understanding of what ecclesiastical abuse was, saying that it "occurs when a church officer, acting in his calling and using the weight of his office, coerces compliance, imposes his personal opinions as church doctrine or policy, or resorts to such power plays as threats and intimidation to insure that his views prevail in a conflict of opinions."[15] Further she noted that in the Latter-day Saint context differences of opinion could turn into the leader assuming there was "moral inadequacy on the part of the member."[16]

With intellectuals in particular, she observed, things could escalate because local church leaders were not usually trained to assess arguments made by scholars. That could lead to those in power

---

13. Lavina Fielding Anderson, correspondence with author, February 7, 2023.

14. Lavina Fielding Anderson, interview with Philip Lindholm, in Philip Lindholm, *Latter-day Dissent: At the Crossroads of Intellectual Inquiry and Ecclesiastical Authority* (Salt Lake City: Greg Kofford Books, 2011), 88. Hereafter Anderson Interview.

15. Lavina Fielding Anderson, "Freedom of Conscience: A Personal Statement," *Dialogue: A Journal of Mormon Thought* 26, no. 4 (Winter 1993): 197.

16. Ibid.

shifting their focus, accusing the church member of not supporting the hierarchy. Then, if the member continued to protest, that protest could be framed as refusing to "yield to the officer's power, then the very act of protest or the expressed desire to continue the discussion is seen as evidence of the charges."[17] Thus dissenters would be caught in a vicious cycle where every act except acquiescence would put their status in the church in further peril.

The vicious cycle was catching more and more of her friends in its movement. Anderson had observed an increasing tension "between the institutional church and two overlapping subcommunities I claim—intellectuals and feminists."[18] This made her want to talk and write about it even more. She hoped to start a conversation because she thought that "both [groups] claim supremacy—the supremacy of institutional authority in one case and the supremacy of the individual conscience in the other." Each one tried "to influence or control historical interpretations, theological understandings, and the nature of the Mormon community."[19] Maybe, Anderson thought, a conversation could help lower the weapons and foster understanding.

To begin that conversation, she presented the incidents of ecclesiastical abuse she had been recording. When she gave her first presentation about her work at a Sunstone symposium, she did not imagine the possibility of it leading to her own excommunication. On August 6, 1992, in a large room at a hotel conference center, she spoke. "When I was through and sat down, I was so emotionally exhausted it took me a few seconds to catch up with myself."[20] The content of her speech was not easy material—in fact, it was incredibly heavy—and yet saying and naming the acts and the people involved in ecclesiastical abuse brought her a sense of relief as well.

At the end of the hour, Anderson recalled, "Leonard Arrington rushed forward, and before I could come down the steps to meet him, seized my hand and kissed it."[21] It was during the audience Q&A when Eugene England argued that the Strengthening Church Membership Committee was undermining the church from its very

17. Ibid.
18. Anderson, "LDS Intellectual Community," 7.
19. Ibid.
20. Lavina Fielding Anderson, "The Church and Its Scholars," *Sunstone*, July 2003, 14.
21. Anderson, "Church and Its Scholars," 14.

foundations (see chapter two).[22] The portion of her research dealing with feminism appeared in the December 1992 issue of *Mormon Women's Quarterly*.[23] Later, she published "LDS Intellectual Community and Church Leadership" for *Dialogue* in 1993. The content of that essay, along with her other work for the Mormon Alliance, was the material for which she was ultimately excommunicated.

Perhaps naively, Anderson felt confident with each of these presentations and publications that "even people who differ sharply can deal with each other respectfully and lovingly." And she knew that failure to do that "is a sign of our humanness, but it is also a marker of the power differential that exists between members and leaders in an organization as hierarchical as the LDS church."[24]

She saw her writing as a matter of personal conscience because she had been deeply troubled by the choices general authorities made. Altogether she argued that the choices created a tidal turn toward anti-intellectualism within the church coupled with a willingness and desire to stamp out voices of dissent. She saw her role and her calling to be a witness in response to what was taking place: "I am not an accuser. I am not a judge."[25] She believed she was simply documenting what happened.

Even though she saw her task as being a witness, Anderson also understood that she had biases against the anti-intellectualism she was witnessing. She recognized that church leaders might tell the stories differently than she would, but, "Despite the lopsidedness I insist that such a record is worth creating and maintaining. It is driven by the search for knowledge. We must not deny that such things exist nor that they are wrong."[26] She believed that if people simply knew the facts, they would recognize their mistakes, apologize for their errors, and commit themselves to a more loving vision of the Restoration.

And for over fifty pages in her *Dialogue* article, she outlined the recent transgressions of the hierarchical church towards its intellectual and feminist members who were seeking out their own truths

22. Anderson, "LDS Intellectual Community," 45.
23. Anderson, "Church and Its Scholars," and "Church in Exile," 172.
24. Anderson, "LDS Intellectual Community," 7–8.
25. Ibid, 8.
26. Ibid.

and attempting to answer their faith questions, listing by name both those she was accusing and those who were their victims. Anderson did not offer analysis of what was taking place. Instead she felt as though the incidents spoke for themselves.

Hers was a distinct understanding of objectivity—the idea that the amassing of incidents would overwhelm the reader to a particular stance. And the lists encouraged her reader to draw conclusions about the problems in the church. She believed that the facts still needed responsible analysis, but also that they would show "ominous" patterns taking place.[27] From blacklisting and censoring writing, from dismissing or firing people from important positions within the church, from cutting off a person's access to religious rituals and community through the act of excommunication, Anderson sought to enumerate every instance of abuse she had encountered.

At the end of the article, Anderson listed seven proposals for what should happen next. "First, we must speak up. We must stop keeping 'bad' secrets when our church acts in an abusive way. We must share our stories and our pain." This goal reflected her belief that problems were best addressed when people knew about and could openly discuss them. The following three proposals required that people protest injustice, expose wrongdoings, and defend each other in the face of the church hierarchy's power. Then, she declared that members should be "more assertive in dealing with our leaders," this meant that they should demand that the church follow its own processes and procedures when dealing with disciplinary issues.

She argued that the institutional hierarchy had been using local leaders as pawns to do its bidding. "The stake president," she wrote, "not the offended general authority, is required to deal with the offender."[28] Thus she wanted to return the church to its own internal system of checks and balances against an abuse of power. The final two proposals framed things more positively. Church members should "support, encourage, and sustain ecclesiastical leaders who also value honesty, integrity, and nurturing," and "we must seek humility as a prerequisite for a more loving, a less fearful, community."[29]

---

27. Ibid, 8.
28. Ibid, 62.
29. Ibid, 63.

Anderson's understanding of transformed community that centered love over fear was also a vision of community that would accept her for who she was. "I consider myself to be simultaneously a loyal Latter-day Saint, an intellectual, and a feminist," she wrote in the conclusion of her essay. "My identity involves all three elements. I cannot truncate my life by excising one or more elements in a misguided search for simplicity."[30] At the heart of the matter was her desire for intersectional and complex identities to be welcomed into her faith community. And because of that, she insisted that "as I hope for forgiveness, so must I offer it. And I do."[31]

Anderson had pulled back the curtain on the culture of silence that reinforced the power of priesthood holders, especially those with important callings in the church. Her calling out individuals by name and expectations for a changed approach went against the very nature of the purity system. Her work showed that the church's opaque system protected those at the top; it was part of how the hierarchy maintained its power. And that maintenance came at the expense of those in the pews.[32]

Disciplinary Actions

Not long after the publication of her *Dialogue* article, Anderson was contacted by her stake president, Marlin S. Miller, who initiated her disciplinary proceedings. She recalled that he saw her work as publicly shaming the church and violating "the confidentiality of Church leaders on the ward, stake and general level." Miller warned her that if she continued to participate in the Mormon Alliance, and if she did not retract the claims made in her *Dialogue* article, she would lose her temple recommend.[33]

Rather than recant, Anderson doubled down. She wrote to Miller, further explaining why her work was important. In addition, she told

30. Ibid.

31. Ibid.

32. For a discussion of these issues in Catholicism, see Megan Goodwin, *Abusing Religion: Literary Persecution, Sex Scandals, and American Minority Religions* (New Brunswick, NJ: Rutgers University Press, 2020), 138–47. See also Anthea Butler, "The Catholic Church Has Yet to Repent for Its Sex Abuse Scandals," *Huffington Post*, September 19, 2018.

33. "Church in Exile," 174.

him that giving up her temple recommend would be an admission of unworthiness. She offered a compromise: she would voluntarily stop her temple worship out of respect for the church and until a resolution was reached. Miller's response was to escalate in reaction to what he interpreted as her insubordination. It was as though her *Dialogue* article had unleashed a self-fulfilling prophecy of ever increasing stakes. In August he notified her that he had contacted the local temple and let the administration there know that they should not honor her recommend.[34]

While this was happening, Anderson tried to meet with Loren C. Dunn, the Area President above her stake president, who, Miller told Anderson, had requested the investigation. Dunn refused to meet with her. Responding to the continued intensification of emotions and responses, Anderson wrote to Miller: "You have control over some aspects of my life as a Mormon, President Miller. You have already deprived me of temple worship. You can restrict or eliminate callings for me. You can disfellowship or excommunicate me. But you do not have control over my spiritual life, my relationship with the Savior, or my identity as a Mormon. I will always be a Mormon, whether I am a member of the Church or not."[35] With this statement, Anderson laid down the gauntlet for Miller. He may have had control as her patriarchal authority over certain things, but not over who she was or how she related to her God. Just days later, she received notification that a disciplinary hearing would be held.

As she learned about the coming council, Anderson thought about what she would like to do. In the event that she was excommunicated, she did not want to accept the idea that she would no longer be Mormon simply because she was no longer a church member. She was especially concerned about Christian, her son. She hoped that what was happening to her did not mean he was "deprived of his heritage as a Mormon." So she went to her bishop to ensure ahead of time that she and her family would still be able to go to church. First, she asked him for a blessing. Then, she "told him that the one thing I wanted from him was for my family to be welcomed

34. Ibid.
35. Qtd. in "Church in Exile," 174.

in church." Her bishop understood and later went to "extraordinary lengths" to make sure that that was the case.[36]

Even as some members of her community were supportive, Miller seemed resolute in his commitment to punish Anderson as harshly as possible. He instructed her that she should not attend the council hearing that had been called about her work. She struggled with this, "because I had things to tell those guys. I had speeches! I would even wake up in the middle of the night with good points to make."[37] Later, she would be glad she did not attend. She realized that her attendance would have caused irreparable damage to her relationships in her community. "Some of those high councilors were in our ward," she remembered. "I would have had to see them and remember that they thought I was unworthy to be a member of the Church. I'm not very strong in some ways. The Spirit knew that and protected me."[38]

Years later, after her husband Paul died in 2018, Anderson found a letter he had written to Miller the day before the disciplinary council. In it he noted that both he and Miller shared something in common. They were caught up in a story that they wished they could reverse. Paul sympathized with Miller who, he wrote, was under instruction to punish his wife from people higher up in the church hierarchy. Paul told Miller that he wished things had been different: "I cannot help wondering what might have happened if the first time Lavina and I met with you, you had said, 'I disagree with parts of your article, but I respect your motives and am moved by the pain you describe.'"[39] But Paul seemed to realize that the middle-ground position that he sought to broker on the eve of the disciplinary council was much too little and certainly too late, if it had ever been a possibility at all. Lavina, his "wonderful, affectionate, sincere, and brilliant" wife, Paul wrote Miller, was likely going to suffer "the harshest penalties that are in your power to give."[40]

---

36. Troy Williams, "Mormon Identity and the Excommunicated," *The Event Newsweekly*, August 16, 2001.

37. Anderson Interview, 91.

38. Ibid.

39. Lavina Fielding Anderson, *Mercy without End: Toward a More Inclusive Church* (Salt Lake City: Signature Books, 2020), 7.

40. Ibid, 5.

The night before her disciplinary council, supporters held a vigil and prayer service at White Memorial Chapel across the street from the Utah State Capitol. Around 200 people sang, prayed, and listened to talks. In addition to encouraging each other in their time of anxiety and concern for what was happening in their church and to their fellow church members, they circulated petitions, one of which was for people wanting to remove their names from church rolls.[41] Paul gave a talk in which he likened what had happened to his family to a car accident on the highway, hit unawares, but irrevocably. Lavina then spoke about the damage that had been done. For her the damage was to the body of Christ which was being unjustly injured. She thanked the people who were church members who disagreed with her but discussed those disagreements, rather than letting them fester.[42]

Anderson did not attend the disciplinary council that excommunicated her on September 23, 1993. Instead she gathered with a handful of friends, eating popcorn and guacamole dip, exchanging the latest rumors and news, watching *A Man for All Seasons* as leaders of her local community determined her future relationship to her church. During the evening, as she and her friends gathered to find comfort together, another friend stopped by with a sad look on her face. Anderson's response was to encourage her friend to see what was happening the same way that she did. "How many times in our lives do we get to take a stand on a question of conscience?" she asked her friend. "I feel *lucky*. This is a privilege that doesn't come to everyone."[43] Here she drew a line, embracing her identity as a witness—as a feminist, an intellectual, *and a Mormon.*

Yet that did not mean that her excommunication did not affect her emotionally. Her church was severing its connection to her, her ritual life, and her community relationships. The morning after her excommunication, when she received the official notification, she had not realized that "no matter how well prepared I was or how carefully chosen my commitment, the blow would be so heavy." It was a personal blow that to her represented "a struggle for the soul of

41. "Six Intellectuals Disciplined for Apostasy," *Sunstone*, November 1993, 67.
42. Anderson, *Mercy without End*, 35–37.
43. Anderson, "Freedom of Conscience," 199.

Mormonism."[44] She realized that her vision of a larger conversation about authority was not as close as she had hoped. And the cost for the lesson was high.

Part of the enormity of the blow happened because the men who had deemed her unworthy were her neighbors and sat with her in church. They had shared communion with her: "They all wore white shirts and ties. Nobody raised their voice. The stake president kept assuring me that he loved me. They made me not-a-member," she remembered, "It didn't feel like love to me."[45] In fact it felt like its own kind of abuse.

Anderson wanted to remember the lack of love that she experienced. She wanted people to remember. It was Miller who had excommunicated her, but it was not his idea. She felt confident that it was Loren C. Dunn, the Area President, who had started the ball rolling and that Boyd K. Packer was behind it all. It was an institutional structure that had set up authority to work in this way. While Anderson followed her personal conscience, there was no room in the purity system for someone with a personal conscience that did not conform to the hierarchy's teachings and publicly spoke out about it, embarrassing the church and leading others astray.

The letter she received about her excommunication did not provide an explanation. It merely stated that she had been excommunicated. It was only after she inquired that Miller said she had been excommunicated for apostasy. He explained, "You are outside of the principles of the gospel and are leading others with you" and so he claimed the action was necessary. But he assured her that her excommunication was "done out of love and concern for you."[46]

Miller's statement reinforced the idea that the power structure was based on love even as it summarily disciplined a member that had stepped out of line. In addition to not listing the reasons for her excommunication, Miller's letter also did not provide a list of the steps she could take to return to full communion with the church. She inquired about the absence of the steps and she heard back from

44. Ibid.

45. Anderson, *Mercy without End*, 80.

46. Qtd. in Jana Reiss, Foreword to Anderson, *Mercy without End*, vii. See also "Six Intellectuals Disciplined," 67.

Miller with "a puzzling answer," saying only that "I couldn't judge the General Authorities or think they were wrong. This topic had never even come up before, and I certainly didn't understand that members had to believe General Authorities couldn't commit errors. I asked him for clarification."[47] "It sounds almost as if you expect me to believe that they are never wrong," she continued. "Is this what you mean? If it is, I think you are asking me to do something that the Church does not require of its members."[48] She never received a response to that inquiry.

Anderson decided to push further with leaders above Miller. Over the next month she quickly drafted a thirty-seven-page appeal, which she sent to several members of the church hierarchy on October 23, 1993. The appeal had three parts. The first was identification of procedural concerns, a primary one being the interference of members of the church hierarchy, especially Loren C. Dunn and Boyd K. Packer, in the disciplinary processes that should be left to the stake and local levels. The second was a discussion of spiritual abuse. She explained how in all of the concern and anger that the *Dialogue* essay had fostered, no one had actually disputed the facts that lay at the center of the article itself.[49] And, finally, Anderson gave a statement about her loyalty to the church.[50]

Even as she was motivated by anger and frustration to dispute the grounds upon which she had been excommunicated, Anderson experienced grief and pain as well. In addition to the pain of community leaders deeming her unworthy of partaking in the church's Sunday sacrament with her local community, she also felt a physical pain at communion. On December 12, 1993, her son Christian was passing the sacrament in their section and continued to glance at her. A distracted Paul took a piece of the bread and then tried to pass the tray to Lavina. "Christian's eyes widen," she recalled, "he grips the tray harder, not relinquishing it. Paul looks up in surprise,

47. Anderson Interview, 100.

48. Anderson, *Mercy without End*, 3.

49. Karen Marguerite Moloney, "Saints for All Seasons: Lavina Fielding Anderson and Bernard Shaw's Joan of Arc," *Dialogue: A Journal of Mormon Thought* 36, no. 3 (Fall 2003): 34.

50. "Church in Exile," 175.

then remembers. His hand drops." Even her son and her husband were taught not to include her in a central ritual of their community.

In that moment she felt a pang of pain, because "these are my husband and my son, the two men I love most, the two men who love me most dearly. My husband began a gesture of inclusion because he forgot. My son completed the gesture of exclusion because he remembered."[51] And so while it may have been intellectually easy to explain why the charges against her were unfair and problematic, Anderson still had to endure the training of everyone in her community, even her immediate family, to exclude her.

In January 1994, Miller notified Anderson that First Presidency members Gordon B. Hinckley and Thomas S. Monson had chosen to uphold the decision for her excommunication. That did not stop her from going on with her life, a life in which she embraced all of her identities. The Sunday after her excommunication she went to church, just as she always did. After the Relief Society meeting was over, she was crowded by other women who wanted to hug her: "'We love you,' one [of] them murmured. 'Keep coming,' said another. 'Did you see how many were in opening exercises at Sunday School?' asked a third. 'I think it's because of you. You're making people search their souls. I know I'm searching mine.'"[52]

Anderson felt overwhelmed with the support and kindness of the people who had been her spiritual community all along. They had not disappeared. Their relationships with her had not changed because of what the church hierarchy had said. "People kept stopping me, hugging me. When I sat down, it took a minute to realize what I was feeling. Pride. I was so *proud* of my ward. They were behaving exactly as you'd hope a Christian community would behave."[53] Though her life continued in much the same way as it had before, her relationship to it all had been fundamentally changed.

Anderson released a public statement that her excommunication "has brought great sorrow upon me and my family, but we feel sustained by the love of God easing our pain." She had faith that in the future everyone who had endured the month of September 1993

51. Anderson, *Mercy without End*, 39.

52. Qtd. in "Church in Exile," 176.

53. Qtd. in ibid.

would realize that "truth and courage meant very different things to very different but equally honorable people. Until that understanding comes, I pray for increased love in our community."[54] While she called for greater understanding, communication and caring, she also insisted on the importance of individual conscience. "God doesn't want little robots," she said in a radio interview. "He sent us here to be free human beings and to use our freedom wisely." She concluded that anything that limited human freedom and conscience was not in line with God's will for humanity.[55]

Anderson remembered her excommunication as a time of profound grief—in the midst of ending and strengthening relationships. She also experienced the excommunication as an opportunity: "[I]t brought me into contact with scores of 'ordinary' members who had never had anyone listen respectfully to their stories and to tell them, with the sacred gift of the Holy Ghost, 'That should not have happened, Heavenly Father loves you. I'll pray for you that you'll have healing and light for the path ahead.' I could tell I was speaking with authority."[56] While she knew that her relationship to the institution had been profoundly changed, she also knew that the Spirit had not left her, and it continued to provide her with the ability to build new and powerful relationships with her community.

Returning to Communion?

Anderson also came to understand the reasons for her excommunication as distinct from the other members of the September Six. Her sin was addressing ecclesiastical abuse, "church leaders who exercise unrighteous dominion over members."[57] She never questioned whether or not she should have done the witnessing she did. Her religious tradition was full of witnesses and she was but one of them. She knew herself to be an orthodox Mormon and so maintained that she was speaking from the center in a spirit and language that her people would understand. Yet those on top perceived her to be dangerous, perhaps more dangerous than any of the other members of the September

54. Anderson, "Church and Its Scholars," 67.
55. "Six Intellectuals Disciplined."
56. Anderson, correspondence with author.
57. Anderson, "Freedom of Conscience," 197.

Six. Her work exposed people who benefited from the silence protecting church leaders. She challenged the system at its core, willing to be public about that which had been under cover for so long.

But she insisted that she continued to be motivated by the Spirit. "I never received any spiritual guarantees that I would be safe or that the church would welcome news and change quickly," she wrote. "But I did receive over and over again the assurance that it was the right thing to do. That assurance has been the single most important factor in the strength I have felt at every step of the process."[58] Anderson embraced the theology of the Spirit that she had learned in church. She felt certain that the presence of the Spirit was with her even as she continued a new path that journeyed away from the church as an institution.

Her confidence in the Spirit made her believe that she would be reinstated as a church member during her lifetime. She knew that future historians of the church would have the distance and perspective to see what was going on. She felt sure that those future historians would "conclude that the church was wracked and rent by a spirit of fear, acting out a nightmare that took the form of scapegoating six of its own."[59] From her perspective the church had distorted what each individual had done to make a statement about orthodoxy and toeing the line. "Masks casting hideous shadows have been placed over our real faces," she wrote. The Six had become monsters in the imaginations of people who were afraid of change in the church. But the time of fear would end, she prophesied. "This time will pass. The fever will break."[60]

In a 1996 speech, Anderson talked about people who offer witness and protest, testifying with their presence. "I want that testimony to say, 'I'm here. I've been excluded from fellowship for speaking the truth and following my conscience, but I'm still here,'" she said. Her continued presence at church was for her own spiritual and relational well-being, but she also saw it as its own testimony. "Don't be afraid," she wanted her community to know, "We don't have to hide

58. Ibid, 198.
59. Ibid, 202.
60. Ibid.

our history, silence our scholars, abuse our members, and marginalize our women."[61]

Anderson continued to write and edit writing that would help the faithful understand who they were through understanding their own histories. In addition, she persisted in her work with survivors of ecclesiastical abuse. As part of the Mormon Alliance, she documented cases, identified ecclesiastical abuse, and called for institutional reform.[62] She did not waver in her insistence that the church had its problems and needed to address the abuse happening to its membership. She also argued that the church had a "well-documented tendency to deny, minimize, or suppress information about inappropriate ecclesiastical response to reported cases of child sexual abuse."[63]

And she observed that the church's choices in its dealings with the September Six was not without its consequences. Excepting Gileadi, she noted in 2003 that the other members of the Six had forty-one children total, 78 percent of whom were no longer affiliated with the institution.[64] Those were children who saw their parents being mistreated and decided that any church that could do that was not going to be their church. "From my perspective," she said, "it's not unrealistic to interpret the last ten years as a litany of losses—losses to individuals and losses to the community."[65]

The ripple effect of the losses did not just extend to family members of the September Six. Anderson argued that "the level of authoritarianism in the Church has increased dramatically." The Relief Society's manual was now the same as the Melchizedek Priesthood's, meaning that "the only voice women hear in lessons is male." Church publications featured the male voices of the hierarchy. The church had increased its emphasis on the importance of obedience to the prophet—an obedience that did not allow for public questioning or disagreement.

In addition, the church had been ramping up its heteronormative teachings about gender and sexuality with its 1995 issuance of the "Proclamation on the Family," a theological stance that was added

61. Qtd. in "Church in Exile," 177.
62. Ibid, 178.
63. Anderson, "Church and Its Scholars," 16.
64. Ibid.
65. Ibid.

"without the benefit of canonization or discussion."[66] Young members had been taught that "history is dangerous," which might well lead to confusion and questions about their faith. Their faith would be challenged and, without an avenue to ask questions or a place to express doubt, their faith would disappear. Anderson thought the institution was actively working against itself: "If the church succeeds in imposing this kind of orthodoxy on its members," she argued "it will end up as a weaker and more fragile organization less able to meet the needs of its members."[67]

In the midst of that consistent criticism, Anderson still went to church and participated in her local community as much as she could. "More than twelve hundred times," author Jana Reiss observed in 2020, "Lavina has sat in sacrament meetings since her excommunication, and more than twelve hundred times, the now-forbidden bread and water have passed her by."[68] In addition, Lavina's husband Paul, who worked as curator at BYU's Museum of Art, was also denied any of the most powerful and public positions in the local ward.[69] While Lavina could see the benefit of this—after all it allowed him more time with his family—it still showed that her spouse was also being pushed to the margins of the community, even as that community continued to support and welcome her.

In 2019, the question of Anderson's return to full membership in the church was raised again. In 2018 she had spoken with both her bishop, Mahonri Madrigal, and her stake president, David McLean. During those discussions she shared with them her personal revelation, brought on by the Spirit, that made her confident that she would be reinstated after "a long time" and that she should stay worthy of membership until that time.[70] At McLean's suggestion she wrote a letter that could serve as the starting point of the discussion about her reinstatement.

In the letter, Anderson articulated her desire for full membership, but she also made clear that she did not fully support everything that was happening in the church. In particular she noted that the church's

66. Ibid.

67. Williams, "Mormon Identity."

68. Qtd. in Reiss, Foreword to Anderson, *Mercy without End*, viii.

69. Anderson, *Mercy without End*, 4.

70. Ibid, 7–8.

exclusion of people in legally recognized same-sex marriages, a November 2015 policy that denied baptism to the children of same-sex parents, and the denial of the priesthood to women were still aspects of the church's teachings and practices that she found unacceptable.[71] Her feminism from the 1970s and 1980s had remained and also evolved, so that by the time of her excommunication and continuing afterwards, she "believed a person's role in the Church should not be circumscribed by gender identity or sexual orientation."[72]

Because of the conversations they had had and his understanding of Anderson, on March 24, 2019, David J. McLean, the president of the Salt Lake Liberty Stake, reconvened the high council in order to reconsider whether Anderson could return to the church. Her son, Christian, wrote a letter to the council explaining that "prolonging Lavina's exile from the ward family she loves and who love her cannot possibly be prompted by a spirit of love and concern for her well-being."[73] Christian made clear that Miller's argument that his mother's excommunication had been done out of love was absurd, and that she had been made an outsider in her community for long enough. And, it seemed the council agreed because they forwarded to the First Presidency their unanimous recommendation for the reinstatement of Lavina Fielding Anderson to full communion in the church family.

In April 2019, Anderson received a questionnaire from church headquarters that she was asked to fill out. After submission, the anonymous reviewer claimed that her statements on the form did not show enough remorse for what she had done in 1993. On August 28, President McLean met with Anderson and read her a letter signed by all three members of the church's First Presidency. "In it they stated they had evaluated the information and were not accepting his recommendation for reinstatement 'at this time.'"[74] While McLean seemed reassured that the letter held open the opportunity for future reinstatement, Anderson wasn't so sure. Part of the

71. Anderson, *Mercy without End*, 10.
72. Anderson, correspondence with author.
73. Anderson, *Mercy without End*, 11.
74. Ibid, 14.

concern of the reviewer and the First Presidency may well have been her continued challenges to church policies.

Lavina insisted that she was not angry or disappointed. This was on the First Presidency as far as she was concerned. They were acting in some of the same ways the First Presidency had in 1993. What she did have control over, namely her personal relationship with God, she was going to continue to nurture. In 2020 she wrote, "Sundays will still find me in the Whittier Ward chapel, third bench from the front on the north side."[75]

Reflecting a few years later, Anderson recalled that when she was denied reinstatement, which came after twenty-five years of "faithful attendance at Church meetings and adherence to Church standards," the Spirit guided her in a new direction. "I felt a clear message from the Spirit that I was 'released' from my obligations to continue seeking reconciliation with the institutional Church." Her efforts at reconciliation had not been accepted. She understood that at the age of seventy-nine she was entering a new chapter in her life.

She still had profound connections to ward members, especially those who had supported her as she grieved the death of her husband. Those were the same people who welcomed her son, Christian, and daughter-in-law, Marina, as the three merged households. But she knew that her connection to the institution was different. "I feel that my history with the Church is an interesting period in my past," she wrote, "and that it IS my past."[76] She had been released from any kind of continued relationship with the institution that had not been willing or able to find a place for her in full communion.

75. Ibid, 15.

76. Anderson, correspondence with author.

9: SEPTEMBER 26

"Dreaming in Color."
—D. Michael Quinn

In mid-summer 1993, and with a church disciplinary council looming, D. Michael Quinn was driving toward the University of Utah one morning and started to sense that a car was following him. This was not a new feeling. Wanting to see if his instincts were correct, he quickly pulled into the parking lot of a supermarket. The car followed him but parked a few rows away, the driver staying in the car. Quinn got out of his car briefly, acted as though he decided in the moment not to go in, and got back into his car to continue driving.

A few blocks away he pulled into another parking lot to see if the car was still following him. It, too, turned into the lot, this one deserted, and stopped several rows away. Neither Quinn nor the other driver got out of their cars. After waiting for a time, Quinn drove toward the other car and flashed his lights at it. Then he drove alongside the driver's side and waved to the woman driver.[1] He did not know who she was, but he felt confident she was following him. And it was not the only time he felt he had been followed. He believed his home had been searched when he was not around and that his daily activities were reported to someone in the church hierarchy. He felt that he was constantly being pursued in order to reveal his private life, a life that did not match with the church's expectations for believers.

Whether or not Quinn's instincts were accurate, each story he told of being watched was part of his growing physical and emotional sense of outsiderness within the institutional church. He felt

1. D. Michael Quinn, *Chosen Path: A Memoir* (Salt Lake City: Signature Books, forthcoming 2023). Hereafter, Memoir.

like a *persona non grata* in many places in Utah. Having been a rising star as a Brigham Young University history professor who had access to the inner sanctums of the church's archives and many of the church's most sensitive documents, Quinn had proven himself untrustworthy from the church hierarchy's perspective. Although he understood his work to be telling the truth about history, exposing the church's attempt to hide what it saw as unsavory aspects of its past, his adversaries saw him as someone leading the faithful away from a sure and narrow path. They thought he caused doubt and publicly criticized church leaders where he could have fostered faith. And so they continued to limit his ability to do his work.[2]

Quinn's path toward finding himself, as a historian, feminist, and gay man, led him farther and farther toward the peripheries of the church he cherished. He found that his identities disrupted all of the life narratives that the church set out for its members.[3] Ending his mixed-orientation marriage in 1986 and resigning from BYU in 1988, Quinn knew he was going to have to forge his own path. He would minimize, as much as he could, the role that the church would play in determining the narrative of his life.

He knew that the institutional church found him wanting. His failure to follow the life story set before him affected him in numerous ways. For the fifteen years prior to his resignation from BYU, he rarely remembered his dreams, and when he did, they were in black and white. Breaking free from the prescribed narratives for his life that the church had taught him, and embracing an unknown but full-of-possibility future, meant that he started dreaming in color. "It's so different now," he wrote in his memoir.[4]

Both Quinn and the church had been hiding aspects of their histories and their identities, portraying only what they thought the world wanted to see. Through the struggle between the institution and the historian, both had facets of themselves revealed that they

---

2. Lavina Fielding Anderson, "The LDS Intellectual Community and Church Leadership: A Contemporary Chronology," *Dialogue: A Journal of Mormon Thought* 26, no. 1 (Spring 1993): 29.

3. Sara M. Patterson, "The *Straight*jacket of Time: Narrating D. Michael Quinn" in Benjamin E. Park, ed., *DNA Mormon: Perspectives on the Legacy of Historian D. Michael Quinn* (Salt Lake City: Signature Books, 2022), 35–45.

4. Memoir, May 1992.

had wanted to conceal. In the end, their encounter meant that both had to come to terms with the private-turned-public aspects of their identities, forced to reconcile who they were with the traits and stories that had once been hidden.

As was the case with other members of the September Six, some have called Quinn a martyr for what he did. While Quinn had a certain kind of naivete that hoped the institutional church would see an accurate account of its history as valuable rather than dangerous, it is problematic to read him as simply a martyr for the truth. Even Quinn knew that martyr narratives were too simplistic. Speaking of the persecution that early Mormons faced, he said, "as appealing as the martyr [story] is for anyone who has been picked on at a personal level or any group historically, usually it is more complex than that."[5]

The portrayal of Quinn as a martyr often ends up robbing him of significant aspects of his life. While he did not find a life partner, Quinn lived a life in community, even though that community took on a very different shape and form after his excommunication. While he may not have been able to maintain the traditional nuclear family that the church expected, he created family networks with his children and others that sustained him throughout his life. While he may have died alone in his condominium, it is unfair to suggest that he was simply *alone* in his life. Narratives that emphasize Quinn's martyrdom suggest that his time at BYU and in a mixed-orientation marriage were the apex of his life, and hint that everything that came after was wandering and loneliness. These narratives deprive him of his agency and relationships in the service of evaluating him with the church's measuring stick, which always found him wanting. Quinn set out on a journey that rejected the narratives of the church about what a good life looked like. While his later life may not have been everything he dreamed of, he was still dreaming in color.

Fashioning a Life

Quinn was born in Los Angeles in 1944. On his father's side of the family he was Roman Catholic and on his mother's side he was a seventh-generation Mormon. It was from this Mormon side that he

5. D. Michael Quinn, interview with John Dehlin, "D. Michael Quinn—21st-Century Enigma," *Mormon Stories* podcast, September 17, 2011, eps. 285–87, mormonstories.org.

learned about religion. Throughout his life he experienced an intense personal relationship with God, feeling that God provided guidance and personal revelations about how his life should proceed.

Quinn's father, Daniel Peña, was born in Arizona, the son of Mexican immigrants. Because of his belief that success would come with being associated with whiteness, Peña changed his name to Donald Quinn, choosing the last name of a childhood friend, Anthony Quinn, who later starred in Hollywood movies. Michael Quinn recalled that, "Marrying my blue-eyed, redheaded, ivory-skinned mother in 1942 was part of his becoming 'Americanized.'"[6]

The marriage only lasted until Mike was four. While he never hid the fact that he was of Mexican descent, he inherited a discomfort with Mexico that persisted even after he spent time in Mexico in his later life attempting to reconnect with his cultural heritage.[7] His discomfort persisted alongside an abiding distrust of any attempts to cover up identity or history in people and institutions, even as he repressed and concealed his own gay identity. Later, Quinn would write, "I now recognize that I saw my father reflected in the Church's official concealment of its controversial past. I was as determined to uncover the secrets of the Mormon past as I was to discover those of my father's Mexican heritage."[8]

Quinn remembered that at a young age he learned a lesson that people would disappoint him, breaking his confidences even when they promised otherwise. He recalled telling his mother something he felt "with the earnestness only a child can feel," and then overhearing her tell the story to a neighbor as a "cute" story. From then on, he wrote, "I let my family and others know me only as a spiritual, talented person, and built emotional walls to keep them from knowing my inner reality."[9] Perhaps related to this effort, Quinn also recalled being told very early in his life and from multiple people that he was special, and that God was preparing him for great things. While members of his church and others contributed to his sense of specialness, perhaps no one did more than his grandmother, who told him

6. Memoir, March 26, 1944.

7. Sujey Vega, "Michael Pena Quinn: A Chicano with Gringo Attitude and Experience," in Park, ed. *DNA Mormon*, 47–51.

8. Memoir, April 26, 1973.

9. Ibid, early 1951.

when he was nine that she expected God would make him an apostle in the church. Quinn heard this idea frequently enough that "from age nine onward, I expected to become an apostle of Mormonism."[10]

Part of Quinn's trust in that vision for the future and a central part of his faith was his relationship with the Spirit. Like all Latter-day Saints, Quinn was taught that the Spirit is an active part of believers' lives, helping them to discern in the midst of choices and providing comfort through hard times. In his memoir written toward the end of his life, Quinn explained: "I cannot remember a time in my life when I have not been filled with assurances of the Spirit."[11]

While his confidence in his faith was strong, Quinn also felt that he was different as he grew to understand his sexuality. When he went to the library to research the feelings he was having, everything that he read was negative.[12] At the age of nineteen in 1963, he confessed his feelings of same-sex attraction to his bishop. "This kindly, blue-collar worker wept with me and was totally reassuring," he recalled. His journal that day read: "Such a load and burden has been lifted from me. I have rededicated my life to Christ and must unfalteringly strive to be worthy of serving Him." Clearly, the meeting with his bishop was a comfort, yet the message he left with reconfirmed that his faith required him to suppress his sexuality, in order to "strive to be worthy of serving Him."[13]

Even though he had experienced these sexual attractions beginning in his childhood and throughout his life, Quinn decided at an early age that he would hide those feelings and live the life narrative the church expected of him: He would serve a full-time mission, marry a woman in the temple, find a career, and have children. At the age of twelve he had made a "conscious choice," one in which he "traded the life of personal fulfillment I wanted to have in a world of risk and vulnerability, in exchange for the life of service to my family and the LDS Church in a supportive environment."[14] He dated a number of women in his youth before asking Jan Latham to be his wife. The two married in 1967 and

10. Ibid, July 1953.
11. Ibid, spring 1953.
12. Ibid April–June 1956.
13. Ibid, January 14, 1963.
14. Ibid, early June 1988.

had four children. Quinn believed church leaders' teachings at the time that having a family and a heterosexual marriage would allow him to overcome his gay desires, but soon realized that was not the case. In 1972, Quinn confessed his attractions to Jan, but the two decided to continue to live together because of their shared love of one another and their family.[15]

In 1976 Quinn began teaching at Brigham Young University, a choice that brought him both great joy and sorrow. He loved teaching and the research that he was able to do during his time there. Even so, he struggled with concealing aspects of his identity. For this reason, his time at BYU was often riddled with tension. He continued to write and research in his pursuit to "uncover the secrets of the Mormon past," knowing well that that pursuit might cost him his career and that his inner self might be exposed.

Quinn's conviction that the attractions he was experiencing were insignificant and could be easily ignored in service of a loftier goal began to wane. He recognized that his sexuality had defined his life anyway, that his choice to ignore his sexual desires in order to conform had only caused more pain for himself and others along the way.

In addition to grasping that his sexuality was an important facet of his identity, he also came to see the exacting toll it was taking on his wife, Jan, to live in such a marriage, calling it a "heavy price for a girl to pay to fulfill a Mormon boy's sense of duty."[16] Describing his decision to follow the only life script offered to young men as a "coward's choice," Quinn was "now forced by circumstance to confront the homosexual realities I avoided as a teenager and young adult."[17]

In January of 1986, a divorce decree finally ended their marriage, which had been under immense strain while Quinn struggled to come to terms with his sexuality. He felt that the decree gave Jan "the only possibility for happiness and fulfillment" that he could offer.[18] He was realizing that his efforts to conform to the life narratives that the church required had resulted in "a failed marriage, my

15. Gary Topping, *D. Michael Quinn: Mormon Historian* (Salt Lake City: Signature Books, 2020), 20.
16. Qtd in Topping, *D. Michael Quinn*, 97.
17. Ibid, early June 1988.
18. Ibid, January 13, 1986.

boys growing up in a one-parent household, all my children out of the Church by their choice."[19]

While the divorce was final, Quinn's BYU employment and relationship to the church still affected Jan and their family, living in Salt Lake City. In July of that year, Jim Allen, chair of BYU's history department, asked Quinn why Jan had stopped attending Sunday meetings. Quinn felt devastated "to know that BYU administrators were kept informed about my ex-wife's religious behavior fifty miles away." In that same meeting, Allen counseled Quinn to be careful because he was being watched. "I've been informed that you were at a homosexual bar last weekend," Allen told him.[20]

At the same time that Quinn's choices in his personal life were being watched, he also experienced a clamping down on the historical investigations that he loved. In May 1986 the church's historical department announced that all researchers must now sign a form that gave the church a right of pre-publication review for archival work completed. Quinn noted that "this was an effort to retroactively close the door on the previous sixteen years of openness in the LDS Church Archives." Quinn understood that refusing to sign the form meant that his and other researchers' work in those archives was over and that church leaders would frame it as their choice, rather than the church restricting historians.[21]

As his relationship with the church started to crumble and he began to distance himself from the institution to which he had committed both his career and his faith, Jan, who decided to relocate outside of Utah, encouraged him to seek out fulfilling relationships with men. She affirmed that their children "loved, accepted, and respected" him and that he would always be welcome to spend time with them during the holidays.[22] Quinn began a personal journey of reconfiguring family and community networks that shifted his emotional well-being away from the institutional church. This offered a renewed sense of kinship and community for him.

Throughout his early career working for his mentor, Leonard

19. Ibid, early June 1988.
20. Ibid, July 1986.
21. Ibid, early June 1986.
22. Ibid, early September 1987.

Arrington, and then at BYU, Quinn had stood between a rock and a hard place. He had to balance the work of a professional historian who was bound by the demands of his profession and the expectations of his faith leaders who wanted a correlated history that bolstered communal identity. Like Arrington, Quinn initially thought that other members of his community would welcome an accurate version of their history. He dove into the topics that fascinated him, working hours on end to add his contribution to the historical narratives of his faith. He learned, though, that his professional demands and the expectations of church leaders were often at odds with one another.

Perhaps no other incident captures Quinn's understanding of this tension better than his response to Boyd K. Packer's talk, "The mantle is far, far greater than the intellect." In that 1981 address at BYU, Packer had cautioned historians against the dangers of "unworthy, the savory, or the sensational" aspects of history, and also against the lure of the idea that historians need to tell everything. In addition, Packer warned that outsider historians had used context to explain away revelation. Quinn had seen that happen and believed there was a middle road. "Not only as a believing Latter-day Saint but also as a historian, I also oppose those who make such conclusions," he stated in a speech he gave at BYU. "One can acknowledge the influence of environment and contemporary circumstance, and still affirm the actuality of divine revelations," he argued, even as he critiqued Packer and Ezra Taft Benson for their understanding of history.[23]

As Quinn navigated this complicated debate, his stake president let him know that several former bishops had recommended that he be called as the new bishop of his ward, but that "Apostle Mark E. Petersen has blocked the appointment."[24] The decision indicated the extent to which the lines had been blurred, at least from the church hierarchy's perspective: Quinn's scholarship and public criticism of church leaders signaled to the hierarchy that he was not worthy of leading his faith community.

Packer's "Mantle" talk was but one example of his commitment

23. D. Michael Quinn, "On Being A Mormon Historian," lecture given before the Student History Association, Brigham Young University, Fall 1981.

24. Anderson, "LDS Intellectual Community," 19.

to the idea that history was perilous to faith. When Packer had earlier interviewed Quinn for his professorship at BYU, Quinn recalled him saying, "I have a hard time with historians ... because they idolize the truth. The truth is not uplifting; it destroys. Historians should tell only that part of the truth that is inspiring and uplifting." Here, Packer claimed that truth in its objective form could be dangerous to faith, that history required hand-selection, with the criteria that it be faith-affirming. Quinn remembered that in response to Packer's statement, he "spoke of balance, perspective, context." Packer shook his head, saying "You'll learn." In his journal Quinn recalled: "I did. And, as the saying goes, 'The rest is history.'"[25]

As Quinn felt confident that historians could contextualize religious experiences, including revelations, without diminishing their significance or their rootedness in the divine, he also argued that Mormons did not need to be defensive about their history. Early Mormons like Brigham Young were unapologetic in how they remembered Joseph Smith, for example. They could acknowledge his weaknesses while also endorsing his role as prophet.[26] Why not do the same in the late twentieth century? Why not acknowledge that prophets were human as well as divinely inspired?

Quinn, part of a group often referred to as scholars of the "New Mormon History," believed he could move beyond pro- and anti-Mormon discourse to a more accurate and fair accounting of the past.[27] He felt that what average Mormons' understanding of history lacked was *context*. The church history that people often received in their church meetings and classes did not contextualize the past because of an underlying assumption that if revelations and prophecies were tied to context, they lost their divine nature—in other words, they could be explained naturally rather than supernaturally. Quinn disagreed. "If we write Mormon history as though its revelations and developments occurred without any reference to surrounding circumstances, we undermine the claims for the

25. Qtd. in Lavina Fielding Anderson, "DNA Mormon: D. Michael Quinn," in John Sillito and Susan Staker, eds., *Mormon Mavericks: Essays on Dissenters* (Salt Lake City: Signature Books, 2002), 329–64.

26. Quinn, "On Being A Mormon Historian."

27. John-Charles Duffy, "Can Deconstruction Save the Day? 'Faithful Scholarship' and the Uses of Postmodernism," *Dialogue: A Journal of Mormon Thought* 35, no. 2 (Summer 2002): 7.

Restoration of living prophets," he argued. "This is one of many areas in Mormon history writing where an alleged defense is actually a disservice to the Saints."[28]

Like his mentor Arrington, Quinn believed that the church lost members because of its inability to give a truthful and fair account of its past. Its leaders were *human,* he always wanted to remind people, and it was dangerous to put them on pedestals for many reasons: First, because it made it hard for people to see the fallibility of church leaders whom they idolized. Second, once they did learn challenging facts, the conflict between the facts and what they had been taught in Sunday school often caused a crisis of faith because the chasm was so large. Finally, pedestals meant that average Mormons did not have good role models for regular, everyday human behavior. Instead, the leaders were cast as demi-gods, making it hard for believers to see that "they, too, were men capable of sin who *did* sin."[29]

What Quinn sought to do was what Arrington referred to as inoculating believers, helping them to understand the broad, accurate, and contextual aspects of their history so that new information could be situated in that broader framework and not cause a crisis of faith.[30] Because his chartered course was fraught on both sides, Quinn ended up writing history that often pleased neither side fully. In the introduction of his 1987 book, *Early Mormonism and the Magic World View,* he affirmed his beliefs as a Mormon: "I feel it necessary to state my biases at the outset. I believe in Gods, angels, spirits, and devils, and that they have communicated with humankind. In Mormon terms, I have a personal 'testimony' of Jesus as my Savior, of Joseph Smith, Jr., as a prophet, of the *Book of Mormon* as the word of God, and of the LDS Church as a divinely established organization through which men and women can obtain essential Priesthood ordinances of eternal consequence."[31]

Even as he offered a testimony, the content of which might be heard at testimony meetings across the world, Quinn added: "I also

28. Quinn, "On Being A Mormon History."

29. "On Writing Mormon History, 1972–95: From the Diaries and Memoirs of D. Michael Quinn," in Joseph W. Geisner, ed., *Writing Mormon History: Historians and Their Books* (Signature Books, 2020), 241. Here Geisner quoted an excerpt from Quinn's personal writings on August 30, 1972.

30. See "On Writing Mormon History," 250.

31. Qtd. in Memoir, late August 1987.

believe that no historical documents presently available, or locked away, or as yet unknown will alter these truths," he continued, "and I believe that persons of faith have no reason to avoid historical inquiry into their religion or to discourage others from such investigations."[32] Again Quinn argued that faith would ultimately win the day and be stronger because of historical inquiry.

While Quinn and other "New Mormon Historians" were making the case that faith and historical inquiry could go hand and hand, scholars at BYU were embracing postmodernism to explain their apologetic position. Using the work of thinkers like historian Peter Novick's *That Noble Dream*, these apologists argued that the pursuit of objectivity was an impossible dream for human beings. Working in the 1980s and 1990s, these professors, including David E. Bohn and Louis Midgley, made the argument that if objectivity was an elusive dream, then perspective was what mattered. In his essay, "Unfounded Claims and Impossible Expectations," Bohn captured the essence of their critique:

> Because Mormons believe that God participates in the unfolding of historical events and will eventually bring them to an appropriate end, every attempt to undermine the historical authenticity of the foundational events of the Mormon past constitutes an assault on Latter-day Saint self-understanding. Even when done with the best of intentions, efforts to de-literalize or mythologize the historical reality of the concrete occurrences that constitute the Restoration are never merely benign attempts to get this or that detail right. Rather they are nothing less than acts of intellectual violence against the believing community.[33]

Bohn's argument that contextualizing and moving away from literal claims was an act of "intellectual violence against the believing community" shows the anxiety around the new modes of history-telling by professionally trained historians. It was not just a different narrative that the New Mormon History were offering; it was perceived as an act of aggression, a narrative that might bring about the downfall of the church.

---

32. Qtd. in ibid.

33. David Earl Bohn, "Unfounded Claims and Impossible Expectations: A Critique of New Mormon History," in George D. Smith, ed., *Faithful History: Essays on Writing Mormon History* (Salt Lake City: Signature Books, 1992), 228.

For these apologists, faith-affirming history was a valid pursuit because all truth claims were made from a particular point of view. But while they used the philosophy of postmodernism, their work was not in line with postmodern intentions because it sought to use the concepts in the philosophical position to draw limitations around what was and what was not legitimate historical inquiry by church members.[34] In addition, they often did not use the methodologies of historical inquiry embraced by postmodernists. They wanted to legitimize their own positionality without recognizing any others.

Throughout his career as a church member who worked at Church Archives and at BYU, up until the time of his excommunication, Quinn pushed back against this understanding. He saw it as the church's attempt to "tell me only good news and happy things," just as his non-Mormon father had consistently told him while masking his true identity as a son of Mexican immigrants.[35] Even as the threat of a church disciplinary council seemed imminent, Michael Quinn remained confident that his historical pursuits would not destroy his or other church members' faith. "Even if Church authorities excommunicate me one day," he presciently wrote in his journal, "it is Mormon doctrine that every ordinance of the Church must be ratified by 'the Holy Spirit of Promise' for the individual, or the ordinance does not have any validity in eternity. I trust in my relationship with God."[36]

Disciplinary Actions

Michael Quinn's excommunication was a long time in the making. When he was still teaching at BYU and chose to publish his April 1985 *Dialogue* article titled "LDS Church Authority and New Plural Marriages, 1890–1904," he set himself on a course leading toward church censure and discipline. The article explored LDS Church leaders' secret sanctioning of and entering into new polygamous marriages after the 1890 Manifesto, in which the church had publicly declared it would abandon the practice. Quinn knew that he was challenging the approved history-telling of his religious

34. Duffy, "Can Deconstruction Save the Day?" 1–33.
35. Memoir, May 1992.
36. Ibid.

tradition: "That alone made me a problem in the eyes of Church leaders, and as a result of that publication, the hierarchy started putting pressure on me directly."[37] This happened despite the fact that he had informed church leaders as early as 1979 that he had been working on this research topic. Even though he had received authorization to examine the First Presidency documents pertaining to the matter, James M. Paramore, a general authority of the church, instructed Quinn's stake president to take away his temple recommend after his article appeared.[38] Apparently church leaders believed that the institution's hard-won reputation was being tarnished. Knowing that Quinn could not retain his position at BYU without a temple recommend, his stake president told Quinn that he would put it away in his drawer but would not revoke it. Even so, Quinn said the loss of the recommend "*really* hurt."[39]

Quinn recalled receiving a letter from Apostle Dallin H. Oaks in May 1985. In it, Oaks was "accusing me of underhandedly obtaining restricted documents at LDS Archives and of preparing to publish the article without notifying my 'file leaders' or the custodians of those documents." Quinn responded by sending copies of letters he had earlier written about his research to Apostle Gordon B. Hinckley—then one of the advisors over the church history division, and G. Homer Durham (the managing director of the division) years before.[40] Clearly the issue was not permissions per se, but rather exposing history that those in power would rather not have exposed.

Quinn was digging up a past the church had worked hard to suppress throughout the twentieth century. Halting the practice of polygamy had set the church on a course of assimilation with the broader culture. For decades the church had worked to de-emphasize its religious differences from its Protestant and Catholic peers. Mormons in the 1980s had been taught that polygamy was part of the distant past and Sunday school lessons rarely, if ever, addressed the

37. D. Michael Quinn, interview with Philip Lindholm, in Philip Lindholm, *Latter-day Dissent: At the Crossroads of Intellectual Inquiry and Ecclesiastical Authority* (Salt Lake City: Greg Kofford Books, 2011), 110. Hereafter Quinn Interview.

38. Anderson, "LDS Intellectual Community," 24.

39. D. Michael Quinn, "Background and Fallout of My 1985 Article 'LDS Church Authority and New Plural Marriages, 1890–1904,'" *Sunstone*, Fall 2015.

40. Ibid.

practice. Yet here was a historian drudging up a history of church leaders who, despite what they said publicly, continued an underground practice for decades after the 1890 Manifesto.

After the article appeared in *Dialogue*, Quinn learned from others that Apostle Packer was denouncing his work in several speeches and to various audiences. In those speeches Packer never identified Quinn by name but described him as "a BYU historian who is writing about polygamy to embarrass the Church."[41] Later, a friend let Quinn know that Packer spoke to the Quorum of Twelve about him, saying, "What Mike Quinn wrote about plural marriage may be true, but no faithful Latter-day Saint would publish what he did."[42] While Quinn believed the truth would allow church members to better understand and reconcile with their past, members of the church hierarchy saw things differently.

Professionally, Quinn felt increasingly unwelcome at BYU and worried that his days there were numbered. After securing a fellowship at the Huntington Library in Pasadena, California, he resigned his position at BYU on January 20, 1988. When the brief fellowship ended, Quinn decided to move to New Orleans, seeking to live outside the tentacles of the church's far-reaching grasp and to pursue his true identity as a gay man. Even as he did, he believed the church would be looking for him and suspected that, if found, he would be excommunicated. Knowing that excommunications and disciplinary hearings are supposed to happen at the local level, he used a post office box rather than a home address so that church officials could not track him down. In New Orleans, he spent time in therapy, which helped him to come to terms with his sexuality and to find peace with what would likely someday happen in church proceedings.[43]

In 1992, fortified by some time away from the centers of institutional power, Quinn decided that he was ready to move back to Utah, where family members and many of his friends lived.[44] Tired of hiding from what seemed inevitable, he squared his shoulders and chose to face whatever was to come. Part of his preparation

41. Memoir, late April 1985.

42. Ibid.

43. David Haglund, "The Case of the Mormon Historian; What Happened When Michael Quinn Challenged the History of the Church He Loved," *Slate*, November 2012.

44. Anderson, "DNA Mormon," 347.

included finally coming out to his parents. In early 1992 he wrote both of them a letter in which he talked about his sexuality. While his father only read part of the letter and expressed no interest in discussing it further, his mother called to say that she loved and accepted him, which would comfort him in the coming months. He recalled that, "Mom phoned to say that my letter had shocked her, but that she loved me unconditionally. I told her that during my whole life I had wanted to spare her the pain of knowing I'm homosexual. 'Why should you carry all the pain?' she said. I cried at hearing those words."[45]

Not long after his move back to Utah and with his increasingly public and critical view of the institution, the church caught up with Quinn. In February 1993, six months after he moved to Salt Lake City, he was visited by his stake president, Paul Hanks, along with Hanks's two counselors. Not there for fellowship, Hanks was "holding a written accusation that my recent historical publications constituted apostasy." At the top of Hanks's list was Quinn's essay, "Mormon Women Have Had the Priesthood Since 1843," an essay in Maxine Hanks's book, *Women and Authority*. Quinn "didn't bother to point out to the stake president that this article was merely a longer analysis of what I had published in the fall of 1981," because he understood that "what was merely controversial back then was apostate in 1993."[46] In addition to that article, the letter also named a piece Quinn had written for *Sunstone* in 1992 titled "150 Years of Truth and Consequences in Mormon History," an essay in which he "wrote about the pressure put upon people who had written about uncomfortable issues or doctrine in Mormonism from the nineteenth century onward." And, finally, the letter noted comments he had made to both the *New York Times* and the *Salt Lake Tribune*, comments in which he said that the church could not "accept the existence of loyal opposition." Instead, Quinn observed that the "LDS leadership wants 'cookie cutter members.'"[47]

When Quinn told Hanks that he was heading to California for continued research at the Huntington Library, Hanks promised that

45. Memoir, May 1992; Anderson, "DNA Mormon," 347.
46. Memoir, February 7, 1993.
47. Quinn Interview, 115.

disciplinary proceedings would happen when he returned. That evening Quinn wrote a letter to Hanks recounting his past experiences with church attempts to discipline him. He explained that he "would never again participate in a process which was designed to punish me for being the messenger of unwanted historical evidence and to intimidate me from further work in Mormon history."[48] Here, Quinn framed the problem as an issue with the facts and the church's unwillingness to recognize the facts as such. Writing to Hanks was not his only act. Quinn "furnished newspaper reporters with copies of [Hanks's] letter and [his own] response, in the hope that publicity would cause LDS headquarters to withdraw its instructions to my stake president."[49]

Even though the church pursued disciplining Quinn, his faith remained. He rejected the idea that the church could determine whether or not he was a believer; Mormonism was both his heritage and his faith. He understood his calling to be his historical work. His work was to reveal what had been unhelpfully concealed in an effort to whitewash and gloss over the church's past. Knowing this, he continued the process of slowly extracting himself from his relationship to the institution that had shaped and given meaning to most of his earlier life.

While he was in California, Quinn received another letter from Stake President Hanks. In his response, Quinn wrote: "Most of all, I resent the fact that everything in your conduct toward me indicates your assumptions of my disloyalty, while at the same time you expect me to loyally conceal your 'personal and confidential' efforts to intimidate me."[50] Quinn wrote that he would not meet with Hanks or any other church officers.

Shortly after Quinn's return to Salt Lake City at the end of his research trip to the Huntington Library, Hanks had appeared at his door, having been notified of his return by the building's manager who, Quinn believed, had been entering his apartment looking for evidence to use against him.[51] Quinn's growing concern that he was being fol-

48. Memoir, February 7, 1993.
49. Ibid.
50. Ibid, March 4, 1993.
51. Ibid, May 11, 1993.

lowed and watched was not simply a sign of paranoia. There had been an effort in the church for decades to find and expose gay church members. Taking lessons from law enforcement, the church had used informants and surveillance in its efforts to stamp out LGBT church members.[52] So it was not surprising that Quinn felt he was being watched. During this visit, Hanks brought with him Quinn's charges of apostasy tied to his writings about women and the priesthood, the conservatism of Ezra Taft Benson, and church censorship.[53]

Boyd K. Packer had recently given his May 1993 talk to the All-Church Coordinating Council in which he identified "three areas where members of the Church ... are being caught up and led away" in "the gay-lesbian movement, the feminist movement ... and the ever-present challenge from the so-called scholars and intellectuals." After hearing about the talk, Quinn felt as though Packer had been describing him: "I was in all of them. Three strikes, then 'Out!'"[54]

After hearing from Stake President Hanks again, this time with an ultimatum about the upcoming disciplinary council, Quinn's reply was both heartrending and telling. "I sincerely hope you are never in the situation of being hunted down by those you regard as Prophets, Seers, and Revelators, but who have defined you as expendable."[55] In the face of what was to come, Quinn reasserted that he had a deep and abiding faith. He wrote Hanks, "Baptism cannot give you a relationship with God, and excommunication cannot take it away.... I can only trust in God's love and in my relationship with Him."[56] Here, Quinn began to assert the theology that he would hold onto for the rest of his life: his faith that God and the Spirit remained with him even as the institutional church attempted to sever its connection with him.

And with that, the disciplinary councils began. The first, on June 6, 1993, put Quinn on probation as a member of the church. This decision was simply the next step after the initial loss of his temple recommend

52. Neil J. Young, "Homosexuality and Politics in Mormonism," in Amy K. Hoyt and Taylor Petrey, eds. *The Routledge Handbook of Mormonism and Gender* (New York: Routledge, 2020), 208.

53. "Six Intellectuals Disciplined for Apostasy," *Sunstone*, November 1993.

54. Memoir, May 18, 1993.

55. Ibid.

56. Ibid.

and therefore his access to the temple.[57] At each step, Quinn was placed further and further outside of the church community and the church's ideas about what one's role in the community should be.

As the first disciplinary council gathered to determine his fate, Quinn decided not to engage. Instead, he chose to see the movie *Super Mario Brothers*.[58] He opted for a silly, pop culture movie based on a video game over participating in the council that would officially break his ties to his faith community. It was after that movie that he reported feeling calm in the face of what was to come. It seems Quinn knew the inevitable and chose to embrace a different understanding of his life's trajectory from what the leaders of his church were offering. Because he did not want his mother to learn about the proceedings from the rumor mill, in late July 1993, he called to let her know what was happening. She described what was happening to her son in a way that perhaps he could not because of his closeness to it all: "They're chopping you off by inches, aren't they?"[59]

In August, Quinn's final disciplinary council took place. The timing of his council and his receipt of the council's decision was slow, and Quinn later suspected that church leaders had postponed his final judgment "to achieve the maximum effect for a message of intimidation from LDS headquarters. Six scholars and feminists in Utah were summoned to disciplinary councils in September." Quinn again refused to participate in this last disciplinary council that would end his ties to the church. He was not even in Utah at the time.[60]

During that final disciplinary council, Quinn traveled outside the grip of the Utah-based institution and entered into the community of Affirmation. There, he mingled with other former and current Mormons who were seeking to forge a new path and find a new identity where sexuality and faith could intersect. They were rewriting the narratives of their lives. At Affirmation, Quinn had star

57. For a discussion of the loss of his temple recommend, see Topping, *D. Michael Quinn*, 111.

58. Haglund, "Case of the Mormon Historian," 12. Quinn was disfellowshipped at this council, an act that meant "placing him on probation, denying him the sacraments and exercise of his priesthood ministry, and even denying him the right to give his testimony in church." See Topping, *D. Michael Quinn*, 119.

59. Anderson, "DNA Mormon," 352.

60. Haglund, "Case of the Mormon Historian," 13. In addition to attending the affirmation conference, Quinn stayed in California for several days.

status because of his research on sexual relationships in the church's past. In 1996, that research would become an award-winning book, *Same Sex Dynamics in Nineteenth-Century Americans: A Mormon Example*.[61] His work offered members of Affirmation a new understanding of their shared past, arguing that the church had once been more tolerant of and even welcoming to queer sexualities and alternative gender identities, but over time had become intolerant and chose to conceal its more inclusive past.

Quinn's work provided members of the LGBTQ+ community with a "usable past," a sense of rootedness in Mormon history and also the possibility of dreaming that things could be different in the future precisely because of that history.[62] His book gave LGBTQ+ Mormons evidence to push back against church leaders like Packer. As John Gustav-Wrathall, future president and executive director of Affirmation wrote, "Most Mormons and non-Mormons today take it for granted that [Packer's] view is consistent with a long history in the LDS Church of viewing homosexuality as an extreme and especially abominable moral transgression... [but] such an assumption is incorrect."[63] Quinn considered his keynote speech at the 1993 conference to be his "last Hurrah as an LDS rebel."[64]

After the disciplinary councils, Quinn received written notice that he had been excommunicated "for my refusal to cooperate with the stake president's inquiry into my alleged apostasy. Bad manners was my conduct unbecoming a member of the Church."[65] The charges had changed. Where once he had been told that his publications made him an apostate, as was the case with other excommunicants, the final charges were simply about failing to follow the hierarchy's

61. D. Michael Quinn, *Same Sex Dynamics in Nineteenth-Century Americans: A Mormon Example* (Urbana: University of Illinois Press, 1996). While Quinn's book provided queer Mormons with a powerful sense of rootedness in history, it was not easily accepted in Utah. Protestors attempted to intercede with the publisher and sought legal channels to prevent its arrival. See Bob Summer, "Latter-Day Dynamics" *Lambda Book Report*, 15.

62. See Alexandria Griffin, "Queer Mormon Histories and the Politics of a Usable Past," *Dialogue: A Journal of Mormon Thought* 54, no. 1 (Spring 2021): 5–9, for a discussion of the past serving as a framework for a possible future where LGBTQ+ folk are welcomed in the church.

63. John D. Gustav-Wrathall, review of *Same Sex Dynamics*, *Journal of Mormon History* 32, no. 1 (Spring 2006): 260.

64. Memoir, September 1993

65. Ibid.

commands, something they identified as "conduct contrary to the laws and order of the Church."[66]

While Quinn acknowledged that his initial response to talking about the excommunication was often snide, he said he was doing so "to conceal the raw pain of the experience." Throughout his life he had experienced that "Mormonism isn't a Sunday religion," but one in which believers had "feeling and experience that fills every part of your life."[67] He was being cut off from a religious tradition and community that was all-encompassing, not just of believers' social and communal existence but also of their internal world. It was a religion that taught people how to *feel* the Spirit, and framed those feelings within a worldview that took up entire landscapes of identity. So it was no surprise that the disciplinary council's decision hurt. "My excommunication was like a death in the family," he wrote, "except I was looking at myself in the coffin."[68] Even as he entered into a period of grief, he noted that "the burning of the Spirit within me made that grief bearable and gave me strength to go on. But the fact remains that the only life I ever wanted to live was dead."[69]

As Quinn struggled to come to terms with the death of the life he had imagined as a boy, the one he had chosen over acknowledging his sexuality, he continued to feel the presence of the Spirit and felt that it sustained him. Later, he said that the excommunication "didn't affect my relationship with God at all. I've actually turned back to the relationship with God that I had as a teenager when I thought, 'It's just you and me, God.'"[70] Recognizing that what he had lost was not a relationship with God, but with an institution, Quinn described himself as a Mormon mystic, who now lived in "a church of one."[71]

---

66. Anderson, "DNA Mormon," 353–54.

67. Troy Williams, "Mormon Identity and the Excommunicated," *The Event Newsweekly* August 16, 2001.

68. Memoir, September 1993. See also E. Marshall Brooks, *Disenchanted Lives: Apostasy and Ex-Mormonism among the Latter-day Saints* (New Brunswick, NJ: Rutgers University Press, 2018), 146–53.

69. Memoir, September 1993.

70. Quinn Interview, 127.

71. Qtd. in Benjamin E. Park, interview with Doug Fabrizio, "The Life and Legacy of D. Michael Quinn, *RadioWest*, February 24, 2022, radiowest.kuer.org. Similarly, in his Mormon Stories interview he referred to himself as "a church of one."

Even when Quinn was later asked to return to the church by his stake president, he knew there was no going back; the relationship had been severed irrevocably. While the church might have come to accept the history Quinn wrote about as common knowledge in the decades following his excommunication, he could not go back because he had made a choice to take an alternative road. When he was twelve, Quinn chose a heterosexual life in order to embrace the life narratives that the church had told him were *the best*, the ones they had promised would lead to his exaltation. But now he had embraced who he really was. He could not return to a life of concealment. "I can't go back because I can't be openly gay in the Church," he said.[72] He had found a new way to be faithful to both himself and to God. He was dreaming in color.

What Comes Next

When telling the story of Michael Quinn's life, people often focus on his financial struggles and search for work after he left BYU. A recent biographer of Quinn described his life after excommunication this way: "From the 1990s until the end of his life, then, Quinn became, like his son Adam, a bit of a drifter. Cut off from his family, his academic position, and his church membership, there was little to hold him in any one place."[73] At times, in story-telling about Quinn, such claims appear to serve as a kind of object lesson, suggesting that after the break in his relationship with the church Quinn struggled to find his place and identity. It seems better instead, to frame Quinn's financial struggles as the persistence of his reputation as a rebel following him, even in an academic world that might be imagined as more tolerant. And yet Quinn's experiences indicate that the church institution's and members' negative perceptions of him pursued him long after he had been formally expelled from the community. His rebel identity could not be left behind.

As a 2002 visiting professor at Yale University, Quinn was slated to speak at a conference, yet BYU told conference organizers that it would not participate as a co-sponsor of the conference if Quinn spoke at it. While Yale supporters insisted that Quinn would

72. Quinn Interview, 127. See also Quinn, interview with Dehlin.
73. Topping, *D. Michael Quinn*, 122.

participate, in the end, Quinn offered to introduce the keynote speaker, rather than speaking about his own research, so that the conference could go on.

The next year, Quinn was the single finalist for a tenure-track position in Utah/Mormon/Western history at the University of Utah, making it appear likely that he would be hired. But several scholars in the history department—most of them not LDS—voted against Quinn's hiring. They wondered if his field of specialization was appropriate, were concerned that he had not served on a teaching faculty for sixteen years, and felt he needed some renewed training on lecturing.[74] But something more was going on. One of his recommenders from BYU, Thomas Alexander, expressed a concern in his otherwise positive letter of recommendation that someone so publicly critical of the church would be hired to teach Mormon studies. As University of Utah historian James Clayton later put it, "There was a concern by several of us in the department that Mike was not the right person to head up any kind of Mormon history or Mormon studies program given the fact he's very publicly excommunicated. There would be quite a number of people in the Mormon community who would look unfavorably on that. That gave me pause."[75]

The following year, the Religious Studies department at Arizona State University wanted to offer Quinn a one-year visiting position but the choice was overturned by the associate dean for personnel. He claimed that Quinn "lacked expertise to teach Christianity and Judaism courses." It was later revealed that the dean had asked another administrator to review the "risks and benefits" of hiring Quinn, the risk being "alienating the Mormon community."[76] The benefits of hiring Quinn did not end up outweighing the risk. The fear was that Latter-day Saint donors would withdraw support for the institution.

At the same time that the financial and political power of Latter-day Saint donors meant Quinn did not have access to full-time financial support at an institution he chose, the private and unaffiliated

74. D. Michael Quinn, email to Gary Bergera, February 3, 2004, Signature Books Collection.

75. Daniel Golden, "In Religion Studies, Universities Bend to Views of Faithful," *Wall Street Journal*, April 6, 2006.

76. Ibid.

graduate institution, Claremont Graduate University (CGU), was raising funds for an endowed chair in Mormon Studies. As part of that work, CGU created an advisory council "composed mainly of believers" who were expected to help fundraise and have a voice in the hiring process. When asked about Quinn's possible role in the program, the dean of the School of Religion at CGU, Karen Torjesen, said, "We don't want any bomb-throwers."[77]

CGU's concern was that the creation of an endowed chair with Quinn at the helm would set up a hostile relationship with the very donors CGU sought. So when asked if Quinn would be considered for the position, the associate dean of Religion, Patrick Horn, said, "Probably not."[78] Here was a secular institution unaffiliated with the church, declaring it would not even consider Quinn's candidacy for a position before the job description even appeared.

As Quinn continued to pursue full-time employment at a four-year college or university, his status as a publicly excommunicated scholar meant that he was perceived as a scandal, a hot-potato, someone not to be touched. His excommunication was more than just a rupture of his social relationships and his relationship to the institution; it meant that his reputation as an excommunicant would continue to follow him.

On February 11, 1999, Quinn attended Leonard Arrington's funeral with his friend Maxine Hanks. Perhaps feeling external pressure or perhaps because of a pressure they created themselves, the two sat in the back. Hanks recalled that Gordon B. Hinckley, then president of the church, praised Arrington as the first professionally trained historian to hold the official position of Church Historian. Yet "it was an ideal that couldn't survive," Hanks later reflected. As he gave his eulogy, Hinckley said, "I don't know where historians will fit into the next life. I don't know what they're going to have to write about. Maybe there's a place in some dusty archive somewhere where they can get together and talk about the past."[79] As he spoke, and probably thinking of her own experiences and

77. Karen Torjesen, qtd. in Daniel Golden, "Expelled Scholar of Mormon History Can't Find Work," *Wall Street Journal* April 6, 2006.

78. Patrick Horn, qtd. in Golden, "Expelled Scholar."

79. "In Memoriam, Leonard J. Arrington," *Journal of Mormon History* 25, no. 1 (Spring 1999): 5.

her friend Quinn's, Hanks wryly wondered "if there's a place for historians in the here and now."[80]

The two friends in the back row knew all too well what could happen when the institution was confronted with a history it would just as soon forget. Hinckley said that "historians are usually concerned with the dusty tomes of history, but Leonard was a happy man. What a marvelous thing to draw happiness out of history."[81] Hanks felt strongly that Arrington should be remembered differently. His legacy was not using history to inspire happiness, rather it was "the search for truth." She was glad they were remembering Arrington fondly even as she noted that the church could not "tolerate his vision of open inquiry." At the same time, though, she felt as though Quinn, the historian she identified as Arrington's heir, was putting his Mormon Studies work behind him. "What does their absence bode for the future of Mormon history?" she wondered.

Quinn thought that another Arrington would arise, but that there would not be another "Camelot," where the church allowed open investigation of its past. Mormon history needed new blood, Hanks thought, but both she and her friend sitting in the back knew that, at that time, "those who publish honest history will pay a price for the truth."[82] So they took comfort in their friendship and pursuit of truth, a path both would continue to follow, even as they experienced the weight of the church's memory about the September Six.

Reflecting thirty years after September 1993, David Wright, who was excommunicated in April 1994, explained that he usually only merited, at best, a sentence in historical accounts of the September Six. Even though he faced the same extreme punishment that most of them had, history-tellers often decided that his story did not warrant mention. Because his excommunication did not happen in that now infamous month of September, he was often simply left out. Wright explained, "On one hand, I wish I were remembered more. On the other hand, I'm glad I'm not, because I really went on to other sorts of things and have had a very happy life."[83]

80. Maxine Hanks et al., Letters, *Dialogue: A Journal of Mormon Thought* 32, no. 2 (Summer 2002): iv–x.

81. "In Memoriam, Leonard J. Arrington."

82. Ibid, x.

83. David Wright, oral history with author, March 2023.

D. Michael Quinn's life stands in stark juxtaposition to Wright's experiences for many reasons. But at the most basic level, the lesson is important. Quinn never escaped the narratives of what happened in September 1993. In terms of social interactions for the rest of his life, his employment prospects, and historical memory, Quinn's life seemed locked into a story of struggle between the institutional church and its members. Wright, on the other hand, was primarily forgotten in terms of the September Six narrative. While that forgetfulness dismissed his experiences, it allowed Wright to move beyond what happened at that time. It was a slight but also profound gift. Wright could live and narrate his life as he chose. Quinn never could.

After their disciplinary councils, the September Six went in different directions, regaining their spiritual and social footing in whatever ways they could. In the end, their journeys represent the range of Mormonisms in the history of the Restoration. Just as there is some diversity within the institution, there is diversity around the margins of, and beyond, the institution.

While Lavina Fielding Anderson continued to attend her ward congregation for decades after her excommunication, her 2019 appeal for re-entry into full membership was turned down by the institutional church. Maxine Hanks, on the other hand, whose own excommunication did not faze her spiritually because at the time she was an agnostic, requested and was granted re-baptism into the church after two decades. Neither she nor the church acknowledged fault in what had happened to her in September 1993. Lynne Kavanel Whitesides moved on from the church spiritually and never looked back. Her spiritual journey took her beyond the bounds of Christianity and toward an eco-theology rooted in feminism and environmentalism. Avraham Gileadi returned to full membership in the church just a handful of years after his excommunication, whereas Paul Toscano lost his faith as he continued to critique the church. Michael Quinn, who remained faithful to the church's theology throughout his life, never returned to nor sought church membership. Though his drive to tell church history as unflinchingly and truthfully as possible might someday become accepted, he believed his identity as a gay man never would be.[84]

84. Quinn quoted this May 18, 1993, journal entry in Memoir.

Yet all of these people remained faithful to their restoration claims in their own fashion. They never wavered in their embrace of individual experiences of the Spirit or Ultimate Reality that led them in their quest for what was true. They remained committed to their arguments that personal conscience and experience were important sources of knowledge. They held fast to the idea that dissent was vital to the life of a healthy community. And they embraced an egalitarian and just vision of the future. They wanted to tell history as they understood it and challenge the abuses of history-telling—and tradition making—that reinforced power structures and demanded compliance. Their spiritual journeys led them down many different paths after September 1993, but they all remained somehow tied to that vision of the Restoration. The Six were insiders and outsiders both before and after September 1993. They embodied the diversity and range of experiences within the Mormon tradition. They exemplified the struggle for the soul of Mormonism.

CONCLUSION
THIRTY YEARS LATER

> *"Does this member have a testimony of The Church of Jesus Christ of Latter-day Saints and its doctrine, including its teachings on marriage, family, and gender?"*
>
> —Ecclesiastical Clearance Office, Brigham Young University

The rise of the internet in the 1990s profoundly changed the decades after September 1993. The internet democratized knowledge that had once been the province of institutions and elites and connected people who would not have known one another before. It had the power to bridge distances and also the power to create them. This shift has transformed the nature of Latter-day Saint communities. Local wards are defined geographically, meaning that people who may not interact with one another on a daily basis, who may come from different racial and ethnic groups, different socio-economic classes, and different political inclinations, need to learn to work together to keep the laity-led community going. Blogger, scholar, and church member Jana Riess explains that at the local level the church puts her "into wards with people I didn't choose and don't necessarily have a lot in common with, and prods me to build a life in common with them anyway."[1] This structure is quite different from many Protestant congregations around the United States that are not organized geographically but rather based on similarities in both theological and political leanings, a combination that can lead to a type of group-think.

While the LDS geographical organizational structure is still very

1. Jana Riess, "Mormonism's Tortured Genius," *Religion News*, August 29, 2022.

much intact, the presence of the internet allows Latter-day Saints who share common theological and political leanings to find one another easily. It may be that a person is the only LGBTQ+ member of their ward, but turning to Twitter and Instagram allows that same person to find a supportive community of LGBTQ+ Mormons who understand some of their experiences. Progressive Latter-day Saints can also find one another, explore their common causes, and organize. In similar fashion, ultraconservative Latter-day Saints like those who are a part of DezNat, short for Deseret Nation, who are influenced by and who embrace aspects of white nationalism, can find and connect with one another. Church members can now find themselves in their own echo chambers, just like anyone else.

As the church continues to define its identity in the twenty-first century, it pushes up against several strong forces. On the one hand, it must work to maintain itself as distinct from other Christian churches. It needs to appeal to potential converts as an institution and community that offers something different. This it must do as surveys show that the fastest growing groups in the United States and in many countries in the world are "Spiritual But Not Religious" and "Nones."[2] These statistics demonstrate that there are more people who are comfortable simply living without religion in their lives or borrowing aspects of different religious and philosophical traditions in order to fashion their own individual spirituality. At the same time, and in its efforts to be viewed as fully American, the church does not want to appear *too different*.[3] The church works to promote an image of Latter-day Saints as the epitome of fine, upstanding, moral people who anyone would want to have as their neighbors.

In this identity negotiation that is happening in a new digital age, the institutional church continues to promote the purity system. Some aspects of that system, such as approaches to history-telling, have changed profoundly in the past thirty years, while others have remained relatively the same. What is clear, though, is that the church hierarchy steadfastly aligns itself with conservative evangelical politics. Because of this choice in allies, the institution works

2. Gregory A. Smith, "About Three-in-Ten U.S. Adults Are Now Religiously Unaffiliated," Pew Research Center, December 14, 2021.

3. McKay Coppins, "The Most American Religion," *The Atlantic*, January 2021.

to support causes that circumscribe the power of and marginalize women and LGBTQ+ members. Nowhere is this more evident than at BYU, a university system that manages to reflect the conservative right's deep suspicion and distrust of intellectualism and higher education, progressivism and activism for civil rights.

History-Telling

One of the effects of the internet is that alternative narratives about the church's history from other sources are much more accessible to believers. While the institution can continue to control access to its historical documents and offer its own narrative of the past, counter-histories abound, at the fingertips of people everywhere. The internet allows believers to find or stumble upon aspects of the church's history that the hierarchy excludes from the stories taught at church and through its educational system.[4] The church has responded to this inundation of unauthorized story-telling with a new approach: to tell its own history in a way that addresses historical research and potentially controversial topics while mitigating the impact of those topics as much as possible and maintaining institutional control over interpretation.

This approach can be seen primarily in the Gospel Topics essays that began to appear on the church's website in 2013. There was no announcement of their presence in church forums or a statement explaining why they existed. Later, Steven E. Snow, a general authority, and the Church Historian and Recorder, called the project a "soft roll out" of essays that would address hard questions people had about controversial church topics. The essays were not signed by anyone, nor were they published in any of the church's magazines, even though they had passed through the church's correlating process.[5]

The essays addressed questions that caused some people to struggle with their faith. Yet the church chose not to make a grand announcement about their existence out of concern that they could cause doubt for church members who had not previously struggled

4. E. Marshall Brooks, *Disenchanted Lives: Apostasy and Ex-Mormonism among the Latter-day Saints* (New Brunswick, NJ: Rutgers University Press, 2018), 74–75.

5. Matthew L. Harris and Newell G. Bringhurst, "Introduction," in Matthew L. Harris and Newell G. Bringhurst, eds., *The LDS Gospel Topics Series: A Scholarly Engagement* (Salt Lake City: Signature Books, 2020), 20.

with questions about the church's past. Because of the fact that the essays just appeared on the church's website without any kind of announcement, though, some people wondered if they were anti-Mormon. These readers had not heard the topics the essays explore discussed in any church setting. And so the institution ended up making an official announcement of their presence and placing its imprimatur on them in late 2015. While there had been talk of an official historical narrative on these topics for several years in the Church History department, the origin of the essays was a November 2010 fireside in Stockholm, Sweden. Over 600 people attended to meet with Church Historian Marlin K. Jensen and Assistant Church Historian Richard E. Turley Jr. in order to ask questions about the church's history and faith.[6]

Not long after the fireside, John Dehlin, Greg Prince, Travis Stratford, and several others, performed a study of people who had left the church. They called the report of their findings "LDS Faith Crisis." The report named the gap between official church narratives taught in church settings and "uncorrelated history" (meaning history-telling that had not gone through the institution's correlation process, often written by outsiders) as a key issue why believers leave the church.[7] The study demonstrated that many Latter-day Saints lost their belief due to a faith crisis brought about by learning church history that they had not been taught in church contexts.

The Gospel Topics essays were in part a response to these growing concerns about church members leaving because of history-telling, the foundation of the church's purity system. Some see the essays, written by professional historians in the employ of the church or at the church's invitation, as progress. They represent the church's attempt to publicly address some of its past that it had previously tried to keep hidden, sometimes so well that many modern members did not even know of its existence. Others are not so sure that progress is being made.[8]

Historian David J. Howlett argues that the new setting in which the church finds itself is a "Post-Correlation LDS Church," a church

6. Ibid, 3–6.

7. Ibid, 7–9.

8. Jana Riess, "For Mormons in a Faith Crisis the Gospel Topics Essays Try to Answer the Hard Questions," *Religion News*, October 2020.

in which "LDS members inhabit a less homogenous and more fragmented church at least as compared to the church of the 1960s." This does not mean that correlation has ended. It is very much alive and in process. Rather Howlett points to an anxiety about memory loss precisely because of the central role history-telling has played in the formation of Latter-day Saint identity.[9] Because of the internet, the church had to adjust the correlation process to respond to the need for institutional story-telling, story-telling that counters and softens uncorrelated narratives.

The Gospel Topics essays represent the church's attempt to respond to a twenty-first century context. Rather than silencing alternative story-tellers as it did in times past, the church now offers to the world its own accounts of its controversial past, even as the essays are still an effort to control the institutional version of the Restoration. The absence of authors' names contributes to the aura that the essays are not interpretive and perspectival, but simply recount the past as it was. They claim a kind of universality, a "here are the facts" message representing *the* way faithful members should understand the church's story. They illustrate that the nature of the Restoration is still very much up for debate.

In the church's introduction to the essays, readers are reminded that Doctrine and Covenants 88 commands believers to learn about the gospel while also recognizing that "not all sources of knowledge are equally reliable." The introduction portrays the essays as "straightforward, in-depth essays" that were approved by the First Presidency and Quorum of the Twelve, reassuring readers that the essays have been through the correlation process and that they can trust the source. It suggests the essays are tools to help believers be "well informed about Church history, doctrine, and practices," at the same time that they attempt to moderate the more troubling aspects of history.[10]

Some of the Gospel Topics essays might be fairly categorized as addressing the differences that other Christians, particularly evangelicals

9. David J. Howlett, "Cultural Work of the 'First Vision Accounts,'" in Harris and Bringhurst, eds., *LDS Gospel Topics*, 160.

10. "Race and the Priesthood," churchofjesuschrist.org, accessed January 7, 2022. See also Brooks, *Disenchanted Lives*, 44–52.

with whom the church has shared political platforms, have identified as the traits that indicate that Latter-day Saints are not Christian. An example of this is a sub-group of essays that manages the history told about the church's practice of polygamy. Each essay in this category frames human history and relationships similarly. Monogamy between "one man and one woman—is the Lord's standing law of marriage," but at times God commands some faithful people to practice plural marriage. In this way, the church tells history that is in line with its co-religionists on the conservative right while also justifying its polygamous past.

Still others tackle the issues that dissenters were previously disciplined, ostracized, or lost their jobs for researching and exploring. One such essay addresses "Race and the Priesthood." While the essay names some of the church's racist past, it uses context to soften the blow. Church members turned away from what God had intended for all people, the essay claims, because of the broader racist society. The essay concludes with a condemnation of all racism, stating that "Since that day in 1978 [when Spencer W. Kimball received the revelation lifting the racial bans], the Church has looked to the future."[11] Just as Lester Bush and Armand Mauss pointed out long ago, the church framed the revelation as a moment for looking forward. It did not attempt to address or redress past injustices. While the essay condemns past racist teachings and acknowledges that the racial bans were rooted in the racist culture in which the church grew, it only goes so far. It does not acknowledge that whiteness in the Book of Mormon and Latter-day Saint teachings has been tied to morality and goodness while dark skin has been associated with bad choices and immoral states.[12]

The essay titled "Joseph Smith's Teachings About Priesthood, Temple, and Women," appeared at the same time that the Ordain Women movement was gathering steam, protesting women's lack of access to the priesthood role. This essay does a lot of historical heavy lifting, addressing several significant topics that have played a major role in the church. The essay begins with a declaration that

11. "Race and the Priesthood."

12. Matthew L. Harris, "Whiteness Theology and the Evolution of Mormon Racial Teachings," in Harris and Bringhurst, eds., *LDS Gospel Topics*, 247–64.

women are an important part of the community. "Because only men are ordained to priesthood office," it explains, "questions have arisen about women's standing in the Church." It then turns to providing historical context for the question of women and the priesthood.

Recognizing the centrality of the priesthood to the claims of the Restoration, the essay explains that Joseph Smith conferred the priesthood on other men. "By the same authority," the essay continues, "Joseph Smith organized the Relief Society." Much like the book *Women and the Covenant*, the essay argues that the Relief Society was established under Smith's authority, who then worked "to give women authority, sacred responsibilities, and official positions within the structure of the Church, not apart from it."[13] The anonymous authors provide an analysis that explains women's position in the church and that Smith used language tied to priesthood authority to describe women's roles, but are adamant that "neither Joseph Smith, nor any person acting on his behalf, nor any of his successors conferred the Aaronic or Melchizedek Priesthood on women or ordained women to priesthood office." In addition, the essay explains that women in the nineteenth century participated in blessings and healings in ways that may seem odd to believers today because "women's participation in healing blessings gradually declined in the early 20th century" as leaders in the church counseled people to involve male priesthood holders in such affairs.[14]

In the temple, it continues, ordinances take place that "were priesthood ordinances but they did not bestow ecclesiastical office on men or women." The temple ordinances provided priesthood power to individuals that would allow them to receive personal revelation and deepen their relationship with God. When men and women are sealed to one another in marriage in the temple, "they enter together, by covenant, into an order of the priesthood." It is through this covenant that they may achieve exaltation, the highest level of heaven.

The essay makes a distinction that highlights the way that men and women in the church are viewed differently: "men are ordained to priesthood offices, while both women and men are invited to

13. "Joseph Smith's Teachings About Priesthood, Temple, and Women," churchofjesuschrist.org, accessed January 7, 2022.

14. Ibid.

experience the power and blessings of the priesthood in their lives." Women can receive some passive advantages of the priesthood, but do not share in the role or the authority that is offered to men. The essay's language softens the patriarchal authority of the institution while also reaffirming it.

Margaret Toscano argues that this softening and reaffirmation is a form of gaslighting. "The thesis of the church essay is that Smith's statements about women and priesthood do not mean what they seem to mean," she argues. The essay asks readers to conclude that: "(1) Smith never ordained women to priesthood and never intended to do so; (2) the temple priesthood does not confer authoritative keys or have any efficacy in the church organization; (3) the Relief Society was never intended to be a priesthood organization; and (4) anyone who thinks otherwise is under a misperception and misguided."[15]

Toscano points out that the essay is meant to align the church's teaching about the priesthood today with Joseph Smith's teaching; thus, it is primarily about the nature of the Restoration. It suggests that "the place of women within the organization today reflects God's will, the same yesterday, today, and, presumably, forever."[16] The contrast with the race essay, then, is striking. Where the essay about race takes context into account in order to explain the changing nature of revelation, the essay about women and the priesthood does the opposite by denying that things have changed—or will ever change—at all. It creates a seemingly insurmountable wall of "tradition." It does so by starting with the apostasy of the church after the death of the ancient apostles in order to affirm that the Restoration was about the return of the priesthood and its keys to the earth. That understanding of the Restoration, Toscano argues, reinforces the idea that current priesthood holders and the church hierarchy are the only ones "who have the right to say what priesthood means."[17]

Yet she offers a counter-narrative, as did several members of the September Six. Smith's goal, she argues, was to bring the priesthood, with its spiritual gifts and its religious authority to *all people*. But

15. Margaret M. Toscano, "Joseph Smith's Teachings on Priesthood, Temple, and Women," in Harris and Bringhurst, eds., *LDS Gospel Topics*, 326.

16. Ibid, 327.

17. Ibid, 339–40, 355.

Toscano contends that the church does not want people to see this, as it would cause those who have been denied those gifts to understand what is rightfully theirs. The church, she says, does not provide all the information that would allow readers to determine for themselves. Instead it offers its own interpretation of history as *the* history. This, Toscano reasons, has profound effects on women's experiences of the faith. The institution has limited their spiritual and institutional authority without providing them the means to interpret for themselves the grounds upon which the claims are made.[18]

Women and the Divine Feminine

While it appears there have been no institutional moves toward granting women priesthood power or authority outside of the temple, aspects of the temple ritual have transitioned to provide more affirming messages to women. Some have interpreted these as nods toward gender equality in the church. In 1990, the institutional church removed the requirement for women to obey the law of their husbands. In 2019, it removed the requirement that wives should hearken to their husbands as their husbands hearkened to God. In 2023, the language of the ceremony changed from portraying Eve (representing all women) as not just a helpmeet to Adam (representing all men), but both as "companions and helpmeets for each other." Even as these instructions gestured toward gender equality in personal relationships, the institution added language about "the blessings Latter-day Saints will receive if they are obedient."[19] Here the greater equality in personal relationships is juxtaposed with the emphasis on obedience to the church, which is rooted in patriarchal priesthood. Church member Sara Vranes spoke of the 2019 changes in mixed terms. While on one hand she thought, "Oh, things can change, things can get better." On the other, she thought that "these were changes that … should have happened so long ago."[20]

Slow change has occurred elsewhere, not just in the temple. The church has begun to expand its understanding of women's social

18. Ibid.

19. Jana Riess, "More Jesus, Less Touching," *Religion News*, February 10, 2023.

20. Daysha Eaton, "LDS Temple Ceremony Updates Aim to Put Women on Equal Footing with Men," *KUER*, January 4, 2019.

roles as well. Deseret Book, a church-owned press, and Brigham Young University's Maxwell Institute co-published a 2023 book edited by Melissa Wei-Tsing Inouye and the late Kate Holbrook titled *Every Needful Thing: Essays on the Life of the Mind and the Heart.* The book celebrates the perspectives of working and faithful members of the church who embrace their motherhood, their faith, and their work lives. This is a far cry from church leaders in previous decades who told women the measure of their calling and salvation was motherhood, most notably Ezra Taft Benson's 1987 speech, "To The Mothers of Zion." Jana Riess says, "What was entirely absent from Benson's talk (which was made part of the 1990 book *Come Listen to a Prophet's Voice* and is still on the church's official website as part of the curriculum for the Eternal Marriage Student Manual) is any notion that women might actually want to work. That they, like men, are called to other things in life besides parenthood and that they deserve the chance to develop their talents and pursue their God-given interests."[21] From her perspective, the slow shift marks an important moment—that the church is recognizing the diversity of women's experiences in its membership.

While slow changes are still change, it is on the theological front and with the figure of Heavenly Mother, that no substantive changes have been made in the past thirty years. In 1991, Gordon B. Hinckley made it quite clear that Heavenly Mother should not be the subject of theological inquiry or relational spirituality, stating, "I regard it as inappropriate for anyone in the Church to pray to our Mother in Heaven." Even with such counsel not to explore the figure of Heavenly Mother, people did anyway. Just as with Mary in the Catholic tradition, it is the laity of the Church of Jesus Christ of Latter-day Saints who have historically contributed the most to the development of theological discussions and questions about the feminine divine. The internet has only served to multiply these discussions.

On April 2, 2022, Apostle Dale G. Renlund gave a speech at a women's session of general conference titled, "Your Divine Nature and Eternal Destiny." His speech marked a significant moment because it had been a long time since someone of such high rank in the church

21. Jana Riess, "LDS Church's Slow Shift Away from Demonizing Working Mothers," *Salt Lake Tribune*, March 1, 2023.

had spoken publicly about Heavenly Mother. Renlund's talk, no matter what he said, was bound to be the subject of intense scrutiny.[22]

Renlund began by emphasizing that even though he was neither young nor a woman, he was going to be speaking to the Young Women's theme for the year. That theme began, "I am a beloved daughter of heavenly parents, with a divine nature and eternal destiny."[23] Renlund reminded his audience of a truth in the statement: that humans have heavenly *parents*, a father and a mother, thus reinforcing the heterosexual nature of the divine realm and eternal progression. He referred to the Gospel Topics essay on Heavenly Mother as the extent of what the church knew about her. That short essay acknowledges that while there is "no record of a formal revelation to Joseph Smith on this doctrine," several women in the early church recalled that he had spoken to them about her. Smith's successors continued to affirm the existence of Heavenly Mother, including the 1995 Family Proclamation. "Prophets have taught that our heavenly parents work together for the salvation of the human family," the essay continues. Just as Renlund was preaching in 2022, the essay emphasized that the church had limited knowledge of her. She exists, he stated, but little else was known.

Renlund counseled that seeking more understanding was positive, but believers needed to be cautious. Speculation about something that had not been addressed through revelation could lead to deception and error. He argued that prophets could not demand information from God who operated on a divine timetable rather than a human one. To do so would be "arrogant and unproductive."[24]

A 2021 article in *LDS Living* outlined the entirety of remarks church officials have made about Heavenly Mother and her

---

22. These publications ranged in theological approach. Two books, *A Girls' Guide to Heavenly Mother* and *A Boy's Guide to Heavenly Mother* appeared in 2020 and were published by Deseret Book. These came after a 2016 children's book by the same authors, Bethany Brady Spalding and McArthur Krishna titled *Our Heavenly Family, Our Earthly Families*. Carol Lynn Pearson wrote a book of poems about Heavenly Mother in 2020 titled *Finding Mother God*. This came on the heels of Rachel Hunt Steenblik's 2017 poetry collection, *Mother's Milk: Poems in Search of Heavenly Mother*. See Julia Duin, "God's Wife? Mormon Women Want to Know More as Church Leaders Insist Faithful Pray Only to the Heavenly Father," *Newsweek*, June 24, 2022.

23. Dale G. Renlund, "Your Divine Nature and Eternal Destiny," *Ensign*, May 2022.

24. Ibid.

attributes. The list was not long. With Heavenly Father, Heavenly Mother "gave your eternal intelligence spirit form," making each person unique.[25] The article discussed Heavenly Mother's creative power and noted that as a mother, she is constantly worried for her offspring. In addition to her role as mother, she also played the role of wife and companion to Heavenly Father. Her identity was her relationships. Together the Heavenly Parents experienced the full-range of human suffering and emotion, and so understand the experiences of the faithful in their mortal lives. Heavenly Mother, in the words of Spencer W. Kimball, is "the ultimate in maternal modesty, of the restrained, queenly elegance."[26]

The content of the *LDS Living* article and Renlund's talk showed that, at least in terms of institutional and official theology, little had changed. Reactions to Renlund's talk ran the gamut. While the church had begun to use the phrase "Heavenly Parents" more frequently in its discourse, nothing of substance—no new information—had been added at the institutional level, even though lay members were continuing to explore. What *had* changed thirty years later was that many members felt more comfortable exploring and critiquing an apostle's talk.

Jana Riess struggled with the talk and studied it carefully. While she felt the affirmation of Heavenly Mother's importance and doctrinal significance from the pulpit by one of the church's top leaders comforting, she also noted that the speech took "a more restrictive turn."[27] She was glad that Renlund did not employ a traditional argument that the church did not speak about Heavenly Mother because Heavenly Father was trying to protect her. Riess called that old argument "codswallop," saying instead that Heavenly Mother "can't be some wilting Victorian flower shrinking under the protective coverture of a strong man. If we believe in eternal progression as we claim to, then Heavenly Mother has already been through a hell of a lot to become who she is. If she made it that far, she's strong. She's holy. She can take it."

---

25. Danielle B. Wanger and Katie Lambert, "11 Powerful Truths about Our Heavenly Mother from Prophets and Apostles," *LDS Living*, February 22, 2021.

26. Ibid.

27. Jana Riess, "Heavenly Mother Are You Really There?" *Religion News* May 6, 2022.

Here Riess described Heavenly Mother as a tough, feminine figure. The value in Renlund's talk, Riess explained, was that Renlund was willing to say "I don't know," rather than engage in speculation. For her that seemed promising. It spoke of the possibility of a day when "the church is less wedded to the sexism of the world." Until that time, Riess would have to live with the irony "that the same church that keeps telling me in various ways not to think like a man or act like a man is also failing to provide me with any other heavenly example to emulate."[28]

Writing for *Religion Dispatches*, Holly Welker felt more pessimistic about the talk. She saw a pattern in the church hierarchy of an unwillingness to explore or offer wisdom about Heavenly Mother. In addition, "they really don't want Latter-day Saints to exercise gifts of the Spirit to learn more about Heavenly Mother on their own." She heard in Renlund's talk a "call to inaction," telling believers that they should do nothing but trust in God's time table. But Welker argued that Renlund and other church authorities should remember the incidents surrounding the 1978 revelation about the racial bans. During that time Kimball did historical research and asked God to better know what God thought about the issue: "It was not enough just to wait until the Lord saw fit to take the initiative."[29] Drawing the parallel, as so many had before her, between the 1978 revelation and hoped-for revelations to create a more inclusive church in terms of gender and sexuality, Welker made her plea for continued contemplation and change to church authorities.

Some changes to the discourse framing women's experience of the temple transformed since the 1990s, creating a more inclusive environment. While the church has started to acknowledge the roles of women beyond motherhood and wifehood, that change comes slowly and has yet to be reflected in how the church community explains and understands the divine realm, except to acknowledge that humanity has Heavenly Parents.

28. Ibid.

29. Holly Welker, "'Always Pray to the Father': Mormon Leader Calls Desire for Knowledge of Heavenly Mother 'Arrogant and Unproductive'" *Religion Dispatches*, April 13, 2022. In June 2022, Danielle Calder organized a conference where those interested could gather and discuss Heavenly Mother called "Let's Talk About Heavenly Mother." The event was in Provo, Utah, a center of Latter-day Saint orthodoxy. The event had several hundred registrants.

What Happens in the Family...

While the church created the Gospel Topics essays in order to manage history-telling and revised the temple rituals to reflect greater gender egalitarianism so that it would not lose believers, it continues to maintain its insularity, its keep-the-dirty-laundry-in-the-family mandate in order to shape its public image for outsiders. On August 4, 2022, that image and that approach were called into question when the AP News published a story titled "Seven Years of Sex Abuse: How Mormon Officials Let It Happen." Written by Michael Rezendes, the Pulitzer Prize-winning Boston Globe reporter who helped expose the Roman Catholic Church's cover-up of clergy sex abuse, the article gave a powerful and tragic example of the extent the institution went to in order to protect itself. The story focused on Paul Douglas Adams, who for years sexually abused his very young daughters, filmed the abuse, and posted it online. His family was described as "deeply involved" in the Latter-day Saint community and, when he met with his bishop, John Herrod, Adams confessed to what he was doing.

Herrod called the church's helpline to learn how to address the abuse, but church attorneys wrongly told him that there was nothing he could do because of Arizona laws protecting clergy-penitent privilege. Herrod tried to work with Adams and his wife to stop the abuse happening in their home. When a new bishop, Robert Mauzy, took on the role, he, too, reached out to church officials. They instructed Mauzy to have a confidential disciplinary hearing and excommunicate Adams. The excommunication happened in 2013, but nothing was done by church members or officials to help Adams's daughters, who remained in his home until Homeland Security arrested him in 2017, having tracked down the source of the online child pornography.[30]

Established in 1995 in the wake of sex abuse scandals in the Roman Catholic Church, the church's helpline that Herrod and Mauzy both called was meant to support church officials who wanted help understanding the steps to take when they learned of abuse. Prior

30. Michael Rezendes, "Seven Years of Sex Abuse: How Mormon Officials Let It Happen," *AP News,* August 4, 2022.

to that time, the church asked bishops to contact law enforcement if they heard of abuse. Also at that time the church's helpline was placed under the oversight of "risk management" (which addresses the protection of members and officials from any emergency, including weather events and fires).[31] Helpline calls fall under the purview of lawyers whose job it is to protect the institution.[32] Information disclosed to those lawyers is always protected by attorney-client privilege. Church handbooks after 2010 explained that church leaders' goal should be helping survivors of abuse.[33] Though Herrod and Mauzy said church attorneys told them that clergy-penitent privilege required their silence about Adams's abuse, the law in Arizona does not say that. It simply says that clergy can choose to keep information from law enforcement.

The church faces legal action because of the process it instituted in 1995. Survivors and their families argue that lawsuits are necessary because the church has "a system that can easily be misused by church leaders to divert abuse accusations away from law enforcement and instead to church attorneys who may bury the problem." Failure to take action leaves the victims of abuse in an abusive situation, just as Adams's young daughters endured for years. One lawsuit against the church explained that the failure to report abuse occurred "to avoid scandals, to avoid the disclosure of their tolerance of sexual molestation and assault, to preserve a false appearance of propriety, and to avoid investigation and action by public authority."[34] Some have suggested that the church is more interested in protecting the perpetrators than the survivors, perhaps in an effort to protect the priesthood role.[35]

The AP News revealed that protocols for the helpline require records be destroyed daily.[36] The protocol they found also tells those who answer the helpline to only have bishops and stake presidents use first names in describing the case, to encourage reporting abuse

31. Ibid.

32. Jana Riess, "How Mormons Are Addressing Sex Abuse: Too Little, Too Late," *Religion News*, August 10, 2022.

33. Rezendes, "Seven Years of Sex Abuse."

34. Ibid.

35. Ibid.

36. Ibid.

by victims, perpetrators, or others who know of the abuse, but also to—and this is in all capital letters— "never advise a priesthood leader to report abuse. Counsel of this nature should come only from legal counsel."[37]

Jana Riess argues that several factors contributed to this situation: "A non-transparent leadership system that is run almost exclusively by men," as well as a culture that expects the church to show "the best parts of our community and hide flaws from outsiders." It teaches that the hierarchy is "not to be criticized." In addition, she names an internal purity culture that often blames survivors. All of this stems from an institutional culture that sees itself as morally superior to the broader culture, a stance that promotes the idea that "it could never happen here."[38] In all of these critiques, Riess echoes Lavina Fielding Anderson's voice from the 1990s. The church system preaches obedience. This required obedience to authority merges with the expectation to keep dirty laundry "in the family." While this cements group cohesion, it often fails to protect the most vulnerable from those who can take advantage of positions of power.

In an initial response to the allegations of creating a system that has enabled abuse to continue, the church explained that its policies were to support survivors of abuse and to allow law enforcement to deal with abusers, even as abuse may also be addressed through church disciplinary means.[39] Further, it pointed to training for church leaders who oversee youth programs, training that explains how to report abuse, as evidence of its care for victims and survivors. The training reportedly takes thirty minutes or less and quizzes leaders on policy.[40]

In an August 5, 2022, statement, the church declared that its process had been "seriously mischaracterized," though it did not provide substantive examples of how. The statement explained that the helpline "is instrumental in ensuring that all legal requirements for reporting are met. It provides a place for local leaders, who serve voluntarily, to receive direction from experts to determine who should

37. Qtd. in Rezendes, "Seven Years of Sex Abuse."

38. Riess, "How Mormons Are Addressing."

39. Brady McCombs, "Former Mayor, Mormon Bishop Accused of Sex abuse of children," *AP News*, September 8, 2022.

40. Riess, "How Mormons Are Addressing."

make a report and whether they (local leaders) should play a role in that reporting. When a leader calls the help line, the conversation is about how to stop the abuse, care for the victim and ensure compliance with reporting obligations, even in cases when the law provides clergy-penitent privilege or restricts what can be shared from private ecclesiastical conversations."[41] Though the institution defended its practices, a system of secrecy, of encouraging silence in the face of abuse, continues.

Pillars of Purity at BYU

While the church has argued for clergy confidentiality in cases of abuse, it has also required that church members wishing to work for the Church Educational System (CES) voluntarily and retroactively give up clergy confidentiality.[42] This sends a contradictory message about the significance and value of clergy confidentiality. Even as changes have occurred in the church's approach to history-telling and to its temple rituals, both to make believers more comfortable and confident in their faith, little has changed in the purity system itself, evidenced best in what has been happening in recent years on the BYU campuses. The CES oversees all of the church seminaries (for high school students), institutes (for college students), and the BYU campuses. For this reason, the CES is a powerful office in the church. Its domain is the faith education of so many young believers. It is here, in the office and its institutions, that the church most loudly and openly preaches and polices the purity system.

While the BYU campuses may be the flashpoint of these issues, it certainly is not the only place where the church is requiring members to conform to the purity system, especially in relationship to bodily purity and sexuality. In November 2015, the church issued what is often referred to as the "November Policy." The policy announced that participants in same-sex marriages were apostates and eligible for excommunication. In addition—and this was the most contentious part—children of same-sex marriages would not be allowed to

41. "Church Offers Statement on Help Line and Abuse," August 5, 2022, newsroom.churchofjesuschrist.org.

42. Peggy Fletcher Stack, "BYU Requires New Hires to Waive Their Right to Clergy Confidentiality," *Salt Lake Tribune*, August 28, 2022.

participate in church rituals like baptism until they were eighteen.[43] For critics, the policy was not just an insult to the LGBTQ+ community, but it also represented theological hypocrisy on the part of the church hierarchy. After all, they argued, the church's Articles of Faith claim that "We believe that men will be punished for their own sins," meaning that children should not be punished for their parents' so-called sins. For some observers, the November Policy confirmed what they had suspected: that despite its shift toward language of compassion and kindness toward LGBTQ+ members, the church still did not accept their full humanity. Just a few years later in 2019, the church switched gears and rescinded the policy. The reversal made clear that individuals in same-sex marriages were not apostate but were rather participating in a "serious transgression." Further, with their parents' understanding of the commitment, children of same-sex couples could join the church and participate in its rituals.[44]

In April 2019, Matt Easton, a graduation speaker at BYU's ceremonies declared: "I stand before my family, friends and graduating class today to say that I am proud to be a gay son of God." He went on to declare that his gay identity did not mean that he was broken or lacking, but instead that "I am loved and important to the plan of our great creator. Each of us are."[45] In both the church and university's institutional and cultural contexts, this was a bold and brave move. BYU's Honor Code does not have a policy about same-sex attraction, but it does state that punishable behavior includes clothing that school officials deem immodest, premarital sex, and same-sex sexual activity. Further, it declares, "Homosexual behavior includes not only sexual relations between members of the same sex, but all forms of physical intimacy that give expression to homosexual feelings."[46] Some observers felt that Easton's speech marked a shift in how non-conforming sexuality would be discussed in the church and on BYU's campuses, while some saw it as a courageous, individual move in the face of unchanging systems of power.

43. Elizabeth Dias, "Mormon Church to Allow Children of LGBT Parents to Be Baptized," *New York Times*, April 4, 2019.

44. Ibid.

45. Dan Levin, "In Commencement Speech, Brigham Young Graduate 'Proud to Be a Gay Son of God,'" *New York Times*, April 30, 2019.

46. Ibid.

In April 2021, a religion professor at the Provo campus of BYU, Hank Smith, had a negative encounter on Twitter with one of his former students, Calvin Burke, who is openly gay. Just after Natasha Helfer, a pro-LGBTQ+ and sex-positive therapist was excommunicated, Smith tweeted that leaving the church meant "leaving the doctrine as well" and that people who left could not continue to believe in Heavenly Mother or the Plan of Salvation.[47] Smith received pushback online from multiple people for attempting to police belief and enforce orthodoxy.

One such response came from Burke, an outspoken critic of the school's exclusionary policies. "On behalf of Mormonism, I apologize for Hank Smith," Burke tweeted. Smith tweeted a one-word response about Burke: "Korihor." In the Book of Mormon, Korihor is an anti-Christ who doubted the existence of God, tried to infect others with his disbelief, and was punished with muteness for demanding a sign of God's existence.[48] Everyone who saw the tweet and knows the stories of the Book of Mormon, would know that Smith was calling a student at his university the anti-Christ.[49] The next day, Smith deleted the tweet and wrote, "I do need to apologize for calling Cal what I did. I deleted the reply. That was unjustified and unfair. My emotions got the better of me. I am very sorry."[50] Smith never personally apologized to Calvin Burke, even though Burke was a former student of his who had previously received a priesthood blessing of comfort from him.

In spite of public concerns expressed to Smith's department and the university, BYU never publicly acknowledged the incident. This, even though one of its faculty member's social media post caused one of its students, a gay young man, to be targeted with hate-filled messages and death threats. Such a post and the resulting comments go against the church hierarchy's teachings that people in the LGBTQ+ community should be treated with love and compassion: "The gospel

47. Qtd. in Courtney Tanner, "BYU Professor Calls Gay Student a Book of Mormon Term Associated with Anti-Christ," *Salt Lake Tribune*, May 14, 2021.

48. Alma 30:6–60.

49. Tanner, "BYU Professor."

50. Qtd. in ibid.

of Jesus Christ teaches us to love and treat all people with kindness and civility—even when we disagree."[51]

BYU's silence about Smith spoke volumes. The church's teachings about kindness and civility did not appear to apply to Burke. "I just need to go to school in a place where I can feel safe," Burke tweeted the next day. "And last night was confirmation, albeit brutal, that even with my testimony [of faith] I am not safe or welcome here at BYU."[52] Burke eventually left BYU in search of a more welcoming campus community.

In August 2021, Apostle Jeffrey R. Holland gave a talk at the Annual University Conference at BYU. The speech represented the three pillars of the church's purity system and emphasized the message that believers should simply trust the church hierarchy and the patriarchal authority of the priesthood. To begin, Holland told the story of the importance of the giant Y painted on the hill next to BYU's campus; for him as an individual, its significance stretched back to when he was seven years old and first came to realize its importance. He described the Y as a "white and bold and beautiful" symbol marking the space as a special one, one that he would call "the greatest university in the world."[53] Even as Holland spoke about the school as a model for the world of merging faith and intellectual life, he noted that some professors were not supporting church doctrine and policy. In an ominous tone, he warned that "there *are* consequences to this."

Holland turned to explaining that "scholars building the temple of learning must also pause on occasion to defend the kingdom," arguing that faculty at BYU had a responsibility to be defenders of the faith. To both build Zion and defend it, he declared in the words of Neal A. Maxwell, an apostle from 1981 to 2004, they would need "both trowels and muskets." And their job in the current world context was to offer some "musket fire" from the sacred bastion of the institution.

This call to musket fire was not new—in his speech Holland quoted apostles Neal A. Maxwell and Dallin H. Oaks. Both had

51. "Church Leaders Counsel Members after Supreme Court Same-Sex Marriage Decision," LDS Newsroom, June 29, 2015, newsroom.churchofjesuschrist.org.

52. Qtd. in Tanner, "BYU Professor."

53. Jeffrey R. Holland, "The Second Half of the Second Century," BYU Annual University Conference, August 23, 2021.

used the metaphor in the previous two decades. Why was musket-fire such an appealing metaphor? It is a metaphor of violence, to be sure, but because they referred to antiquated muskets rather than modern weapons, the call to violence seemed to conjure up a romanticized past where Latter-day Saints had been persecuted and, in the midst of that persecution when they were just trying to survive, felt they needed to carry weapons to protect themselves as they built Zion. Yet for a church with significant political and economic power to call upon that metaphor in the twenty-first century is to call for violence in defense of the church's purity system. In this instance to police the boundaries between insiders and outsiders based around the doctrines of familial and bodily purity—to violently respond to those seen as transgressive or non-conforming.

Holland's primary concern was those at the institution who felt that the church's teaching on family and sexuality were problematic. He explained that he loved LGBTQ+ people, but that even Jesus, who loved everyone, did not find everyone's behavior acceptable: "Musket fire? Yes, we will always need defenders of the faith, but "friendly fire" is a tragedy—and from time to time the Church, its leaders and some of our colleagues within the university community have taken such fire on this campus. And sometimes it isn't friendly—wounding students and the parents of students who are confused about what so much recent flag-waving and parade-holding on this issue means."[54]

Once he explained why he found the metaphor of musket-fire appropriate, Holland then lifted up Clark G. Gilbert, commissioner of the CES, as a bastion of love for BYU and education in the church. He explained that both he and Gilbert understood that if BYU replicated what other universities offered, it would not be special or stand out. He went even further to declare that there may be a time in the future when BYU would have to forgo its position in professional academic organizations to defend its own destiny and future. It had to live up to that Y on the hill and the promise that it spoke of to his seven-year-old self.[55]

It was no coincidence that Holland highlighted the whiteness

54. Ibid.
55. Ibid.

of the Y. Without directly naming it, he was referring to symbolic protests on BYU's Provo campus. Earlier in 2021, students and local activists had lit up the giant white Y on the mountain in rainbow colors as a sign of welcome to and recognition of LGBTQ+ community members. Organizers assigned each protestor a light color and a spot on the Y. When all seventy-six flashlights were lit, the rainbow could be seen for several miles. Bradley Talbot, a gay student who organized the event, explained that the demonstration sought to communicate to the school that "We're here ... part of this institution."[56] In 2021 that happened twice, once before and once after Holland's talk. In December 2021, the school deemed future displays to be against the rules. While the school owns the trail up to the Y and the property around it, the school, which bought the surrounding land in 2014 from the US Forest Service, must provide public access. The school framed its prohibition against future demonstrations as a concern for public safety on a steep trail. Anyone caught could be subject to school discipline and possible arrest.[57]

Further, the school updated its policy declaring that campus members could not oppose church doctrine or "deliberately attack or deride" the church in a protest.[58] In addition, a school spokesperson noted that unacceptable public displays of protest "could include two people wearing rainbow items or two professors putting rainbow signs on their doors."[59] Even small acts of support for the LGBTQ+ community were re-read as challenges to the authority and truth claims of the church.

In 2021, the church sustained Clark G. Gilbert, a past president of BYU–Idaho, as a general authority and later that same year he became the Commissioner of the CES, a powerful position because of all that it oversees. Gilbert had earned the position and its oversight of the purity system on the church's campuses. Under his 2015–17 leadership as BYU–Idaho president, he fended off what

---

56. Courtney Tanner, "LGBTQ Students at BYU Light Up the 'Y' in Rainbow Colors," *Salt Lake Tribune*, April 14, 2021.

57. Courtney Tanner, "BYU Bans Protests on Y Mountain Year after LGBTQ Students Lit It up in Rainbow Colors," *Salt Lake Tribune*, January 12, 2022.

58. Ibid.

59. Courtney Tanner, "A BYU Professor Says She Was Fired after LGBTQ Advocacy," *Salt Lake Tribune*, February 14, 2022.

he saw as threatening liberalism in the broader American culture by not renewing the teaching contracts of some professors. One was fired after she posted a message of support for the LGBTQ+ community, as well as a critique of the church's stance on the issue, on her private social media page.[60] Juxtaposed with the administration's lack of response to Hank Smith's public social media posts and their dangerous outcomes, the two instances highlight the university's commitment to the purity system.

Similar dismissals happened again in the coming years. Soon after Gilbert became the commissioner in August 2021, the Provo BYU campus did not renew the contract of a writing professor, Sue Bergin, in spite of her nearly thirty-year career at BYU. Her department chair told her that he did not know why she was being dismissed, but Bergin suspected it was because she wore a rainbow pin to class and spoke openly and positively about her two gay brothers. She wore the pin because her father, Allen Bergin, had been a psychology professor at BYU who taught the idea that gay church members could change with therapy, discipline, and mixed orientation marriages. He publicly apologized for those teachings in 2020. She wore the pin because it allowed some students to feel comfortable enough to approach her outside of class about their own or a family member's sexuality. She would tell them, "I respectfully disagree with the church position on marriage equality. And I wrestle and struggle with that."[61] And so Bergin felt she knew precisely why she had been dismissed, yet she still could not believe it.

In February 2022, Clark G. Gilbert gave a devotional address on BYU's Provo campus titled "Christ's Peace in Perilous Times." Gilbert explained that attending BYU as an undergraduate was "a refuge and a source of strength" that also trained him to stand up for his beliefs and values. He drew upon his own personal history, telling a story of being mocked by high school peers in Phoenix for his religious beliefs. The story ended triumphantly, though, with Gilbert singing a beloved Latter-day Saint song, "I Am a Child of God," for the entire high school. This memory functioned several ways in the speech: it aligned Gilbert's personal history with the broader history of the persecution

60. Tanner, "BYU Professor."
61. Tanner, "BYU Professor."

of the church, it called on audience members to connect their own sense of self to the group through the persecution narrative, and it invited them to remember their own stories of love for BYU.

Gilbert explained that BYU was a school with a "unique spiritual mission," a place where the community could "perform at the highest levels, engage with the world, and never compromise our values or beliefs." In fact, he said, "BYU taught me that we can do this not in spite of our faith but *because* of it."[62] He reminded his audience that BYU was "a religious university with a religious purpose." He proclaimed that it would always be so, even though other religious institutions of higher education had changed. Prophets had spoken, he said, about the unique role that BYU "will play in the kingdom of God." Because of that role and because its governance is tied to the institutional church rather than being independent of it, Gilbert knew that BYU would stand the test of time as a *religious* institution long after others had disappeared.[63]

Gilbert declared that BYU was especially important in the perilous times the church was facing in the twenty-first century. Satan no longer felt the need to hide what he was doing. His plan was to whip up temptation and danger while also pacifying believers, making them apathetic to the evil in the world. Students might be fearful about their future and it was no wonder. The world was a scary place. But they also needed to trust that their faith was the foundation that would help them weather whatever storm they faced.

As he made the speech, Gilbert portrayed the outside world as dangerous and frightening, while BYU represented peace, faith, and orthodoxy. Under his leadership of the CES, BYU campuses continued to rid themselves of faculty who would not toe the orthodox line. In 2022, BYU–Idaho was not transparent about the reasoning behind its decision not to renew the contracts of two more faculty members. Both believe that it was because of their open and inclusive stances toward the LGBTQ+ community.[64] They were not expressing any radical ideas; they simply stated that members of the LGBTQ+ community should be valued and respected, an idea not

62. Clark G. Gilbert, "Christ's Peace In Perilous Times," February 8, 2022.
63. Ibid.
64. Colleen Flaherty, "A Chill at BYU," *Inside Higher Ed*, December 1, 2022.

out of line with official church teachings.[65] Theirs was a basic argument for equity and inclusion.

Ben Buswell was one of these faculty members. Buswell, who is trained in business and entrepreneurship, went to his bishop when he heard he had been dismissed. Stunned and surprised, his bishop said he would share with Buswell what he had told the Ecclesiastical Clearance Office (ECO), a new office created for the BYU campuses that monitors the schools' hiring and faculty review processes. Buswell had recently spoken to his bishop about his growing discomfort with the church's policy about LGBTQ+ members. The conversation, which happened in a church hallway and that Buswell thought was an exchange between friendly church members, ended when Buswell told the bishop that he would figure it out and that "it's not a big deal." When the bishop completed the ECO's form about Buswell, that conversation was on his mind. He explained the conversation, ending with a comment that Buswell "is honest in his desire to understand the Lord and will come to the right decision on this."[66] When the bishop revealed what he had written, Buswell felt he finally understood why he had been dismissed. It was simply no longer acceptable to have doubts about the church's stance on gender and sexuality.

While the BYU campuses have been tightlipped about the reasons behind professor non-renewals, other changes have occurred that demonstrate their continued commitment to the purity system. Where they have long required all Latter-day Saint employees to have ecclesiastical endorsement, or a bishop's statement that they are acting in line with the university's expectations, they now require a temple recommend for new employees. A temple recommend demonstrates employees' fidelity to the church's policies and doctrines. In addition, candidates for new positions have to agree that their local bishops can openly speak about issues shared with them confidentially, just as Buswell's bishop had. In this new climate, job seekers must waive their access to clergy confidentiality, a protection previously promised to all church members.

65. Ibid; Sam Brunson, "BYU and Cryptic Standards," *By Common Consent*, December 9, 2022, bycommonconsent.com.

66. Tammara Kemsley, "BYU-I Instructors Fired for Failing 'Ecclesiastical Clearance,'" *Salt Lake Tribune*, November 28, 2022.

BYU also relies on the work of the previously mentioned Ecclesiastical Clearance Office, overseen by Commissioner Clark Gilbert. While the purpose of the office is not entirely clear, there seems to be a focus on rooting out those who speak or act in ways that challenge church doctrine, especially on LGBTQ+ issues.[67] Created in 2020, the Ecclesiastical Clearance Office (ECO), was designed to ensure that employees maintain doctrinal purity and their temple recommends. Some believe that the office is responsible for the university severing its ties with the faculty discussed earlier as well as others. The office and the new requirement to waive confidentiality work together. The institution can look into people's pasts and explore any conversations they have had with their church leaders without alerting the applicant. The ECO "contacts current and former ecclesiastical leaders concerning the ecclesiastical worthiness of all candidates." In its determinations, it "also considers factors such as public positions or statements related to leaders, doctrine, and policies of, and an individual's overall activity in, the Church of Jesus Christ."[68] The ECO removes some of the power of the local structure of the church. In the past it would have been up to the discretion of the current, local church leader to provide a temple recommend. Someone the person knew at that moment would be determining their worthiness. The ECO's purpose and its secrecy operate to police the behavior of everyone, using fear of not getting a job, to promote doctrinal orthodoxy.[69]

The clergy waiver and the expectations for faculty, are tied to the institution's "mission alignment standards," which state that an employee must demonstrate "a pattern of public expression that faithfully promotes the mission and doctrines of the church; is devoid of contradicting or opposing church doctrines, policies and general leaders; and refrains from expressions and behaviors that are dishonest, unchaste, profane or disrespectful of others."[70]

In March 2022, the Church Educational System issued new questions that ecclesiastical leaders could use in their interviews. "It

67. Flaherty, "Chill at BYU"; Kemsley, "BYU-I Instructors Fired."

68. "Ecclesiastical Clearance and University Standards Compliance Verification Policy," BYU-Hawaii, byuh.edu, accessed January 3, 2022.

69. Flaherty, "Chill at BYU."

70. Qtd. in Stack, "BYU Requires New Hires."

is critical that each [church] employee represent the mission, values, and goals of The Church of Jesus Christ of Latter-day Saints," said Commissioner Gilbert. He argued that the new questions and updates reflected the institution's goals and the need to have employees "engage fully in the spiritual mission that is central to each CES institution."[71] While some of the questions are fairly innocuous, asking about the leader's relationship to and knowledge of the candidate, others are clearly tied to the maintenance of the purity system.

Most obvious in this matter is the question, "Does this member have a testimony of The Church of Jesus Christ of Latter-day Saints and its doctrine, including its teachings on marriage, family, and gender?" This question embodies the three pillars of the purity system already discussed—doctrinal, familial, and bodily. Yet it also demonstrates the new truth about the purity system: tests of levels of orthodoxy now revolve around an individual's willingness to affirm church teachings about gender, family, and sexuality. Or rather, the familial and bodily *are* the doctrinal standards of purity.

Other questions include: "Does this member support current Church policies and practices and sustain the leaders of the Church?" and "Has this member demonstrated an exemplary and extended pattern (at least one year) of avoiding pornography?"[72] Overall, the questions demonstrate a renewed commitment to ensuring that those who do not uphold the purity system are not hired, keeping them away from influencing younger people of faith. The justification for the new policies and programs is tied to the education of young members of the church. "No institutional decision is more important to us," said Gilbert, "than the selection of employees, including faculty, as it has the greatest potential to impact our students."[73] They are warding off future D. Michael Quinns, Cecelia Konchar Farrs, David Wrights, and Sue Bergins, who are upstanding church members but may encourage students to ask questions about their church, its history, and its policies.

In addition to upholding the purity system, the institution and

71. "Ecclesiastical Leader Questions for New CES Hires," LDS Newsroom, newsroom.churchofjesuschrist.org, accessed January 3, 2022.

72. Ibid.

73. Ibid.

its new employee expectations reinforce the idea that the temple and worthiness to enter the temple are at the heart of a faithful life. The temple is the font of the purity system, structuring and authorizing its claims. In an October 2021 general conference talk, President Russell M. Nelson affirmed this, stating "Everything we believe and every promise God has made to His covenant people come together in the temple ... (the Lord) is providing opportunities for each of us to bolster our spiritual foundations more effectively by centering our lives on Him and on the ordinances and covenants of His temple."[74]

The emphasis on the purity system is evident not only in BYU's hiring practices, but also in its expectations for faculty in their research methods, topics, and conclusions. At a talk in November 2022, Justin Collings, the new associate academic vice president of faculty development at BYU, encouraged department chairs and deans to revise their expectations for promotion in order to promote and reward faculty whose work aligns with and enhances the church's teachings. Collings quoted First Presidency counselor Dallin H. Oaks, who had previously told faculty members that their research should support church policies. Collings encouraged topics for research that addressed such issues as "languages, family, religion and constitutional government." He declared that rank and status documents "should not 'merely mimic analogous documents at other schools' but should 'reflect, reinforce and propel our unique and inspired mission.'"[75]

The shift has raised concerns about academic freedom at BYU. While some faculty at the university, the ones for whom the call made sense both in terms of faith and research, embraced the call for new standards, others are concerned and see the move as part of an attempt by the church to encourage particular research topics and conclusions in faculty research—an approach that could damage the institution's reputation in the world of higher education.[76]

The world of higher education, though, is not the place where church leaders want to fit in. Their allies for decades now have been

74. Tad Walch, "BYU, Other Latter-Day Saint Schools Will Require Temple Recommends for New Latter-Day Saint Hires," *Deseret News*, January 27, 2022.

75. Tamarra Kemsley, "BYU Faculty Members Urged to Align Their Teaching, Research Better with LDS Tenets," *Salt Lake Tribune*, January 29, 2023.

76. Ibid.

political and religious conservatives. This continues to be true today. In the early months of 2023, Ron DeSantis, the governor of Florida and would-be 2024 Republican presidential candidate, is seeking to change the way US history is told so that the country does not have to reckon with its racist past. Florida has extended its "Don't Say Gay" bill to cover the entire time a young person attends public schools. Around the country, white Christian nationalism is on the rise, pushing for the country's return to a romanticized and imagined past. White privilege and power work to erase the experiences of marginalized groups from mainstream attention. Conservative Christians and politicians push anti-LGBTQ+, anti-trans, and anti-choice legislation through state legislatures. In this context it is not surprising that the church that has been steeped in the politics of the right for decades continues to maintain its purity system. It is the system that helped the institution claim a mainstream identity and shore up its political power.

It is also no surprise that, just like conservative Christian churches have clung to the idea of religious freedom in order to support their claims about gender and sexuality, so, too, has the LDS Church. In its statement about same-sex marriage, the church hierarchy states: "Just as those who promote same-sex marriage are entitled to civility, the same is true for those who oppose it. The Church insists on its leaders' and members' right to express and advocate religious convictions on marriage, family, and morality free from retaliation or retribution. The Church is also entitled to maintain its standards of moral conduct and good standing for members."[77]

Similar statements appear in the church handbook and are scattered throughout church resources. In this way the church, once an oppressed minority whose first amendment religious freedom protections were not respected in the *Reynolds v. United States* (1879) Supreme Court case, now is using the cloak of religious freedom to protect itself from legislation for equal rights for the LGBTQ+ community.

It should also shock no one that it is at the BYU campuses that much of the debates about orthodoxy and intellectualism are taking place; it is simply a microcosm of the divisions in the broader culture.

77. "Same-Sex Marriage," Gospel Topics, churchofjesuschrist.org, accessed May 10, 2023.

In DeSantis's Florida similar issues have been raised at its premier public liberal arts college, the New College of Florida. There DeSantis has stacked the board of trustees with politically and religiously conservative members. Because of this, five faculty members who had their departments' support for tenure were denied that status by the trustees. The higher education world that haunts DeSantis is one that reckons with the nation's past and current racism, accepts all sexualities amongst consenting adults and all genders without question, acknowledges that history-telling is a political act, and asks questions about anything, including religious belief. Ron DeSantis and Clark Gilbert share many of the same dreams and nightmares.

As the church hierarchy continues to maintain its authority, it is turning to offices like the Ecclesiastical Clearance Office to make sure that local church leadership is authorizing only non-questioning Latter-day Saints to teach at church universities. The new system for hiring BYU professors suggests that the institution feels it is not enough to contact an applicant's current bishop for an ecclesiastical endorsement, but that past local leaders need to be contacted for endorsements as well. The institutional church is trying to ensure that purity and orthodoxy remain standards in local communities everywhere.

But at the local and communal level, the church is changing, prodded in part by online communities and connections. Some people are leaving the pews because of the church's policies about LGBTQ+ identity and its gender expectations that are rooted in a patriarchal system.[78] Others are staying in the pews but demanding a more inclusive vision of the Restoration. At that level of the laity, people are embracing their sense of personal revelation, driven by the Spirit toward a more egalitarian community. At that level, the September Six and their legacy continue on, shaping people's memory of individuals willing to stand up to the institution in the struggle for the soul of Mormonism.

78. See Part II of Jana Riess's *The Next Mormons: How Millennials Are Changing the LDS Church* (New York: Oxford University Press, 2019).

PHOTOGRAPHS

Lynne Kanavel Whitesides. *Courtesy Salt Lake Tribune.*

Avraham Gileadi. *Courtesy Salt Lake Tribune.*

Maxine Hanks. *Signature Books Collection, Busath Photography.*

Paul Toscano. *Signature Books Collection, Busath Photography.*

Margaret Merrill Toscano. *Signature Books Collection, Busath Photography.*

Lavina Fielding Anderson. *Signature Books Collection, Busath Photography.*

D. Michael Quinn. *Signature Books Collection, Busath Photography.*

First Presidency, 1992. Front Row (L to R): Gordon B. Hinckley (First Counselor), Ezra Taft Benson (President), and Thomas S. Monson (Second Counselor). *Courtesy Salt Lake Tribune.*

Dallin H. Oaks. *Public domain.*

Boyd K. Packer. *Courtesy Salt Lake Tribune.*

Leonard J. Arrington. *Signature Books Collection.*

D. Michael Quinn, 1994, signing a copy of *The Mormon Hierarchy: Origins of Power. Signature Books Collection.*

ACKNOWLEDGMENTS

"Stories are vulnerable things."
—White Lies

It seems like yesterday that Barbara Jones Brown spoke with me about writing a book about the September Six. This is the first time that I worked with Signature Books and I want to thank all of the folks at the press who helped make this possible. In particular, John Hatch provided excellent editorial advice and Jason Francis helped to keep everything on schedule in addition to making the material reality of the book as wonderful as it is. Thanks to Sophia Snyder for her careful proofing. I am especially thankful to Barbara Jones Brown who as director of Signature helped me to imagine the project, encouraged me to use the Signature archives and reading room, spoke with me countless times about ideas and arguments, and helped me find and gain access to important sources. That she then became my content editor for the project was a true delight. Her feedback and knowledge of the field is astonishing. Her hard work to invite and prod Mormon Studies in new directions is a real blessing to the field.

An episode of the podcast *White Lies* reminds us that "stories are vulnerable things." They are vulnerable because in sharing them, we open ourselves up to others. They are vulnerable because they make us who we are. For this reason I want to express my profound thanks to the people who allowed me to interview them for this book. They graciously shared their time and stories with me and entertained the idea that not everything has been said about the time surrounding the disciplinary councils of the September Six. To trust someone with your story is a powerful gift and I am so honored and grateful for those who shared those gifts with me. Many thanks especially to Lavina Fielding Anderson, Christine Jeppsen Clark, Cecilia Konchar Farr, Maxine Hanks, Lynne Kanavel Whitesides, and David Wright.[1] Thank you.

Throughout my time at Hanover College I have received support in so many ways from so many different people. I want to thank the Faculty Development Committee for its support of my project. Jennifer Sterk in the Provost's Office helped me keep up with the technology necessary for this work. I've also benefitted over the years from a lively and thoughtful scholarship group: many thanks to Dominique Battles, Paul Battles, James Buckwalter, Saul Lemerond, Alejandra Rodriguez Villar, Mandy Wu, Xialong Wu, Mi Yung Yoon, Fernanda Zullo. In addition, I have been graced with the help of fabulous librarians at Duggan Library, especially Jen Duplaga, Michael Ellis, Kelly Joyce, Patricia Lawrence, and Sarah Verkamp. I have a departmental home that has always been supportive and encouraging in my pedagogical and scholarly pursuits. Many thanks to Dave Cassel, Mike Duffy, and Beatrice Marovich. Finally, I am thankful for my students who keep me on my toes and engaged in questions about how to best live in the world.

In the field of Mormon Studies, I've received great encouragement and welcoming community from so many people. Special thanks go to Quincy Newell, Benjamin E. Park, Taylor Petrey, and Joshua S. Smith for reading portions of this manuscript and providing excellent feedback. David Howlett offered valuable advice on several key issues. Katie Ludlow Rich helped with finding a source. Matt Harris shared important sources from his own files. Joey Stuart put together a wonderful index for the book. My thanks as well to the people at the Church History Library who helped when they could.

My friends help to make my life full and meaningful. I would like to thank Sharon Benton, Jeff Brautigam, Don Carrel, Dave Cassel, Mike Duffy, Ashley Eden, Joyce Flanigan, Katy Hadley, Amy Hoyt, Natalia Hubbs, Amir Hussain, Steve Jobe, Terry Jobe, Kate Johnson, Tina Jones, Jamie Kepros, Sara Moslener, Jennifer Naccarelli, Quincy Newell, Zephirin Ryan, Robyn Ryle, Katy Lowe Schneider, Nasrin

1. For health reasons, Anderson did not feel up to an oral history interview, but she very generously offered to answer some questions in a written format.

Shahinpoor, Steve Steiner, Kay Stokes, Ruth Turner, Karla Van Zee, and D.J. Walch. I am especially thankful for Katy Hadley, Robyn Ryle, and Karla Van Zee's willingness to listen as I mulled over the arguments in this book. Their feedback and questions helped deepen my thinking. Thank you as well to Katy Hadley who read and asked questions about portions of the manuscript. Our escapades over the years—for social justice, teaching, crafting, and travel—have been such a joy. Thank you for all of the laughter and companionship.

My family also helped to support and make my life full. First, and always, thank you to my parents Evan and Veronica Patterson who unwaveringly support their daughters in their pursuit of their dreams. Thank you to Veronica for reading and commenting on large portions of this manuscript. Your questions and comments always helped me to keep going. Thank you to my sister, Carrie Lee, who is a remarkable and creative person, always supporting me in my studies of religion even as those religions make absolutely no sense to her.

I would also like to thank several others for the warm welcome of family: Betsi and Russell Cunningham, Katie and Dave Staubach, Angie Chandler, Virginia and Jeff Chandler, and Larry Chandler. Special thanks to Betsi who provided me with an unlimited supply of pens to get me through the project!

Thank you to Willow whose laughter is magic and medicine. Who can't keep a secret. And who shares my delight in rocks, leaves, walks, art, and saying no.

And, finally, thank you to Eli for encouraging me to do this project, cheering me on throughout, and providing the laughter and companionship that I need. I'm looking forward to all of our plans when I write a book that earns Netflix royalties. Until then, I am grateful for the swap meets, the ridiculous questions, the mad lib walks, the laughter, the inside jokes, and the company—for the exquisite company most of all.

INDEX

Numbers marked in italics denote photographs

B

C

D

I

J

Q

R

Y

Z

About the Author

Sara M. Patterson (she/her) is a professor of theological studies and gender studies at Hanover College, where she holds the inaugural Barron Professorship in Social Justice Education. She is the author of multiple articles addressing the intersections of gender, sexuality, and religion. Her research also explores the intersections of religion, space, and material culture, a topic she most recently explored in *Pioneers in the Attic: Place and Memory Along the Mormon Trail* (Oxford University Press, 2020). She is a former board member of the Mormon History Association.